HUMAN HISTORY AND THE WORD OF GOD

BY JAMES M. CONNOLLY

The Voices of France

JAMES M. CONNOLLY

Human History and the Word of God

THE CHRISTIAN MEANING OF HISTORY IN CONTEMPORARY THOUGHT

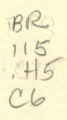

THE MACMILLAN COMPANY, NEW YORK

COLLIER-MACMILLAN LIMITED, LONDON

The author wishes to thank the following for permission to reproduce copyrighted material: Abingdon Press, for *The Kingdom of God*, by John Bright; and *Christ and History*, by George A. Buttrick. Association Press, for *The Place of Bonhoeffer*, by Martin E. Marty. Bruce Publishing Company, for *Catholic Thought in Crisis*, by Father Peter Riga. Cambridge University Press, for *The Bible Today*, by C. H. Dodd. Desclee Co., Inc., for *The Word, Church and Sacraments in Protestantism and Catholicism*, by Louis Bouyer; and *A Study of Hebrew Thought*, by Claude Tresmontant. Doubleday & Company, Inc., for *Portrait of Karl Barth*, by George Casalis, copyright © 1963 by Doubleday & Company, Inc., reprinted by permission of the publisher; and *The Opium of the Intellectuals*, by Raymond Aron, copyright © 1957 by Raymond Aron, reprinted by permission of Doubleday & Company, Inc. Dover Publications, Inc., for *Whitehead's Philosophy of Civilization*, by A. H. Johnson. Duquesne University Press, for *Faith and the World* and *Contemporary European Thought and Christian Faith*, both by Albert Dondeyne. Farrar, Straus & Company, Inc., for *The Meaning and Matter of History*, by Martin D'Arcy, S.J. Fortress Press, for *Biblical Problems and Biblical Preaching*, by C. K. Barrett; *The World: Its Creation and Consummation*, by Karl Heim; *Fact and Faith in the Kerygma of Today*, by Paul Althaus; and *The Living Word*, by Gustaf Wingren. Harper & Row, for *The Divine Milieu*, by Pierre Teilhard de Chardin, S.J.; *The Phenomenon of Man*, by Pierre Teilhard de Chardin, S.J.; *The Theology of St. Luke*, by Hans Conzelmann; *The Scope of Demythologizing*, by John Macquarrie; *Pattern and Meaning in History*, by Wilhelm Dilthey; *History and Eschatology*, by Rudolf Bultmann; *The Twentieth Century in Europe*, by Kenneth S. Latourette; *Rebellious Prophet*, by Donald Lowrie; *Twentieth Century Religious Thought*, by John Macquarrie; *Jesus of Nazareth*, by Günther Bornkamm; *The Historical Jesus*, by Heinz Zahrnt; *Searchlights on Contemporary Theology*, by Nels F. S. Ferre; *Christ and Culture*, by H. Richard Niebuhr; *Christian Apologetics* and *Introduction to the Theology of the New Testament*, both by Alan Richardson, reprinted by permission of Harper & Row and SCM Press Ltd.; *Modern Catholic Thinkers*, by A. Robert Caponigri, reprinted by permission of Harper & Row and Burns & Oates Ltd.; and *The Apostolic Preaching and Its Developments* (2nd ed.), by C. H. Dodd, reprinted by permission of Harper & Row and Hodder & Stoughton, Ltd. Harcourt, Brace & World, Inc., for *The Sacred and Profane*, by Mircea Eliade. Alfred A. Knopf, Inc., for *What is History*, by Edward H. Carr. The Johns Hopkins Press, for

Acknowledgments

From the Stone Age to Christianity, by William F. Albright. John Knox Press, for *Salvation History*, by Eric C. Rust; and *A Theology of Proclamation*, by Dietrich Ritschl. Loyola University Press, for *The Intent of Toynbee's History*, edited by Edward T. Gargan. The Macmillan Company, for *Reinhold Niebuhr*, by C. W. Kegley and R. W. Bretall, copyright © The Macmillan Company 1956; *Ethics*, Copyright © The Macmillan Company 1955, and *Prisoner for God*, copyright © The Macmillan Company 1953, both by Dietrich Bonhoeffer; *Darwin's Vision and Christian Perspectives*, by Walter J. Ong, S.J., copyright © The Macmillan Company 1959, 1960; *Communism and the Theologians*, by C. C. West, copyright © SCM Press Ltd. 1958, reprinted with the permission of The Macmillan Company; *Christian Initiation*, by Louis Bouyer, copyright © Burns & Oates Ltd. 1960, reprinted with the permission of The Macmillan Company; *New Testament Theology*, by E. Stauffer, published by The Macmillan Company; and *American Thought*, by Morris R. Cohen, copyright © 1954 by The Free Press, used with the permission of The Free Press of Glencoe. McGraw-Hill Book Company, Inc., for *History, Archaelogy and Christian Humanism*, by William F. Albright; and *Theology of the Christian Mission*, by Gerald H. Anderson. Penguin Books Ltd., for *The Old Testament Prophets*, by E. W. Heaton; *God's Living Word*, by Alexander Jones, copyright © 1961 Alexander Jones, published by Sheed & Ward, Inc.; *The Christian Commitment*, by Karl Rahner, S.J., copyright © Sheed & Ward Ltd. 1963, published by Sheed & Ward, Inc.; *Theology of History*, by Hans Urs von Balthasar, copyright © Sheed & Ward, Inc., 1963; *The Splendor of the Church*, by Henri de Lubac, S.J., copyright © 1956 Sheed & Ward, Inc.; *Catholicism*, by Henri de Lubac, S.J., published by Sheed & Ward, Inc.; *The Resurrection*, by F. X. Durrwell, copyright © Sheed & Ward Ltd. 1960, published by Sheed & Ward, Inc.; and *The End of the Modern World*, by Romano Guardini, copyright © 1956 Sheed & Ward, Inc. University of Notre Dame Press, for *The Bible and the Liturgy*, by Jean Daniélou, S.J.; *Liturgical Piety* and *The Meaning of Sacred Scripture*, both by Louis Bouyer; and *God's Unfolding Purpose*, by Suzanne de Dietrich, copyright © W. L. Jenkins 1960. The Westminster Press, for *Christ and Time*, by Oscar Cullmann, copyright © 1950 W. L. Jenkins, the Westminster Press; *History Sacred and Profane*, by Alan Richardson, copyright © SCM Press Ltd. 1964, used with permission of The Westminster Press; *The Christology of the New Testament*, by Oscar Cullmann, copyright © SCM Press Ltd. 1959, used with permission of The Westminster Press; *Genesis*, by Gerhard Von Rad, copyright © 1961, W. L. Jenkins, The Westminster Press; *The Bible in the Age of Science*, by Alan Richardson, copyright © 1961 SCM Press Ltd., published in the United States by the Westminster Press, 1961, used by permission; and *Agape and Eros*, by Anders Nygren, translated by Philip L. Watson and published in 1953 by The Westminster Press, used by permission. SCM Press Ltd., for *Christian Belief and This World*, by Alec R. Vidler; *A New Quest of the Historical Jesus*, by James M. Robinson; *Biblical Words for Time*, by James Barr; *The God Who Acts*, by G. E. Wright; *The Biblical Doctrine of Man in Society*, by G. E. Wright; and *Four Anchors from the Stern* by Alan Richardson and others, all published in London by the SCM Press Ltd., distributed in the United States by Alec R. Allenson, Naperville, Ill. Philosophical Library, Inc., and Longmans, Green & Co., Ltd., for *Insight*, by Bernard Lonergan, used with the permission of the Philosophical Library, Inc., and Longmans, Green & Co., Ltd. Random House, Inc., for *The Last Things*, by Romano Guardini, copyright © 1954 Pantheon Books, Random House, Inc.; *The Faith and Modern Man*, by Romano Guardini, copyright © 1953 Pantheon Books, Random

Acknowledgments

House, Inc., and used with permission of Burns & Oates Ltd.; and *The End of Time*, by Josef Pieper, copyright © 1954 Pantheon Books, Random House, Inc., and used with permission of Faber & Faber Ltd. Newman Press, for *The Fourth Gospel*, by Louis Bouyer, Westminster, Md.: Newman Press, copyright © 1964 Newman Press; *The Bible and the Universe*, by Evode Beaucamp, O.F.M., Westminster, Md.: Newman Press, 1963, copyright © 1959 Les Editions du Cerf, English translation copyright © 1963 Burns & Oates Ltd.; *The Christian Message and Myth*, by L. Malevez, S.J., Westminster, Md.: Newman Press, 1958, copyright © SCM Press Ltd. 1958; *The Apocalypse of Saint John*, by H. M. Féret, O.P., Westminster, Md.: Newman Press, 1958, copyright © 1958 Blackfriars Publications; *Further Paradoxes*, by Henri de Lubac, S.J., Westminster, Md.: Newman Press, 1958, copyright © 1958 Longmans, Green & Co., Ltd.; *St. John's Prologue*, by M. E. Boismard, Westminster, Md.: Newman Press, copyright © 1957 Newman Press; *Karl Barth*, by Jerome Hamer, O.P., Westminster, Md.: Newman Press, copyright © 1962 Newman Press; and *Lay People in the Church*, by Yves M.J. Congar, O.P., Westminster, Md.: Newman Press, 1956. University of Chicago Press, for *Meaning in History*, by Karl Löwith, Phoenix Books, University of Chicago Press, copyright © 1949 University of Chicago; and *Culture and Faith*, by Richard Kroner, University of Chicago Press, copyright © 1951 Richard Kroner. The Liturgical Press, for *Theological Dimensions of the Liturgy*, by Cyprian Vagaggini, O.S.B., Collegeville, Minn.: The Liturgical Press, 1959, copyright © 1959 Order of St. Benedict, Inc. Oxford University Press, for *Towards a Theological Understanding of History*, by Eric C. Rust, copyright © 1963 Oxford University Press; *The Conflict Between Paganism and Christianity in the Fourth Century*, by Arnaldo Momigliano, Clarendon Press, Oxford University Press, copyright © 1963; and *Existentialism and Religious Belief*, by David Roberts, edited by Roger Hazelton, Galaxy Books, Oxford University Press, 1959, copyright © 1957 Oxford University Press. Oliver & Boyd Ltd., for *The Christian Doctrine of History*, by John McIntyre, Edinburg: Oliver & Boyd Ltd. 1957, copyright © 1957 John McIntyre. SPCK, for *Paul and Rabbinic Judaism*, by W. D. Davies, 1962, 2nd ed. 1955, copyright © W. D. Davies, 1948. Henry Regnery Company, for *The Lord of History*, by Jean Daniélou, S.J., copyright © 1958 Longmans, Green & Co., Ltd.; *Power and Responsibility*, by Romano Guardini, copyright © 1961 Henry Regnery Company; and *The Lord*, by Romano Guardini, copyright © 1954 Henry Regnery Company. C.W.K. Gleerup Publishers, Lund, Sweden, for *Nature and History*, by Bernhard Erling. Charles Scribner's Sons, for *From First Adam to Last*, by C. Kingsley Barrett; *Faith and History*, by Reinhold Niebuhr; *Oswald Spengler*, by H. Stuart Hughes; *The Philosophy of History*, by Jacques Maritain; *The New Testament in Current Study*, by Reginald Fuller; *Christianity and the Problem of History*, by Roger Shinn; and *The Hinge of History*, by Carl Michalson. Image Books, Doubleday & Company, Inc., for *The Meaning of Man*, by Jean Mouroux, 1961, copyright © Sheed & Ward, Inc., 1948. Helicon Press, Inc., for *Christianity and Culture*, edited by J. Stanley Murphy, C.S.C., 1960, copyright © 1961 by Helicon Press, Inc.; *The Scandal of Truth*, by Jean Daniélou, S.J., 1962, copyright © 1962 by Helicon Press, Inc.; and *Theological Investigations*, Vol. 1, by Karl Rahner, S.J., 1961, copyright © Darton, Longman and Todd, Inc., 1961.

The author also wishes to thank the following periodicals for permission to quote copyrighted material: *The Bible Today*, for "The Idea of Progress in the Early Church," by George T. Montague, February, 1964, pp. 640–641, published by The Liturgical Press, copyright © by the Order of St. Benedict, Inc.,

Acknowledgments

Collegeville, Minnesota. *Catholic Biblical Quarterly,* for "The Christians' Union with the Body of Christ," by Barnabas Ahern, Vol. 23, No. 2, April, 1961. *Cross Currents,* for "From the Logic of History," by H. I. Marron, Vol. 11, No. 1, Winter, 1961. *The Dunwoodie Review,* for a review by W. F. Martin, Vol. 3, No. 2, May, 1963. *The Harvard Theological Review,* for "The Biblical View of Time," by James Muilenberg, Vol. 54, No. 4, October, 1961. *Theological Studies,* for "The Word of God in the Old Testament," by John L. McKenzie, S.J., Vol. 21, No. 2, June, 1960; "The Ecclesiology of Johann Adam Möhler, by Peter Riga, Vol. 22, No. 4, December 1961; "Kingdom to Church," by David M. Stanley, S.J., Vol. 14, No. 1, March, 1955; "The Relationship of Love to Faith in St. John," by Thomas Barosse, C.S.C.; "The Protestant Preacher and the Prophetic Mission," by Avery Dulles, S.J., Vol. 21, No. 4, December, 1960; "The New Testament Doctrine of Baptism," by David M. Stanley, S.J., Vol. 18, No. 7, June, 1957; "Eric Voegelin," by W. F. Albright, Vol. 22, No. 2, June, 1961; a review by Vincent T. O'Keefe, S.J., Vol. 21, No. 4, December, 1960; a review by R. O. Johann, Vol. 24, No. 2, June, 1963; "The Philosophy of the Human Person in Karl Rahner," by Gerald A. McCool, S.J., Vol. 22, No. 4, December, 1961; and "Christian Philosophy of History," by Paul Henry, S.J., Vol. 13, No. 3, September, 1952. *Theology Digest,* for "Time in Theology," by M.D. Chenu, O.P., Vol. 10, No. 4, Autumn, 1962; "Christian Values at Mid-Twentieth Century," by Walter Ong, S.J., Vol. 4, No. 3, Autumn, 1956; "Secular Knowledge and Revealed Religion," by Walter Ong, S.J., Vol. 6, No. 2, Spring, 1958; and "The Sacraments: An Encounter with God," by E. J. Schillebeeckx, O.P., Vol. 8, No. 2, Spring, 1960. *Theology Today,* for a book review by Neill Hamilton of *Jesus of Nazareth,* by Günther Bornkamm, April, 1963; a book review by Walter E. Weist of *The Rationality of Faith,* by Carl Michalson, January, 1964; and "Is the New Quest Docetic?", by Paul J. Achtemeier, October, 1962. *The Atlantic Monthly,* for "The Quest for Christian Unity," by Barbara Ward, Vol. 210, No. 2, August, 1962. *The Commonweal,* for "Christian Worship and the Historical Dimension," by Joseph L. Cypriano, No. 19, August, 1962, p. 468.

FOR MYLES M. BOURKE

to whom I am indebted for my
training in the Word of God

ACKNOWLEDGMENTS

The author wishes to express his appreciation and his debt of gratitude to all those who made this book possible, particularly to the Reverend Maurice Carroll of Monsignor Farrell High School; the Reverend Donald Hendricks of Cathedral College; the Reverend Robert E. McNally, S.J., of Woodstock; the Reverend John D. Gerken, S.J., of John Carroll University; and, for his continual encouragement, to the Very Reverend Myles Bourke, Dean of St. Joseph's Seminary in Dunwoodie, Yonkers, New York.

CONTENTS

Contents

PREFACE

THE IMPORTANCE of having a feeling for history, the fact that history is leading somewhere, that it has some meaning, are concepts that we have grown accustomed to expressing daily, even if we don't know exactly what we mean by them. On the other hand the phrase "history of salvation" has become familiar to us only recently. At an audience given by the present Pope to the observers at the council, Dr. Skydsgaard, a leading Lutheran theologian, said that nothing could be more important at the moment for ecumenism than a common study of the *Heilsgeschichte,* and the Pope himself replied that he would favor the institution of some special school that would make this the object of its researches.

How are we then to understand all that? There is no simple answer. The present volume will give some idea of a very controversial book written by a French Jesuit a few years ago, *De l'actualité historique.* Father Fessard in that book openly challenged the Thomist theologians with the bold assertion that a major weakness of Thomism was its exclusion of both a philosophy and a theology of history. Immediately not one but two massive answers were launched against that intruder by two leading figures of contemporary Thomism. They were in complete agreement on the point that Father Fessard had grossly misinterpreted Saint Thomas; but one demonstrated that there are indeed a philosophy and a theology of history in Saint Thomas, while the other established no less brilliantly that, thank God, there is none of that stuff in a man who has thought out, once and for all, the problems of all generations. This may give some idea of the difficulty of the question.

Father Connolly, who is always extremely well informed on any given subject, has no pretension toward solving all those riddles at a stroke. But he will give us something perhaps more fruitful: the necessary information to see the meaning of the questions raised before trying to provide the right answers. How what we call the "sense of history" made its first appearance in human thought after the Renaissance and began to be molded into more or less majestic systems in the nineteenth century, how modern exegesis in its turn has rendered us more and more sensitive to the fact that Christianity, precisely, is a fact before being a fine network of ideas—these are some of the things his wide review of the field will make us able to realize. After that we shall be at least in a better position to follow and understand one of the capital debates among modern thinkers and to grasp the wonderful opportunity it provides us, not only to answer the most burning of all the questions asked by men today, but also to reach some deeper apprehension of the essentials of Christian faith.

Louis Bouyer

INTRODUCTION

The Challenge of Human History

WHEN MAN considers human history and attempts to assess its direction and to arrive at its meaning, he touches upon a strain of human thought that has remained constant to the human experience from primitive civilization to our modern era. In attempting to present the varieties of man's thinking and, in particular, contemporary theologies of history, we are faced from the outset with the ambivalence of the term "history" itself. At the beginning one must set down quite clearly just what he conceives that term to designate. Simply speaking, history can embrace the total course of human events—the complete inclusion of all human actions—so that history embraces the whole of the human reality. But although it would be legitimate for one so to designate the concept of history, it is not that which man has come to mean by the term.

The term has a narrower meaning; it denotes man's record of significant events, meaningful events, in the total course of human events. Thus it is that we frequently speak of men and events as historical in the sense that they have had a special significance for mankind. The historian, properly speaking, devotes his time and his efforts to the study of meaningful events, and the philosophers and theologians of history devote their explanations of history to the course of these meaningful events. It is this that we mean by "history": meaningful events that explain each succeeding era in the total course of human events.

It is on the crucial moments of human history that philosophies and theologies, explanations of history, are centered. Thus the experience of Israel in the age of the covenant, of the Prophets, and of the exile are the moments in which a profound understanding of the history of God's people is proclaimed. It was when Christianity emerged at the time of Constantine and seriously threatened to replace the older paganism that an Augustine wrote a *City of God*. The passing of the Christian order that began with the age of rationalism and the Enlightenment produced a Voltaire and his attacks upon the older Christian theologies of history. In our own time two world wars and the seemingly senseless course upon which human history reels make for the popularity of a Toynbee or a Spengler. Current history, the post-Christian era, demands from the theologians the articulation of a theology in which the place of the believing Christian in the world and in its history is evident. Thus it is that the explanations of history, of the meaningful events that mark man's progress through time, are themselves provoked by the historical process.

Considerations of history, attempts to find therein ultimate meaning and purpose for the total course of human events, have been a feature of Christian thought since Augustine. The end of the nineteenth century saw a shift in emphasis and a properly scientific concern about the laws of historical research that dominate modern thinking on the problem of history. Thus even the problematic has been confused by a changing conception of history itself. When one asks about the "meaning" of history or a "philosophy" of history, ambiguity, determined by these shifting concerns of historians and philosophers, results. First, one may consider the philosophical and theological concern which attempts to establish the purpose and ultimate rationale of the historical process as the point of inquiry; or, second, one may consider the concern of the professional historian, who seeks to establish the methods, the laws, the "critique" of investigation. Our concern here is not with the establishment of critical history but rather with the broader problem of the pursuit of meaning in the whole course of human history.

Here again a number of problems must be met. What is the origin or source of human history? What is its chronological end, that is to say, the end point in time at which human history will cease? What is, from beginning to end, the teleological import of human history, its ultimate meaning or purpose? And, finally, what is the significance of history here and now? What does a consideration of history tell me about myself, about my times, the place and meaning of my own share in the process? Thus if the Christian maintains that the end or purpose of history lies in some extrahistorical reality such as the Kingdom of God, what is to be said of human achievement, that is, of man's work, his culture? A theology of history that speaks of the beginning and the end, of ultimate purpose, must also speak in the here and now of a theology of culture and of the values—if there are any—of man's work in time.

When in the course of our discussion we come to an extended treatment of the theology of history, we shall see part of the curious ambivalence of the "historical" resolved in a consideration of the biblical revelation. When we speak of the Bible and the events of that revelation, we mean by "historical" that they are actual, real events that have a place in time; they have truly occurred and are historical because they possess a real place in the course of human history (that is, "historicity," the quality of having happened). In addition to this they will be called historical because they are meaningful, significant, important in understanding the course of history in which they occur. These real events will be meaningful events because they will themselves be the ultimate explanation of the process of history itself. In addition to their actuality they possess their significance from the fact that they are the revelation of God. Certain facts within human history will be the "acts of God," the "wonderful works of God," and in these events of history will be found God's exposition of the meaning that the entire process of history possesses.

But is it necessary that history have a meaning? That there is a point to the whole process? Many historians ask the question, and they are content with a record of the facts and an explanation of the causes of events that are evident from the record. To ask many a professional historian the question about the meaning of history itself is to ask a philosophical question beyond his own sphere of study. Yet a man's sense of history, his grasp or nongrasp of its ultimate meaning, demonstrates his own attitude to philosophy. For modern man the meaning of history is the most vexing of questions. In fact, the interpretation of history is a major factor in our time in the scheme of every ideology which claims the allegiance of man's mind.

Today we have tasted the bitter frustration of two major wars and innumerable small ones; we have inherited senseless weapons of universal destruction; scientific progress has been crowned by bigger and better bombs. Popular existentialist philosophies demand of us an introspection that borders on self-obsession. These are major factors in modern history, and from them an urgency has been conferred upon the problem of history. Modern man has a sense of history; he cannot avoid it. The meaning that he sees in his history determines his conduct and has repercussions for every man.

In our own time Adolf Hitler appealed for a broken and divided Germany to return to her greatness; he evoked a conception of history in which he called Germany to her destiny. His emphasis upon race and racial purity and Aryan superiority provided for many Germans a mystique; it surrounded the movement of Nazism with an attractive theory of historical importance. Nazism promised a future. We tend to forget this appeal of Nazism, to evaluate it solely by the incredible toll of misery it produced. We forget the meaning and purpose of living that it conferred upon a disillusioned people, particularly the young men and women of post-World War I Germany. To the hopeless, Nazism was a movement in which they could contribute toward the construction of human history; it offered them a share in the future.

The hope and appeal of the Nazi period dims by comparison with the sweep and pull of communism. The Marxist theory today provides for its adherents the same sense of participating in the future. It claims to give each man's life a significance in terms of present sacrifice for an ultimate goal. More than this, the economic theory upon which it is based provides seemingly unquestionable evidence for its inevitability in human history. This is the intellectual attraction that Marxism offers—an ineluctable pattern that human history will take.

The eighteenth and nineteenth centuries have not witnessed the passing of the age of nationalism. The drive of Asia, Africa, the Middle East, to national identification is reaching its peak in our time. Nationalism represents fundamentally the driving force of a people for a place in history; in a sense one might say that it is the nationalist who rises to the fever pitch of history.

The conflicting ideologies of modern man—politics, economics, philosophies—reflect his interpretations of history. In the West the ideologies of democracy and capitalism are considered the products of historical process that best provide for the political and material needs of men. Each in turn, communism and democracy, socialism and capitalism, appeals to history for vindication. To a degree they are all alike in that they seek to give meaning to history, to the duration in which man finds himself.

The place and significance of man and his history have become the arenas in which the rival philosophies of man do battle. Positivism, scientism, Thomism, existentialism are all ranged upon the battlefield of the meaning man is to give history. Thus the Christian today in a very real sense faces the challenge of human history. The Christian must witness to his contemporaries by answering the questions concerning history. Does it, can it, have meaning? If it does, what is its meaning?

Not only does this challenge exist for the Christian, it quite obviously possesses enormous urgency. A Christian witness to God and Christ must be a witness taking account of history; thus it is a witness not only to the Christian fact but to the relevancy of that fact for man caught up in the flow of an apparently uncontrollable force to which he has given the name "history."

The aim of this book is to introduce the reader to the various concepts of history in the Western world, and in particular to show how men in our time have attempted to answer the question history poses. In this we will attempt to survey the heritage of thinking about the problem. We will give some attention to the question of the possibility of a philosophy of history, specifically of a Christian philosophy of history, and to the philosophers both secular and Christian who have posed the problem. With these preliminaries surveyed, we can turn toward the idea of a theology of history, to the popular Protestant theories and the Catholic views of history. In conclusion we shall try to coordinate definite elements of the Christian theological view to enable the Christian as an individual to live in awareness of the full Christian dimension of history that has come to us in Christ.

If this work should seem hasty and at times sketchy, we beg the reader's indulgence. This study is not intended to explore completely all the efforts man has made toward the creation of philosophies and theologies of history. But it is hoped that the work will introduce and explain the problem posed by the theology of history, that it will present solutions currently in vogue among Christian theologians, and finally, that it will indicate a coordinated view of the elements from which a theology of history may be presented.

JAMES M. CONNOLLY

New York, 1963

PART ONE

MAN AND HIS HISTORY

Chapter 1

FROM PHILOSOPHY TO HISTORY:
THE DEVELOPMENT OF THE PROBLEM OF HISTORY TO OUR TIME

MANY CHRISTIAN writers in presenting the Christian view of history and time have vividly contrasted it with the ancient pagan pre-Christian conceptions. It has been fashionable to denigrate the cyclic conception of time common to the pre-Judaic and pre-Christian civilizations. The eternal recurrence, the doctrine of the cycle as an expression of human history, is found in the earliest communities of men.[1] The common Christian criticism of cyclicism is based upon the concept of human freedom that is believed concomitant with the Christian linear view of time. Beginning and end, creation and the final intervention of God are Judaeo-Christian contributions, but they are not so strongly contrasted with cyclicism that the latter can only be pictured in terms of frustration and despair.

The actual conditions that governed the primitive cyclical view of time were quite different from the despair that Christian writers normally attach to that conception. Mircea Eliade and other scholars have pointed out that while primitive man did naturally draw on the cyclic conception of nature for a cyclic conception of human history, nevertheless, far from leading man to despair, such a concept actually served to liberate man and gave meaning to his life.[2] The cycles of time were placed within a framework essentially religious, so that the sacredness of cyclic time lay in its ability to grant the rebirth of the world and man.

Thus through such a rebirth the religious man could recover the original holiness of this world: a recovery through cosmogenic myth, a periodic repetition and reliving of the cosmogony. Escape was possible for man in the sacred calendar, in the religious commemoration of the acts of the gods. Through his religious observance and in the cycles of time the sacred time of the primeval gods could be actualized. There was then to be found in temporal cycles the eternal return to the sources of the sacred, of the holy; and thus man's temporal existence could be saved from frustration and meaninglessness.

It was when the initial idea of the holiness of the world was lost that the ancient cyclical conception of time led to an intolerable pessimism. The evolution of more intellectual cultures, the growth of reasoning concerning the world and nature, led to the loss of religious content in the repetition of the cycles of time. The loss of the religious framework deprived cyclic time of its value of reintegration with the primitive cosmogony; the cycles ever returning upon themselves to infinity became terrifying. Thus the Eastern doctrines of cosmic cycles—as, for example, among the Hindus—inevitably see the world and time as essentially illusions, from which escape is to be sought. The loss of a religious framework for the cyclic conception necessarily brings some such theory of escape to nirvana as the ultimate goal of a man.

The Greeks and the Romans were in turn dominated by this cyclic view of time. For them the world was repetitive, an eternal return. According to Plato the soul is one and consequently eternal because indestructible; the world of which a man is aware is but a land of shadows, man lives in a cave, he is an exile. Human history goes nowhere—forever changing, it ever remains the same; human history is meaningless on its own terms. Furthermore, man is not free in such a system, his acts are determined by the gods. It was to this world dominated by terrifying concepts of determinism, cycles, the meaninglessness of human acts, that the Judaeo-Christian concept of linear time came.[3]

In short, the point in human history at which the contrast between the meaninglessness of cyclical time and the purposiveness of the linear conception is most vividly evident is that point at which the cyclic conception lost its religious framework and usefulness in putting man in touch with the sacred time of the gods. It is to an era that may be characterized as the prison house of cyclic time that Christianity brings a universal doctrine of the meaningfulness of history.

THE JUDAEO-CHRISTIAN REVELATION

The revelation of the Old Testament presents to man an entirely new concept of human history. This is based upon a belief in the one God as the Creator of the world and all therein. This world is the creation of God, the free and gratuitous and effective action of God. Thus in the Bible eternity is not to be thought of as some infinite time before history but rather as the measure of God's perfect fullness. When God creates, time begins: it is a measure of creation. Time is creation still in progress. For the later Old Testament authors time has a beginning, and it will also have an end, that is, in the sense of a new beginning. Time has a direction; the actions of human history are, therefore, irreversible—they do not return through a constant cycle; human actions are performed once and for all.

Thus human history as based upon the biblical concept of creation may be seen as linear. It is a fixed line having beginning and ultimate goal. Furthermore, in this fixed period of historical time the eternal God acts; He manifests Himself in actual historical actions, and these acts of God in time are a theophany, a revelation of Himself.

The New Testament revelation completes the Old. Here the variable factor of human history, freedom, is stressed. Mystery develops and enshrouds history itself as the New Testament also emphasizes the constant of history, namely, the providence of God, His free and eternal purposes. Thus providence and freedom maintain between them a field of unbearable tension: from one viewpoint they constitute in Christian thought the mystery of human history.

The New Testament reveals further a God-Who-Acts and enters time in a marvelous theophany. The Son of God comes in the flesh; there is revealed an Incarnation in time. The Christian fact, the divine event, is God's saving purpose accomplished in Christ: for this event did history move to an ordered fullness, this event now dominates history, and again, it is this event that determines the ultimate end of history.

Thus the biblical revelation of God as the God-Who-Acts gives to the Christian not so much a philosophy of history as, properly speaking, a theology of history. To this theology of history, a linear conception of man's duration in time, Christian thinkers have turned throughout the ages. In the second and third centuries of the Christian era the Fathers, especially Clement of Alexandria, Julius Africanus, and Hippolytus of Rome, proclaimed a divine Providence ruling the world, and to the Hellenistic idea of chronography they added a Christian completion by recording the apostles and their successors. The crucial moment in early Christian history was October 28, 312, marked by Constantine's victory at the Milvian Bridge; it signified the emergence of the Christian religion as a factor in world history. Thus in the fourth century, Christian thinkers such as Lactantius, Eusebius, and Athanasius emerged with works that showed "concern with the pattern of history rather than with the detail." [4] Lactantius in his *De mortibus persecutorum* (c. 316) attributes Constantine's victory to God's punishment of the pagans; Eusebius emphasizes chronography; Athanasius' *Life of St. Anthony* (c. 360) marks the beginning of hagiography.

The last gasp of pagan scholarship in the fourth century was evident in the growth in number, quality, and authority of the pagan histories in their *breviaria*. These made an intellectual demand upon the Christian that required a comparable answer. It was provided by Augustine, Sulpicius Severus, and Orosius. The educated Roman convert to Christianity in the fourth century was ignorant of Jewish and Christian history; conversion demanded not only a theology but also a history. "People learnt a new history because they acquired a new religion. Conversion meant literally the discovery of a new history from Adam and Eve to contemporary events." [5] Thus it was that the Christian had to explain the Old Testament history leading to Christ, so that he presented Christianity as something totally new but as something intellectually respectable.[6] It was in this stage of the fourth century that the first of the great theologians of history, and probably the greatest, Saint Augustine, emerged. His linear conception of time and his theory of the two cities in history dominated Christian thinking until modern times.

AUGUSTINE TO BOSSUET

It is in the monumental work of Saint Augustine (354–430), *The City of God*, that we find the elements of a Christian sense of history ordered around the specific theme of history itself. The Christian fact is opposed to the pagan theories of recurring cycles. Augustine was quite specific about this linear conception of time, and his treatment of history was dominated by its inevitable end, the world to come. This eschatology of Augustine was built upon the Genesis imagery of the six-day creation, so that we now live in the last day.

According to Augustine, there are no philosophical principles to be abstracted from human experience around which an orderly conception of history might be constructed. There is only to be found sin—the city of man in human history. Against this must be placed in present time the building up of the City of God. Augustine did not look upon the history of man, nor did he find there any cause for cheerful optimism or inevitable progress; he found in human history only the brutal fact of sin. Augustine believed that man must turn away from sin, that he must renounce the city of man in time and contribute toward the building up of the City of God, whose perfection he confidently awaits.

Augustine's view of history was the one commonly held in the Church and in intellectual circles until the seventeenth century. In no small measure did his renunciation of the city of man give impetus and substance to the growth of monasticism; in fact, the monks of the Church frequently drew flight from the world and a driving force of asceticism from his principles of the theology of history.

It would be erroneous to see in Augustine and his intellectual preeminence in the Church a complete Christian rejection of the cyclic theory of time. A number of Church Fathers and theologians, even into the Middle Ages, held to a cyclic conception of time. While they would accept creation and parousia as the poles of human history, they would see within these spheres a historical motion dominated by cycles of action, as nature was dominated by cycles. During the Middle Ages this historical attitude was finally abandoned in favor of the Augustinian view. In 1157 Otto of Freising published his *The Two Cities,* a universal history of man reflecting concern for historical facts but dominated by the eschatology of Augustine. For Otto, however, the Church was to be identified with the City of God. He also gives an interesting geographical sweep to history in that he maintains the destiny of humanity always lies to the west. (Thus Christianity began in Jerusalem and constantly moves to the west.)

In the thirteenth century, as Martin D'Arcy has remarked, the Thomist system, built around the principles, insights, and thought of Saint Thomas, provided not a theology or philosophy of history but only the necessary materials for a Christian philosophy of history based on the concept of man as a free moral agent, of man as a free cause of events.[7] Yet no major Christian thinker after Thomas found these materials in Thomism directable toward such an understanding of history, that is until the contemporary revival of neo-Thomism in philosophy and theology.

The variable element of human history, freedom, and the constant of God's providence became the focal points of the major theological battle of the later Middle Ages. The energies of Thomist and Molinist were spent upon the vexing and ultimately unanswerable question of God's predestination and the consequences of grace and sin as they resolve in the life of the historical person.

Jacques Bénigne Bossuet (1627–1704) marked the chronological high-water mark of the Augustinian conception of history. In his celebrated *Discours* Bossuet, stressing the providence of God, saw in the disasters of history the chastisements of God. Again, this view of history was based upon faith, impossible of purely rational demonstration on the basis of the facts of history alone. Bossuet, like Augustine, in whose tradition he moved, was a theologian of history.

This interpretation of history soon collapsed beneath the hammer blows of the rationalist Voltaire. Voltaire brought reason to human history and ridiculed the invocation of a divine Providence to explain historical events. The defects inherent in a simplistic view of history as propounded by Bossuet became all too evident. The stage was set for the philosophers, the scientists, the wise men of the world, to explain the meaning of history.

VICO TO VOLTAIRE

The seventeenth century was dominated by the philosophy of René Descartes, and with it by a fundamentally antihistorical attitude. Descartes denied to the study of history any standing as a branch of knowledge, for, he maintained, in the description of events that history claimed to provide, no description ever exactly covered the event. Thus, because of the contingencies of its subject matter, history could never attain to truth. A growing movement of thought marked by a strong historical sense was not, however, so easily to be set aside, and later thinkers, detecting this fatal weakness of the Cartesian philosophy, used it as a fulcrum to overthrow Cartesianism.

The Italian Giovanni Battista Vico (1668–1744), a skilled historian with a brilliant mind, led the onslaught against the Cartesian theory of truth.[8] Where Descartes had begun with the disjunction of fact and idea, Vico as a historian began with the given facts of the past; to these facts he brought a critical method and principles for the establishment of historical knowledge.

Vico divided history into periods, and taught that these periods tended to occur again and again in a certain order; he believed that he had found a pattern to history. The recurrence of historical periods was not a rigidly conceived cyclical movement, self-enclosed, as it had been for later pre-Christian thought, but rather a spiral movement, pre-eminently one of ascent. Vico was a Christian who believed that history had beginning and end, that periodization did not mean the cyclical trap of an enclosed eternal recurrence, but he did believe that in history one could trace through these periods observable phases and laws. Because this motion of history is to be envisioned as a spiral, the historian could not from his knowledge of the patterns predict the future; each state of history possessed its own peculiar qualities.

In effect, what Vico was seeking was a "scientific" history embracing not only a philosophy of history but also an empirical method for the historian. He deliberately set aside the revelation, in which he devoutly believed, in order to study human history with reason alone. In this manner he discovered what he believed to be a certain law immanent in history—divine Providence. For

Vico the historical process reflected the gradual unfolding of the divine Will. In addition, one was to find in history abundant evidence of the freedom of will possessed by man. This twofold existence of human freedom and divine Providence forbade any certain predictions of the future by the historian. The development that exists in the stages of human history is a real development in which the eternal law of God emerges; but this law, this divine Providence, is also continually opposed by man's evil disposition.

This philosophical insight into history had little influence at the time, but it demonstrates for us the first serious or, at least, adequately presented Christian philosophy of history. Vico marks a new stage in Christian thinking on history, that of Christian philosophy (the use of reason, guided by revelation, in exploring the meaning of history) rather than of theology (the use of revelation to explain the meaning of history). In the course of his thought one also finds the first elucidation of principles of historical method that are of interest to the historian rather than to the philosopher.

To this historical thought of Vico, particularly to his principles of method, was soon joined the empiricism of Locke, Berkeley, and Hume. Empiricism added little to the developing tradition of historical thinking, but it did provide philosophical bases for the overthrow of Cartesianism, and with it the Cartesian disdain for history. The road had been opened for historical thought to develop; first, however, it was to pass through the fire of the Enlightenment. The ideas of the English empiricists were avidly seized by the Enlightenment, and by François Voltaire (1694–1778) in particular.

The Enlightenment stood foursquare against revealed religion; the new historical thought was utilitarian in this opposition and considered "revelation" of little value in itself. In the new empiricism Voltaire found the principles with which he could reject Cartesian thought and at the same time destroy the oversimplified theology of history represented by Bossuet. For Voltaire reason was the key to history; there was no need to invoke the providence of the deity. Subject to his withering attack, the concept of theology of history slowly ebbed away from the forefront of Christian thought until it reappeared in our own time.

But Voltaire was as doctrinaire about reason as Bossuet had been about providence. Voltaire disdained any idea of history prior to the fifteenth century; all else was to be regarded as artifice and myth. He had no sense of man's historical development. History was used by Voltaire as another stick with which to beat the Church, and the Enlightenment never rose above the level of Voltaire. No real developments in historical knowledge, method, or philosophy were made by the period.

It did have one enormous effect: in its rationalistic rejection of any concept of providence in human history it set the stage for the period of the philosophers of history. History was now emptied of meaning, and the emerging generation of idealist philosophers would feel a necessity to discover in the entire process of history some meaning, some reason beyond externals, some real pattern and law.

THE IDEALIST PHILOSOPHERS OF HISTORY

In the era that followed the Enlightenment the history of man had become a "scandal." Theories of human perfectibility and progress were advanced in an attempt to see a pattern or meaning in the course of historical change. That which had at one time been the task of the theologians, the reconciliation of evil within the framework of a divine Providence, had now become a problem central to the work of the philosophers.

These men looked upon the growing critical history of the past as purely fragmentary; they saw it as a catalogue of unrelated facts; they felt the need of something better to display the meaning of the historical process itself. In a word, these philosophers wanted history to be intelligible. The vicissitudes of life, the miseries of man, these had to be seen as stages in the process of something better, steps toward a higher goal. History simply had to have meaning, there had to be a teleological end; if not, they were "morally outraged."

The professional historian had, and even today has, little or no interest in these moral demands of the philosophers. When the philosophers had finished advancing their theories, the historians more than ever wanted nothing to do with what they regarded as no legitimate domain for the historian. The historian interested himself in the facts of history; he denied the existence of pattern. The intelligibility of history was the catalogue of various casual factors surrounding a historical event, admittedly incomplete and always provisional. But the philosopher of history saw this only as superficial and incomplete: he saw the schema of facts and factors as something beyond which he must go—indeed, beyond which he was compelled to go. It is in this light that we can see how the late eighteenth- and early nineteenth-century philosophies of history originated as necessary creations designed to fill an intellectual vacuum and a moral need.

The first of these philosophers was the idealist Immanuel Kant (1724–1804). He was not a historian, but primarily a philosopher. An essential ingredient of his philosophy was morality; and in this philosophy a divine Providence was the necessary basis for a life in conformity to moral laws. Human history must, then, have a meaning in itself, and must be explicable from a philosophical point of view.[9]

The meaningfulness of history was constructed by Kant along the eighteenth-century theories of progress. Man was continually making progress, the line of human history was always ascending. However, there was one difficulty with this view—the real-life shocks of the individual. The individual could suffer evil and setback in history; how was this to be reconciled with Kant's view of ever-ascending progress? Kant transferred his vision of human history and its concept of progress to the whole, not to the individual. Human history must be seen in its long-term plan. This plan of nature, this definite progress, was to be elucidated by the historian; it was his proper job, just as natural laws were the object of investigation for the scientist.

The obvious weakness inherent in the Kantian system was the a priori nature of history that it envisioned: history could be explained by the philosopher without reference to the actual course of human events. In addition to this outrageous conception Kant saw the determination of this historical process in the future. Yet the historian must object as historian that the only legitimate purpose of his study of the past is to be enabled to demonstrate in historical terms the meaning of the present. No one, least of all the historian, can know the future.

The poet Friedrich von Schiller (1759–1805) interpreted and worked with Kant's theory of history. Schiller was himself a university professor of history, and like Kant he conceived an idea of universal history on the lines of progress. Schiller, however, placed Kant's futuristic goal in the present. For Schiller universal history explains the present. Johann Fichte (1762–1814), another pupil of Kant, agreed with Schiller and refined his view of universal history into periods, or stages, in which the idea of freedom develops. Both Schiller and Fichte, like their master Kant, vitiated their work by a priori principles or frameworks, into which history was made to fit. While the historian may object that Kant's goal of progress in the future neglects the present, the philosopher may legitimately object to the patent error of claiming that this transitory and conditional present (the Prussian *Sitz-im-Leben* of Fichte and Schelling) is nevertheless the goal of that process.

Another of Kant's pupils, Johann Herder (1744–1803), even more than his master became the first of the great nineteenth-century philosophers of history. He began the publication of his *Ideas For a Philosophical History of Mankind* in 1784, the year of Kant's publication of an article spelling out his views of history. Herder's position was that one must understand the universe and man's place in it before the problem of understanding history can be broached. The study of the cosmos impressed Herder with its wide varieties of gradation. These gradations of existence led him to propose a universe animated by a singular force, the object of which was the "freedom of the spirit."

For Herder the spirit of man, the spirit of the peoples of world history, is the spirit of freedom and the internal unifying force of the cosmos. It is quite evident to him, however, that this spirit is in conflict with the external forces of environment and milieu. History proper is the product of this interaction of internal and external forces. As a result of this, Herder attempted to be more historical and more attentive to the details and facts of human history. These events of history were, like the events of nature, governed by law: Herder conceived of them as having some general purpose. Therefore the processes of history had meaning, and this was the attainment of a state where man could be "truly human," truly himself. It was a state where the spirit of freedom emerged perfectly. The vagueness of this perfection of man being "truly human," the indefiniteness of this state was never adequately clarified by Herder and presents one of the greatest difficulties of the theory.

Like Kant, Herder must labor under the critique of the historian. His theory is deliberately constructed on lines of a priori thinking. To his credit it must be said that Herder attempted to start with facts, but he moved all too quickly from some facts to a development of general laws of history. Moreover, while appreciative of the distinct genius of nature to be found in various peoples and cultures, his principles, if carried to a logical conclusion, would defend narrow theories of racial supremacy.

The idealist philosophy of history reached its acme in the work of Georg Wilhelm Friedrich Hegel (1770–1831).[10] Hegel's concept of history was based upon his philosophy, and primarily upon the dialectics of that philosophy. To grasp his idea of history it is necessary to examine some of his philosophical concepts.

Thought for Hegel was fundamentally built upon a system of triads. This dialectical nature of thought is built upon thesis, antithesis, and synthesis. Logic, or the Idea of a thing, known in this triadic process, is itself part of a supertriad of Idea as thesis, Nature as antithesis, and Spirit as synthesis. The Idea demands reification in Nature, and returns to itself as a concrete in Spirit.

The World, then, is not simply a reflection of ideas, it is the development of Idea. The philosopher through his knowledge of the Idea (acquired through the laws of the dialectic) bears in upon history and elevates its empirical contents to the rank of necessary truths. The key to history is the idea of freedom, developing itself, and finally realizing itself. Spirit is the consciousness or ultimate realization of this idea of freedom. This triadic process was completed in world history according to Hegel by the Germanic nation of his own time.

Hegel thus harnesses the idea of progress to his philosophical system; he makes sense out of history by progress through the dialectic. He finds a pattern in history, and yet is able to recognize a distinction in the development of historical events. The difficulties of human freedom and responsibility are resolved by demanding the "long view" of history—the importance of the ethics and morality of society rather than of individuals.

Again, Hegel faces the charge of a priori judgment; furthermore, there is the unacceptable cynicism of denying morality to individual conscience in favor of the long view of society. But despite these shortcomings, Hegel has influenced historians, not by giving them a philosophy of history, but by concentrating upon the sense of the importance of the past. The eighteenth century displayed a considerable lack of real historical ability; Hegel rectified, albeit from an erroneous philosophy of history, this lamentable lack of the historical sense.

> But for all the arbitrary and romantic elements in Hegel's philosophy of history, both philosophers and historians must remain forever in his debt. For the first time he brought together the data of history in a rational synthesis, exhibiting the progress of humanity from its Asiatic cradle to modern western Europe and clearly recognizing the fact of cultural evolution. The connecting thread might be inadequate and the resulting construction badly lop-sided—yet an imperfect classification is better than no classification at all.[11]

POSITIVISM AND AUGUSTE COMTE

The empirical point of view came to a position of dominance over historical thinking in the nineteenth-century movement of positivism. The progress in natural science and the scientific method led to the development of the positivist mind and its intervention into the realm of historical studies. The scientific notion of evolution directed a major blow at Hegel's conception of nature as well as at his conception of history. Historical thought and scientific thought had the explication of evolutionary progress as their object.

Auguste Comte (1798–1857) applied to history the strict positivist method of the natural sciences. With his law of the "three stages" Comte offered to make sense of history. For Comte progress is signified in three stages of civilization: at first man attempts to attribute effects to the direct causality of God; then, as civilization progresses, these effects are attributed to metaphysical principles; and finally, in the ultimate stage of progress, they are rightly attributed to nature via the empirical sciences. Throughout this system one finds an unquestioned assumption of progress and a simplistic and naïve view of it.[12]

The positivists following Comte became obsessed primarily with the necessity for facts as raw materials, and secondarily with the framing of laws for these facts. Through this system their conclusions obviated any criticism of a priori thinking. Thus they provided a great incentive for the gathering of the materials for serious critical history; and this was no small contribution to historical studies. As a matter of fact, this critical sense of the need for facts has been the major and lasting contribution of positivism.

However, the critical historians began to stop at this first stage of the positivist method; they were content to rest with the facts as they could ascertain them. For this they were strongly criticized by positivist philosophers; the historian, they thought, should get on to the second stage of the process, the stage of framing the laws of history, as the scientists were doing in their fields. Their charge against the movement of critical history that they had brought into being was that the historians were now being "nonscientific."

As a matter of fact, though positivism did bring about this first stage of the critical historians, and men like Mommsen, Acton, Maitland, Von Ranke became masters of detail, yet the idea of seeing laws in history or even of framing universal histories was lost. With these men also appeared a perfection of method.

This became the great contribution of the positivists: the appearance of a critical method of handling historical sources. The historians using it turned to the discovery of facts, and saw no point to the positivist injunction to get on to the second stage of framing laws of history. Their positivism, or better their heritage of positivism, consisted simply in *the fact*—the fact knowable in itself and independent of other possibilities. Thus the historian felt he must pass no judgment upon these facts; the historical fact was envisioned as a natural fact.

The growth of this "historicism," a scientific history that stopped with fact, had unfortunate consequences. The historians refused to deal with the history of thought that created the facts they investigated; no history of religion or of philosophy or of the thought that produced these facts was undertaken—only purely political history. As a result the historians became distrustful, and as they remain today, opposed to any idea of a philosophy of history. Philosophy of history as the search for the ultimate reason of human history itself was rejected; but the philosophy of history that determined the why and wherefore of historical thought, of the norms of the subject of history itself, was the only philosophy of history they would accept.

KARL MARX

If we were to judge nineteenth-century thought about history by the results it produced, no name would be more significant than that of Karl Marx (1818–1883). For good or for ill, it is Marx and his conception of history that have most sharply affected the world in which we live and that today most seriously challenge the Christian view of history.

Marx was a Hegelian. From Hegel he derived the basic elements of his system, particularly the dialectic of thesis-antithesis-synthesis. But Marx introduced a substantial change in making the dialectic the nature of *things,* not the nature of *thought.* Hegel's concept of the various aspects of society as having an organic relationship to one another also seriously affected Marx's thought. His system (dialectical materialism) was at its base materialistic, and yet it contained the strong bent for history that a sense of the organic nature of society would convey.

In addition, Marx united to this the empiricist strain of thought that went back to Voltaire and the Encylopedists, and the positivist thought associated with Comte. Marx was not only interested in understanding history, he was equally desirous of shaping it. He brought a concept of social dynamics, a desire to use history for certain ends, to his system. Marxism became under his guiding genius an amalgam: the inverted idealism of Hegel, the empiricism of Voltaire, the positivism of Comte, and his own intense practical interest in the uses of history. The end product was a strong theory of history, a theory that not only made sense of history but of what was happening in one's own time as well.

The only real influence that existed in human history, Marx believed, was economics. On these lines he has made a lasting contribution to our understanding of one of the major historical forces. No serious historian since Marx has been able to ignore the economic influence upon the course of human history. But it must be said that the dialectical process at the heart of the system remains unproven. It was not testified to by fact in the Marxian presentation, nor did Marx ever attempt to provide an a priori justification of the dialectic according to principle.

While the dialectic remains an assumption, and his interest in the economic forces of history remains an accomplishment, Marxism, as conveyed to the modern world, maintains the hallmark of dynamism. More than a system of conceiving history, it is a faith; and with it goes all the commitment that the word "faith" implies. The Marxist has faith in the inexorable processes of history, in the certainty of the ultimate term of history in a socialist reality. It is this terrible attractiveness and sureness of purpose that creates the contemporary intellectual appetite for Marxism.

KIERKEGAARD AND EXISTENTIALISM

The severest reaction against the work of Hegel that appeared in the nineteenth century was that of Sören Kierkegaard (1813–1855). Kierkegaard's critique was motivated by an acute sense of Christian faith, and the anti-idealist movement of existentialism that he set in motion was not destined to flower until the twentieth century.

The absence of morals or ethics as a controlling factor for the individual to be found in the Hegelian demand that one take the long view of human history revolted Kierkegaard. This Hegelian viewpoint he felt to be the degradation of both God and man. History, Kierkegaard maintained, had meaning and purpose—in this he agreed with Hegel—but such knowledge of the ultimate meaning of history was reserved to God alone, and was not to be found in the philosophical creations of man.

This outlook was essentially the result of Kierkegaard's metaphysics and epistemology; it was predetermined by his attitude toward being and knowledge. The processes of human history, he said, are "becoming," therefore they are contingent: in them divine Providence and the contingencies of human freedom remain at work. This contingency of human history based upon human freedom makes any real philosophy of history impossible. In the process of becoming, assent to or realization of becoming—and consequently of historical events—is only possible through an act of will. At most, it is only through this act of will, through faith, belief, that one may grasp an event. Consequently, true knowledge of human history is impossible and, what is more, so are scientific laws.

Although for Kierkegaard there can be no philosophy of history, no real rational explanation or perception of both the processes of history and its meaning, he does proclaim a definite theology of history. The touchstone of such an explanation is the historical event of God's coming in Christ—the Incarnation. As a historical event, it is therefore known only by belief or assent; but as the unique historical event, it is known only by a second order of belief, a unique historical belief that we call faith.

Through faith, which is man's assent to God in Christ, through this grasp of the fact of the Incarnation, a man becomes "contemporaneous" to Christ. This act of faith is the gift of God; it is the means of *becoming* a Christian. The only real possibility of knowledge of and actual possession of the meaning of history is with God, and by grasping in faith God in Christ, the Christian's world view is actually a theology of history. It is through faith in Christ that he sees the point to human history. It is not accomplished through reason; thus there is no philosophy of history. It is accomplished through the unique faith that is a gift of God.

This view has become, as we shall see, extremely popular in the twentieth century, particularly among the "crisis" theologians of Protestantism. It is to Kierkegaard and his spirit that they look as their master. We shall see later elaborations of this view, and its difficulties and deficiencies from the Catholic theological standpoint. We shall also see that this existentialist tradition stemming from Kierkegaard has given rise on its principles to a contemporary atheistic movement with its own nihilistic conception of history. The twentieth century has made the importance of Kierkegaard and his tradition, insignificant in his own time, most evident.

Thus, up to our own time, has the problem of history developed. It has passed from concepts of cyclical time to an era of theological thought embracing a linear conception, through a period of philosophers, and, eventually, empiricists. Many of the trends established throughout the long history of man's thought are now evident in the world and bid in the intellectual market place for the adherence of the modern intellectual. The theological revival, based upon studies in Scripture and the sources of the Christian religion, has restored the theological conception of history (and in some cases, a Christian philosophy of history) to a place of respectability; the idealism of the philosophers has been modified and yet retains its influence. The Marxist challenge is more than evident; and the crisis theologians of Protestantism have drawn enormous vitality from their dynamic conception of a new theology of history.

Chapter 2

FROM HISTORY TO PHILOSOPHY:
THE PROBLEM OF HISTORY IN OUR TIME

BOTH PHILOSOPHERS and theologians who devote themselves to the explanation of the meaning of history are well aware of the traditional lines of approach to the problem of history. Before we can examine the elements of the theological viewpoint in the explanation of history, it is well also to be aware of current thinking about history. The complexity of this subject should not be missed in the necessarily sketchy presentation that follows, but the presentation of this current thought is a logical prelude to a theology of history, for it is necessary to see how historians interpret their discipline, how they interpret the historical process itself. Philosophers, particularly the moderns, are marked by their consciousness of history. The problem presented by the historian's view of the meaning of history and by the philosopher's conclusions about history will in no small way allow us to appreciate the relevance of the theological preoccupation with history.

There remain also the questions raised by definitions—of history as a "science," or of the philosophy of history—which will be dependent upon and reflective of the traditions of thinking that have dominated historical thought. As we have remarked, "history" itself is that term embracing the study of the meaningful events of the past. Thus while the occurrence of an event is sufficient to bring it within range of the term "historical" as having happened, the study of these unrepeatable events called history does not embrace every simple occurrence, but rather those "meaningful" events that through cause and effect give insight and understanding to the whole movement of the historical process.

The historian, he who limits his vision to the historical occurrence and its relation to the process itself, has as the object of study the human events of man in time. History has as its subject matter the individual and singular acts of the past, the particular and the concrete. The historian is the thinker who faces, investigates, and evaluates the concrete moments of the past. Such a study has its own means of investigation, roads to knowledge of the past, that have been developed by man: a method that found its first definitive formulation in the nineteenth century. Historians have formulated and established critical laws and principles for the study of the process itself, for arriving at a more accurate perception of past events. This legacy of method, of controlled and critical use of the sources from which history is recorded, compiled, and understood is a legacy of the nineteenth-century movement of historicism. And because many of these historians have arrived from these critical studies of history at certain conclusions concerning history itself, they and their opinions must be evaluated.

Distinct from history, then, is the philosophy of history. The philosophers of history utilize the raw material of the historian, they direct their gaze upon the total process of history itself and seek to abstract from the process those laws or patterns that they feel give meaning to the process of history. But not even the philosophy of history has now been saved from the threat of ambiguity. The failure to maintain this strict definition has led many, and these principally among the historians, to deny the existence of a philosophy of history insofar as that connotes the attempt to "explain" the process itself. They nevertheless use the term to designate the branch of historical studies that justifies critical history, determines its norms, and erects what may be called an epistemology of history. Since this latter discipline is directly related to the historian and history, and since it is well to avoid terminological difficulties, we shall include such studies under their proper subject, history, and use the current definition of the philosophy of history to refer to the attempt to present the "meaning" of history as abstracted from its processes.

The subjects, history and the philosophy of history, which have such preliminary importance in the development of a theology of history, and which so seriously mark man's thinking today, have their immediate origins in the nineteenth century. From our investigations of the nineteenth century we shall be able to turn to the modern historians and their view of the history of men, then to the idealist, positivist, and existentialist strains of thought in the philosophy of history, and finally to the question of the Christian philosophy of history.

THE NINETEENTH CENTURY: INTELLECTUAL WATERSHED OF HISTORICAL THOUGHT

At the end of the last chapter we saw that the empirical studies of nature led inexorably to the framing of laws; and under the aegis of this type of thinking, historians looked to the establishment first of the historical fact, and thence to the framing of the laws of history, to the definite patterns of history that full historical knowledge would lay bare. The nineteenth-century historians soon became quite content with the establishment of "facts"; they perfected their methods of historical research, and fearful lest they fall into the a priori conceptions of history that dominated idealist thought from Kant to Hegel, they became skeptical of any ability to construct a philosophy of history. In the first fervor of achievement they were content to look upon their discipline, their conquests of history, as a science. History as a discipline was born in the nineteenth century, and its preoccupation with itself, with its own methods and finally with its own judgment of itself as a science we call the tradition of historicism.

Historicism, then, stated the historian's point of view. This was that there was a critical method for the study of the past, that theology and philosophy had nothing to say to the historian, and that there could be no a priori approach to the historical process for a historian. In short, human history was the object of the study of the historian as was the world of nature the object of study for the natural scientist. From the simple naturalistic view of historicism the historian came to regard his field as a science and its practitioners as scientists. Physicist and historian were each in his own way scientists—only the object of their study differed.

Who were these men? No one would deny that the founding father of historicism, the first historical scientist, was the Prussian Leopold von Ranke (1795–1886). Not only because of the initial impulse that he gave to historicism, but because of his method and his aims, Ranke has long been regarded as the father of modern historical scholarship. His was the ideal of "pure" history, concerned only with the penetration of a particular event; a subject and a discipline strictly distinct from either philosophy or theology. Von Ranke tried to remove himself from his work, to abstain from judgment, to have as a standard nothing outside the historical process itself. The historical event, he maintained, could be explained by no category outside of history itself. Of necessity, then, his historical study was a separate and distinct subject from the other fields of knowledge, with its own methods and standards of evaluation; it was, simply speaking, a science.

That which Ranke began, others took up. Noteworthy among these first great historicists were Buckle, Acton, and Bury in England, Mommsen in Germany, and Berr in France. Thomas Buckle (1821–1862) alone of the great scientific historians attempted to go beyond the event in itself to the establishment of laws of historical development, to attempt to find if there are patterns in history. For this Buckle long suffered the criticism of his fellow historians. Lord Acton's (1834–1902) influence was to carry well into the twentieth century the ideas and ideals of scientific history. Theodore Mommsen (1817–1903) brought the genius of historicism to bear in his classic history of Rome, and Henri Berr (1862–1954) may be termed the last in a long tradition of scientific history, the last link in the historicist chain that Ranke began to forge. Throughout these years such men and many others in the historicist camp carried to perfection the methods of historical study and research.

There is a point here at which we must stop and reflect not only about what Ranke and the historicists did but also about what they wanted to do. Is the subject of history, the pursuit of the facts of the past, a science? Is its object, in fact, knowable? Are the methods of historical knowledge really critical and scientific? Are the conclusions of history as certain as those of the physical sciences?

Let it be stated that first of all the method, the laws governing the study of the subject itself, the critique established for the exploration of evidence and the mining of sources, certainly does establish history as scientific. But does method alone suffice to bring any intellectual discipline within the scope of what is to be regarded as science? Here we reach what is fundamentally a semantic problem. History is a science in the older Aristotelian sense of that word, but this is established because history does arrive at some knowledge. Today, however, "science" is not a term that we use in an Aristotelian sense in any branch of human knowledge; it has a specific meaning for the mind of modern man. From the limited sense in which the word "science" is used today, history can only be regarded as scientific in its methodology: it is certainly not scientific in view of its object (the past event), and is most certainly not scientific in its conclusions (a knowledge of past events based upon available sources and conditional information).

The physical sciences, aiming as they do at the establishment of universal and necessary truths, are not in the same category as history, which attempts to understand the singular and the unique. The knowledge of an event is never finished, never completed, always conditional, always based upon the supposition of having exhausted the sources of information. Physical science may arrive at some certainties, and what is more important, it may test by controlled experiments those certainties and conclusions. But history is never certain; there are few positive conclusions to which a historian can point.

The complicating factor for the historian is, of course, human freedom. The ability of man to choose, his freedom to act or not, in the long view deprives historical knowledge of any possibility of achieving certainty. History is not a science, for the historian cannot test his conclusions by experiment and cannot therefore predict actions or the term of the historical process. On the basis of his limited knowledge of the past, no matter how exhaustive that may be, the historian cannot in view of freedom refer to the future. The historian must in the end be satisfied with the statement of past ontological facts and conditional judgments of their causes.

It would seem, then, that Ranke and the scientific historians after him erred in their belief that history was a science and that the historian could successfully place himself outside of his study. The personal consciousness, the subconscious, the philosophy, experiences, and beliefs of the historian as a man all influence his selection, treatment, and conclusion in historical investigation. The total self of the historian (personality, and environment) must affect the end product of his study. There can be no really "pure" history, for not only is history affected by the evidence available, it is also substantially affected by the historian himself.

It can be seen, therefore, that the intellectual discipline of history cannot be regarded as a science. To deny this is to accept the naturalistic presuppositions of history prevalent in the nineteenth century, and it is also to ignore the different types of conclusions arrived at. The inherent weaknesses of "pure" history were soon evident in the products of scientific history. These were abstract and lifeless presentations, not at all adequately reflecting the dynamics of the historical process. Later nineteenth-century historians were shaken by these obvious failures of scientific history, and their consequent reflections upon the work of history and the historian's function soon led to the crisis of historicism—the rejection of the notion of history as a science.

If the edifice of science in which Ranke attempted to make history dwell has collapsed, historicism has not, for all of that, ended. The approach to identity with the physical sciences is today overwhelmingly rejected by the historians. As a matter of fact, present-day references to "scientific historians" are only to trained and competent professionals who use the critical method. When the opening to science closed, the historicist movement turned toward an opening to the realm of philosophy, and as Ranke signaled the first, or scientific, stage of historicism, the second, or philosophic, stage is marked by Wilhelm Dilthey.

Wilhelm Dilthey (1833–1911), a German like Ranke, faced the problem set in motion a generation earlier by his countryman.[1] Like others seriously reflecting upon the nature of history, Dilthey came to reject the conclusion that one could make of history a science pure and simple. There remained for him the problem of establishing the subject of history upon its own footing as a form of knowledge. To do this, Dilthey initially distinguished the branches of knowledge into sciences of culture and sciences of nature, a distinction fundamental to his theory of history and one that has long influenced other historical thinkers. History for Dilthey was unlike the physical sciences; in that it possessed the power to live the experiences of the past, history could be meaningful.

Step by step Dilthey analyzed the temporal and historical structure of human life and the way in which meaning arises in it, how this meaning is expressed and how it can be understood. He then proceeded to an account of how the meaning rooted in the awareness of individuals becomes embedded in the meaning of institutions, organizations, and historical processes, what form it takes there, how it can be recaptured through historical evidence and lead to historical understanding.[2]

Dilthey's long labors in historical studies contributed much to nineteenth-century developments in methodology; to this methodology he added the use of descriptive psychology and the phenomenological approach. He never actually completed his initial labors in working out a complete system in which he could definitely fix the places of human knowledge—science, history, philosophy. He sincerely hoped that historical studies would liberate man's mind from theology, philosophy, and even science. The position Dilthey occupies in the intellectual tradition is one of influence upon later historicism and especially one of symbol, for it was Dilthey in his rejection of the "science" of history who fathered the second stage of historicism.

Historicism after Dilthey, and because of him, passed to the thinkers of the idealist strain (Croce and Collingwood); and it is the tradition of Ranke, modified by Dilthey, and then in turn modified and explicated by Croce and Collingwood, that dominated twentieth-century historicism. In addition, however, it must be emphasized that Dilthey's influence was not limited to the idealist thinkers only, but was received by the growing and emerging existentialist philosophies. These two strains, historical idealism and existential thought, emerged with great vigor in the twentieth century.

THE TWENTIETH CENTURY: FROM HISTORICISM TO IDEALISM

The historicist tradition after Dilthey soon fell into the hands of the idealist thinkers. The first and most popular of these was the Italian philosopher Benedetto Croce (1866–1952), the most influential Italian thinker of his day.[3] Although the classification would be seemingly abhorrent to him, Croce was actually in the Hegelian tradition. He conceived of history as the living out of thought; history was the stage upon which the universal and particular met, history alone was real. The historian, Croce said, experienced history only in the present; and reality, since it was purely the present experience, was history. Thus the Absolute, or the Spirit, or Him whom older thinkers named as God, was the historical process itself. Croce rejected any notion of history as a record; rather it was to be envisioned as a slow movement toward an ideal world, and the Absolute, or God, of this process was the spirit of liberty. "Liberty," he said, "is the eternal creator of history." The principle of history, the ideal of historical motion, the eventual goal of the historical process was the absolute explication of this spirit of liberty.

Thus it can be said that Croce actually formulated an idealist philosophy of history. Its weaknesses were, however, more evident to historians than to the idealist philosophers. Croce's ever-progressive realization of freedom said nothing about the actual existence of evil in human history; it destroyed both the reality and the uniqueness of any past event. His historical idealism, in which all history was contemporary, did stress the value of past events for their importance to the present. The relationship of history to present life, however, while a contribution by Croce in his accenting a forgotten theme, did not, for all of that, exhaust the importance of history as the intellectual discipline. Its value in the hands of later historians was a pragmatic basis for their subject.

That which had begun as a crisis for historicism in the critique of Dilthey, and had continued as a philosophy by Croce, reached full flower in the lifetime and work of the most influential twentieth-century historicist, the English professor Robin G. Collingwood (1889–1943).[4] Collingwood always maintained the existence of history as a subject autonomous in itself: it was, in his theory, reenactment in the mind of the historian of all past thought. Since he denied such a philosophical reality as human nature (that is, human nature as an unchangeable essence continually found in history), philosophy could not contribute to historical understanding. Historical knowledge was to be envisioned as the reliving of the thinking found in the past. The difficulty of fixing Collingwood's precise thinking on this subject lies in the fact that his own thought developed over the years and was constantly fixed upon what he regarded as the ultimate question, namely, the relationship of history to philosophy.

The final achievement of Collingwood's work was to identify history as a subject with philosophy. The mind investigating historical realities, according to Collingwood, really faced only one essential question, not a theological or philosophical one, but an essentially historical operation. To discover the thought of a man is to discover, he said, the questions that a man asked, and to discover the solutions a man has proposed is to discover the problems he has faced. That which is philosophical, then, is intrinsically linked with that which is historical.

Philosophy and history for Collingwood did not become problems to be placed in balance on the scales of human knowledge, but rather philosophy was subsumed into history. The radical distinction in Collingwood's earlier thought was between natural science and history, philosophy being essentially a part of the latter and in no way a separate discipline. In commenting upon the later extension of Collingwood's historical thought, Professor T. M. Knox has remarked that perhaps the only reason Collingwood so extended history as the ultimate form of knowledge, even to the point of embracing the natural sciences, was the fact that Collingwood himself never really worked in the fields of natural science.[5]

The essential difficulty in Collingwood's approach to history, and indeed the essential difficulty in any such idealist approach (Croce's, for example) is that while it may indeed recognize the perduring element of human freedom in history, it errs by excess. If history be but the history of thought, then man alone, without the influence or determination of natural forces, makes his own history. Human freedom may indeed be a determining factor, and at times *the* determining factor in events, but no serious historian would ignore the real forces outside of freedom (nature, geography, demography) and those free but external forces (economics, society, politics). Indeed, the Christian disclaimer to Collingwood's thought would include not only these historical factors, which he feels Collingwood does not face seriously enough, but also the knowledge the Christian has of divine Providence, which rules all history.

In the tradition of Croce and Collingwood, but in his own way, the American philosopher Paul Weiss has attempted to right this excessively philosophical bent toward history.[6] His work examines with sympathy and insight the work of the historian, and he then proceeds to check the results of historical study against the actual world. Although the ultimate thrust of this work of Weiss is one of reconciliation, it does not seem that he has succeeded. He has managed, however, to open the door to a new dialogue—a dialogue more cognizant of inherent difficulties—between the historians and the philosophers.

THE TWENTIETH CENTURY: THE EXISTENTIALIST EMPHASIS

Although the contemporary philosophical movement of existentialism draws its original impulse and initial insight from the work of Sören Kierkegaard, it has also contracted a debt to Wilhelm Dilthey for many of its basic statements about human history. At the outset it must be stated that within this wide philosophical movement there are many different points of view about specific problems. Merely the invocation of the names of its prominent representatives indicates these variations: Marcel, Jaspers, Heidegger, and Sartre. Although the movement has had a profound impact upon contemporary theology and provides elements for Christian theologies of history (to which we shall return later), we are here basically concerned with its view of the meaningfulness of human history. What is common to existentialism in its contributions to the philosophy of history is its insistence upon the experience of personal awareness of existence, of the instant, of man's incompleteness, and finally, its insistence upon the awareness that man's achievement of knowledge is through the experience of existence.

In the light of our pursuit of the meaning of history, and later of the theology of history, it is most important that among the existentialist thinkers some time and attention be given to the German philosopher Martin Heidegger (b. 1889). It is both the totality of his system and the influence he has had that dictate some study of his position. Inspired by Kierkegaard and admittedly influenced by Dilthey, Heidegger has made the major existentialist contribution to the philosophy of history. He is one of the most original and influential thinkers of our time, but his thought is extremely difficult to pursue and is complicated by his construction of totally new terms. Incomplete as such a short presentation must be, and inexact as it may be, nevertheless some sketch of Heidegger's ideas is necessary to understand historical thinking.[7]

Being (*Sein*) as the object of intelligibility is so only for a being whose mode of being is the search for this intelligibility. This being is a human existence (*Dasĕin*). Therefore, to understand being is itself part of human existence; and the being of the human *is* itself part of the being of human existence, and the being to which the human is related is called "existence." Thus existence can only be understood by existing, and this understanding is the proper meaning of "existential." Human existence is in the world and is, simply, being-in-the-world or "thereness." The end of human existence is death, and therefore the being of this human existence is a being-unto-death. The traditional essentializing process of philosophy by which we speak of "man" reveals not truth but rather an unauthentic form of human existence, for it is an escape from the anguish (*Angst*) in which we are aware of the fundamental thereness of the human existence as a being-unto-death. This unauthentic form of human existence can be avoided only in choice, that is, commitment of the self to the possibilities of being. Conscience is the interior call from anxiety, from human existence, to authenticity. It is human existence that is first and foremost historical, and therefore historical occurrence may be defined as the occurrence of being-in-the-world. Man as a being in history finds in history (which involves choice) the meaning of his own existence. History, therefore, serves a man in the achievement of authentic existence by allowing him decision. The historical process must not be envisaged as including a man as an "item" (and this is historical study as we traditionally know it), for this is escape, an unauthentic form of existence, since the potentialities of choice are lost sight of. There is not then a truly "objective" study of history, for it is only in the offer to decision, in the cataloguing of potentialities worth repeating for freedom, that history has any validity. So David Roberts has written of the problem of history in Heidegger:

> The facts which an historian studies are meaningless unless they can be related to his personal decisions and to the decisions of the men in the past who produced those monuments, documents, and other materials which he has to interpret. All this must be taken into account if the historian is to study the past in such a way that its implications for the future can be understood. The selection of what is to be studied and interpreted requires an existential choice on his part.[8]

It is obvious that with Heidegger we are not facing a philosophy of history as such, but rather, simply speaking, a philosophy. Upon his metaphysics, his intuition, and his definition of human existence Heidegger has built a world view. For good or for ill this total view of existence is one of the major intellectual voices of our world. It presents within it, and indeed as part and parcel of it, a dynamic conception of the meaning of history. His disciple, Rudolf Bultmann, has spelled out the meaning of this philosophy of history: "The meaning of history lies always in the present." [9] It is a position in the tradition of Dilthey, like that of Croce and Collingwood, but unlike theirs, nonidealistic, it is dependent upon an organic and total world view so peculiarly their own that its only proper label is "existentialism."

THE TRADITION OF THE HISTORIANS

The drift to idealism via Croce and Collingwood was not the only road followed by historical thought in the twentieth century. Concurrent with the rise of the historical tradition of these men, still another group of professional historians vociferously maintained the impossibility of a philosophy of history. For them the historical process under the critical eye of the historian yielded no information about its ultimate meaning. Furthermore, this rejection of the a priori patterns into which eighteenth- and nineteenth-century idealism forced history included as well the rejection of even the possibility of such a philosophy of history.

In the United States such nineteenth-century philosophers as Charles S. Peirce (1839–1914) influenced the historians by emphasis upon the concept of chance. Because of the primacy of chance it could be said that Peirce made "novelty and time real and history truly autonomous." [10] Following the lead of Peirce that no laws existed to explain events—although they might aid in making intelligible phases of events—the influence of Alfred North Whitehead (1861–1947) served to buttress a sense of historicism rather than a philosophy of history. For Whitehead "God does not impose any particular pattern on the course of historical events. What happens in history is the result of the selective process going on in the experience of the individuals who exist during the historical period under discussion. God exercises a purely persuasive function." [11] Divine Providence, according to Whitehead, was not to be invoked, nor were eternal laws of history to be sought—the future was perfectly "open."

For the most part the realist historians of today, admitting that history as an object exists outside the mind, remain uncommitted to any philosophy of history and share with the early historicist school the denial of ultimate explanation in history. The brunt of the argument about the philosophy of history advanced by most historians is, in simple terms, that there is no philosophy of history, nor is such a philosophy possible. The eminent American historian who restored the influence of economics to historical studies in this country, Charles A. Beard (1874–1948), denied meaning to history, going so far as to state that as a historian he had arrived at a position of "historical relativism." [12] For him history yielded up no patterns, but demonstrated only the relativity of events and the particular historian's point of view. The Dutch historian Peter Geyl states that all the historian can render as the fruit of his labor is his own impression of history, there being no patterns, no laws, no goals.[13] The distinguished Raymond Aron of the Sorbonne commits himself firmly neither to the camp of historical relativism nor to that of positivism. The historian, he says, is selective, and his selectivity is based purely upon his own values; history in itself provides him with no values. "The historian," Aron remarks, "can bring out the meanings of action, institutions, and laws. They cannot discover the meaning of the whole. History is not absurd, but no living being can grasp its one, final meaning." [14] For Aron the new philosophies of history witnessed by our time are no more nor less than "secularized theologies."

The British historian Alan Bullock argues the meaninglessness of attempting to abstract from the study of history any meaning or universal laws, and states that such an attempt "is a kind of speculative activity which many professional historians eye with distrust and dislike." [15] The extreme version of meaningless history against the philosophers of history is represented by the positivist philosopher Karl Popper, who although denying to the philosophy of history even consideration, nevertheless concludes this denial with the affirmation of a principle worthy of Dilthey, Croce, and Collingwood, and the existentialism of Martin Heidegger: "Although history has no ends, we can impose these ends of ours upon it; and although history has no meaning, we can give it meaning." [16]

Edward Hallett Carr is the latest of the historians to enter the lists. Delicately choosing his way, he has rejected the idealism of Collingwood, and goes on to reject the extreme positivism of Popper. History he sees as a "continuous process of interaction between the historian and his facts, an unending dialogue between the present and the past." [17] History, "both the enquiry conducted

by the historian and the facts of the past into which he enquires,"
is to be envisioned as a social process, and the dialogue of the historian and the past is a dialogue between the society of yesterday
and the society of today; so that the dual function of history is to
understand the society of yesterday and to increase man's mastery
over the society of today. "So far as I am concerned, I have no
belief in divine providence, world spirit, manifest destiny, history
with a capital H, or any other of the abstractions which have sometimes been supposed to guide the course of events." [18]

If so many historians, if such distinguished practitioners of
the craft of history so consistently deny a meaning to history from
their own historical viewpoint, one would indeed seem rash to
persist in looking for such a meaning. Nevertheless there has been
no end of the making of philosophies of history. Despite the cau-
tions so frequently and so eloquently entered by the professional
historians, our age has witnessed attempt after attempt to make
meaningful the entire process of history. It is to some consideration
of these endeavors that we must now turn.

THE PHILOSOPHIES OF HISTORY

As historical visions widen and as historical knowledge gains still
greater victories over the past, man consistently tries to find the
constant, the recurring, the inevitable pattern that subsists in history. Perhaps the causes of these undertakings are as manifest as the
undertakings themselves, and perhaps the uncertain nature of the
stage of history in which we dwell has influenced these pursuits.
But no matter what has given rise to these constant attempts at a
philosophy of history, they have arisen. Although the philosophies
of history meet with the scorn of historians, they are attempted, and
they do seem to mark a disease endemic not only to philosophers
but, strange as it seems, to historians.

Modern historical thought has been increasingly influenced by
the science of sociology; instigated by Comte and Spencer in the
nineteenth century, it has been definitized by Durkheim in France
and Weber in Germany. Émile Durkheim (1858–1917), insisting
upon the explanation of social life in its own terms, turned the
historians toward the study of social forms; Max Weber (1864–
1920), while highlighting the interdependence of historical factors

(religion, economics, politics), called the historian's attention to the facts of man's societal life and provided the basis for later organismic philosophies of history such as Toynbee's. This sociological tradition culminated before World War II with Professor Pitirim Sorokin's four-volume philosophy of history, *Social and Cultural Dynamics.*

Sorokin found in the history of man four basic forms of society —the "ideational" and the "sensate," the "idealistic" and the "mixed," thus demonstrating that "as a philosopher rather than an historian, Sorokin is more interested in abstract types than in concrete phenomena." [19] Moreover, Sorokin's study was marked by a constant use of statistics, which constitute a methodical element unlike that of any other philosopher of history. His overall conclusions concerning the oscillation of Western culture strongly parallel the historical curves graphed by Vico in the eighteenth century.

The sociological approach, mediated by Sorokin, has affected such works as Alfred Kroeber's *Configurations of Culture Growth,* which tried to delimit statistically the fundamental patterns of cultures, and Philip Bagby's *Culture and History.* The great contribution of the sociologists to the philosophy of history has been, however, in the emphasis it has placed upon the varieties of human societies as organisms, and upon history as the study of the life of those societies. The recent work of Ernest Cuneo, *Science and History,* recalls these sociological efforts. Cuneo, however, attempts to argue from a scientific analogy of motion and velocity to the possibility of scientifically predictable patterns of energy expansion within history.

In the early twentieth century the most celebrated philosophical attempt to pinpoint the meaning of history was *The Decline of the West* by Oswald Spengler (1880–1936).[20] The pessimism that dominated the immediate pre-Christian conceptions of history returned to haunt modern man in Spengler's work. *The Decline of the West* was first published in 1918 and was significantly influenced by the period of crisis that the date represents. A prophet of doom, Spengler delivered his message quite simply: Western civilization had entered upon the period of its decline. Every culture passed through the states of nature: spring, summer, fall, and winter. No real progress was to be found in human history, only the temporal reflection of the cycle of nature. Modern civilization was marked by the phenomena of decline: crowded cities, the power of money, and

the domination of the masses of the people. This was a civilization
grown old and facing only its death; to be optimistic in the face of
this inevitable historical phase of decline was only moral cowardice.

For a world long fed upon the concepts of an irresistible evolutionary drive at work in history and upon ideas of inevitable progress, the endurance of the world conflagration of 1914–18 made
Spengler's conception of history in these meaningless cycles quite
attractive. Spengler helped to make the real current difficulties
tolerable by presenting them as part of an inexorable process. *The
Decline of the West* may have been bold, and indeed from a point
of view may have been an explanation, but one thing it was not,
and this the historians repeatedly charged—it was not history.
Spengler's work could not in any true sense be regarded as historical: it did not account for all the facts of history, it was seemingly an a priori pattern into which the historical process as it has
actually developed was made to fit. It was synthetic work, and no
serious historian can give it any serious credence; he can only be
aware of it and note the persistent human demand for explanation
that gives it historical importance.[21] The philosopher must also be
aware of its serious deficiencies and its basic assumptions; unlike
the historian, however, he can regard it with the importance that its
construction and influence demand.

Arnold Toynbee, more careful than Spengler and more attentive
to historical realities, has presented us with the most celebrated
philosophy of history in our time. The first three volumes of *A
Study of History* appeared in 1934, three more in 1939, and the work
was completed with four additional volumes in 1954. In 1961, after
his critics had thoroughly dissected his work, he published his *Reconsiderations*. No study of human history in modern times has
been more widely heralded, avidly read, and universally disputed.[22]
No contemporary philosopher or historian has subjected the history
of man to such intensive investigation. His massive history surveys
more than six hundred primitive societies and twenty-one civilizations. From this enormous compilation Toynbee has attempted to
illustrate the enduring principles of human history, to draw the
elements for a philosophy of history based upon an empirical study
of the facts of history, and to highlight elements that provide a
groundwork for tentative predictions of the future.

In this study Toynbee has not rejected the uncertain factor of freedom—that basis for indeterminism that is part and parcel of human history. The determinism and pessimism of Spengler are rejected because of freedom, and the ultimate mystery involved in the "meaning of history" is affirmed.

> For this is the crossroads at which he could have taken the way of Spengler into the tragic experience of civilizations as a spiritually unrelieved, organic rhythm of birth and death, of growth and decay. When, in universal states and churches, he recognized something more than byproducts of a disintegrating civilization, he was informed by a sensitiveness for the presence of the Spirit in history that is so signally absent in Spengler.[23]

The historical societies and civilizations that Toynbee traces do not indicate a cyclical determinism but rather give evidence of certain common elements. The key factor in the historical process is that of challenge and response. Western civilization as we know it is not fixed in a Spenglerian determinist cycle of doom; on the contrary, it finds itself in a state of challenge. The response that Western man is to make to that challenge will now determine the continuance of Western civilization, perhaps not as we have known it but as transfigured into a totally new situation.

From history Toynbee draws four possibilities of response. Our civilization may now freely choose to enter a period of reaction (idealizing some past era and thus dooming itself to archaism) or a period of revolution (idealizing some future utopia and thus dooming itself to the fallacy of futurism) or a period of detachment (suspending judgment and thus entering a period of despair and withdrawal), or finally, it may enter a period of transfiguration. This last course is the one to which Toynbee points and that he gently urges upon our civilization. By this period of transfiguration we mean that man must move his total situation into a new frame of reference; he must move on to a vision of wider context and give new meaning to his civilization. This meaning he finds in a selective use of the New Testament teachings on the Kingdom of God.

Throughout this lifetime work Toynbee constantly maintains the validity of his conclusions as a historian; these, he insists, are based on historical evidence empirically arrived at. Although the work has been well received in many quarters, not only for its content but also for its literate presentation and incisive appreciations, it has also received some strongly worded censures. The most vocal of

Toynbee's critics have been the professional historians. While they would certainly distrust his announced purpose of arriving at the meaningful patterns of history, since they regard such as, a priori, impossible, they have devoted long and attentive criticism to the historical basis of Toynbee's conclusions. If Toynbee's magnificent attempt collapses, it collapses precisely, in their view, as history. Any serious attempt to appreciate the value of Toynbee's achievement must take this criticism and its several points into account: Toynbee is continuously selective, he frequently begs the question, he is involved in internal contradictions, he is unappreciative of history's uniqueness, he has little sympathy for basic historical forces such as nationalism, and finally, while this amalgam of reasons makes him unacceptable on a historical basis, it is obvious that Christian thinkers must reject his basic conclusions.

The brilliant Dutch historian Peter Geyl has persuasively pointed out the historical flaw in Toynbee's work: Toynbee's continual emphasis upon the empirical nature of his research. His selectivity toward facts dominates his method and deprives his study of history of its empirical claim; the events that support his thesis are called as evidence, but what is left unsaid is to be regarded in fact as of equal importance to that which is cited. Furthermore, the theories he is attempting to prove are invoked as evidence in his discussions of the breakdown of civilizations. In discussing Western civilization as he finds it now, Toynbee predicates of its symptoms that he has definitely stated as belonging to two distinct periods, the stage of growth and the state of disintegration. Toynbee maintains the idea of a "civilization" as a unit for study, but when explaining his challenge-response theory cites as evidence smaller units of singular civilizations that he has already rejected as the unit for study. Finally, nationalism, as he conceived it, is a roadblock to his ultimate goal of human unity, and is to be judged only as a destructive force, of no real value in itself; from this position he is led to the preposterous equation: the Jewish displacement of Arabs in Israel is equivalent to the Nazi mass murder of six million Jews.

That, however, which many students of history find most difficult in Toynbee's work is his unhistorical treatment of the uniqueness of human events. The broad parallels, the brilliant analogies of historical events, these serve only to sweep the reader along the powerful currents of Toynbee's arguments. But on sober reflection one must always recall the absolute uniqueness of any historical event, the concreteness of a historical fact, its singular place in time, and all its attendant and individual circumstances. Toynbee's parallels may be striking, they may also illustrate and not infrequently illuminate historical movement, but for the historian they are not decisive.

There are some eminent Christian thinkers who have, for all of Toynbee's shortcomings, taken away from *A Study of History* certain observations, such as the law of challenge and response, that they regard as valid and that they utilize in the construction of a Christian philosophy of history. It must be pointed out that although such observations may at times be compatible with what Christian revelation tells about human history, they remain just that—observations. If the Christian philosopher endows them with certainty and a probative value, he does so at his own peril, for the ultimate source of certainty in Christian thinking about the meaning of history is divine revelation, not the historical events themselves. One may use certain observations or laws of Toynbee, but this should be done at all times with the full awareness that their historical significance as abstractions is precisely that of observations, not strict historical certainties empirically arrived at or strictly proven. Toynbee may have stumbled upon certain truths, but such certainty is conferred from a higher order, not from the study of the historical process itself.

A Christian philosopher may know with full certainty of divine Providence and human history. But he may border upon a blasphemous intrusion upon divine mystery if he attempts to find the "how" of their balance from a purely empirical study of the historical process. It is one thing to formulate the problem in these two terms—and even here a demurrer may be entered as to a historical demonstration of providence; it is quite another to explain them.

For many persons, then—historians, philosophers, and theologians—Professor Toynbee's work is to be judged a tour de force, interesting but unacceptable. No Catholic thinker, from the theological certainties of his faith, could even hope to find in Toynbee's conclusions about an ultimate syncretic religion a proposition consistent with the unique historical revelation of God in Christ.[24]

In 1961 Toynbee published his *Reconsiderations,* in which he tried to face the voluminous works of his critics. He has modified the strongly Hellenic character of his civilization types and his earlier judgment of religion as a social factor. Nevertheless he still maintains the empirical character of *A Study of History,* with all due allowance for the subjective and arbitrary nature of any human study. Toynbee's self-defense is perhaps best understood and ana- lyzed by H. Stuart Hughes:

> Yet this chastened and sophisticated Toynbee finds it difficult to main- tain with any consistency his new subjectivist stand. He is constantly relapsing into his old positivist phraseology and biological metaphors. . . . If he had *really* changed that much, he would have had to ask him- self whether he should have embarked on his life's work at all, or rather, whether he should not have cast it in quite a different form, as a series of essays or suggestions, instead of a monumental work which purported to give a tight explanation for the whole course of human history.[25]

THE CHRISTIAN PHILOSOPHERS OF HISTORY

Most Christian thinking concerning the meaning of human his- tory should, of course, be dominated by the theologies of history. But the ability of Christian thinkers to present what may be termed a Christian philosophy of history has come to the fore in our own time. The obvious cause for this is the twentieth-century thrust of philosophies of history. On this level of presentation the problem admits of a number of possibilities, for Christian thought reflects fairly closely the wide divergence of secular scholarship over the possibility, nature, and content of a philosophy of history. At one extreme we have the work of Jacques Maritain, who not only admits the possibility of a Christian philosophy of history but indeed has sketched the elements of the problem that such a construction would embrace. At the other extreme we have such distinguished Christian thinkers as C. S. Lewis and Christopher Dawson, who deny even the possibility of such a philosophy.[26] Between these poles lies the work of such brilliant men as Martin D'Arcy and Her- bert Butterfield, who admit the guidance that the extrahistorical knowledge of revelation represents toward at least a possible Chris- tian construction.

The problem is, however, tied to a number of a priori considera- tions. If the data for constructing this Christian philosophy of history is known only through revelation, and not by reason, or if only the data used as the controlling factor is known only through revelation, is the resultant construction more properly a philosophy or a theology? From the very first there is involved in this problem the old question of the possibility of a Christian philosophy.[27] There are many who would state that one has either a philosophy or a theology, and that the control exercised by revelation for the Christian thinker deprives one of the possibility of Christian philosophy. On the other hand, Étienne Gilson speaks for the majority of Thomist philosophers when he states that the philosopher in his construction of a philosophy can utilize the Christian revelation, not in the sense of providing for him the *data* of his construction (since, properly speaking, this would be the object of reason alone), but as providing the guiding star of his construction.

Again, assuming the settlement of the initial problem of Christian philosophy as such, even to the point of admitting the thesis of Gilson, there still would remain a problem for a Christian philosophy of history. Can the thinker who utilizes the *empirically achieved data* of historical study stand, as it were, outside the historical process and see pattern or meaning in the whole historical process itself? In this case of the Christian philosophy of history, revelation is no guiding star but is itself involved in the data for the Christian philosophy of history. This problem, fundamental to any Christian philosophy of history, will recur again, but let us now turn to our Christian thinkers, ranging as they do from those who affirm this Christian philosophy of history to those who deny it.[28]

Regarding an oppressive naturalism as the connatural enemy of true historical thinking, A. Robert Caponigri calls for the initial clarifications of history. As a realm of meaning, he tells us, history "emerges as the enunciations of self-conscious spirit in defiance of the necessities and limitations of nature." [29] The temporal process, history, is fundamentally distinguished from the natural process by the freedom that is the essence of the spirit. The problem of the philosophy of history, Caponigri states, lies in the initial supposition. Historicism, naturalism, and the idealism of Croce have been the rocks upon which the philosophy of history has foundered in the past, and the disengagement from these suppositions is only possible by the establishment of the suppositions proper to the problem of history. This, he says, is first, and negatively, disengagement from the supposition of excessive analogy (fallacy is introduced by nonhistorical descriptions of history—for example, the biological). Second, and positively, the time factor must be intrinsic and constitutive in any characterization of historical phenomena. For Caponigri these are the lines along which investigation is to continue; solutions are not possible until the initial questions they raise are solved. Only then may history and philosophy achieve the rapprochement so keenly desired in our contemporary culture.

The moving spirit of neo-Thomism, Jacques Maritain, has not only affirmed the Christian philosophy of history but has indeed contributed an extremely thoughtful work toward its construction.[30] As a necessary preliminary to his view of what the Christian philosophy of history entails, Maritain has met the objections of historians that history renders only knowledge of the singular. He maintains that the formal object of history is not the same as that of the philosophy of history. The philosophy of history has the same subject matter as history, but its formal object is the abstract universal or the intelligible *raisons d'être* in historical knowledge; these in turn are to be checked against one's philosophy of God and man. Thus the philosophy of history uses both induction (historical facts) and deduction (verification by reference to one's metaphysics and moral philosophy). Maritain strenuously denies that a philosophy of history as he envisions it implies any a priori conceptions, but says that both the inductive and deductive methods are to be used in its construction—"intelligible data and connections which have been drawn from facts by induction, but which are checked and verified by a rational analysis."[31]

Maritain maintains the essential mystery of history, its supra-intelligibility, insofar as it depends upon the purpose of God. The philosophy of history will neither rationally explain the historical process nor provide a reconstruction of history along the lines of necessary laws. Its humble task will be to interpret, to characterize, certain general aspects or directions in history; it will enlighten us about historical events but never necessitate them.

Thus he accepts free will as a central problem in history, and he denies necessitating laws within the historical process. Those "laws" that he does affirm, those provisional interpretations of human history that the philosophy of history arrives at, are of two particular types: first, functional laws, or axiomatic formulas, always verifiable at the various stages of human history; second, typological formulas, or vectorial laws (stating the extent, direction, and significance of determined sections or periods of history).

Maritain strenuously opposes any a priori rejection of a philosophy of history such as proposed by Dawson. But in his own work it does not seem that Maritain has come to grips with the problem of a philosophy of history, since he approaches the question with the a priori assertion that a philosophy of history is not only possible but even necessary. Furthermore, it may be asked if Maritain's thinking really fulfills the definition, even his own, of a philosophy of history? Does he make history meaningful, intelligible, with empirical historical evidence? It seems that Maritain does give us the techniques or intrinsic forms for a formal philosophy of history and that he does take care to avoid the danger of rationalizing the ultimate mystery of the divine purpose in history, but on the point at issue, the philosophy of history, it would seem that his construction falls short of the goal.

The distinguished scholar and eminent archeologist William F. Albright of John Hopkins University has proposed what he refers to, in the tradition of Toynbee, as an organismic philosophy of history.[32] Albright's Christian commitment and acknowledgment of divine Providence have not kept him from pursuing the general laws of human history. The historian, he says, must begin with the fundamentals of man's social life as basic data. "As we ascend the hierarchic scale from plane to plane of variability, our laws become progressively less general and less binding or more uncertain —in both history and science—until we reach a plane where the number of variables makes prediction impossible, as far as the finite mind can tell." [33]

Thus from philosophers of history Albright adopts what he regards as the valid insights represented by basic philosophers, "provided only that one fully recognizes the limitations of their use and does not attempt to deduce binding conclusions from their analogical application." Obviously influenced by the sociology of Durkheim and Weber, Albright has stated with regard to his "modest" system: "An inductive organismic philosophy is the only proper way in which to approach the problem of the relation of historical contexts to one another." The understanding of history, therefore, does not depend solely upon the establishment of empirical relationships; and this understanding of *entire* history leads to the affirmation of "an Intelligence and a Will, expressed in both history and nature." [34]

If it can be so frequently stated that Marx took the Hegelian system and stood it on its head in his own system of dialectical materialism, we might well congratulate Eric Voegelin for his use of Hegelian "spirit." Thus far three volumes of Voegelin's work, *Order in History*, have been published, the "order" of the title substituting for "spirit" in Hegel. Voegelin has spelled out meticulously his dependence upon Hegel, his own faith in the transcendent and absolute God of the Christian tradition, and his Augustinian and existentialist leanings. The guiding principle of history is order, and the historical manifestation of being is distinct and dependent upon the transcendent divine being. Albright has written: "It is precisely his theism which permits him to treat historical data as important in themselves. In other words, his recognition of the extra-historical source of the ordering principle helps to give him a respect for the facts of history which is rarely, if ever, found among those students who try to derive an over-all principle of organization from the historical experience itself." [35] However, there is the disturbing doubt that Voegelin's claim to support his argument from the empirical data of history justifies the view of order emerging in history, or of the absolute God as the *fons et origo* of that order.

It is in his startlingly incisive and literate book, *The Meaning and Matter of History,* that Father Martin D'Arcy demonstrates the transitional stage in modern Christian thought about history. D'Arcy does not deny outright the possibility of a philosophy, for to do so would be to demand from the philosopher the same formal object and critical method demanded of the historian; this, then, is the basis for a philosophy of history, that such a philosophy has a different formal object from that of history. The philosopher seeks the meaning of history, not simply its content. As D'Arcy states his case, the presence of moral judgment in history opens the door from the strict empiricism of the professional historian to the domain of the philosopher of history.

D'Arcy finds himself in agreement with Professor Geyl's rejection of Toynbee only insofar as Toynbee maintains his work is the result of empirical historical method. But D'Arcy does justify Toynbee's attempt as distinct from history as such. Toynbee's initial question about the rise and fall of civilizations is primary to any real philosophy of history; his consequent recognition of both providence and freedom, and finally, his general law of challenge and response are all taken by D'Arcy as legitimate conclusions for the philosopher of history.

Yet it is in the work of Vico that D'Arcy finds the forerunner of true philosophies of history; D'Arcy considers him among those philosophers who take history as a whole as their object and the laws, patterns, and meanings of the whole as the object of their research. Thus Vico is acceptable both for his stress upon freedom and providence, and the notion of development in history.

When D'Arcy speaks of the idea of progress through challenge and response he relates the growth evidenced in history to basic facts known in the Christian revelation. The crisis of the Cross has significance for each man, as it has for the historical process, and this is the crucial point for a Christian understanding of history. Love and sacrifice, human values that exist because of creation, the building up of the body of Christ until the parousia—all these distinctively Christian factors are necessary to see history as a whole. These are, according to D'Arcy, admittedly theological facts, but it is their implications that open the possibility of establishing a Christian philosophy of history.

What is the Christian philosophy of history for D'Arcy? He does not spell it out, rather he calls upon a number of sources to indicate the elements in history that are to be utilized in such a Christian philosophy of history. D'Arcy tells us that this will be distinguished on the one hand from the strictly empirical methods of history, and on the other hand from the revelation that establishes theology. It is, then, a possibility, not an accomplished fact. But it is toward the elaboration of this Christian philosophy of history that D'Arcy would direct the efforts of the Christian intellectual of today in order to give a stable philosophical basis to human values, a truly lasting humanism reconciled to the eschatological or "unworldly" element of Christianity.

The borderland between the denial and the affirmation of a Christian philosophy of history is marked by the work of Herbert Butterfield. In the first book in which he took up this problem, *Christianity and History*, he put forward the thesis that complete historical study of human events does not in itself explain the entire process; for this explanation one must turn to the data of Christian revelation. The Christian beliefs—for example, the Fall and effects of original sin—give man law and pattern for history, they give meaning to the observable evil in human history.[36] Butterfield says that the fundamental Christian beliefs in the Fall, divine Providence, and God's redemption are theological facts, but they are more adequately illustrated in the strict historical study of man. Patterns or laws are not abstracted from history; rather, the ideas of various philosophers of history give some intimation of the real meaning of the historical process, though none can be described as exhaustive. Thus it is that the historian can find in the Christian affirmation of divine Providence and human freedom the perduring and variable elements of history.

With his later work, *History and Human Relations,* Butterfield moved more firmly into the camp of the antiphilosophers rather than that of the philosophers of history. The historian, he now concludes, is bound to his empirical study of unique events, and he cannot find in the process of history itself any law, pattern, or meaning. Thus Butterfield's maturing reflections upon history as an object of study have moved him closer to that body of Christian thinkers who, in the words of D'Arcy, have placed an embargo upon the philosophy of history, Christian or otherwise.

Professor Bernard J. Lonergan of the Gregorian University in Rome is considered by many to be one of Roman Catholicism's most stimulating and original thinkers. A mathematician and philosopher, the Canadian Jesuit is now actively engaged in erecting a new theological synthesis based upon his original philosophical work of some years ago entitled *Insight.*[37]

In speaking of the history of man it would seem that Lonergan feels that his rule of "emergent probability" would be a controlling factor, for "human actions are recurrent; their recurrence is regular." Within a mathematical overview of the world process Lonergan speaks of this emergent probability as "the successive realization in accord with successive schedules of probability of a conditioned series of schemes of recurrence." Thus within the succession of world situations they are characterized by schemes actually functioning, those possible and those probable. Within this world view, however, he quickly goes on to state that "the world process is open. It is a succession of probable realizations of possibilities. Hence it does not run along the iron rails laid down by the determinists nor, on the other hand, is it a non-intelligible morass of merely chance events." [38]

While human history falls within this law of emergent probability, it does so in its own way, influenced by insight, communication, and decision. Here we find in Lonergan's thinking a basis for the philosophy of history: "Because they [the events] are intelligible, they can be understood as are the workings of emergent probability in the field of physics, chemistry, and biology." This seemingly organismic view of history has for Lonergan serious reservations: "But because they are increasingly intelligent, increasingly the fruit of insight and decision, the analogy of merely natural process becomes less and less relevant." And so, in history "common accessible insights, disseminated by communication and persuasion, modify and adjust mentalities to determine the course of history out of the alternatives offered by emergent probability." [39]

While Lonergan seems to speak of and, indeed, to imply a philosophy of history, this nevertheless remains but a door in his own thought to a deeper dimension. This is the theology of history that is specifically Christian. For him the theology of history is built upon the conception of the Church in history as the mystical body of Christ. Thus he writes of the contemporary theologian:

> So too it may be that the contemporary crisis of human living and human values demands of the theologian, in addition to treatises on the unique and to treatises on the universal common to many instances, a treatise on the concrete universal that is mankind in the concrete and cumulative consequences of the acceptance or rejection of the message of the Gospel. And as the remote possibility of thought on the concrete universal lies in the insight that grasps the intelligible in the sensible, so its proximate possibility resides in a theory of development that can envisage not only natural and intelligent progress but also sinful decline, and not only progress and decline but also supernatural recovery.[40]

A very striking denial of the possibility of a Christian philosophy of history is made by the most important and distinguished Catholic historian in the English-speaking world, Professor Christopher Dawson. Commenting upon C. S. Lewis' denial of a Christian philosophy of history, Dawson maintains that Thomism, reflecting a Hellenic and Aristotelian tradition, has never devoted much attention to the problem of history. He sees in the Hebraic tradi-

tion of the Christian faith the tradition of a Christian interpretation of history.

> The Christian view of history is not a secondary element derived by
> philosophical reflection from the study of history. It lies at the very
> heart of Christianity and forms an integral part of the Christian faith.
> Hence there is no Christian "philosophy of history" in the strict sense
> of the word. There is, instead, a Christian history and Christian theology
> of history, and it is not too much to say that without them, there would
> be no such thing as Christianity.[41]

Dawson goes on to state that the elements necessary to an understanding of the Christian view of history can only be grasped in
faith, and "if we cannot accept them, it is useless to elaborate
idealistic theories and call them a Christian philosophy of history,
as has often been done in the past." [42]

A historian like Dawson, Henri-Irénée Marrou, professor of the
history of Christianity at the Sorbonne, is one of the most respected
Catholic thinkers in France. He is the author of the penetrating *De
la connaissance historique,* in which he has posted the boundaries
to both historical relativism and positivism, and in which he finds
himself in substantial agreement with Aron on the limits of history.
Marrou stresses the subjective element in the historian's dialogue
with the past and believes that it is within this dialogue that the true
historian is ulimately bound to pursue the elaboration of the
"central problem of his existence, the solution of which involves
his life and entire person." The study of history, then, becomes "an
empirical manifestation of that 'original projection,' that fundamental desire by which the human person incarnates itself and
seeks to realize itself." [43]

For Marrou it is not from the study of history that the solution
for man's fundamental problems comes but from the philosophy *or* theology of history. "The truth of the history is a function
of the truth of the philosophy professed (implicitly or not) by
the historian." [44] Thus Marrou reverses the trend that flowered
in Collingwood (when all thought and philosophy was to be taken
under history) by stating that as history uses auxiliary sciences it
must itself become an auxiliary science to thought. What, then, of
a philosophy of history? This Marrou definitely rejects. It is man
who uniquely exists and possesses reality; all the organisms, civilizations, and systems are abstractions. The historian has only the

probable—no certainties, no experiments of verification. "The proper mode of an historical judgment is the possible." [45] In his denial of the philosophy of history there is also the denial of a Christian philosophy of history, but not of a theology of history. This theology is arrived at by faith, and its verification or "proof" cannot be found in the labors of the historian or empirically deduced from past events.

The distinguished historian of primitive religions Mircea Eliade has said of the positivist historians that they are a "decomposition product of Christianity," for they stress the importance of historical events (a concept Christian in origin) while denying to such events "any possibility of revealing a transhistorical, soteriological intent." [46] Eliade goes further in his critique, placing himself firmly outside the pale of the philosophers of history: "Christianity arrives, not at a *philosophy* but a *theology* of history. For God's interventions in history, and above all his Incarnation in the historical person of Jesus Christ, have a transhistorical purpose—the *salvation* of man." [47]

What is the Christian to make of all this? Is a Christian philosophy of history possible or not? Does it exist or not? From the variety of opinions that face a thoughtful Christian today, it would seem the earlier Butterfield or the D'Arcy midway point would be the most comfortable, namely, to affirm its possibility but deny that it has been actually achieved. Truth does not, however, always stand in the middle. While this view is attractive, it does not really come to grips with the problem as it is clearly stated by the affirmed Christian philosophers of history, who proceed to work out its application, or as it is denied by the Christian historians.

Does the position of affirmation, as we find it in Maritain's philosophical approach, or in Albright's "organismic" attempt, or in Voegelin's study of order, seem conclusive? Hardly. For again, once we examine the affirmative view of the possibility of a philosophy, and ergo, of a Christian philosophy of history, we find that there are as many Christian philosophies of history as there are Christian philosophers. A most serious attempt to bring this problem to a solution has been made by the distinguished German Thomistic scholar Josef Pieper.[48] His "essay" on a Christian philosophy of history bears little resemblance to any we have seen and is more striking in its reliance upon fundamentally theological insights. We shall take up in some detail Pieper's argument when we come to the Catholic theologians of history. As far as we are concerned here, suffice it to say that his sparkling defense of a Christian philosophy of history does not ring true.

It is not, however, on the basis of the works of these reputable authorities that we find ourselves confused by the notion of a Christian philosophy of history and rejecting it, but because of the intrinsic value of the argument. Christianity is by definition a historical religion—tied to the unique historical event of the Christ. But it is also a transcendent religion, whose basic witness to the Christ event is of its nature above and beyond reason, above and beyond the empirical, whose basic witness is a call to faith in God's deed in the Christ. This is not to say that history is not a servant of the Christian faith—it has many and varied services to perform, as we shall see—but rather it is to say that the Christian religion does not await its verification from the historian, or the philosopher, for that matter; it is not, and indeed it maintains it cannot, be proved by any purely rational or empirical inquiry. If the elements apprehended in faith are "used" to construct this nebulous "philosophy of history," and if these elements are apprehended only in faith, then it is indeed hard to see how this process may be labeled a "philosophy" of history. As Dawson has said, Christians possess a theology of history, and it is here that their thought must be exercised. It is time that Christian thinkers, meeting the challenge to establish a basis for humanism in the Christian revelation, moved on to their articulation of history as theologically meaningful.

PART TWO

THE JESUS OF HISTORY
AND THE CHRIST OF FAITH

Introduction

CHRISTIANITY as a religion is primarily historical. It finds the revelation of God not only in man and in nature as the handiwork of God ("For since the creation of the world His invisible attributes are clearly seen—His everlasting power also and divinity—being understood through the things that are made" [Rom. 1:20]), but essentially and primarily in history. The revelation of God for the Christian has occurred in the realm of history at a specific time and in a specific place. The God who reveals Himself is a God-Who-Acts.

The intention of the New Testament authors is to proclaim the signal event of Jesus Christ as the saving work of God in that same Jesus. It is told as history—in particular, concrete, and specific events. Since the historical order is essential to the New Testament documents, and to the Gospels particularly, it follows that to deny the historical facts to which it links itself and to which it bears witness is to destroy the New Testament revelation of God in Christ. Without the solidly established historicity of Jesus there can be no theology of history.

The Gospel documents narrate facts and their meanings; therefore these documents are both historical and theological. To deny either aspect is to destroy the Christian tradition. Consequently the affirmation of the historicity of the Gospels, of the having-happenedness of the New Testament account of Jesus, is an essential affirmation of the Christian, as is the explication of the meaning of those events in Jesus as the Lord of history.

The distinguished New Testament scholar C. K. Barrett, on the occasion of his inaugural lecture as professor of divinity at Durham University, offers us an instructive commentary on the relationships of history and theology in Christianity.[1] In the New Testament proclamation of Jesus as the Lord of history we are confronted not only with the problem of historicity but also with the problem of history itself—the purposes of God, the meaning of history, and the place of each Christian in history. The intrinsic link is spelled out by Barrett:

It will not do to say *either* we can prove the history true and, therefore, accept the faith; *or* we know the faith is true and therefore accept the history. To argue in either of these ways is to assume that we know the logical priority of the two factors in the question, and priority is just what each seems unwilling to claim for itself. The problem of historicity (the question how we may get at what really happened), and the problem of history (the question of the meaning of what really happened, and of "happening" as such), thus refuse to be separated. We cannot get at what happened without being compelled to consider what it meant.[2]

The problem of stating a Christian view of history is further complicated by the New Testament, for it presents as the meaning of what happened an eschatological view of history; thus a new thread must be woven into the pattern of the whole. Historicity, meaning, and eschatology so interrelate that the statement of the Christian view of history must treat each very carefully in order that damage is not done to the whole.

Any Christian view of history, therefore, must be in some sense eschatological; we cannot, as we shall see, follow simply where Bultmann has led us and "demythologize" the eschatology of the New Testament into some existentialist view of reality. Barrett comments very perceptively on this eschatological sense that must be present for the Christian commentator:

> The narrative tradition has its place in the gospels, not in spite of the eschatological preaching, which is the groundwork of the New Testament, but because of it. Eschatology, which has long seemed the baffling and disruptive factor in New Testament studies, may perhaps come to be regarded as the creative and unifying element in our work, holding history and theology together, and making both intelligible and dynamic. The problem of historicity and the problem of history come to rest here, and come to rest together. The eschatological convictions of the primitive church account for the existence of a historical tradition, and they also account for theological development.[3]

What we will attempt to do in this section is to relate the conclusions of the scholars of our time concerning the historical Jesus as presented in the New Testament; then we will turn to the basic elements (theology) to be found in the New Testament teaching about history. Part Three of the book will examine the actual theologies that the scholars have developed concerning the Christian meaning of history. Although we are thus introducing a division in our study between historicity and theology, it is a necessary and, to a degree, a logical division, in order to clarify basic conceptions involved in stating the theology of history.

As we have remarked, any real Christian theology of history is based upon the historical figure of Jesus Christ and His meaning for history as proclaimed in the New Testament. We propose to follow in this chapter a chronological survey of the problem of the historicity of Jesus in contemporary Protestant theology. To understand the Protestant theologies of history presented later it will be necessary now to see how Protestant thought about historicity has proceeded in our time. We will then submit what might be called a "critique" of the literary and historical problems dealing with historicity from a Catholic point of view. Finally, this chapter will deal with the Catholic point of view on the historicity of Jesus, giving careful attention to the crucial problem of the Resurrection.

Chapter 3

THE JESUS OF HISTORY

IN THE NINETEENTH century the work and tradition of Ranke produced the "historicist" school of history. The members of this school brought to perfection a critical and methodical approach to historical studies. Their object and goal became determination of the fact; they simply strove to discover what had happened. Ranke's discovery of "pure" sources led him and the historicist school to believe in the possibility of a pure noninterpretative history. To this classical historicist assumption was joined a method that stressed a classification of sources in which some could be clearly distinguished as "pure" and objective.

At the turn of the century this critical method was first applied to the Bible. Its initial application to the Gospels led to their rejection by the critics as historical documents—the trouble lying of course in the word "historical." The result of this application was to jeopardize seriously the traditional Christian apologetic.

This traditional apologetic for Christianity was, in brief, presented in this manner: the existence of God, the possibility and significance of miracles, the claims of Christ, the proof adduced from miracles, and the Church established by Christ. This apologetic always stressed the initial assumption of the Gospels as historical documents, and after the demonstration of the Church the guarantee of those documents as "revealed." Obviously the critical rejection by the historians of the Gospels struck a major blow at the keystone of this apologetic arch.[4]

A number of scholars, proceeding from the bases of their own philosophies and a priori assumptions, and cognizant of this historical critique, moved in to fill the gap. Solutions to the "problem of Christ," ranging from allegations of his nonexistence to mere affirmations of his human existence, mushroomed within a few years. In the Church some scholars, using the historicist assumption and the critical method, provoked the widely ranging crisis known as "modernism." It should be remembered, however, that this era of liberal Protestantism and Catholic modernism was not one of historical criticism alone; rather, it was the era of historical criticism as combined with manifold philosophies and theologies, each attempting to force a meaning of and explanation for the Christian phenomenon.

Among the more significant problems produced by the era was one central to the Gospels and essentially literary: the Synoptic problem—the relationships of the three Synoptic Gospels (Matthew, Mark, Luke) and their possible influences on one another. At this time the problem was as productive of as many solutions as there were scholars. Most of these solutions relied on the existence of two sources: Mark (the oldest) and a Q document, or collection of sayings (Logia). At this time, through historical and literary criticism, there began an earnest pursuit of the historical Jesus, Jesus as He actually was, what He really said and did. This was the era of liberal theology, and its quest of the historical Jesus was dominated by the historicist critique, the literary examination of the documents, and not least by philosophical presuppositions (as, for example, the impossibility of miracles).

A Protestant scholar, Heinz Zahrnt, has recently commented upon the necessity of facing the problem of historicity in Protestant theology: "History has become our fate. We must, therefore, pass everything which we think, say and believe about Jesus through the sieve of strict methodological consideration, through the fire of historical criticism." [5] It is to this Protestant passage through the fire of historical criticism that we now turn.

THE QUEST FOR THE HISTORICAL JESUS

The end of the nineteenth century witnessed the demise of Hegelianism and a revival of Kantian thought in the theology of Albrecht Ritschl. Ideas of value and morality dominated the Ritschlian school; Ritschl himself reduced religion to a series of value judgments. One of the major figures in this school was Wilhelm Hermann (1846–1922), who definitely jettisoned the traditional Christian concept of dogma and saw in Jesus the embodiment of the highest religious experience. While the Ritschlian tradition via Hermann was followed closely by theologians such as Theodor Haering (1848–1928), Hermann's disciple Adolf von Harnack (1850–1930) reduced Christianity to the built-in and exorable demands of the Ritschlian system. Harnack, who possessed great ability as a historian and a knowledge of Christian antiquity, spelled out his conception of the Christian religion as a pure ethic: dogma and Christology were worse than nonsense, they were a positive hindrance in knowing the Jesus of history. In Harnack's hands Jesus turned out to be the very model of the Ritschlian system, a religious genius who taught the fatherhood of God and the ethical ideal of the Kingdom of God. Harnack marks the high-water mark of the movement called "liberal Protestantism," a movement not only doomed in the new biblical criticism of Alfred Loisy and Albert Schweitzer but also destined to be discarded in the wake of World War II.[6]

With liberal Protestantism, that movement concentrating upon eschatology was also growing. It began with Johannes Weiss (1863–1914), who utilized the eschatological nature and expectation of Judaism at the time of Christ to challenge effectively the Harnack conception of the Jesus of history. Wilhelm Wrede in 1901 published his study of the Gospel of Mark, *The Messianic Secret,* in which he demonstrated the fallacy of the Harnack supposition because the sources were completely theological. It was left to Albert Schweitzer to destroy Harnack's concept in his *The Quest of the Historical Jesus.* According to Schweitzer the attempts to isolate the historical Jesus from the ecclesiastical Christologies were doomed to failure, for the sources, even the "pure" source of Mark, as Wrede had demonstrated, were all tainted with a Christology, an eschatological world view of Jesus' own time. Moreover, according to Schweitzer, Jesus was Himself an eschatologist. Schweitzer's renowned philosophy of "reverence for life" was, however, his own attempt to isolate the teaching of Jesus from its eschatological framework. Thus Schweitzer accepted the suppositions of the old quest while at the same time contributing to its downfall (that is, he presumed one could deal with the documents as historical).

Actually, the full brunt of this new criticism represented by the eschatologists served to point out the fatuousness of the historicist concept of the "pure" source as applied to the Gospels. They made it quite evident that all sources concerning Jesus were "interpretative," and in the first bloom of success seemed to prevent forever any possibility of achieving a knowledge of the historical Jesus.

While the new school of eschatology was tilting fairly successfully at liberal Protestantism and the quest for the historical Jesus, historians themselves were shifting positions about their own science. This now led the historians to more secure grounds and a more accurate conception of their subject. All historical writing, they realized, was from a particular point of view, all history is to some degree interpretative. Not every event or fact that occurs is the object of the historical record or the goal of the historian's labor, but rather, primarily those events or facts that have meaning. In short, the historian interprets as well as records. From this point of view the New Testament, and the Gospel documents in particular, might be restudied as a form of history.

Why did the quest for the historical Jesus fail? Basically, for two reasons, theology and history. As for theology, Heinz Zahrnt maintains that the quest attempted to place the basis of faith in scientific history and to make the historical Jesus the object of that faith. The theological end of the quest is described thus by Professor James M. Robinson: ". . . the discovery of the *kerygma* at the center of the Gospels. . . . It was this rise of the *kerygma* to the center of our understanding of primitive Christianity, and to the normative position in contemporary theology, which was the underlying cause for questioning even the *legitimacy* of the original quest." [7]

From the historical point of view the quest was doomed, for, as Schweitzer demonstrated, the New Testament documents were faith documents; they all reflected a theology and not a "neutral" picture of Jesus. The "lives" of Jesus produced by the earlier generation of critics and theologians were their own inventions, and they were lives of Jesus as those critics a priori conceived Jesus to be. The destruction of the Jesus of history in the liberal tradition was achieved, as Zahrnt points out, by the work of historical criticism, not orthodoxy. Again we have Professor Robinson's comments:

> We have come to recognize that the objective factual level upon which the nineteenth century operated is only one dimension of history, and that a whole new dimension of the facts, a deeper and more central plane of meaning, had been largely bypassed. . . . The dimension in which man actually exists, the "world," the stance or outlook from which

he acts, his understanding of his existence behind what he does, the way in which he meets his basic problems and the answer his life implies to the human dilemma, the significance he had as the environment of those who knew him, the continuing history his life produces, the possibility of existence which his life presents to me as an alternative— such matters as these have become central in an attempt to understand history. It is this deeper level of the reality of "Jesus of Nazareth" as he actually was which was not reached by "the reconstruction of his biography by means of objective historical method." Consequently, the two meanings of the term "historical Jesus" no longer coincide.[8]

The archeological and linguistic progress of the late nineteenth century coupled with the new historicism gave rise to a new school of theology based upon historical research, the History of Religions school. In their examination of Christianity they compared it historically with other contemporary Oriental religions, and like the Ritschlians, whose Jesus of history they helped the eschatologists destroy, they were doomed to disappear by the late nineteen thirties. The major representative of the History of Religions school was Ernst Troeltsch (1856–1923), who set in motion later sociological investigations of religion and influenced the movement of the social gospel in the United States. In accord with his historical methodology, Troeltsch felt that Christianity "was to be placed in the context of its historical basis, shorn of its supernatural element, and denied any final or absolute character." [9]

Another representative of this school, Wilhelm Bousset, declared, in his *Kyrios Christos,* the Hellenistic character of the Christian religion. The titles of Jesus (Lord and Christ) of his title indicated the work of Hellenization. A point of continuity with modern scholarship was established in the work of two distinguished scholars of the History of Religions school, Gunkel and Weiss; they isolated and used the "literary forms" of biblical material, a process which we shall see Bultmann perfect in modern times. Although form criticism has remained as a constant method in biblical criticism, the History of Religions school ceased to exist. The ultimate failure of this school was due to its inability to explain in its own terms the survival and success of Christianity as distinguished from all other religions at the time. These men forced the question, "How and why is Christianity unique?" and then found themselves unable to answer it.

The initial result of this type of form criticism was an increasing historical skepticism. More and more scholars concluded that all that could be known was the faith of the community (*Gemeinde-theologie*). The impression gained ground that Jesus as He actually was could not be found in the splintered library of books arbitrarily signified as the New Testament. Into this setting in the 1930's came the revolutionary work of the British scholar C. H. Dodd.[10] Dodd carefully studied the significance of preaching for the early Church, and having turned to the sermon outlines of the first apostles as recorded in the Book of Acts, he discovered a common unifying core for the New Testament community's proclamation. This proclamation, titled from the Greek for "preaching," *kerygma,* was the essential outline of the Church's preaching of the Christian faith in its state of mission. It consisted essentially in the proclamation of a series of events (the life, death, and resurrection of Jesus) in which the glory of God is revealed. In the kerygma is proclaimed God's saving work in Christ to man. Dodd demanded, as the early Christians consistently demanded, the historical, the having-happenedness, of the facts narrated. For Dodd the Jesus of history and the Christ of faith were essentially identical.

The isolation of the kerygma, the proclamation of the saving work of God in Christ, did not at first destroy the historical skepticism of the form critics. Rather, coupled with a historical cynicism, it created the intellectual matrix for a new movement, namely "demythologizing," associated with the name of Rudolf Bultmann.

As we have pointed out, it was the recognition that the Gospels were sources impregnated with the ideas of the kerygma that definitely ended the old quest for the historical Jesus. Dodd, in isolating and identifying the kerygma, attempted to demonstrate its connection with the historical Jesus. According to Robinson, however, Dodd neglected the existential function of the kerygma as a call to faith, a fact that accounts for the significance of the kerygma in contemporary theology; furthermore, Dodd makes the error of interpreting the kerygma in "terms of a positivistic view of history." [11] Also, as Ulrich Wilekens has pointed out, the speeches in the Book of Acts that Dodd used reflect the theology of Saint Luke.[12]

Between the two wars Protestant theology began to tack to more orthodox positions, rejecting the old liberal distinction between the Jesus of history and the Christ of faith. Bultmann had yet to present his now renowned position, and the work of Dodd was complimented by the growing *Heilsgeschichte* (salvation history) school. This school, which is still vital, centers its concerns about the acts of God in the history of salvation. So Rudolf Otto traced the interpretation of Christ (Christology) of the early Church back to Jesus Himself, thus establishing a continuity between the Church's faith and Jesus Himself.[13] Otto's work has since faced the critical scorn of the Bultmannians, for "it cannot be demonstrated from the tradition by a critical examination of the sources."[14]

The continuity between Jesus in history and the proclaimed Christ marks the works of this period by Dodd, Otto, and the *Heilsgeschichte* school and is still represented today by such scholars as Alan Richardson, George E. Wright, Floyd Filson, Joachim Jeremias, and Ethelbert Stauffer.[15] Stauffer's theology of the New Testament and his life of Jesus are regarded by the Bultmannians as the destruction of all that scholarship has achieved since 1900, for they maintain Stauffer does not take account of the relationship between the proclaimed and the historical Jesus.[16] The Bultmannian critique of Stauffer has been supported by even so distinguished a Catholic critic as Rudolf Schnackenburg.

Before we move on to the work and place of Rudolf Bultmann in the contemporary discussion of the historicity of Jesus, it is well to sum up briefly. We find in the immediate tradition of the twentieth century this three-stranded thread: Ritschlian theology and its liberal Protestantism, thoroughgoing eschatology, and finally, the methodology of the History of Religions school. For all their shortcomings, they have left an enormous heritage. The first of their contributions was the awareness of the importance of historical as well as literary criticism; the second, the recognition that the earliest Christian witness to Jesus is theological and is set within a framework of thought quite different from our own; third, the invaluable service of recognizing the eschatological element in the New Testament and early Christianity; fourth and last, the motivation that lay behind their work: the conviction that an attempt should be made to isolate the core of the Christian religion from primitive ways of thinking and present it to the modern world.

In the twentieth century the extremely important contribution of C. H. Dodd in isolating the kerygma of the New Testament, and the existentialist emphasis in the Kierkegaardian tradition set in motion by Karl Barth, have been fused both with the tradition of the turn of the century and with the growth of the physical sciences. Science has contributed not only to the investigation and mounting control of modern man over nature and man's environment but also to methodology and the formation of a new world view in the mind of modern man.

In speaking the Christian message to the modern mind Rudolf Bultmann represents one of the most influential figures in the field of Christian theology in the twentieth century. His influence is measured in terms of his coming to grips with the problem created by Barthian theology, namely, the relationship of the Word of God to human history, a relationship Barth declared to be absolutely discontinuous. Bultmann, in company with Martin Dibelius, inherited the form-critical method (*Formgeschichte*) from Weiss and developed it into an important critical tool. The conclusions of Bultmann's rigorous form-critical application were very skeptical about the Jesus of history as we find him in the New Testament. Why? Because, according to Bultmann, Jesus in the New Testament is presented in the "myths" of the first-century mind, whose world view was a simplistic and naïve three-storied universe. Within the New Testament and its myths, however, is the kerygma, the proclamation of God's Word to us; the New Testament must, therefore, be demythologized so that we may confront God in the kerygma. Bultmann's theological system of kerygma closely reflects the existentialist concept of man in Martin Heidegger, which we have seen. Here, however, we must be concerned with Bultmann's interpretation of the historicity of Jesus Christ.

The form-critical method used by Bultmann presumes the editorial nature of the New Testament books: they represent collections of different materials ("forms") that were later edited and redacted within the Church. Thus the Gospel of Mark represents the oldest of the Gospels, and through Mark one may arrive at the oral stage of tradition. The isolated forms of pericopes represent the oldest tradition, and they were used by the community in its preaching of the Gospel, the proclamation of Christ in liturgy and catechesis. But the usage of these forms always reflects the Easter event of the Resurrection. "The understanding of the History of Jesus in the Gospels is governed by the Resurrection to such an extent that the boundaries between His actions before Easter and His actions after Easter are blurred. . . . We always have Jesus only in the kerygma i.e., in the faith and proclamation of the community." [17]

The difficulty of Bultmann's position, then, is that we have only the Jesus enshrined in the kerygma, and what is there to prevent what seems a logical step among the "left-wing" Bultmannians, a process of "dekerygmatizing," so that the historical Jesus evaporates into symbol? "Does not the history of Jesus finally dissolve for us, this time not in the fire of historical criticism but in the fervor of faith?" [18]

Both critics and the disciples of Bultmann from Marburg are fond of pointing out the work of Martin Kahler, who had demonstrated at the end of the first quest that the kerygma is the final entity that is historically apprehensible. For Kahler, Jesus was historical precisely because He is proclaimed the Christ of faith and is effective in that proclamation. Bultmann's work and his indifference to the past history of Jesus (the historicity of the Resurrection is called "irrelevant") has simply put Kahler's original profession of the Christ of faith on a firm critical basis. For Bultmann, Jesus is, however, not a myth but a real event in which God's saving action occurred and still occurs when He is proclaimed. To seek beyond the proclamation, the kerygma, to the historical Jesus is pointless for Bultmann, and, what is worse, is an attempt to provide historical justification of the kerygma, an action contrary to the demand of faith.

The post-Bultmannians, especially Dahl, Käsemann, and Bornkamm, are highly critical of the master for allowing his historical agnosticism concerning Jesus to run the risk of reducing Jesus to a symbol. When demythologizing occurs, "does one encounter in the *Kerygma* a symbolized principle, or interpreted history?" [19] Robinson makes explicit the interest in historicity and Jesus:

> Hence the decisive point with regard to the *kerygma* and history is not whether the *kerygma* preserves detailed historical memories about Jesus, but rather that the *kerygma* is decidedly an evaluation of the historical person. The *kerygma* does not commit one to assume the historicity of this or that scene in Jesus' life, but it does commit one to a specific understanding of his life. Thus the *kerygma* is largely uninterested in historiography of the nineteenth-century kind, for the *kerygma* does not lie on the level of objectively verifiable fact. But it is decisively interested in historiography of the twentieth-century kind, for the *kerygma* consists in the meaning of a certain historical event, and thus coincides with the goal of modern historiography. [20]

The criticism directed at Bultmann apropos his disregard for the historicity of Jesus is of course shared by the large bulk of non-Bultmannian biblical scholars and theologians.

Bultmann's critics embrace not only—as would be expected—Catholic theologians but also many of the modern theologians of eminence in Protestantism.[21] Primary to their criticisms is the location of the Christ event. "Did it take place 'in the years A.D. 1–30,' or as some wag has put it, does it take place when Dr. Bultmann ascends the pulpit at 11 A.M. on a Sunday morning?"[22] Saint Paul's first letter to the Corinthians springs to the lips of every critic dealing with Bultmann's reference to the Resurrection as mythological: "And if Christ has not risen, vain then is our preaching [kerygma], vain too is your faith" (I Cor. 15:14).

The foremost representative of Bultmann's critics is Paul Althaus. It is precisely on the point of the historicity of Jesus that Althaus directs his stinging criticisms: "the *kerygma* and the historical Jesus are torn apart, and the importance of the latter is minimized in comparison with the *kerygma.*"[23] Althaus thinks that for Bultmann to "parenthesize" the historical Jesus because of his belief that past events as past are irrelevant is to miss the importance of historical fact in I Corinthians 15:14. The Bultmannian justification on the basis of an existentialist concept of history is a departure from the concept of history in scholarly usage and is "the product of caprice, and makes it hard to come to an understanding with the historian who investigates past history."[24] With the sense of the critic who has found the vital supposition of his opponent and at the same time his most vulnerable position, Althaus bears forward:

> The presence with us of the past, insofar as it has contributed to produce the situation in which we live today, is quite different from the presence to which the existentialist conception of history and the historic refers. . . . True, the "historic" is distinct from the merely factual, and means more than mere fact, but it does include the notion of historical fact, and *does not exist* without it. Let the past have the power to make itself present to the existence of men today, it is for all that *also* past. The historical is not the same thing as the historic in the modern sense of the latter concept, but the historic is never without the historical, it is also historical, and as such it is the object of historical inquiry and knowledge.[25]

The essential quality of Bultmann's disciples from the University of Marburg (the post-Bultmannian school) is their affirmation of the importance of the historical Jesus for the kerygma and, in consequence, a "new quest for the historical Jesus." This new quest of the Marburgers officially began with an address given in 1953 by Ernst Käsemann, and its necessity is rooted in their belief that without the historical Jesus there can be no Christology. Two prenotes to the new quest are commonly set: first, that it is necessary to investigate the continuity of the proclaimed Christ with the Jesus of history; second, that this service of historical scholarship cannot provide by itself the basis for faith.[26]

The methodology of the new quest reflects a radical form-critical approach. The assumption is made that "sayings" of Jesus in the Gospel accounts hold a priority in historical accuracy over narrative; traditions that do not reflect the Judaic or early Christian background are presumed more historical than others. This methodology guarantees what Zahrnt calls a "critically insured minimum,"[27] which serves as a principle of validation for the rest of the material. Professor Macquarrie speaks of a "minimal core of factuality ascertainable by rational inference which can be tested by anyone."[28]

The distinctive characteristic concerning Jesus to be drawn from this material, according to Zahrnt and Bornkamm, is His "sovereignty," His characteristic authoritativeness that marks His discontinuity from all others in His milieu. This recognition "is a decisive point in the understanding of the historical Jesus." The sovereignty of Jesus derives from His awareness of Himself as the decisive factor in the appearance of the Kingdom of God. "In the person of the historical Jesus, then, eschatology, consciousness of his person and existential understanding belong inseparably together. Each conditions the other; they run together like three parts of a ring."[29]

The question of the Resurrection, for the Marburgers, belongs to the realm of faith, for it transcends history and cannot be grasped except in faith. Historical criticism verifies only two facts: the change in the disciples, and their allegation that the risen Jesus appeared to them; the implications of these facts are, however, significant. But the truth of the Resurrection remains limited to faith, and the New Testament inseparably joins the Resurrection accounts to faith; the term of faith is the person of the risen Jesus, not the verifiable facts. The Resurrection is the point of continuity between the historical Jesus and the Christ of faith; it is here that "Jesus enters the proclamation of the community and Himself becomes its content."[30]

The best known example of the new quest for the historical Jesus by the post-Bultmann school is to be found in Gunther Bornkamm's *Jesus of Nazareth*. According to Bornkamm we possess no words of Jesus that do not "contain at the same time the confession of the believing congregation. . . . This makes the search after the bare facts of history difficult and to a large extent futile." [31] But lest this should seem to indicate on Bornkamm's part only a study of the early Christian community theology, he nevertheless pursues through the Gospel records an understanding of the history and person of Jesus, and he remarks that Jesus is to be found in the record of his words and deeds rather than in any messianic consciousness or claim. Bornkamm claims of the Resurrection stories that they evidence the faith, they are not the basis for the faith. And yet, once again Bornkamm the Bultmannian draws the reader up short with the assertion: "But it is just as certain that the appearances of the Risen Christ and the word of his witnesses have in the first place given rise to this faith." [32] As one perceptive reviewer has said: "This statement shows a sharp and irrevocable break with an extreme branch of form criticism. It would seem that what has led the author to this position is a rejection (after diligent study of the source material) of the Humean apriorism that no testimony is sufficient to establish the historicity of a miracle." [33]

The new quest for the historical Jesus, then, not only follows upon the Bultmannian suppositions as a logical pursuit but it demonstrates the intrinsic difficulty for the Bultmannian system. This is illustrated, for example, in the comment of Neill Hamilton about Bornkamm's *Jesus of Nazareth:*

> By balancing each apparently negative consideration with a complementary positive one, Professor Bornkamm still comes out where the Gospels do. I think this is amazing. I also think it is impossible. This is something like a Cullmannian superstructure built on a Bultmannian foundation. Now the new quest elsewhere argues that this is where Bultmann was really heading all along. I cannot agree. The man is still alive and he has said no.[34]

It would seem that if a "pure" Bultmannian position exists, it is held by Bultmann alone. The implications of his view inexorably lead either to the antikerygmatics of the left (Buri, Ogden, and so on) or to the right (the Marburgers). There could be no clearer indication of the intolerable position of Bultmann than the course of biblical criticism that he has so strongly affected. The heart of the dilemma that Bultmann has posed for those who would follow him seems to lie essentially in his tearing apart the factuality ("happenedness") from the meaningfulness of those facts.

Eric Rust in commenting upon the new quest has pin-pointed the theological danger inherent in Bultmann's position: "What is significant in the new approach is the recognition that without some emphasis on the historicity of Jesus, our faith lapses into docetism, and the gospel becomes an abstract form of universal truth." [35] This theological criticism of docetism so well aimed by Professor Rust at Bultmann may even be extended to the post-Bultmannians, despite their new quest for the historical Jesus. In their definition of faith they follow Bultmann's lead and will not allow their new quest or its achievements to provide even a basis for faith. "This very emphasis contains within itself the thrust which ultimately and, it seems, inevitably must render the Christian faith docetic." [36]

Toward a Christian Apologetic: I. History and Historicity

The rejection of the older historicist assumptions by the historians and the discoveries of the form critics provide new material and new viewpoints from which to examine the historical claims of Christianity. The perfection of historical method has caused many to see the necessity of reading a historical witness (whether a literary form or a document) in the context in which it was used. In order that they may grasp the essentials of past events, those of a later age and different culture must avoid reading historical records from their own point of view. The witnesses must be read and/or examined as part of the past that produced them. In short, historical method and all the critical faculties it brings to its investigation must be adapted to the source at hand. Though the witnesses available to the historical Jesus are *committed* Christian witnesses, whether in the oral traditions of the early Church or in the Gospel documents themselves, they are not for that reason any the less witnesses to the historical facts. They are witnesses to events, witnesses that record in their own way the meaning of those events.

As we have seen, the result of the evolving understanding of history and the historical problem presented by the Gospels was a new pursuit of the historical Jesus. In such a pursuit one must always remember that primary factor present in the evidence available: there is and has always been preserved *in the Church* the distinction of the Gospels as separate from apocryphal writing. The Gospels, because of their content, their careful mode of transmission, and the proclaimed intention of their authors, must be examined as real historical sources of the Church's tradition. As such they are easily distinguishable from the apocryphal writings, which are intentional fabrications of history representing a new world view of some Christians. The examination of these documents has been both literary and form-critical; the strata of tradition have been ably sketched. But while the literary examination of the Gospels as witnesses to Jesus provide illuminating information for the historian, there is still a fundamental problem of determining the historicity of the facts they relate.

The problem of historicity and Christian belief revolves about two elements: the historical records and the older tradition their literary components reflect. From these elements an answer must be sought to the historical problem, "Is there a complete and evident distinction between what actually happened (event) and what the early Christian Church believed had happened (meaning)?" The question involves not only the renewed modern Protestant quest for the historical Jesus but the entire apologetic question involving every Christian. As we shall see, the Gospels do reflect, in their own way, authentic tradition, and it is a legitimate supposition to accept the historical reality of that to which they bear witness.

The late nineteenth and early twentieth centuries saw a fruitless quest for the historical Jesus; that quest was doomed *in semine* because of its suppositions. It is a more proper procedure, and indeed more historical, to examine the Gospel documents and the history they contain while keeping in mind the particular nature of that history, the particular religious purpose of their authors. History does not stand in a vacuum, but as a record it always includes the *event* and the *meaning of that event* for the people who shared in it. Selectivity and interpretation are constitutive elements of history, and if the Christian apologetic seeks to handle the Gospels as historical documents, it must do so with an eye to the purpose of the authors, to the selectivity they demonstrate, to the meaning they witness, and to the contemporary forms in which these were cast.

It is quite evident that the Gospels were not written for our modern idea of historical purpose. They are not biographies of Jesus; they were not meant simply to record for later ages the events of a past time. Rather they were written to testify to a suprahistorical meaning that lay in events the authors witnessed and in which they were involved. They were written to testify to the suprahistorical fact of God's intervention in human history in the saving work of Jesus Christ.

The Gospels, in looking upon the history of man, do not find social, political, or military events to be the significant elements of man's history, but rather see history as a mystery, a mystery essentially composed of two stages, the Old and New Testaments. History for the Evangelists is salvation history, and they have not only witnessed and recorded historical events, but also—and primarily— the meaning of those events.

Thus these eyewitnesses, the Evangelists, are interested in writing salvation history rather than simply history. The genre of salvation history and its form as the primary object of the Evangelists do *not,* however, exclude the historical (have-happened) factor. The concept of salvation history serves to illustrate and explain the purpose of the Gospel documents, the meaning of the events recorded, but it does not exclude the reality of the events, which we call, strictly speaking, the factual.

Again, from the viewpoint of history in the sense of historicity alone, can the recital of the events in Christ's life, presupposing their actuality as recorded in the Gospels and their accuracy in every detail, provide a historical *proof* of Christ's divinity? It seems not, for the divinity of Christ is not subject to reason: Christ as divine is not the object of the purely rational witness, whether he be an eyewitness or an accurate historical recorder. History in itself, simply as a record, cannot conclude affirmatively as to the divinity of Christ, for such is not and cannot be the object of a historical or rational investigation. It is and can only be, since it is suprahistorical, the judgment of faith. And it is to this that the Gospel witness is addressed: the revelations of the Christ, leading the reader to the realization of Christ's divinity; these revelations are the occasions of saving faith, the gift of God. This is indeed the very meaning of the word "gospel," the "good news"; the good news of God's saving work in Jesus Christ His Son.

There is then only *one* Gospel: that of God's work in Christ, a work accomplished through a series of real historical having-hap-pened facts: the life, death, and Resurrection of Jesus. This is indeed the common core of all the New Testament documents. These facts of the Christ constitute the apostolic sermons of the Book of Acts; they are found in books earlier than the Gospels (Pauline Epistles); and these same interpreted facts, this "gospel," is itself the unifying core of all the four Gospel documents. The historical recording within the community of Christ's historical existence, coupled with the meaning of Christ's work as the saving action of God in history, constitute the kerygma, or the one "gospel."

This kerygma, this message or proclamation of God's work in Christ, is intimately related to the having-happenedness of certain specified events, and constantly appeals to their having-happened-ness wherever and whenever it is proclaimed by the Evangelists and Paul. The events were known to all in Jerusalem, and the kerygma is their proclamation in the light of their meaning. The factual or historical claims of those who preached this kerygma were avail-able for refutation by either the Jews, who reacted against it, or the Romans. No one contradicted the facts; none were able to lay to rest as myth the words and life events of Jesus. It was because of lack of faith that the unbelievers were unable or unwilling to accept the full kerygma, namely, the meaning of those events— the work of God in Christ.

The having-happenedness of these events is, as a major constitu-tive element of the kerygma, demonstrative of the fact that the intent of the Evangelists in presenting salvation history is also to a large part historical in our sense of treating of the having-hap-pened. The kerygma points to history, and while, as we shall see, in some of its *forms* it may modify what we consider as historical, nevertheless in the minds of its preachers it stands or falls on fact. "And if Christ has not risen, in vain then is our preaching [*kerygma*]. . . ."

From another point of view, what the Christian states is simply that the determination of the facts recorded in the Gospels is a determination based upon a theological principle; the Gospels are written by believers for believers, they are written "from faith to faith." The identity of the Jesus of history and Christ of faith is affirmed in fact, but at the same time having-happened events are not chosen indiscriminately, but for a purpose. "Many other signs also Jesus worked in the sight of His disciples, which are not written in this book. But these are written that you may believe that Jesus is the Christ, the Son of God, and that believing, you may have life in His Name" (John 20:30, 31).

TOWARD A CHRISTIAN APOLOGETIC: II. THE "FORMS" OF THE NEW TESTAMENT

The question of the forms in which the kerygma is expressed brings us subtly to a change of emphasis—from the question of the historicity of the facts upon which Christianity is built to the actual historicity to be applied to all the forms in which the kerygma is expressed. One must be cautious in handling material from the first and second centuries lest one leap too quickly from a judgment of form to a judgment of historicity. While the historical having-happenedness of the kerygma is evident, and while we claim historicity for the essential Gospel narrations, a more careful literary examination of the Gospel documents must now be pursued. In the various literary forms of the Gospels there is a serious manipulation of material, and the historicity of a fact used in a special way and for a special intention may indeed differ from the actual fact historically evidenced by the form.

In this literary problem of the forms in which the kerygma finds expression the importance of the intellectual matrix in which the Gospels were written becomes evident. The ideas current in the first and second centuries, the illumination of the times provided by the Dead Sea Scrolls, the traditional handling of the material by Hebrew authors, all become of overwhelming importance in establishing the literary forms and, consequently, in judging the degree of historicity such forms may reflect.

Any literary examination of the Gospels must lead to knowledge of their formation and of the editorial procedures involved in their composition, and also to an understanding of their real nature and intention as not simply history, but specifically salvation history. Literary procedure arrives at the establishment of the text, now fairly unanimously agreed upon. Next is a criticism of the sources, which is based upon the elements common to the three Synoptic Gospels. The Synoptic problem itself has found tentative approaches toward solution in the widespread agreement upon our present Mark as the oldest of the Gospel documents, upon the independence of Matthew and Luke, and upon their joint dependence in some cases upon Mark. From these common points of agreement hypotheses are advanced for the solution of the Synoptic problem.

The procedure of form criticism in our own century, whereby the oral traditions of the Gospel have been subjected to minute scrutiny, has created far more difficult problems. The legitimacy of such a study must, however, be maintained in the light of our knowledge of the importance in the period of the Evangelists of oral tradition. A number of conclusions may be stated upon which some common agreement has been obtained. The first of these is the affirmation of the existence within the Gospels of literary forms: the Gospels are envisioned as a number of examples of these forms, previously existing in fragmentary fashion, joined together and at times editorialized. This joining together is represented by the redactional, or editorial, work of the Evangelists, in which for some a seemingly chronological succession is achieved. Therefore, beyond the documents as we have them are many of the older literary forms. Because some form critics, such as Bultmann, having worked from a priori philosophies or dogmatic presuppositions rather than by critical method alone, may have arrived at radical positions of historical skepticism, the real lights that such critical methods may throw upon the Gospels should not be neglected. This study of redactional procedures reflected by the Gospels is called *Redaktionsgeschichte.*

In a sense we may state, then, that the Gospels are the culmination of oral transmission in the community of Christians. This tradition, this handing down of teaching in fixed oral forms in the Church, demonstrates under investigation an enormous care and fidelity in the actual tradition itself. The tradition has its origin in the Church; there it is understood and controlled; there great fidelity to the account of the eyewitnesses is maintained in the transmission. The extreme variations and obvious clumsiness of the apocryphal writings demonstrate the destruction of tradition when it is removed from the control of the original Christian community and its historical memory.

The substance of the New Testament accounts evidences a discontinuity in history, such as the uniqueness of Jesus and the completely different content given to the traditional messianic themes, and this discontinuity can be accounted for only by the impact of facts. The supposition that the Church created the content of the Gospels, which was put forth by the earlier form critics, may be answered by pointing out the discontinuity discovered in the oldest examples of these forms, which helps us to see that the Church did not create the Gospel content. The creativity necessary to account for the Gospel accounts was hardly able to exist in the community, but itself depended upon the fact. While the Church may have reflected upon what it was given, it did not itself create the kerygma, but rather received it from the actual event of God in Christ.

Again, this presupposition of the Church's creativity in regard to the Gospel content that so vitiated the work of the earlier form critics neglected an essential element found not only in the Gospel documents but also in their older forms. The Church's consciousness of the having-happenedness of the events the Gospels narrate demonstrates that the Church did not create this material. While witnessing to the words and work of Jesus the Church interpreted their meaning, but the actual historical nature of those words and work is frequently appealed to and determines the interpretation that is found in their narration. It is objected that this interpretation was forced by the Church upon the facts, but it seems far more evident that the Church itself was created by the facts related in the kerygma, that her interpretation was imposed by the facts themselves as they were experienced in the concrete historical situation. It is at this point that reason has run her course, and the movement of faith, the acceptance of these facts and their meaning, seems to enter the scene.

This formation of the Gospels within the Church demonstrates, in the oldest examples of the forms that are traceable, an intimate connection between fact and meaning. The oldest forms demonstrate not just historicity (event) but history (event plus meaning). These oldest oral forms reflect Jesus as an object of adoration and cult. Thus it can be stated as a result of the most careful examination of the oldest ascribable forms that the Gospels were written in faith: they were written by believers, and as such are not to be seen as "purely" or solely the object of historical method. Nor is this to be wondered at, for of its nature the Gospel proclaims the work of God (a supernatural action transcending time) in human history, in events (of their nature spatial and temporal). To investigate such documents on the basis of historicity alone is to divide them falsely; faith and fact are intimately related and cojoined in these documents as fact and meaning; historicity stops at the facts and can never achieve the essentially suprahistorical meaning that they reflect. The existence of the Church, the community in which these documents were formed, can find as the cause of its existence only faith in Jesus as the Christ. The essential meaning of these documents, then, is the object of faith; their essential meaning can never be the object of historical method alone.

Furthermore, all the separate literary genres that we find in the Gospels are joined by one unifying fact—this belief in Jesus. And as we have pointed out, this faith is, in the kerygma, intimately related to fact. To make these statements is not, however, to deprive the Gospels of their proper historical significance (having-happenedness), for this is as essential to them as is the meaning of the having-happened. The Gospels do intend to include that which is called the strictly historical, but the redactional procedures involved in composition have reflected the Old Testament tradition of writing documents for the community, so that the facts presented through various forms are joined together in a documentary, rather than a chronological unity. If the properly historical examination of the Gospels is incomplete in itself, if it leads to questions that the Gospels cannot answer and are not intended to answer, by the same token the examination of historicity must be concluded and completed in an examination of the meaning of the facts witnessed to. Jesus, the Christ of God and the Lord of history, must concurrently be the object of investigation. Thus in the next chapter we shall turn from this historical Jesus (the fact) to the relationship of Jesus to all history as Lord (the meaning of the fact) that constitutes the Gospel witness.

TOWARD A CHRISTIAN APOLOGETIC: III. BULTMANN, HISTORY
AND THE RESURRECTION

Rudolf Bultmann poses for the Catholic a challenge to the traditional apologetic for Christianity. An apologetic would in itself be meaningless for Bultmann, since it would imply the lack of faith, an attempt to validate or justify the kerygma. Bultmann, then, is far more the Lutheran in his emphasis upon the *sola fides* and the absolutely nonrational nature of the encounter demanded in the kerygma than he is usually given credit for being. But the challenge presented by Bultmann is the theological and historical challenge faced by Catholic scholarship in contemporary theology. It simply will not do for the Catholic to dismiss the work, the insight, and the vast critical achievements of Bultmann and his school by merely reaffirming the constant tradition of the Church, a tradition that identifies the Jesus of history with the Christ of faith. Properly understood, this tradition of the Church is itself and of itself a sufficient theological argument, but the Bultmannian thrust, everywhere evident in New Testament studies, is being met as it were from within the structures of Bultmann's presentation of the problem. An attempt is being made by Catholic scholars to see Bultmann's point as Bultmann has intended to make it, rather than engage in a fruitless polemic in which neither side is really talking to the other. Many current observers have remarked, along with Macquarrie, that the treatment of Bultmann at the hands of Catholic scholars has in many instances been far more appreciative and knowledgeable than in the Protestant community.

But it is in this dialogue that serious attention must be given by any scholar, Catholic or otherwise, to certain assumptions made by the Bultmannian school. The critical assumption is historical, that is, it concerns the nature of history. Bultmann assumes a purely existentialist understanding of history; and along with his followers, in their brutal but incisive criticisms of positivistic history, he forces the subjective element, the sense of "communion" in the event by the historian, to the peril of the event as a happening. If, therefore, the existentialist distinction and its emphasis upon the subjective are applied in fullest rigor to the event of Jesus Christ, the empirical nature of that event will fade in importance.

In the kerygma we do not have two elements (the happening and its meaning) as the existentialists would affirm them. To state that one element, in this case meaning, is exclusively history is the reverse of the positivistic sense of history, in which factuality is affirmed to the peril of meaning. Rather, we receive these two elements *together,* simultaneously; one cannot be separated from the other, as each group in its own way (positivists and existentialists) attempts to do, without doing damage to the true conception of history.

We do have in the kerygma an eschatological encounter, but it is still the eschatological encounter attached to a real event, which event possesses—as "happening"—an empirical character. Using the Cross as an example, we must agree with the Protestant scholar Althaus: "It is decisive that He died as the Christ, for all of us; and faith alone knows this. But it is not less essential for faith that this so-called Christ event is not a myth, but that the real man Jesus died. That is a historical question. Faith cannot declare it a matter of indifference." [37] And if Bultmann, in his radical conception of faith, will maintain the necessity of not attempting to validate the kerygma, we must also affirm with Althaus the traditional Catholic concept of the *praeambula fidei.*

> There is always an element of *fides humana* included in our certainty about the Jesus Christ of the *kerygma.* It certainly must be sharply distinguished from the *fides divina,* the certainty of our faith concerning the presence of God and His salvation in the history to which the *kerygma* bears witness. The *fides humana* can never create the *fides divina,* but the latter is never without the former.[38]

Finally, we must be aware that in the Christian apologetic the resurrection of Jesus from the dead can never be other than the keystone of the apologetic arch. The Catholic can in no way admit the conception of myth with regard to the Resurrection nor countenance the Bultmannian assertion of the irrelevancy of the Resurrection. This is not to say that the difficulties involved in the Resurrection as a *motive* of faith and as an *object* of faith are not significant. Within the Resurrection accounts of the New Testament there are historical (having-happened) facts that are legitimate objects of investigation for the historian (the empty tomb, the appearances, the distinctive change within the apostles). In short, the New Testament evidences continuity and discontinuity, so that the Resurrection is basically the pre-eminent exemplification of the essential difficulties faced by Christian faith and purely historical investigation. As Father Vincent O'Keefe observes:

> We are dealing with mysterious and superhuman events which in their totality do not issue from an historical proof but are the object of faith. Some of the effects are perceptible and can be the object of testimony. The empty tomb and the apparitions are subject to some control by the historian. They illuminate each other and can be united in one coherent explanation which is the extraordinary event whose roots are supernatural and divine but whose visible effects have the value of a sign.[39]

Toward a Christian Apologetic: IV. The Work of Alan Richardson

The nineteenth and twentieth centuries produced a tradition in Protestant thought by introducing a distinction between the Jesus of history and the Christ of faith. It has been a distinction that has not left unaffected even the work of Catholic theologians, and especially apologetes. It has also served the Church, however, in provoking a number of attempts by traditional Christian apologetes to restore the identity that the Jesus of history and the Christ of faith have always possessed in the historic Christian faith. These new attempts at an apologetic have been marked by the rather considerable contributions of the Anglican theologian Alan Richardson, professor of Christian theology at the University of Nottingham. The literate and articulate Canon Richardson has crowned his labors of many years with the Oxford Bampton Lectures of 1962. These are a first-rate study of the problem and a significant contribution in contemporary Christian apologetics. They have been published as *History Sacred and Profane*.[40]

Richardson brings to his apologetic a strong sense of the historical development of Christian theology. His treatment of the past is replete with incisive and telling criticisms and assures the reader of his ability, constantly evident, to avoid the errors of his predecessors. His critique is leveled not only at the now defunct liberal theology of the nineteenth century but also at many of the figures that dominate contemporary theological thought. The burden of his attack upon the "neo-orthodox" theology of Tillich, Brunner, Barth, Bultmann, and the post-Bultmannians is precisely the ground of history. He maintains these theologians represent "in one form or another a disengagement of theology from history." The modern Bultmannian preoccupation is burdened by a nineteenth-century positivist conception of history, "the view that history is a naturalistic continuum of causes and effects, in which 'miracles' do not happen, and in which the activity of God cannot be a factor in causal explanations." [41] Richardson affirms in clear and unmistakable language the historical nature of the New Testament kerygma:

> The kerygma of the whole Bible is a proclamation that God is a God who intervenes in history and is Lord of history. The biblical language about God's mighty acts in history certainly needs interpreting; but it

does not need demythologizing, because it is not a myth. It does not speak in mythological terms of an existential meaning disclosed in a certain historical situation, but of how God intervened in the stream of events and altered the course of history. Existentialist hermeneutics does not salvage the historical element in the biblical kerygma from the wreckage of the historic faith in the shallows of positivist philosophy.[42]

Richardson has seen the necessity of basing an apologetic in our times upon the character of historical thinking. This has always marked his major works and comes to complete fruition in *History Sacred and Profane*. The key question for the historian is one of "involvement" in the history he explicates. Without this involvement there can be no full sense of history. "The truth is that 'scientific history,' the establishing and the collecting of 'facts,' is only part of history-writing . . . the historian must bring to the facts that he handles a perspective, a point of view, a scale of values. . . . In this sense all history is *somebody's* history: impersonal history is not so much history as chronicle." And again: "The root fallacy here is the not uncommon assumption that the historian must derive the criterion of his judgment, or the scale of values by which he selects and interprets his facts, from the study of the facts themselves." [43]

Relying upon what he regards as an "Anglican" school of thought in this matter from the time of Edmund Burke through Ranke and Burckhardt, and the insights offered by Dilthey, Croce, and Collingwood (which insights he carefully distinguishes), Richardson builds an apologetic upon an understanding of history that presupposes the involvement of the historian. Prior to his apologetic he takes up the fundamental question of the nature of historical thinking itself:

History, unlike science, does not progress by making wider and wider generalizations; it progresses by giving more coherently rational explanations of the available historical evidence, so that in the end we are bound to agree that "it must have been like that." Historical method does not rule out the possibility of an event's having taken place because it does not fit into a system of generalizations; it decides that an event has *probably* taken place because the assumption that it has done so makes better sense of the evidence. There are no historical generalizations (or laws of history) which determine in advance of the historical enquiry whether an event may have happened or not; historical generalizations arise out of the evidence and are not a priori conditions of thinking which precede it. . . . Still less are there any laws of history (such as the law of progress) which can be used to answer historical questions without the fatigue of having to look at the evidence. History is not a generalizing science which tells us that if such and such circumstances occur, then such and such results will follow; it does not attempt to formulate general propositions of the type "any such thing must be so and so." [44]

Richardson calls to witness the distinguished American historian Carl Becker for support of his assertion that "history is not a direct knowledge of past events, but it is rather a mental construction made by historians in order to comprehend the traces of the past which have come down to us." [45] When this understanding of history is applied to the crucial question of the resurrection of Jesus, Richardson demands two inseparable conditions for the argument: first, credible witness (and here he relies upon the traditional apologetic and the new biblical scholarship); and second, the historian's own experience and understanding (so that the historian's final judgment is determined by the kind of man that he is). Thus the resurrection of Jesus cannot be *observed*, for the historian's judgment is an *inference* from the evidence; it cannot, because of the nature of historical judgment, be *demonstrated*, for "the only form of demonstration in history is a demonstration that this judgment of the evidence is more rational than that one." [46]

The historian, then, must seek a known feature of history in which he may place the Resurrection (thus observing the second of Richardson's two conditions), so that it is intelligible in historical terms. This known feature, which he calls a "covering law," is to be found in the history of Israel, which offers the observer a number of "disclosure-situations"; that is, "there occurs at certain 'historic' moments the discernment of a meaning which provokes a response to what is discerned, an acknowledgment of an obligation, a commitment to an overriding purpose." [47] Thus the resurrection of Christ, which as an event falls within this category, can be delineated in historical terms.

The Catholic theologian faced by Richardson's attempt to provide a firm base for a Christian apologetic cannot but be impressed by his efforts. Few professional theologians have really attempted to come to grips with the problems of the historicity of Christ on the grounds of the historians themselves. However, while the work of

Richardson remains admirable for what he has attempted to do—
and, indeed, much of it is useful for a Christian apologetic in the
twentieth century—there are some difficuties and some new questions that he opens up. One is tempted to ask if he has not too
closely tied his apologetic to one particular modern conception of
historical thinking. Historiography has not as yet reached a definitive plane of self-explanation; in fact, a glance at the major historical journals indicates that historians themselves are still far from
agreement about Richardson's basic problem—the nature of historical thinking. Here the problem is also affected by the area of history
the historian is investigating. The fluctuations of American and economic history in which Becker was so deeply involved have certainly
influenced his judgment about the nature of his task as a historian.
Again, one is tempted to ask whether Richardson's use of the Old
Testament "disclosure-situations" is an adequate historical category
within which one may place the crucial subject of the Resurrection.
How dependent is the Old Testament "disclosure-situation" on the
faith of the observer? And if the Old Testament events, themselves
revelatory, necessitate faith by their disclosure value, has not Richardson simply pushed the question of faith and the Resurrection
back one step? What are the categories through which the historian
qua historian may perceive the historical understanding of the Old
Testament events? While Richardson has indeed offered some
startling insights into the apologetic problem, he has also raised and
provoked new avenues of thought. For this, the Christian theologian
is certainly in his debt.

Conclusion: The Eschatological Nature of the New Testament Witness

In any consideration of the Gospels and their narrative of events
one special element must always be kept in mind. The meaning
of these events is eschatological: in them history has reached its
fulfillment by an act of God. Thus the Gospel narratives have always
this suprahistorical element, the God-Who-Acts in human history.
The one Gospel proclaimed by the Evangelists is always eschatological as well as historical: it proclaims real events, but events that give
history itself meaning. The new age, the revelation of the Kingdom
of God, in short, the eschatological form of the kerygma, is the

essential link between the historical facts narrated and the meaning
all history has received from those events. The eschatological framework, then, bears out and illuminates the essential historicity of the
Christian proclamation, for history is fulfilled and given meaning
precisely in specified historical events, the words and work of the
great eschatological figure, Jesus Christ.

Throughout the New Testament documents eschatology is clearly
present. In the Pauline Epistles, in Paul, in Acts, in the Epistle to
the Hebrews the death, resurrection, and ascension of Christ are
the decisive eschatological events, and this reflects what critical
method tells us about the most primitive preaching of the kerygma.
The Gospels in their redactional formation undertook a thoroughgoing eschatological evaluation of the entire life of Jesus; thus, for
example, the stress on the fulfillment of prophecy accounts for the
Infancy narratives, particularly for the emphasis on the Virgin Birth.
The growing Christian awareness of a "time between" the fulfillment of history in the Christ event and its revelation in the Second
Coming led Paul to explicate the doctrine of the Church as identified with Jesus, so that we see "the whole territory of the Church's
life as the field of the eschatological miracle." [48] John's Gospel sums
up the whole of Christ's life in an eschatological sense, whereas his
apocalypse climaxes the realization of the futurist or Second Coming
element in Christian eschatology. The cause of these eschatological
developments of the New Testament authors must be seen through
the illumination of the Spirit of God and not solely as a purely
rational response to the stimulus of a historically developing situation brought about by the fact that the parousia did not occur
simultaneously with the eschaton of the Christ event.

This eschatological element, present in all strata of the New
Testament documents and their formation, itself presents a problem.
At the time of the New Testament there was an enormous eschatological tradition and a seemingly vast Jewish heritage of apocalyptic
teaching. The earliest scholars most intent upon seeing this tradition
as the situation in life in which the New Testament was produced
(Schweitzer, Loisy, et al.) have frequently objected to the historicity
of the central tradition represented by the kerygma. Thus, it is
alleged, the main lines of the Christian kerygma were the creation
of men living with the apocalyptic traditions; the Christian kerygma
is envisioned as having been produced by imaginative minds defi-

nitely shaped by this eschatological heritage. These arguments are based upon (a) the enormous amounts of Hebrew eschatological literature deriving from the Old Testament heritage and apocalyptic literature, and (b) the strong interest the Gospel writers had in applying this tradition to Jesus (thus, for example, they would maintain that the Infancy accounts resulted *solely* from this search for fulfilled prophecy).

Actually one can hardly deny the existence of what may be termed an apocalyptic matrix for the intellectual milieu of the Evangelists, but this in itself proves little toward discrediting the substantial historicity of the Christian narration. The argument depends upon the allegation that the evident attempts to apply the older Hebrew eschatological traditions to Jesus forced the production of the historical facts asserted. But it is upon this very point that the argument collapses, for the New Testament authors do not use all these messianic predictions to be found in the eschatological tradition. In fact, quite few are used, and even whole eschatological areas of the Old Testament, certainly known to these men, are not used. What is demonstrated by New Testament eschatology is a principle of selection, a norm for the usage and application of the eschatological tradition.

What is this norm, or principle of selection, that is the controlling factor of New Testament eschatology? It is obviously the historical tradition, the accurate and controlled memory of what Jesus taught and did. Only those elements of the older eschatological tradition were used that actually agreed with what they knew to be the words and work of Jesus. The selectivity evidenced by the New Testament authors toward the eschatological traditions serves rather to bolster the historicity of their account, for no other reason can explain their selectivity.

That the Christ was the Messiah was not the conclusion of eschatologically-shaped minds without facts, but it was the conviction inevitably resulting from the historical experience of Jesus upon their inherited eschatology. The New Testament presents us with a tradition of the having-happened proclaimed in eschatological terms. Thus, as Dodd remarks, "Eschatology is not itself the substance of the Gospel, but a form under which the absolute value of the Gospel facts is asserted." [49]

Finally, the reader of the New Testament should be aware of the central problem of Jesus and history that the eschatological form of the New Testament proclamation produces. Here we move from historicity to history, from event to meaning. The problem centers upon the "time between," upon the era in which we live between the first coming of Christ and the second coming, the parousia. In a sense all time is involved in this mystery: the past (the historicity of the Christ event), the present (the meaning of the Christ event), and the future (the eschatological fulfillment and its relation to the parousia).

The Old Testament tradition of the Day of the Lord, of the fulfillment of history in the eschaton, was based upon the prophetic teaching of God's providence ruling the world and giving meaning to human history. This meaning, however, was never to be found in recorded history itself, although this is the field in which God's purposes are worked out. The Day of the Lord as a final term of the historical process would be that day on which God's meaning would be evident. The eschaton, the last day, the Day of the Lord, is thus envisioned in Jewish tradition as both historical (the end term of the historical process) and suprahistorical (the explication of divine purpose). The eschaton expresses the real internal meaning for history, and it also inaugurates a new age, the "age to come," and realizes God's eternal purposes.

In the New Testament this tradition is repeated, but with one significant difference—it is presented as having occurred. In the particular historical event of Jesus the eschaton is inaugurated. The prophetic symbol for the explication of God's meaning in history, the "age to come," is now initiated in Christ. But the problem of the "time between" remains. The passage of time from the realization of the Christ event to the parousia presents a problem to the Christian. Both the first and second comings of Christ are actually the one act of God, but are separated in time, and it is in this separation that the Christian finds himself. The problem that New Testament eschatology presents is this "time between," or to use Oscar Cullmann's phrase, the "even now—not yet."

The "time between"—it is herein that the Christian must walk. He is aware in faith of the finality and eschatological significance of Christ, and yet he must also look forward to the termination of the historical process in the parousia. The world in which he lives, the human history in which he partakes, the faith he professes, and the hope he confidently bears are all related to the problem of the "time between." To illuminate his passage in what he knows to be the eschatological age, bounded by the Christ event and the parousia, the Christian must look to Jesus, the Lord of history, the same yesterday, today, and forever. Here the Christian must search for the meaning of history and his own place in it. It is to this problem that we must turn in faith.

Chapter 4

THE CHRIST OF FAITH

THE CHURCH from her initial state of mission, when the Holy Spirit was given at Pentecost, has throughout history professed her faith in Jesus Christ as the Incarnate Son of God and as her crucified, risen, and ascended Lord. No modern line of investigation from the era of liberal Protestantism through the form-critical school has produced a "historical" Jesus who adequately explains this traditional faith. The Church has always based her profession of Jesus as the Lord not upon one or another of many human a priori philosophies but upon the facts of the Gospel history.

Historical investigation cannot be taken as the sole method of investigation of the Christian religion. By itself historical method provides not a positive and demonstrative proof for the Christian allegation, but rather a negative demonstration of its legitimate claim to historicity. The historian finds in the Christian proclamation an unceasing and uncompromising assertion of the having-happenedness of the events it witnesses, and at the same time, involved in that proclamation, he finds that the meaning of these events is not attainable by critical method alone. The meaning of the events proclaimed is suprahistorical, and consequently lies beyond the means of historical method, that is, in the realm of faith.

What the Christian maintains of the New Testament is also maintained of the Old Testament. It is not only the apostolic preaching of Christianity but indeed the whole Bible that is concerned with the proclamation of the God-Who-Acts.[1] In the Bible the saving action of God throughout human history culminates in Jesus Christ. These actions are the objects of historical study, but precisely as *God*'s actions they are not verified by historical investigation, or indeed by any other human process. We have through historical investigation a reputable attestation to the having-happenedness of biblical revelation; we have an impressive demonstration that no theory has an adequate explanation of the historical occurrences witnessed to, other than the explanation given by the witnesses themselves; but we do not have, and indeed *cannot* have, historical proof of those actions as being of God.

There are historians who a priori rule out the miraculous and consequently find other explanations for what is attested as God's action in history. It is not primarily as a historian, however, that one adopts such a position. The historian cannot know in advance of his evidence what can or cannot happen. Rather he must take the evidence as he finds it and then attempt to render a historical explanation for what has occurred. When God acts in history, the historian's capability ends with the event as having happened. He cannot affirm by empirical historical method, but also he cannot deny, the meaning of the event. The actions of God in history are historical events that transcend his investigatory powers. When the historian attempts to explain these events without allowing the possibility of miracle, then the basis from which he acts is not that of history but of an a priori philosophical belief.

Still further, it must be constantly stressed that the one sure historical fact that the historian possesses when he faces the biblical witness to the God-Who-Acts is the fact of the testimony itself. "God acted in history thus and so." The historian is now in the realm of faith, but the statement of the particular witness to God's action, the allegation, is itself the adequate object of his investigation. This witness itself he cannot explain away. The meaning of the event as it occurs in the testimony of the witness is an integral part of the event in any historical appreciation of the developments that follow from it. The acceptance of the biblical witness of God's action in history is faith; it is faith that accepts the totality, an event inseparable from its meaning. This faith, then, is not anti-historical or unhistorical, but suprahistorical; it is, for all that, based upon history. Faith as the reception of the God-Who-Acts is not opposed to reason, but supplements it and goes beyond it.

Moreover, a growing number of historians today realize that to understand an event of the past and its witnesses one must allow them to speak on their own terms. Thus in a sense there must be for the historian an "existential encounter" with the past. This encounter becomes in the Christian fact a transcending one. The biblical proclamation of God's saving action, in particular the apostolic preaching throughout the era of New Testament Christianity, is not only the testimony of witnesses to the action of God in history but has remained even until today the Church's summoning of the hearer to encounter God in those actions.

Consequently faith must be seen as more than intellectual assent to verbal revelations; it is a personal encounter with God. The nature of the biblical revelation is precisely historical. Revelation, the object of faith, does not terminate in propositions but in events, in God's actions, and this termination involves the believer in those saving actions. God is not known in faith as He is through reason. Reason acquires a natural knowledge of God through creation: supernatural revelation is distinguished by history, by God's action throughout history culminating in Christ, an action, as we shall see, that is continually presented in the Church through its proclamation. Revelation is man's encounter with God, faith is the response of man, and the Church is the historical place of that encounter and response. Thus faith is required as the *sine qua non* for the adequate examination of the meaning of human history in the light of God's action.

It is, then, precisely from a basis of faith that the examination of God's action in history begins. It is with Christian faith and membership in the Church, wherein God's actions have been proclaimed and in which the response of personal belief and involvement with those actions has been made, that history falls under a new light. God's action in history culminates in the New Testament kerygma, the proclamation of Jesus as the Lord of history. The explication of the meaning of the Christ event is possible only for the believer; and thus we have crossed from the proper boundaries of history into theology, from the investigation of history as such to history illumined by faith. This is, in short, the realm wherein the Jesus of history is identified as one with the Christ of faith.

If we move from the area of history to that of faith, from the historical figure of Jesus to the meaning of Jesus as the Lord, in no less a manner will this new area of investigation constantly tend to move back again to the area of history. For, as we have remarked, God's supernatural revelation is inseparable from history. The God-Who-Acts reveals Himself in history: it is constantly maintained as the arena of God's action throughout the Bible. Christianity is historical because it is not an abstraction, because revelation did not terminate in concepts but rather in God's action in time. This protestation of the historical nature of Christian revelation is not the theory of occasional scholars but an essential part of the entire biblical proclamation of God as the God-Who-Acts.

For the observer the Bible itself as a book and the biblical revelation as a history will bear from the start the difficulty that is intrinsic to the Christ in whom they culminate. In short, we have the existence of mystery—the historical and suprahistorical elements of the Christian proclamation and their essential combination in the unity of the event. Alan Richardson comments on this difficulty: "This is the 'scandal' of the biblical witness, as it is the scandal of the Incarnation: that the Eternal should have become historical and that, therefore, the historical should become the bearer of the eternal Word. The historical Jesus Who is the eternal Word is part of the history of our world. The Word became Flesh. The factuality of God's action in the events to which the Bible testifies is . . . the historic Christian faith." [2]

SALVATION HISTORY

The essential nature of the Christian proclamation is the same as that of the entire biblical revelation. The Bible proclaims God's saving action directed toward men; it recites God's actions in human history, actions that have their motive in love and their purpose in man's salvation. It is for this reason that we properly speak of the biblical revelation as salvation history. The term bears reference both to the idea of the history of man's salvation and to the idea of the sacred history that saves. For the Christian both ideas are to be identified.

The Bible deals with the continual proclamation of specific historical events that are the acts of God Himself. In the Old Testament there is present a kerygma, a unifying and common core of events whose proclamation constitutes the essential nature of the entire Old Testament. It is, as we shall see, not unrelated to the New Testament kerygma, but both are identical as the process of salvation history, both essentially proclaim God's saving acts.

A word of caution must be entered. We are dealing here with the essential elements of salvation history cojoined with an emphasis upon the fact that the biblical revelation always terminates in

God's actions. Thus God is known through His actions; it is what God has done that lies at the basis of any theology of the Bible, or indeed of any theology based upon His supernatural revelation. But at the same time this does not mean that theological disciplines that translate the biblical revelation into the abstract and conceptual order are in any way less biblical or less accurate. The philosophical presentation of God through abstractions and through the instrumentality of dogmatic formulas and definitions is a legitimate function and at times a necessary presentation of the biblical content by the Church. What the Church does—the means she uses, the theological disciplines that present and preserve and explore what has been confided to her in revelation—needs no defense. What is given here is an attempt to follow the historical nature of biblical revelation through the methods proper to biblical theology. Salvation history serves to follow closely the biblical pattern, to utilize the dynamics of biblical language and thought, and to emphasize the historical nature and reality of God's actions. It also reflects the oldest form of the Church's presentation of her belief: the proclamation of God's actions in history.

In the Mosaic revelation priority is given to the *creative activity of God*. In the narration of creation history is given its beginning, and central to this revelation is the place of man as the ruler of creation. But man created in freedom used his freedom to sin, and it is toward sinful human nature that God turned in love in order to repair that sinfulness. From the sinful race of man one group was chosen by God as His people to prepare for the salvation of the race. This group, the people of Israel, were created by God's action in history in the Exodus.

The Law, the Prophets, and the worship, indeed the entire religious history of Israel, center about the memory of God's action in the Exodus. The kerygma, or proclamation, that gives unity and meaning to the Old Testament is the continual proclamation of the Exodus as the experience of redemption and covenant. The biblical witness to God's action in the Exodus is one that is created by historical fact and one that continually appeals to that fact, namely, the actual deliverance from Egypt.

Throughout the Old Testament the expressions of Israel's faith in God always take the form of proclaiming God's saving action, and always refer to the Exodus redemption that God accomplished with "His mighty hand and with an outstretched arm." Literary critics, form critics, the great numbers of biblical scholars today tell us that the explicit reference to the Exodus is the common feature of the oldest parts of the Old Testament, and indeed of the oldest oral traditions reflected in the biblical texts. In the prayers of the Psalter almost every psalm re-echoes God's saving action, "for it is always from the fact of the Exodus that the devout Israelite draws his unconquerable trust in the protection and nearness of God, which is at the heart of his most personal piety." [3] The greatest of Israel's feasts, the heart of her liturgical calendar and the most meaningful celebration of worship, was the paschal meal, the recollection of God's action in the Exodus.

The significance of the Exodus as God's saving action lies in the creation of Israel as the people of God. This is the first realization of the divine plan for man's redemption: God creates a people and enters a covenant with them. In the proclamation of God's action in the Exodus Israel recalled her birth as the people of God. Thus the Prophet Osee said: "Because Israel was a child, and I loved him: and I called my son out of Egypt" (Osee 11:1). The creation of Israel is the supernatural birth of God's people, and God's action in history again illustrates its creativity. The birth of this people is accomplished by the work of God, not of man.

When the recitation of God's saving action was performed by a devout Israelite, he recalled the great action by which his people were constituted and with which he identified himself. Thus the Israelite received a sense of history and of destiny, and through the proclamation of this kerygma he encountered the living God. "History has determined his very existence, and his father's experience of encounter with the Lord of History has become his own personal means of encounter with Israel's God." [4]

The Passover celebration, annually recalling the Exodus, regarded the deliverance of the past as a promise of a definitive deliverance to come. While it recalled and made present for the sharers of the meal the action of redemption, and thus afforded an opportunity for the encounter with God, this meal was also eschatological in nature, that is, it looked forward in the future to a new and final saving action of God. The expectation, like the recollection, was historical: what God did foreshadowed what He would do; the action of God in history as Redeemer was the sign of a final redemption in history.

The age of the Prophets was in many senses the most critical in Israel's existence. From a literary point of view it would seem to be the most productive era in the shaping and composition of the Old Testament. Preprophetic material (the older histories, chronicles, laws, written and oral traditions) were reworked and redacted, so that the basic shape of the Old Testament as we know it was definitely cast. Central to this work and the focal point of prophetic teaching was a constant appeal to the Exodus, a kerygmatic proclamation of God's decisive actions. But in addition to this the Prophets were also concerned with God's past action as the pattern of the future.

Human history itself is envisioned by the Prophets as under God's sovereignty. The incompleteness of history and the seeming lack of meaning in the processes of history (which they saw as a moral order under God) turned their gaze upon the future. In this vision of the future the clue to what God would do was what God had done, and there came to the prophetic tradition a central element, the conception of a climax to history—a final and decisive act of God. God's sovereignty over history, and the necessity that history itself should bear out that sovereignty, was affirmed in faith, for it was far from evident in fact. The doctrine of the eschaton, or end, in which would be revealed God's sovereignty in His final and decisive act, well fitted the Exodus-covenant tradition.

It was Jeremias who, looking forward to the completion of God's work in history, spelled out his vision in detail:

> I will make with the House of Israel and with the House of Juda a new Covenant, not like the Covenant I made with their Fathers on the day when I took them by the hand to bring them out of the Land of Egypt, the covenant that they have broken, although I was their spouse. But here is the Covenant that I will make with the house of Israel, after those days I will put my law within them, and I will write it in their heart, and I will be their God, and they shall be My people.[5]

Throughout the remainder of Israel's history this doctrine of the end, eschatology, had an enormous influence. It led in later times to an apocalyptic literature centering upon the revelation of God's Lordship over history in the last age. Such books as Daniel, provoked by the crisis of persecution, presented this eschatological climax to history through various literary devices—symbols, visions—that is, in a poetic and vivid language. The apocalyptic action of God is to be accomplished in the community He called into existence; and as Jeremias teaches, while it will be an action that is decisive and final, it will nevertheless culminate in a new covenant, so that as it was in the beginning so also in the end God's action will be creative.

The revelation and culmination of God's sovereignty over history in His people was an action foreshadowed in the Exodus experience, it was explained and confidently looked for by the Prophets, and it dominated the Old Testament kerygma until the coming of Christ. Its significance is historical, for Old Testament history is itself looked upon as prophetic, and the actions of God in history afford some clue as to His action in the "age to come."

That portion of salvation history recorded in the Old Testament bears an intrinsic relationship to Christ proclaimed in the New Testament. The Old Testament is in fact intelligible only if read in the light of the New: and in turn the New Testament cannot be rightly understood without reference to the Old. Both Testaments are united in their essential core as salvation history, as the proclamation of God's saving action in time.

The direction of Old Testament history toward the "age to come" was fulfilled in Jesus Christ. The finality of God's work in the eschaton proclaimed by the Prophets is enacted in Jesus Christ. The earliest written documents of the New Testament, the Pauline Epistles, like all the documents of the New Testament, bore witness to the final decisive action of God in history. The various witnesses of the New Testament, the Evangelists, the authors of the Epistles, manifest a common core of preaching, an essential proclamation, or kerygma, namely, that in the death and resurrection of Jesus Christ the prophecy of the Old Testament was fulfilled. Christ inaugurates the new age in which, because of His death and resurrection, He is the Lord.

The essential elements of this Christian proclamation that constitute the earliest preaching of the one Gospel or "good news" are these: first, Christ fulfills the prophecies and the "age to come" begins; second, He was born of the Davidic line, died, and was buried; third, He rose again on the third day; fourth, He has been exalted to the right hand of the Father as Lord and Christ; fifth and last, He will come again. Throughout its manifold expression the Christian proclamation of God's salvation effected in Christ used many of the terms and symbols derived from Old Testament eschatology. The crucial difference between Old Testament and New Testament eschatology is the New Testament's insistent proclamation of fulfillment and accomplishment. God's saving action in history culminates in Jesus. "God, Who at sundry times and in divers manners spoke in times past to the fathers by the prophets last of all in these days has spoken to us by His Son." [6]

It should be noted that Old Testament history, recording the birth and successive crises of God's people, Israel, as it strained forward toward completion in the Day of the Lord, always regarded that day as the inauguration of an age in which Israel would be perfectly God's people. The perfection of Israel as the people of God would then occur through the intervention of God in history. This forward reference, however, was also accomplished by an ever-narrowing conception of God's people. Oscar Cullmann's exposition of God's plan in salvation history as a *Hielsplan* provides us with an illuminating illustration. Within Israel, chosen for the salvation of the world, there was a further reduction to the "pious remnant," a group later reduced to one man, "the servant of the Lord" (see Isaiah), who represents the people; and this person entered history as Jesus Christ: salvation history to Jesus Christ is progressive reduction, and now the process is reversed; it is a progressive expansion in the Church. Thus the two Testaments reflect the movement of salvation history: from the many to the one and from the one to the many. In Christ the Old Testament not only culminates but, as it were, concentrates. Christ is the perfected Israel of God, and His extension through time is the Church, identified as His body and the inaugurated Kingdom of God in time.

Because in the New Testament Christ is perceived as the Israel of God, the Old Testament history is itself regarded as prophetic. It is the fulfillment of the Old Testament in Christ that lies at the basis of that peculiar biblical interpretation called typology that we find in the New Testament.

The relationship of the New Testament to the Old as the action of God in history that fulfills His earlier saving work is best expressed by typology.[7] This typology is actually more than a relationship, it is the essential connection-in-fact that demonstrates the "fulfillment of the Scriptures." "All that is meant by typology is that the New Testament writers see in the events of the life, death and resurrection of Jesus the fulfillment of those historical situations in Israel's past in which already the saving purpose of God had been disclosed. They interpret the past in the light of the present, for now they see clearly the true significance of what had formerly been discerned only dimly." [8] The importance of typology in interpreting the biblical presentation of salvation history lies in its demonstration of the continuity of salvation history as essentially the proclamation of God's saving action from the light and vantage afforded by the New Testament culmination of that history.

The typological interpretation of Old Testament events found in the New Testament demonstrates that the categories of the New Testament proclamation are drawn from the Old Testament, and that there is a direct historical continuity in salvation history as it reaches a climax in Jesus Christ. The New Testament proclamation of God's saving action is the same as that of the Old Testament, and the essential distinction between them is eschatological. The Old Testament has a forward reference to God's final action; it is the New Testament that declares its definitive presence.

TOWARD A THEOLOGY OF HISTORY

The serious Christian who finds in the history of the human race problems of meaning and destiny possesses in the biblical revelation and the salvation history it proclaims the key to understanding the total process of human history. From the revelation of God in His saving actions one may disengage certain elements and use them as elements to illuminate his investigation of the meaning of human history. The destiny of the race, the ultimate problem of meaning in history, is not the object of his reason alone, but remains to be grasped only because God's revelation affords an understanding of them and a declaration of their meaning by God.

These elements of biblical revelation, as they are disengaged from salvation history, enabling the Christian to give meaning to human history, may be stated, for the sake of order, in eight propositions. The lights they offer and the insights they render to the Christian in regard to history do not of their nature completely settle the problems that exist in history. They have implications; their exploration opens new avenues of investigation; and, as we shall see, their apprehension poses new questions. Thus in the statement of these elements we have facts that contribute to the theology of history and indicate some understanding of history. They are points of disengagement from which further development of a theology of history follows, a development that presupposes and includes them.

1. The Bible Demands the Viewpoint of Faith. Faith is the required biblical prelude to any study that seeks to find meaning in human history; faith is a radical shift in the position of the observer. To study human history with the means provided by reason and historical method alone will never produce an adequate explanation of history. It may provide a useful awareness of the elements that constitute history, but it will never comprehend them in a meaningful totality. Much may be seen there through reason, but no edifice emerges, only the loose stones of a foundation. The meaning of history does not lie within the historical process itself; it lies ultimately with God and is to be found in His revelation. It is through faith in God's action in history that one finds the ultimate meaning of life, the significance of human history, and encounter with the Lord of history. Thus there can be no philosophy of history, only a theology of history.

Over and above the apprehension of God's plan through faith, a complete explanation of history still remains impossible. Through faith the meaning of history lies open, but by definition a total and perfect knowledge of that meaning of history, which embraces the totality of human actions in time, is impossible. For the object of faith is ultimately the mystery of God's love; this is a mystery that may be known and apprehended through faith, but it cannot be exhaustively explained. Thus even in a Christian theology of history, as on all levels of Christian theology, significant problems must remain, and the theologian in exploring them reflects the ancient motto of his profession, *Fides quaerens intellectum.* In all the affirmations it makes about history, in all the insights it offers, the biblical revelation remains revelation and consequently mystery. For every light it sheds on the vision of the believer, new problems will arise and difficulties grow, and the ultimate mystery of God perdures.

2. *God is the Eternal Ground of Being.* Before all else, God is. God is prior to and cause of every form of existence. Ethelbert Stauffer comments: "The fundamental datum of any theology of history, the primary fact to which the old biblical tradition always goes back, is not sin, nor even creation, but the absolute priority of God over the whole world and its history: the priority of the Divine." [9] This priority of God demands the affirmation of the traditional Christian conception of predestination. So it is that Christ was "Foreknown, indeed, before the foundation of the world, he has been manifested in the last times for your sakes," [10] and Saint Paul thus summarizes God's plan in history:

> Blessed be the God and Father of Our Lord Jesus Christ, who has blessed us with every spiritual blessing on high in Christ. Even as he chose us in him before the foundation of the world, that we should be holy and without blemish in his sight in love. He predestined us to be adopted through Jesus Christ as his sons, according to the purpose of his will.[11]

The New Testament insistence is one upon God's absolute priority and rule over the events of history, and is an insistence upon the purpose of God's authorship of history, His glorification. It must not be thought that this doctrine of God's absolute priority makes of history, so to speak, a prepared script simply unrolling to an end in which God already is. There are other elements to be incorporated in a Christian view of history, and these factors (as for example, freedom) will complicate what seems on the face of it so simple an explanation of history.

3. *The Bible Envisions a Linear Organization of History.* History has a beginning (creation) and a termination (parousia); it also has a center, or hinge: Jesus Christ. The end of human history can be understood in different ways, as either the meaning or the term of the historical process. The intrinsic identity of meaning and term constitutes an eschatological problem for the Christian viewpoint. If Christ is the end of history as its meaning and fulfillment, why does a future term to the process of history (parousia) remain?

The linear organization of history imposed by the events of salvation history demands the historical order as the scene of God's activity and as the place of man's encounter with God. In this line of history time takes on a particular significance, having a place in

God's plan and pattern. Time "is not a thing opposed to God, but is rather the means of which God makes use in order to reveal His gracious working." [12] Throughout the New Testament a number of words are used to refer to time as an age, as a process of duration. One particular word used in a special sense is *kairos,* a point of time, a moment most favorable for an undertaking. By divine decision these special points of time have a special place in God's plan: as isolated from other references to time, the specific points called *kairos* constitute salvation history. Thus, for example, we have Jesus' message: "The Master sends word. My *kairos* [time] is near." [13] So now in time, because of the death and resurrection of Jesus, there exists in the Church's proclamation of that event a *kairos* for the believer. If that redemptive event was the *kairos* of Christ, the meaningful moment in time for the accomplishment of the divine plan, so now the presentation to the believer of that event by the Church is the *kairos,* the meaningful moment in time, for the believer. So Peter says, "The *kairos* has come . . ." [14]

4. The Bible Testifies to Divine Providence and Human Freedom. Two seemingly irreconcilable principles emerge in the biblical view of human history. God is the sovereign Lord of history, all history fulfills His providential purposes. Yet within history that unique element of man, his freedom, makes history what it is. How can man be free in an order in which God fulfills his purposes? The reconciliation of God's providence with man's freedom constitutes the heart of a mystery of which we are aware in faith. The problem is complicated by the existence of evil, not only moral evil as the result of man's freedom, but physical evils. The profession of God's providence and the evidence of evil cannot be reconciled by, or worked out in, a purely historical or rational line of inquiry.

Granting the necessity of faith and accepting the knowledge that faith brings, the problem remains. For centuries theologians argued the "how" of human freedom and the effectiveness of God's grace by which salvation is attained. Explanations of grace have erred in overstressing either the effectiveness of grace, or our human freedom; and, in like manner, rational explanations of human history come and go, erroneously stressing one factor. Explanations of history, whether deterministic or voluntaristic, are rejected by the

Christian who affirms both providence and freedom in history through faith.

5. *Man Has Used His Freedom to Sin.* The Bible tells us that man's history from the beginning is marked by sin, a free act of man against God, which has brought in its wake suffering and death. The biblical revelation teaches that man's sin has opened the gates of history to the adversary, Satan, and his power. The consequences of sin are cosmic, and Christ's appearance is, in His own teaching, the invasion of the cosmos and conquest of the satanic power and its control over the world. Saint Paul clearly teaches: "For the eager longing of creation awaits the revelation of the sons of God. For creation was made subject to vanity—not by its own will but by reason of him who made it subject—in hope, because creation itself also will be delivered from its slavery to corruption into the freedom of the glory of the sons of God." [15]

6. *The Bible Proclaims the Redemptive Action of God Within a Divine Plan.* The dogmatic affirmations of God's grace have always stressed for the Christian the divine initiative. Thus the redemptive action of God is always initially God's motion, and it is always regarded as God's saving work. It was Reinhold Niebuhr who once remarked that the fundamental error of modern man in relation to history was the conception of the historical process itself as redemptive. The Bible has constantly stressed the suprahistorical nature of redemption.

Biblical revelation as salvation history proclaims a redemption of history in history effected by the work of God in Christ. It sees the events of salvation history as meaningful and as offering an encounter with God. Thus it is that God is met in history. The divine plan possesses one unique element that unifies these concepts in the present historical situation: the Church.

The Word of God is creative, and the Church is constituted by it, as was the witnessing community of the Old Testament covenant. In the Church Christ is present in the proclamation of Cross and Resurrection, the saving event. Through the work of the Spirit Christ is made present in Word and sacrament, and thus the Christian, in a new people of God, is afforded the opportunity of encounter with God in the saving event.

The relationship of the Church to human history, which is the presence of the inaugurated Kingdom of God within the historical process, gives rise to the serious problem of their proper positions. The Church is salvation history, and it is present within secular history, but it cannot be known or judged by the purely empirical process of history. The problem perennial to Christian thought has been the proper contribution of sacred or salvation history to a historical knowledge of the world, or secular history.

Quite obviously sacred history exists within secular history, not as a separate or "second" history but as a series of meaningful events. Since their meaningfulness is essentially supernatural and is directed toward man's salvation, they lie of course beyond the legitimate scope of the historian. But the real effects that Christianity has had in the secular order, the contributions it has made, its meaningfulness as a factor within secular history—all of these are legitimate factors for historical investigation. While there is a distinction in the eyes of some theologians between secular and sacred history, the two do interact, and the Christian must affirm the primacy of sacred history, both absolutely in its own right and also in relation to secular history, to which it gives purpose and meaning. This enlightenment of secular history that the perception, through faith, of salvation history affords, also allows one to see a pattern within the meaningless confusion of secular history.

7. *The Purpose of History is the Revelation of the Glory of God.* Man is called into being to glorify God, as is the creation itself.[16] The purpose of creation and history is to reveal His glory and to have His creatures proclaim His glory. This, then, is man's vocation—to glorify God. In his sin, man refused this vocation, rebelled against God, and introduced into history the conflict of the glory of God and the glory of this world, and it is this conflict that culminates in the Cross.

So it is that Jesus' work manifests the glory of God; it is revealed in Him. Throughout John's Gospel, Jesus is presented as the manifestation of this glory; even the Cross is the means by which He must glorify God.[17] That is why in the very beginning of his Gospel John declares of the Word made flesh, "and we saw His glory, glory as of the only-begotten of the Father." [18]

The Church, the body of Christ in history, those joined to Him as Head through faith and the sacraments, are the hidden though present realization of the original destiny of mankind—the glorification of God. All will be completed when every creature glorifies God, when the whole cosmos becomes the temple of God [19] and time becomes the New Sabbath.[20] Ethelbert Stauffer expresses it thus: "The antiphony of universal history leads into a symphonic doxology. At last God has attained the *telos* of his ways: the revelation of the *gloria dei* achieves its end in the hallowing of His name." [21]

8. The Bible Possesses One Constant Element in Its View of History: Eschatology. The essentially eschatological element of the biblical revelation not only dominates salvation history but unifies all the elements of biblical history. Biblical eschatology affords an insight into all the principles we have enumerated and establishes a relationship between them. The finality of salvation history in Christ is absolute and definitive, and serves as a revealed denial of any concept of indefinite progress. The fulfillment of history in Christ makes a belief in progress categorically different from Christian hope. But if Christ inaugurates the eschaton, if we truly live within the "last days," then a definite relationship for this "time between" must be established for the Christian.

Eschatology places before the Christian his most challenging problem in the face of history—the problem of the time between the eschatological event in Christ and the parousia.

PART THREE

HISTORY AND THE THEOLOGIANS

Introduction

APOSTOLIC Christianity regarded the life, death, and resurrection of Jesus Christ as the inauguration of the eschaton, the last days. Thus the Christ event of the New Testament is spoken of as an eschatological event. Christ is the final and crucial moment in history. But the apostolic age also expected an apocalypse, the revelation and perfection of the Kingdom of God established in Christ. The Old Testament confusion of eschatology (finality) and apocalypse (revelation) is understandable from this historical point of view, for, looking forward to the future, prophetic proclamations of God's action in time were identified as historically contemporaneous actions. Thus from their point of view the Old Testament writers were unable to appreciate the temporal stages in the working out of God's action.

It is in the New Testament that we find the immediate realization of the eschatological nature of Christ's life and resurrection. Christ's strictures in attempting to clarify the inherited apocalyptic concepts of the apostles, cojoined with the giving of the Holy Spirit and the passage of time, allowed the Apostolic Church to become aware of the distinction in historical time of the inauguration of the eschatological age and its apocalyptic perfection. This is the growing Christian awareness of the "time between," the interval in historical time between the first and second comings of Christ. It is this mysterious period of the "time between" that constitutes the nub of the problem of history for the Christian.

There have been Christian thinkers so absolutely convinced of the eschatological nature of the Christian revelation that they believe there is no problem of history. Time and the historical process, they maintain, are meaningless; the individual salvation of the Christian is exclusively important. Is the Christian, therefore, to condemn as ultimately irrelevant his work and his culture, his accomplishments in history? Are politics, society, knowledge, progress, and human endeavors generally, meaningless in view of the finality of Christ?

The arena of settlement for this problem has been well delineated by Roger Shinn: "The problem of the Christian interpretation of history is to make its conception of the fulfillment of human life (the Kingdom of God) relevant to history without confusing it with historical accomplishments which are of ambiguous worth." And in speaking of the modern Christian living in history today, John Cogley has placed the question in the realm of the Christian facing human culture: "The challenge is to show the relevance between the authentically secular and the authentically sacred. . . . Our deepest problem then arises from the fact that while we are required to remain *in* the world, we have been solemnly warned not to become *of* the world." [1]

The problem of history is essentially as old as Christianity itself. It is involved in mystery, in the delicate balance of the Gospel injunctions to serve in the world and to await the coming of the Bridegroom, and in the theological affirmation of God's providence on the one hand and man's freedom on the other. It is not an easy problem, and it will not do for an age dominated by a sense of history to write it off simply as mystery without some attempt to explore and illuminate it. Mystery it surely is, and like every aspect of the Christian mystery there is a demand upon the Christian to investigate it and to relate the elements of that mystery to one another. Proffered solutions, as we shall see, will stress one element rather than another; but, be that as it may, it still behooves the Christian to consider seriously the elements of the problem and the solutions, to look for possibilities, and finally, to see its relevance to daily life.

This part of our inquiry is divided into two chapters. In the first we shall attempt to see the answers that are to be found in the dominant theological thinking of the Protestant community. The problem of history has aroused perhaps a far greater interest among Protestant theologians than among their Catholic counterparts. Many elements of the Protestant recognition of and responses to the problem have given to modern man fresh insights and appreciations of the biblical view. The second chapter is devoted to the Catholic theologians of history. Within the Church, owing to the progress in historical and biblical studies, the problem of the Christian interpretation of history is exercising a greater number of scholars; and these in turn are dividing along the two specifically distinct lines of thought provided by the Christian conceptions of the Incarnation and eschatology.[2]

Chapter 5

THE PROTESTANT THEOLOGIES OF HISTORY

To APPRECIATE fully the Protestant response to the question of history it is necessary to understand the proper insights and peculiar emphasis of Protestantism. Such a comprehension of Protestant theology should be approached from a historical point of view. One must see Protestantism make its way through history from the time of Luther and Calvin; see it here united, with one element dominant in its face to the world; find it again fractured, suffering an ineradicable split into two or more positions; watch as positions wane or move together under one single impulse. To appreciate the Protestant answer to history today one must look to the diversity of the Protestant theologians and to the systems they advance. The systems and approaches that underlie and structure the thought of these theologians have to be grasped not only in order to see how they answer the question of the Christian meaning of history but also how they pose the question itself.

Before giving our attention to the voices that dominate Protestant theology, let us turn to the historical traditions and influences that have formed the Protestant heritage and that in their own ways affect Protestantism today. The founding fathers of Protestantism, Luther and Calvin, and the systems they propounded bore elements relevant to the problem of the Christian in history. For Luther, in revolt against a corrupt scholasticism, there was a new emphasis upon the historical derived from two major sources of his thought: the Bible and the apocalyptic view it presented, and Augustine with his concern for two cities of man and God. Luther's insistence upon God's absolute transcendence and man's essential sinfulness recognizes that human history is incapable of saving itself and that the Kingdom of God within history is destined to triumph on the last day. The individual Christian, for Luther, lived within the City of God through faith, within an invisible Church; he also lived in the

city of man, the kingdom of the wicked. The two cities were, however, irrelevant; they had no point of contact, and their intrinsic
separateness denied from the beginning anything other than a
purely Augustinian interpretation of history.

Calvin, akin to Luther in stressing God's absoluteness over and
against sinful man, yet envisioned the Kingdom of God in history
as being built, as God's work in history. Calvin positively denied
any significance to history in itself other than as a place where God
builds His Kingdom. The element of transforming history, according to Roger Shinn, has given to Calvinism an enormous sense of
mission to refashion human history.

Traditional Protestantism, despite sectarian division, remained
at heart a single movement from the viewpoint of its basic principles. Under the burden of the Enlightenment, however, infected
with the subjective methods of Descartes, Protestantism slowly
divided into a movement bearing two opposed traditions: one emphasizing God's transcendent authority, and another reflecting a
growing antisupernaturalism. The antisupernatural element sought
to place religion upon a firm basis of reason and science, and consequently shifted with every breeze prevalent in the field of secular
knowledge.[3] By the nineteenth century Protestantism had again
regained a monolithic appearance, but this was achieved by an
antisupernatural dominance and a lapse in the Protestant memory
of the religious insights of Luther and Calvin.

Empiricism, Kantianism, positivism, evolutionary progress each
in turn slowly attained respectability within Protestantism, and each
served to bolster and confirm the antisupernatural tradition. Hegel
and his dialectic, Schleiermacher and his religious consciousness,
Ritschl and the progressive realization of the Kingdom of God each
manifested the tendency to identify the emerging ideal of evolution
with Christianity. The growth of scientific history and of biblical
criticism coincided to erect the edifice known as liberal Protestantism. At the heart of this structure was its essential involvement
in theories of knowledge, and it was here that the Christianity of
liberal Protestantism was at its weakest. "The inner inconsistency
of liberalism could not be detected so long as it was itself carried
along on man's human confidence and general cultural achievement." [4] The peak of "progress" was reached in 1914 when the world
went to war.

Now the edifice of liberal Protestantism collapsed. Its demise was signaled in 1919 by Karl Barth's *Commentary on the Epistle to the Romans*. With Barth the Protestant experience of God's otherness and man's sinfulness reasserted itself, and the new reformation of Protestantism initiated by Barth maintains itself even today under the misleading title of neo-orthodoxy. Ferre has pointed out that liberal Protestantism was inconsistent in its theological structure and in its accommodation of the Christian message to scientific method, and that it was not only the new supernaturalism of neo-orthodoxy that contributed to the collapse of liberal theology but also a new movement of the left. The latter was more thoroughgoing in its rationalism, and is represented, in Ferre's opinion, by Bultmann and Tillich; it is this movement that served to complete the destruction of liberalism initiated by Barth.

It would be a mistake and an oversimplification to state that Protestantism today can be so easily divided and pin-pointed as Ferre would have it. There are the theologians of the Scandinavian school and the numbers of biblical scholars who represent the historic Christian faith; these have to be fitted within any coherent picture of Protestantism. Yet we must attempt to organize a presentation of modern Protestantism in which to present the divergent views of history.

It is for this reason that we have adopted the following divisions: *neo-orthodoxy* (beginning with Barth and the rejection of liberal Protestantism he represents, and including those theologians who may be said in a wide sense to follow his tradition); *existentialism* (reflecting a more thoroughgoing alignment of Christian theology and biblical scholarship with existentialist philosophy); *biblical theology* (representing the more orthodox and traditional among the biblical scholars); and finally, the *theologians of history* (those who, from various traditions, have written *ex professo* treatments on the problem of a Christian theology of history).

Neo-orthodoxy

The movement in contemporary Protestant theology that bears the name of neo-orthodoxy finds in Kierkegaard its predecessor and prophet, and in Barth its founder and systematic apostle. It signifies and is itself signified by the rejection of liberalism in theology. It rejects the attitude toward history reflected in that theology: the tradition of man's goodness, the evolutionary emergence of religious consciousness, and the progressive nature of the realization of the Kingdom of God on earth. However, the neo-orthodox rejection of liberalism must not be seen as successful solely as the result of reaction to the First World War and because of its convenient substitution of an existential theology. There were many other factors —biblical scholarship, the knowledge of the eschatological nature of the Christian revelation, the growth of the historical and psychological sciences; all these served to provide methods of criticism toward the unwarranted progressivism that dominated the historical thinking of liberal theology. Neo-orthodoxy combined these elements to provide a theological critique of progress that, in the view of one of its practitioners, "far from being merely a pessimistic reaction to temporary historical difficulties or a retreat into religious obscurantism appeals to facts and judgments corroborated by much of secular thought." [5]

The foremost exponent and founder of neo-orthodoxy, and perhaps the most significant single Protestant theologian today, is Karl Barth. The theology he has erected and the viewpoint this theology implies for the Christian meaning of history must be understood against Barth's background and theological development. A young minister at Geneva, Barth began his career in the tradition of liberal Protestantism, strongly influenced by the views of Schleiermacher on the importance of man's emerging religious consciousness. The First World War, as it served in the secular order to destroy the easy concepts of man's progress prevelant at the turn of the century, served also to lead Barth to a rejection of those ideas in the theological order.

This rejection of Schleiermacher and liberalism was signaled in 1919 by Barth's *Commentary on the Epistle to the Romans.* Now strongly influenced by the writings of Kierkegaard as he had been formerly influenced by Schleiermacher, he began to structure his theology with existentialism. Barth developed a dialectical theology—a knowledge of God through crisis, the encounter of man and God through God's gracious entrance into history. Barth denied that God could be known in propositions, that he could be limited by concepts, and so he demanded the area of encounter for man's knowledge of God. This phase of Barth's thinking culminated in

1932 with the publication of the first volume of *Church Dogmatics*.

Barth at this juncture came to see that he was subordinating the Word of God to a philosophical system in the existential nature of his dialectical theology. As once he had rejected Schleiermacher and liberalism, so he jettisoned Kierkegaard and existentialism in order to affirm the absolute and total transcendence of God and the completely free and unfettered notion of His Word. This position was indicated by his rewriting of *Church Dogmatics*. His theology now became a Christology, and central to it was an insistence upon the incarnate nature of Jesus Christ. From Barth's restatement of incarnational theology flowed a re-examination of his theology of encounter. Jesus Christ is God's encounter with man. To hear and participate in Christ was God's Word to man, and this could only be accomplished in the Church through the proclamation of the Word and the sacraments. From Christology Barth inevitably developed an ecclesiology.

In the dimensions of Barth's theology the problem of history is related to the eschatological event of the resurrection of Jesus, itself the historical core of Christianity. In the risen Christ the Christian is made a new creature, and the world and its history become meaningless and irrelevant. The Kingdom of God is radically discontinuous with the world. There is no point of contact between the Kingdom of God and man's politics, his society, and his culture.

Man is warped, sinful, ignorant. In Christ he is a new creature. The distinction is absolute, a new "creation" demands the radical difference between historical man and the Christian. Sacred history, therefore, can have no relationship to secular history.

Thus Jerome Hamer comments on Barth's doctrine of the Word of God:

> [The Word] cannot be identified with an historical fact (Geschehen); for historical fact is limited by nature. Everything which appertains to history is bound to a continuity from which it cannot detach itself. Every fact depends upon some cause and is itself associated with the entire unfolding of history, which serves as its frame. This is true not only in the order of nature but equally in the order of history and humanity. So we must not think that man's liberty is an exception; it, too, is inserted into history. Without falling into the error of absolute determinism, we must admit, says Barth, that practical realities limit man's choice to certain possibilities, and that man, when facing a decision,

does not have an unlimited scale of choices. He is limited, first of all, by his capacities; moreover, his choice must rely upon what has gone before and consider the future as somehow continuous with the past. . . . The Word of God is not enclosed within the continuity of history; though it intervenes in history, it never allows itself to be absorbed by it. Sometimes, it will be *in* history, without ever being a part *of* it. If the Word of God were able in some way or another to identify itself with definite occurrences enclosed within the succession of human events, it would no longer be the Word of God; for it could no longer claim identity with the Uncreated Act.[6]

The background for Barth's theology vis-à-vis history may be seen in his *Church Dogmatics,* where he distinguishes between the two German words for history, *Historie* and *Geschichte,* a distinction not easily implied in the use of the ambiguous English word "history." *Historie* is that which is perceptible to man, the series of created events that can be represented as related created events; *Geschichte* is the salvific activity of God, His mighty acts by which He accomplishes His eternal economy. As Father Hamer has remarked, "the opposition between *Historie* and *Geschichte* contains not only the antithesis of created and uncreated, but also of profane and sacred." [7]

The innate difficulty in such a theology is that in its absolute expression it "snuffs out all human effort and makes naught of the Christian message." [8] Barth's theology depends upon two essential elements of Christianity: eschatology and unworldliness. The first implies the refusal of any ultimate sense to history after Christ; the second is the essential denial of all human values. The radical discontinuity between God and man, while it serves to settle the question of the Christian meaning of history in a negative way, would seem to be at base unbiblical; and it is against this radical discontinuity that all of Barth's critics rail. It makes no provision for the essential nature of man, who, despite his sinfulness, is made in the image and likeness of God, or for the Incarnation, which itself provides in Christ the supreme action of God in history; finally, history remains the place of decision and is redeemed by Christ. Barth's assertion of discontinuity does not offer a solution for the problem of values in human history since Christ; it simply denies it. And, ultimately, in this denial Christianity becomes irrelevant to human history.

Barth's influence has not diminished, and his disciples maintain the relevance of his dogmatic emphasis for man in the world. Thus there are attempts such as the following to evaluate the impact of Barth upon theology today:

> Time will do its work, lessening the impact and present interest of the whole, while putting the different parts of Barth's work in perspective and assigning them their proper place in history. But one thing is clear. Barth is and will remain the theologian who rediscovered the message of the sovereign grace of God in Jesus Christ and forced the church to hear that message at a crucial moment in its life. He stressed the inevitable implications that flow from that message for the life of the Christian who is called by his Lord to be a true man, fully involved in the world and acutely conscious of all the problems that are posed for men by the troublesome questions of their earthly destiny.[9]

The Barthian rejection of meaning and value in human history has had its clearest exposition in the eloquence of Karl Löwith. For Löwith, man's sin and God's saving purpose "alone require and justify history as such, and historical time." [10] Human history, then, is only an interim, the period of decision. The events of human history in the time between the first and second comings of Christ have meaning only in the perspective of judgment and salvation; consequently the attempt of theologians and historians to relate secular and sacred history is in effect a blasphemous effort to destroy the difference between man and God. Thus the Christian understanding of history and time is solely the object of faith, not of reason or of philosophy or of empirical knowledge.

If, Löwith maintains, history has a redemptive meaning, a progress, a realization of greatness, it is only insofar as Jesus is the Lord of history and has accomplished His victory. The theology of the New Testament cannot be expressed in the terms of any philosophy of history, for "the problem of history as a whole is unanswerable within its own perspective." [11] The modern age suffers from a progressive alienation from the New Testament revelation, so that its great concern for secular history is made the area of man's destiny; the importance of secular history will decrease as man becomes more intensely aware of God and himself. Systems come and systems go, each attempting to work out God's providence, but all forget that God's providence is a transcendent principle that can never be the subject of interpretation—even in the framework of the history of the Church.

Löwith's rejection of any but a theological interpretation of history is refreshing, and this is the service that with other neo-orthodox thinkers Löwith performs for the world today. But for Löwith as for Barth there is the persistent danger of considering Christianity irrelevant to history. This irrelevance is the problem of all Christian thinkers who base their affirmation of faith as the only key to history upon a radical and absolute discontinuity between man and God. For the Catholic, mindful not only of the discontinuity but also of those areas of contact between man and God, the Church, as people of God, as the mystical body of Christ and the Kingdom of God in history, provides a more meaningful view of history and the relationship that does exist between secular and sacred history. This view is closed to Löwith, who makes Christianity solely the highly individualized drama of personal salvation, without reference to community or Church as an essential element in that drama: "In Christianity the history of salvation is related to the salvation of each single soul." [12]

The objection of irrelevance laid at the door of Barth and the neo-orthodox has been most seriously taken by Emil Brunner, and its consideration has dominated his work. A crisis or dialectic theologian, Brunner has been more consciously existentialist and a more influential figure in American theology than Barth. The major features of Brunner's theology are to be found in his Christology published in 1927 in *The Mediator*. Attention to the element of crisis is to be found in *The Divine-Human Encounter* (1938) and *Revelation and Reason* (1941). In the past few years Brunner has systematized his work in three volumes of *Dogmatics*.

Much of Brunner's work is obsessed with the relevance of the Christian message to the life of modern man, the negation of which is a weakness that he feels vitiates Barth's presentation. The traditional Christian faith must ever be in communication with the world in which it finds itself. This faith, he believes, has been best mediated to man by the Reformation because of its central doctrines of God, man, and the Bible. Thus he regards himself as a "Reformation theologian." Central to his concept of history is the place of the Church and the constant contact in the Church between the Kingdom of God and human history. But, as a Reformation theologian, Brunner maintains that this Church must in history always be under the continual judgment of God's Word in the Scriptures.

In the tradition of neo-orthodoxy, and extremely influential in the United States, is Reinhold Niebuhr. It is difficult to give a coherent presentation of Niebuhr's thought, for in many ways he is a picture of "living theology," and positions he has adopted in later and more mature years are strikingly different from those of his earlier years. As a young theologian, following a Detroit pastorate, he soon succeeded Rauschenbusch as the leading witness of the social Gospel, but with a difference, for Niebuhr rejected the popular doctrine of inevitable progress. Stressing the essential ambiguity of decisions in the social order, he affirmed that a univocal moral order for both man and society was impossible and would deprive social actions of their effectiveness. Social problems do not fall under the same norms and moral apprehensions as those of the individual, and thus he titled one major work *Moral Man and Immoral Society,* in which Christian love is normative for the individual, justice is normative for society.

Niebuhr's theological concern for the present situation of man has led to his frequent and bitter quarrels with Barth, whose theology remains too Olympian and removed from man. *The Nature and Destiny of Man, Faith and History,* and *The Self and the Dramas of History* reveal Niebuhr's fundamental concern and his outlook on the problem of history. Like Barth, however, and the neo-orthodoxy in which he may be located, Niebuhr denies that history has a meaning in itself: there are no patterns, and there is no unity in human history. Any significant meaning in the historical process derives from faith, not from reason. From this basis of faith in the Christian revelation Niebuhr's explication of history has a primary emphasis—that of man's sinfulness. The evil in history, when recognized, can keep one from seeing the historical process itself as redemptive; it is when one denies the existence of sinfulness that one implicitly affirms a salvation in this world.

Unlike Barth, however, Niebuhr does not demand a radical discontinuity between this world and God, so that man can glimpse in the tragic processes of history some faint glimmer of destiny, an intimation that it all somehow has meaning. To go beyond this (awareness of the possibility of meaning by reason) to its achievement is accomplished only in faith. It is the eschatological nature of the Christ event to disclose the whole meaning of history. This position is arrived at through dialectic theology embracing the experience of history and the experience of faith. A Christian interpretation of history through the dialectic is the most comprehensive; it is, for Niebuhr, a total view and in its dialectic embraces the insights of all other views, in themselves partial.

Charles West has written of Niebuhr's vision of history:

> In all this, Niebuhr's pattern of history is one of continuous dialectic between the absolute standard of God's *agape* and the ambiguous pattern of man's search for self-fulfillment. History develops ever greater human capacities for creative accomplishment, and equally great corruptions of these capacities. The pattern does not reorganize itself when God's act in Christ enters it. Christ rather illuminates it in all its ambiguity, like a divine searchlight. The Cross stands, in Niebuhr's phrase, "on the edge of history," showing its true meaning, establishing a new hope by faith, and setting up a new tension between imaginative love and the world. It shows the judgment over all history to be one of grace. But the Cross leaves man where he was before in the complex of historical forces. It lifts no burden from him. It clarifies, but does not essentially change his responsible action toward the powers of this world.[13]

Niebuhr's view of history, one might say, is distorted by his viewing it continually through the looking glass of man's sinfulness. He has little to say of the grace and the power of the Christian witness in history; the culminating tragedy of the Cross has darkened Niebuhr's vision and never quite allows him to view history in the light of the Resurrection.

Further, Niebuhr's concern for the seemingly irreducible elements of incoherence in history has led him to positions of extreme relativity with regard to the law of God; thus, for example, he denies the existence of natural law. Moreover, "the pretensions of the Catholic Church are intolerable for Professor Niebuhr because his vision of the gospel excludes final authority in anything historical." [14] And yet the Catholic critic must admit that Niebuhr, for all the weaknesses of his theology, has been an enormously effective Christian voice in our time. He has unceasingly recalled modern man in the America of today from intellectual and political idolatries to the sure ground of Christian revelation. "Often he has spoken the truth with a fierce courage; sometimes he has spoken the truth in love; but just as often, though unheralded, he has been content to let truth rest in silence under the discipline of love." [15]

A transition in modern Protestant theology may be marked here by the mention of the remarkable Lundensian school of theology, in the tradition of orthodoxy, but with a renewed sense of biblical

themes. To the orthodox tradition is added an intense sense of relevance and the import of preaching as a confrontation of modern
man. Thus this Scandinavian school adequately prepares us to move
from the more orthodox elements of modern Protestantism to the
storm center, Bultmann.[16]

Gustaf Aulen, a Swedish theologian, has revived the ancient
patristic view of Christianity as basically the conflict and victory
of God's saving act in Christ over the powers of evil. He sees in his
concept of Christ as victor the central idea in the presentation of
Christianity to the world of today; [17] and consequently history is
envisioned in the terms of conflict-battle centering upon the decisive
victory of Jesus in the Cross and Resurrection. Anders Nygren, the
Swedish bishop of Lund, developed the theological method of motif
research. The fundamental motif "is that which forms the answer
given by some particular outlook to a question of such fundamental
nature that it can be described in a categorical sense as a fundamental question." [18] The religious motifs he distinguishes in Judaism,
Hellenism, and Christianity are nomos (law), eros (need-love), and
agape (gift-love). Agape is the new and highest form of love, revealed
by God in Jesus Christ. The discontinuity of Barth is expressed in
Nygren as an absolute discontinuity between eros and agape, so that
Father Martin D'Arcy comments: "The real problem is to work out
how both nature and the supernatural life survive in their integrity
in the Christian order. . . . There is nothing human or personal in
the response, nor can there be in this interpretation. In the elimina-
tion of *eros* man has been eliminated." [19]

The task of critically revising and carrying on Nygren's method of
motif research has been taken up competently by Bernhard Erling.
The method of Nygren, he maintains, is apt for the interpretation of
the concreteness of man's historical existence. The actualities of history are meaningless unless they are structured; and both history and
philosophy are joined in motif research that moves in one line from
historical chaos to chronicle, thence to history, thence to history of
ideas; it moves in another line from chaos to caricature, thence to
characteristic, thence to systematic. By working along each line one
rises to a broader context, and ultimately both investigations join in
motif research. The motif is the presupposition for the interpretation of history, as the principle of causality is in nature. Employing
this method, Erling maintains that the ultimate meaning of history

is religious, and the proper theological task is the interpretation of history. "Consequently history rightly understood becomes *Heilsgeschichte*." [20]

Erling follows Nygren in his critique of Bultmann, not with regard to biblical criticism but with regard to Bultmann's demythologizing; it is the twentieth century that must be demythologized, since it is prevented by its presuppositions from understanding the New Testament. The motif research is always, even in the recognition of the motif, open to the possibilities in which the divine activity, represented by the agape motif, may realize itself. "Not only does motif research take the broader view, defining the agape motif in terms of the whole history of salvation to which the Christian faith bears witness, but it is prepared to consider alternate ways in which the love of God establishes its sovereignty, particularly as far as the structures of the natural order are concerned." [21]

Gustaf Wingren, professor at the University of Lund, has presented a penetrating criticism of the difficulties in the system of Nygren, as well as those of Barth and Bultmann, and he has attempted to weld the valid insights of each to his own thought.[22] In *The Living Word (Die Predigt)*, however, Wingren presents the dynamics of the *Heilsgeschichte*. Salvation history centers upon Christ, the Word made flesh, and upon his life, death, and resurrection. The present period of this salvation history, our period, is marked by the preaching of His Cross and resurrection, and the incorporation of all those who "hear" this Word of God. The entire *Heilsgeschichte* is stated in Aulen's terms of a battle, between Christ and Satan. Through preaching, according to Wingren, the power of Christ's victory reaches out to all men and hastens the end when He will come again. "It is the task of preaching to speak about God and the Satanic power in such a way that everyone listening can detect the point in his own life where the battle is being waged and where he is enslaved and bound . . . at this point we have to make clear that when the New Testament puts Christ's death and resurrection in the center, that is bound up with the conviction that there the enemy of humanity was beaten." [23]

Thus Wingren adopts the traditional biblical concept of salvation history and Aulen's concept of Christus Victor to explicate human history, and affords a dynamism to preaching by his consideration of our period as that of the preaching of Christus Victor.

EXISTENTIALISM

The dynamic sense of preaching as a confrontation of man with Christus Victor that Wingren's presentation offers affords us a transition to the most dynamic of modern Protestant theologies, that of Rudolf Bultmann and his followers. Like Barth and Brunner, Bultmann early rejected the old liberal tradition of Harnack. A New Testament scholar, he took up the work of Weiss, and contributed in a major sense to the development of *Formgeschichte*. Bultmann is also at home with Christian origins and bears the distinction of historian as well as biblical scholar. The impact he has made upon modern religious thought derives precisely from his contribution as a theologian.

Bultmann, in facing the question about the meaning of history, finds the beginning of an answer in the fact that the subject of history is man. Further reflection upon man leads him to assert that the life of man is always directed toward the future. Never content with the past, never fixed in the present, man's life always stretches out to the future; life is to be apprehended, it is to be realized. This constant challenge of the future "means at the same time that the real essence of all that man does and undertakes in his present becomes revealed only in the future as important or vain, as fulfillment or failure." Thus a human personality, the self, becomes aware that its selfhood depends upon its decisions, and the "personality experiences its own history within the frame of universal history and interwoven with it, but nevertheless as a history which has its own meaning and is not merged into universal history." [24]

Christianity, according to Bultmann, has something to say to man about his historicity: that man is not free, that he is bound by his own past and its decisions. A radical freedom would be a freedom from the self, and in recognizing his necessity to be free from himself he understands that his genuine self can only be offered as a gift by the future. The Christian believes that he receives this gift of freedom. The Christian message "does not proclaim the idea of the grace of God as a general idea but addresses and calls man and imparts to him the grace of God which makes him free from himself." This is the meaning of preaching and of faith. Jesus Christ is the eschatological event, "not as an established fact of past time but as repeatedly present, as addressing you and me here and now in preaching." [25]

The paradox of Christian living, then, is that while the Christian achieves freedom and is taken out of the world, he nevertheless remains within the world. But his faith belongs to the eschatological event, it never becomes a "fact" of the dead past, but is a reality constantly repeated. "In his faith the Christian is a contemporary of Christ, and time and the world's history are overcome. The advent of Christ is an event in the reality of eternity which is incommensurable with historical time." [26]

In short, Bultmann denies that the history of man, as history, has any meaning. Man cannot, since he is within history, understand its meaning. But we can say that the meaning of history lies in the present, and that the meaning of history can be realized in the present in Christian faith in the eschatological event, Jesus Christ. "In every moment slumbers the possibility of being the eschatological moment. You must awaken it." [27] Throughout Bultmann's presentation runs the rich strain of existentialist thought from Kierkegaard to Heidegger; in his approach to history and his understanding of it Bultmann reflects the thought of Collingwood, whom he constantly cites. Interwoven, then, in the problems of a theology of history in Bultmann are the problems that inhere, as well, in a philosophy of history.

It is this dependence upon a philosophy that is the Achilles' heel of Bultmann's entire breath-taking structure. It is the constant theme of his critics, and is well stated by Father Léopold Malevez:

> To claim that the only valid element in the Christian Message is that view of existence which it gives us, really amounts to saying that the human mind, a priori, dictates to the Word of God the conditions on which he will believe; by that very fact the Bible is placed under the control of a preparatory philosophy; this means putting the Word of God under the domination of human learning, thus robbing God of his sovereignty. If we decide in advance that God can only will to reveal to us the conditions of our authentic existence, it seems that we are infringing his absolute sovereignty, both in his Being and in his action upon us.[28]

The fact that Bultmann maintains throughout his exposition of the New Testament a consistent existential philosophy derived from Martin Heidegger comes as no surprise, for he has long regarded the essential truth of the New Testament as being identical with the insight into the human situation that Heidegger's philosophy presents. The point of the Christian preaching of the New Testament is to allow man to see the problem of personal existence and to direct men through decision to a solution. In short, both the Bible and Heidegger's existentialism speak to the same understanding of personal existence.

The existentialist philosophy, explicated by Bultmann in New Testament terms, derives from an existentialist view of the time. In this view of time the present is looked upon as the dimension of one's meaningful living. The past is over and done with, as unique event it is dead, because it is a place in which freedom and decision and, consequently, life do not exist. The future is always in the realm of the possible; it does not represent necessity, and since it is decision that shapes the future, the present is made meaningful. From this viewpoint, as we have seen, Bultmann maintains that questions of historicity about the New Testament are pointless, they are meaningless regard for the dead past. It is the present "preaching" that confronts man in his situation, that demands decision, and that offers existential freedom. Consequently the New Testament message of existence must be proclaimed in its purity to modern man; it must face man in his situation, and without myths, the intellectual baggage of other eras.

The revelation of God as a continual future brings to man a meaningful present; as preached, this future becomes a possibility to be decided in faith. For each generation of men the Christian message of freedom from man's existential anguish must be reinterpreted. Preaching is that reinterpretation, and makes the deed of God's salvation present. Thus a major portion of Bultmann's biblical scholarship is devoted to demythologizing the New Testament. These myths have located God's saving action in the dead area of historical fact, and thus they falsify their meaning and are unable to be the basis of faith. It is important, however, always to keep in mind that Bultmann's process of demythologizing is not simply the stripping away of myths but rather one of reinterpretation, necessary in every age so that God's Word can be clearly heard.

As we have seen, Bultmann, according to his critics, does not offer the New Testament proclamation of God's saving work but Heidegger's proclamation of an existential salvation for man's situations clothed in the terms of the first proclamation. Beyond this basic criticism of Bultmann, theologians and biblical critics have entered the serious objection that the historical Jesus is not irrevelant to the Christian proclamation of the kerygma but is the object of that kerygma. The critics maintain, therefore, that Bultmann assumes two things: first, an existential structure of reality, and second, and unwarrantably, that the theology of the New Testament derives from the early Christian community and not from Christ Himself. As for the latter assumption, it is indeed hard to see New Testament theology as other than one controlled in the community by an accurate historical memory of that which Christ did and said.

If Bultmann suffers the rejection of those who follow the historic Christian faith, it should be remembered that beyond all his erroneous assumptions he has contributed something of value to Christian thought today. First, he has turned biblical scholars and Christian theologians to a reaffirmation of the significance of God's Word for each person today. He has stimulated the New Testament theologians to a renewed emphasis on biblical scholarship in which its real relationship to man in history is asserted; in short, he has made relevance a key concept in theological and biblical scholarship. Second, he has also recalled Christian theologians to the restatement of an ancient truth too frequently lost sight of in theological circles: that the Christian dogmas, the Church's statements, the theological propositions about God are not in themselves, as verbal formulas, the terminal ends of faith, but that however inadequate *ex parte dei* they are means of attaining to God. His error has recalled the truth of Christian faith terminating in the living God, not in propositions alone.

Bultmann has set in motion a great movement in contemporary religious thought. His former pupils, the Marburgers (Gunther Bornkamm, Friedrich Gogarten, N. A. Dahl, Ernst Käsemann, Erich Dinkler, Herbert Braun, Hans Conzelmann, Gerhard Ebeling, Ernst Fuchs), have, as we have seen, set in motion a new "quest for the historical Jesus." The Marburg disciples are not the only representatives of the Bultmannian school; among English-language scholars are the influential Scottish theologian John Macquarrie and the American biblical scholar James M. Robinson. In addition, it is safe to say that all major theological works—Catholic, Protestant, or

Rationalist—utilizing the biblical sources are today in one way or another affected by the thought set in motion by Rudolf Bultmann.[29]

The Bultmannians have taken Bultmann's fusion of existentialism, historicism, and biblical theology to develop significant contributions to theology with serious implications for any theology of history. In a study of the theology of Matthew, Gunther Bornkamm maintains that the delay in the parousia is presented by Matthew as a new period in history, the period of the Church.[30] History in Matthew, according to Bornkamm, is divided into three periods: promise (Old Testament), fulfillment (Jesus), and mission (a rather short period); then would come the end.

Professor James M. Robinson has developed the theology of history in Saint Mark's Gospel.[31] According to Robinson, Mark presents a struggle between the Spirit and Satan that is transcendent to history and occurs in history in Jesus. The divine power is present in history in Jesus, and there propels history to its end. The most important part of this history is the Christ event, in which the Spirit of God decisively conquers the power of Satan. God's Kingdom is established in history in the Resurrection, and the time after the Resurrection continues the conflict although the decisive battle has been won. Robinson's presentation of Mark's theology of history will accord well with Cullmann's conception, which we shall examine, and also reflects the Christus-Victor theme of Aulen.

There is also present, according to Hans Conzelmann, a theology of history in Luke's writings (the third Synoptic Gospel and the Book of Acts). It is in Luke that a real line of demarcation is drawn between the period of Jesus and the period of the Church, as distinct epochs in salvation history. These two periods are distinct, yet systematically interrelated, and this affirmation by Luke is arrived at "from the problem of the existence of the Church in a continuing period of time . . . in other words, Luke is confronted by the situation in which the Church finds herself by the delay of the Parousia and her existence in secular history, and he tries to come to terms with the situation by his account of historical events." [32] The historical pattern of salvation history in Luke emerges as three stages: the period of Israel, the period of Jesus' ministry, and the period since the Ascension, which is the period of the Church. The middle of time *is* the mission of Jesus, the decisive period of history. The ecclesiastical dimension of Luke allows the individual Christian to draw the strands of the Christian conception of history together.

> Luke does not directly define the position of the individual in the course of redemptive history. Instead his position is defined as a mediated one, for he stands within the Church, and thereby in a definite phase of the story. The Church transmits the message of salvation. . . . This transmission by the Church makes it possible for the individual's remoteness in time from the saving events of past and future, from the time of Jesus and from the Parousia, to be no hindrance to him. Instead of the nearness of these events there is the Church with its permanent function. . . . Thus the individual has a link in time through the Church with a definite stage of history, whereby he is granted the assurance of salvation, and he also knows the actual realization of faith in the fellowship, in sacrament, in prayer, which makes him independent of definite periods of time. For Luke the believer must be indissolubly bound to the Church, if he is not to sink either into speculation or into eschatological resignation. Just as Luke's eschatology provided a plan which could stand regardless of time, in his account of the Church we find something similar in regard to the realization of the message in the midst of the continuing world.[33]

Conzelmann observes that Luke does not consider the Church to be part of the object of faith, part of the saving act, but only the necessary medium of the message. The basis is laid, however, by considering the Church within the categories of redemptive history for this eventual recognition.

The other disciples of Bultmann also contribute to a theological tradition in his wake. Gogarten has attempted to harness the Bultmannian theology to traditional Lutheran thought, and he remarks in his *Demythologizing and History* that the existentialist realization of man in history allows us to state the content of the Christian religion in terms of history and not philosophy. The Norwegian N. A. Dahl has pointed out that the eschatological event in Christ implies an eschatological community, a people of God. But in this view the Church, recognized as part of the eschatological event, is not the organizational Church as we know it but rather the end result in history of the people of God formed in the Christ event. Käsemann has joined Dahl in criticizing Bultmann for ignoring the existence of the eschatological community and its importance as a factor in history.

There is also another trend in post-Bultmannian thought to be noted. Its principal representative is Fritz Buri, professor at Basel, who regards his position as the inevitable conclusion of the Bultmannian system. Buri thinks that Bultmann has stopped short at the kerygma, and that what now remains is the coupling of dekerygmatizing to demythologizing. The kerygma is, for Buri, the last myth. As Macquarrie has pointed out, "Here Buri adheres closely to Jaspars, who stands in relation to his theology much as Heidegger stands in relation to Bultmann's."[34] In Buri's thought we have the ultimate resolution of Christian theology to existentialist philosophy and its view of history. Christianity is but a religious myth expressing the philosophical concept, and the circle begun at the start of the twentieth century in the History of Religions school has come full round.

Bultmann has been fortunate in having as a spokesman and follower in the English-speaking world Professor John Macquarrie, now teaching at Union Theological Seminary in New York. Macquarrie has attempted to rescue the Bultmannian theology from the critics of the left and right and to solidify its basis precisely as a theology. The difficulty of this position, illustrated by the attacks from both sides, is, according to Macquarrie, a bifurcation in Bultmann's thought; this must not be seen as inconsistency but as a paradox verifiable in religious experience.

Macquarrie's procedure in this Bultmannian apologetic is to begin with Bultmann's negative attitudes, which he regards as stemming from Bultmann's view of modernity. In the process of demythologizing, recognition was taken of the world view implied in the mythical matrix; now the Christian message is to be communicated to modern man, who also possesses a world view, based upon the enormous progress of his science. But Bultmann confuses the modern world view, based on science, with modern man's self-understanding, largely secularized. To convey the Christian message to the first is laudable, but it is hardly possible to the second. "If the modern self-understanding is secularized, then it can never understand anything to be an act of God. If it can understand the New Testament at all, this teaching must be transformed for it into a humanistic philosophy. The teaching would have to be expressed purely in terms of the possibilities of human existence and never as a *kerygma* or proclamation of some decisive saving act of God." In this sense we can recall Nygren's admonitions that it is the twentieth century that

must be demythologized. For Macquarrie the modern self-understanding, secularism, is as much mythological as that of the world
view two thousand years ago, and indeed even more alarming. "Here
we are dealing not with an attendant circumstance of the New
Testament teaching, as the ancient world-picture is, but with the
very heart of this teaching." [35]

In summary, Macquarrie reviews the three key concepts of Bultmann's theology: the concept of God (absolute, not as an "object,"
totally transcendent); the concept of an act of God (both objective
and subjective, neither to be emphasized over the other); and the
concept of existence itself (always being-in-the-world, encounter,
thus invalidating any criticism that Bultmann is subjective). The
Christian faith embodies the polarity of the relationship between
God and man, and in Christianity this polarity must always be
affirmed. This is precisely the beauty of Bultmannian theology, that
"this is truthfully reflected in the paradox of existential interpretation and kerygmatic proclamation." [36]

Thus we have seen the Christian conception of history and its
meaning in Bultmann and in the work of his disciples, and the
apologetic erected for the Bultmannian structure. Now we turn to
another existentialist theologian, Paul Tillich, who has erected a
total philosophical and ontological structure to house the existentialist viewpoint.[37]

Tillich, like his contemporary Rudolf Bultmann, is German-born.
He is now an American by adoption, having emigrated to the
United States in 1933, and is professor of divinity at Harvard University. Like Bultmann in so many ways, he is also one of contemporary Protestantism's most formidable theological voices. Tillich's
basic concern has been to reformulate the Christian faith so that its
truth might be communicated to modern man and speak to his situation. Thus his system is in aim and temper much akin to Bultmann's
process of demythologizing. Tillich is the most systematic of modern
Protestant theologians and has erected the most formidable synthesis
of doctrine. In his consistency and vibrancy of thought he has sur-
passed Bultmann, who relies so heavily upon the work of Heidegger.

Tillich strongly reflects the existentialist tradition of Kierkegaard,
so much so that one of the touchstones of his method is his denial of
truth to the abstract proposition. For Tillich theological formulation, even the biblical, must speak to the human situation, and un-

less it does so it is not true. Truth is the correspondence of the structures of reason with the structures of reality.

The human situation in Tillich's thought is a meaningless one. Its meaninglessness derives from man's limited and concrete nature and is reflected in modern man's philosophy, psychology, and art; nevertheless it is his situation. This situation of contingency, or limited being, has a necessary correlative—anguish; and it is the discovery of anguish that is essential in any confrontation of the life situation. The cause of anguish, of contingency, is the separation or estrangement from God, the "ground of being." Man is haplessly tossed into existence and finds himself there naked and alone. His activity in history is an attempt to avoid decision, a foredoomed effort to evade a face-to-face encounter with his situation as it is. Precisely as avoidance of decision this activity is an endeavor by man to overcome his situation, and precisely as such it is ultimately futile and inevitably unsuccessful. Man is both helpless and hopeless.

The solution of this situation lies in Christ as the "new creation," wherein there is no separation from God, wherein humanity has completely conquered its alienation from the ground of being. The destruction of separation and the participation in the new creation is, in short, salvation. This cannot be achieved by any human activity, it is always a "grace." Faith is the realization of God's acceptance of us, and it is always a gift. This new creation reconciles the deep existential estrangement of man.

In human history Christ represents the unique and supreme *kairos* (meaningful moment) in which man encounters God. History itself is the interminable succession of *kairoi,* the climactic *kairos* being Christ. From this unique *kairos,* when God, the unconditioned and the ground of being, enters time and history, there is a new being in Christ. History is to continue, only now it is forever determined by the Christ event. History, as the succession of *kairoi,* is providing each man with the opportunity to recover his real being in God: it is the battlefield in which man finds himself thrown as a limited being estranged from God yet capable of conquering that estrangement in his own *kairos* determined by the Christ *kairos.*

Traditional Christianity must, of course, object that this is not the theology of revelation, it is rather a theological philosophy—in fact, an anthropological philosophy with theological trappings. As to Tillich's biblical method, historic Christianity must object to Tillich's usage of biblical revelation as symbol. It objects that the biblical images, symbols universally adequate to the religious situation of man, are used not only because they are adequate to that situation but also because they express the meaning and significance of real events. Even where the Bible uses obviously mythological symbol, as, for example, the Leviathan in the Old Testament, the biblical revelation uses it not as a symbol for an existential situation but to mediate a real, witnessed historical event, the action of God.

The distinguished William F. Albright has written:

> There is no place for history in such a system, and Tillich himself, followed even more obviously by his pupils, shows the same indifference toward history as is shown by other idealistic and existentialist thinkers in America. . . . It has, however, proved impossible to reduce Tillich's vague and often contradictory ideas to any system, since theology is largely dissolved into existential judgments—which are too often nothing but introspective psychological constructs without any experimental basis whatsoever. The revelation of God in history is replaced by direct intuition of God as "ultimate concern" and of one's current aesthetic preference as "ultimate reality." [38]

Again, like Bultmann's, Tillich's system and its insights have this advantage, that they force the Christian scholar to accent the relevance of the Christian message for modern man. Furthermore, the historical conception of *kairoi* dominated by Christ *kairos* is, with proper demythologizing, able to bear the traditional Christian truth.[39]

In concluding this section, a word remains to be said about one whose influence in Europe has been enormous and whose unsettling theology is now coming into vogue in America. He is Dietrich Bonhoeffer (1906–1945). He was executed by the Nazis at the concentration camp of Flossenburg on April 9, 1945, and as Martin E. Marty has remarked, "If his name appeared at first as a hero or saint, in the second phase he is being taken seriously as he would wish to have been: as a professional theologian." [40] Bonhoeffer lamented the lack of any sense of the natural in Barth and the dialectical theologians, and stated: "So long as Christ and the world are conceived as two opposing and mutually repellant spheres, man will be left in the following dilemma: he abandons reality as a whole, and places himself in one or other of the two spheres (the sphere of the rule of grace or the sphere of the rule of nature). He seeks Christ without the world, or he seeks the world without Christ." [41]

Bonhoeffer restores a sense of the relatedness of man's nature to grace by speaking of the "ultimate" and the "penultimate." The "ultimate" is God's saving grace, and the "penultimate" is man's nature, his situation in the world, which is preserved until the "ultimate" breaks through and redeems man. One cannot exist without the other. "Christian life is the dawning of the ultimate in me; it is the life of Jesus Christ in me. But it is also life in the penultimate which waits for the ultimate." [42] The Christian Church, then, for Bonhoeffer, is here in the world for the sake of the world.

Bonhoeffer spoke of the Church in history, that it was to be understood there in terms of mission and not pattern, and that the age in which we live is a postreligious one. Bonhoeffer's theology was a radical, incarnational one. He writes: "It is not with the next world that we are concerned, but with this world as created and preserved and set subject to laws and atoned for and made new. What is above the world is, in the Gospel, intended to exist for this world." [43] Christianity is now to be communicated to the world in which we live in a worldly way, that is, by living for others. This must now also be the way of the Church, so that in this secularist society she goes down to the death of the Cross, losing everything that she may gain life. This moment in history calls every Christian, and the Christian Church, according to Bonhoeffer, to a perfect discipleship of the Lord.

One can be carried along too easily by the latest vogue in theological thought as in other fields. A serious look at Bonhoeffer's view of man, and particularly Christian man in the world, while it may be a critical look, does not indeed cast any aspersion upon Bonhoeffer. Indeed, he would have preferred, as Martin Marty has said, to be taken as a professional theologian. It is here that one must quarrel with the dour pessimism of Bonhoeffer, for the Christianity that he preaches is ultimately a faith in an irrelevant Christianity, in flight from the world and history. James Richmond has perceptively commented: "In Bonhoeffer's case, it is beyond all reason why modern man should listen to the Gospel. He is religionless, possessing no contact-point for the Gospel in his thinking, his spiritual longings and ethical dilemmas. Therefore, for Bonhoeffer, the Christian can only practise his *disciplina arcana,* live for others and look to God for an act of sheer grace. From the manward side nothing else can be done." [44]

Before going on to see the treatment of history and its Christian meaning in the work of the biblical theologians, we may well find a logical transition for this type of treatment in the work of contemporary Russian Orthodox philosophers and theologians. There is a remarkable strand of thinking in Russian Christianity most concerned with the problem of the Christian and his relationship with history. [45] In modern times this has been best represented in the work of Nikolai Berdyaev (1874–1948). [46] His thought reflects not only contemporary philosophy but also the genius of predecessors like A. S. Khomyakov, F. Dostoevski, and V. Soloviëv, and the Russian Orthodox tradition of the redemption and restoration of every creature. Although he consciously rejected Soloviëv's later eschatological sense and historical "agnosticism," Berdyaev was strongly affected by the idea of unity of man's history and its catastrophic end. His eschatology looked to an age of pure Christianity when the material needs of man would be fulfilled. The three epochs of history as Berdyaev saw them were creation, Christ, and man as cooperator with God. He decried the secularization of culture and the dehumanization of man that marks our era and demanded that man and history refer to some center. "And to Berdyaev it was self-evident that the central figure of history is Christ. Only by the spiritual revolution in every man that an acceptance of the Master's teaching would mean, can the purpose of history be achieved. And thus in one sense the meaning of history lies outside history. It is 'God's eternal purpose.' " [47]

A more richly embroidered eschatological interpretation of history is given by Evgenii Lampert, a Russian Orthodox theologian whose thought has been influenced by Berdyaev. For Lampert time acquires meaning, not a logically evident rationality, in a divine-human event, and "that is what renders time History, for History is Time which has acquired meaning within itself through having transcended itself." [48] The New Testament presents a view of history that is vectorial, not punctual (Lampert is using a mathematical illustration): ". . . that is to say, its symbol is to be found in a directed magnitude, as of a force or a velocity, or in a directed line which receives its orientation or, since it is a very uneven and broken line, its reorientation from an end. . . . The New Testament, then, testifies to the fact that every point in Time has its own 'situation,' not to be repeated or compared with others and moving towards the *telos,* which is within Time and yet beyond it." [49]

Thus the events of man—of individual life and of society—are judged by the light thrown on them from the end. The eschatological orientation of orthodoxy therefore does not conceive of the Christian as crusader or reformer, but rather as one given the power to change the world from within as a part of it. This eschatology must also be regarded as inaugurated in Christ. For the Christian, according to Lampert, the end is coming, and the end is already here, and "from this End Time acquires meaning and History is being fulfilled. The Christian lives not *at* the End of Time, but rather *from* the End and *in* the End of Time." [50]

Contemporary Protestant theology houses its theology of history not only in the dialectical theologies (the neo-orthodox and the thoroughgoing existentialist), it has provided very striking shelters and edifices for such theologies of history among its biblical theologians.[51] Consciously eclectic in drawing on the insights of Barth and Bultmann, provoked by the concern for man's historicity, biblical theologians within Protestantism have given more attention to the meaning of history itself in the Bible. The Catholic, alarmed and disturbed by the vocabulary and striking statements of the existentialists, frequently finds himself more at home among these biblical theologies and their categories, since he finds biblical renewal so basic a part of the contemporary theological movement within his own faith.

The biblical theologians have provided for modern Protestantism three major themes related to any developed theology of history: community, encounter, and the significance of history. The sense of community, derived from a living concept of covenant, has produced an increasing ecclesiology, an awareness of the Catholic tradition, and an ecumenical concern. The divine-human encounter effected in the Christian proclamation of the kerygma in the Church has led to developing theologies of the Word of God. The traditional statement of Christianity as historical has come to mean not only a faith centered upon God's action in history but also a faith that gives history its meaning. These insights of Church-encounter-history are correlative—one evokes the others, none can be grasped without the others—and they remain basic to the work of the biblical theologians.

Common to these biblical theologians is the concept of *Heilsgeschichte,* the German word that means both "history of salvation" and "history that saves." It indicates the working out in history of God's saving work, culminating in Jesus Christ, continuing in the Church, and culminating in the parousia at the end of time. Thus for these theologians the *Heilsgeschichte* has become, in the words of Otto Piper, the "organizing center" of history.

As we have mentioned, Professor Charles H. Dodd published his slim book *The Apostolic Preaching and Its Developments* in 1936.[52] Few books have ever created such an impact upon biblical studies. Dodd recalled the theological world to the central core of the Christian religion, the kerygma, the Christian message, the proclamation of God's act in Jesus Christ. We have seen earlier the elements of the kerygma as Dodd indicates them. Theologically Dodd proposes in this central core his theory of "realized eschatology": in the Cross and resurrection of Jesus the Kingdom of God is established, the eschaton—the end—has taken place, the judgment of God has been rendered. Thus history is realized, and its meaning stands exposed. In Christ we have the teleological end of history, its meaning, not the temporal end. The one event that gives meaning to all others has entered the historical process, and the meaning of history is in that event, not at the end. The Kingdom of God has been established.

Thus in this theory of realized eschatology we do not look forward to the Last Judgment, for that has been realized in the life, death, and resurrection of Jesus; the Last Judgment remains as a convenient symbol of the ultimate universal salvation. The apostolic preaching grew, Dodd tells us, out of the preaching of Jesus, but the futurist sense of a second coming was a deviation; in the later works of John and Paul we find a true grasp of the profound meaning of Jesus' preaching.

Dodd bases his system upon the exegesis of a number of passages (especially Mark 1:15 ff. and 9:1, Matt. 12:28, Luke 11:20), which he translates from the Greek original as the "Kingdom has come," rather than "has drawn near" or "is at hand"; and he systematically eliminates any futurism from Christ's eschatological sayings. Dodd also interprets the Parables to demonstrate this lack of futurism and the realization of the Kingdom in Christ.[53] Why did the early kerygmatic formulations deviate? Precisely, says Dodd, because Jesus used the apocalyptic imagery of the Old Testament in which the temporal end of history and the eschaton were identified. This is to be found in the Synoptics, Acts, and early Pauline writings. The passing of time led the Christian Church to understand the present reality of the Kingdom.

Although there have been a number of objections to Dodd's thesis, most critics have not rejected it outright but have attempted to rectify it. Dodd's exegesis of the Greek for the "Kingdom has come" has been seriously questioned by a large number of scholars. The theological objection to realized eschatology by R. H. Fuller is that Jesus' ministry is directed to a future event, the Cross, and that if He preached a Kingdom *now*, before that Cross, then Dodd's interpretation along those lines "destroys the cruciality of the Cross." This is also the criticism of W. G. Kümmel and James M. Robinson.[54]

A large number of biblical scholars—among them Frederick C. Grant, Kümmel, Cullmann, Rust, and Manson—attempting to save the valid insight that Dodd presents, have tried to purify it.[55] They would prefer to speak of it as the "inaugurated eschatology," taking their cue from the work of Joachim Jeremias; this concept thus preserves the futurist element that they maintain is to be found in the Scriptures. These biblical theologians feel there is a tension in Christianity of the "even now—not yet" that must be preserved. Dodd himself in his *Fourth Gospel* has accepted Jeremias' rendering of "realized eschatology" as "inaugurated eschatology." [56]

Dodd has also considered in the light of the Christian revelation the entire meaning of history, for which he sets down immediately certain principles of interpretation. First: God is sovereign in history. Second: The biblical revelation does not allow any a priori fixation to the process of history. Third: This lack of a priori fixation is due to the biblical insistence on the moral responsibility of man within the framework of providence. Thus the biblical revelation, according to Dodd, "encourages a sober agnosticism about the actual unfolding of that purpose in the future course of events." [57]

In our present situation when the Word of God is addressed to us there are two effects—judgment and renewal. Judgment is a negative effect "denying false values expressed in the situation as it has developed historically." This judgment of God upon us introduces an element of moral value, it implies our responsibility. Renewal is a positive effect and the first intention of the Word of God, which is creative. This creative act of the living God "does not simply pass over the wreckage of past failures, but transforms and utilizes it." [58] In all of this the address of God's Word to us depends upon the initiative of God, and it is always a concrete possibility in the here and now. This, for Dodd, is the meaning of the Church:

> The place where history is made is the place of encounter between God and man, where the Word of God is heard and man responds in obedience. Such is the purport of the whole biblical history. That history is alive in the Church, which was brought into being by it, and continually witnesses to it. In our time history is being made in the Church. . . . If so, it is not because the Church has a superior plan of reconstruction; or because its clergy speak with authority upon political or economic questions; or because its members are exceptionally virtuous or intelligent. It is because the Church, however low it falls, bears the indelible marks of its origin. . . . The Bible deals all through with the conception of a *people* of God, which is the point of application of God's creative Word, and the place where history is made through man's response to it.[59]

Oscar Cullmann, professor at the Sorbonne, holds a distinguished position among New Testament scholars today. His theology of history, like Dodd's, reflects the *Heilsgeschichte* and is presented in his *Christ and Time*. Cullmann manages to weave the basic insights of his theology of history into the wider context of his Christology, formulated in *The Christology of the New Testament*.[60] Both his biblical and theological works are complimented by his careful research into primitive Christianity, so that Cullmann reflects one of the finest personal syntheses of Scripture, theology, and history among modern scholars.

For Professor Cullmann all history is to be understood from its mid-point, Jesus Christ, who is the decisive turning point of history. He thinks that the problem of history arises from faith in the history of revelation and redemption. Thus "here in the final analysis lies the 'offense' of the primitive Christian view of time and history, not only for the historian, but for all 'modern' thinking, including theological thinking: the offense is that God reveals himself in a special way and effects 'salvation' in a final way within a narrowly limited but continuing process." [61]

Cullmann sees the importance of the Christian conception of time in the fact that salvation is bound to a continuous time process, all points of which are related to their historical mid-point. Time has an unending extension both backward and forward, and our present age is a specific limited time within this unending time between creation and parousia. The New Testament, he maintains, then knows no "eternity" in our philosophical sense of God's measurement, but rather only an unending time. The qualitative difference between time and eternity is no doubt a great contribution, but it is, for all of that, a distinction foreign to the New Testament.

What does the New Testament present to us? There are in New Testament theology three ages: the age before creation, the present age (creation to parousia), and the "coming age" which is visualized as the unending time of the new creation. "All this can take place only in a time framework that continuously moves straight forward; it cannot occur in the framework of a dualism between time and eternity." However, the mid-point of the second age (the eschatological Christ event, signified by the Lordship of Jesus) now superimposes a new two-part division of time upon the three ages. The faith of the Christian, his sharing in Christ the Lord, allows him to begin sharing the future age. "This to be sure does not mean that the development of the redemptive process in time has become unimportant in its time quality for him who believes." [62] History, therefore, remains for the Christian his age and the place of importance, for time preserves its significance for redemptive history. Revelation leads the believer to understand the stages of this redemptive history and to see that the Christ event has not changed the three ages of time but has put its decisive mid-point in Jesus, so that in Christ time is divided anew. Thus the Christian understands in faith that the war with Satan continues, but he perceives also that the decisive battle has been won.

There is a tension, and a significance, to the present stage of redemptive history in which we find ourselves.

It is already the time of the end, and yet is not *the* end. This tension finds expression in the entire theology of Primitive Christianity. The present period of the Church is the time between the decisive battle, which has already occurred, and the "Victory Day." To anyone who does not take clear account of this tension, the entire New Testament is a book with seven seals, for this tension is the silent presupposition that lies behind all that it says. This is not the dialectic and the only dualism that is found in the New Testament. It is not the dialectic between this world and the Beyond; moreover, it is not that between time and eternity; it is rather *the dialectic of present and future*.[63]

This present stage of redemptive history is the period of the Church and takes for its meaning in redemptive history the preaching of the Gospel to all peoples. The Church also reflects the tension of the "even now—not yet."

> The time tension is manifested in the Church through the continuance of sin, which nevertheless has already been defeated by the Spirit. The Church is God's highest gift of salvation in this intermediate period, and yet it is composed of imperfect, sinful men. Just as the entire redemptive history as such can only be believed but not proved, so above all the Church also can only be believed, and it really takes a quite special courage of faith to see the center of the present Lordship of Christ in this Church, which from its very beginning is so imperfect and all too human.[64]

The Christian centers his theology of history, then, upon the Church, whose missionary proclamation, whose preaching of the Gospel, gives to this period between the Christ event and the parousia its meaning in the history of salvation, a meaning that it possesses through its connection with the present Lordship of Jesus Christ. The Church must, therefore, be seen in its eschatological dimension, an eschatological reality that is uniquely actualized in the celebration of the Eucharist, for "in the Supper celebration there is concretized, so to speak, the present's entire situation in redemptive history: its simultaneous and particularly close relation to both the mid-point and the end." [65]

Cullmann's work has met with wide acceptance among New Testament theologians, the bulk of neo-orthodox Protestantism, and, with reservations, among many Catholics.[66] He occupies a major position among modern Christian thinkers about the theology of history. But Cullmann has not escaped severe criticism by some modern scholars. John Macquarrie comments that "what will trouble the modern reader is that the view of time and history advocated by Cullmann seems to be indissolubly linked with an outmoded geocentric cosmology. . . . Perhaps Cullmann's view could be made more plausible

by a process of demythologizing, but he himself will not have this." [67]
And elsewhere he says:

> We could accept Cullmann's views only if we were prepared to surrender
> the hard won distinctions which thought has made among such concepts
> as "time," "process," "history," "myth," and to relapse into the confused
> undifferentiated thinking of two thousand years ago when these various
> ideas were still confounded and unseparated. But why should we be
> asked to return to such an outlook? Is there any virtue in confusion?
> Can the historical claims of Christianity be made more plausible only
> by "willing suspension of disbelief" so that we can once again see history
> as a cosmic drama of redemption? It may be reasonable to ask for such
> a suspension of disbelief in literature, but surely not in religion. [68]

Cullmann meets such objections as these by referring to Macquarrie's demurrers as the "scandal," or offense of the Christian view
of history. But a far more serious challenge to Cullmann is posed
by James Barr, professor at Princeton. [69] Cullmann makes a strong
case for his work from a use of New Testament words, and it is here
that Barr strikes with a detailed examination of the words chosen.
"The distinction between *karios* and *aion* is the basic element in this
lexical structure. . . . The fact that significant cases occur where
kairos does not mean 'a point of time defined by its content,' and
that the opposition to *aion* is thus quite wrongly stated by Cullmann, thus greatly weakens or entirely destroys the connection between this theory of time and the facts of lexical usage in the New
Testament." [70] In his critique of Cullmann's lexical usage Barr
maintains that Cullmann does precisely what he accuses others of
having done, bringing a philosophical framework to the Bible and
fitting the biblical vocabulary to the framework. His warning is
aimed at the biblical theologians as well as at Cullmann:

> What is more important is that Cullmann, while repudiating philosophy
> and with it all theology that uses philosophical insights, and while insist-
> ing that the concrete biblical material is the sole foundation of truth,
> by his lexical method has hypostatized and conceptualized the words,
> assimilating them to mental concepts and concealing their actual lin-
> guistic function in usage. By de-syntacticization of them he has produced
> a structure out of his words which fits precisely with his view of time,
> although the words are nowhere used in the texts to *state* this view or
> anything similar to it. In fact the hypostatization of vocabulary items is
> one of the principal ways in which modern biblical theology has forced
> dogmatic and philosophical schemata upon biblical material, while at the
> same time professing on the one hand to be non-philosophical and non-

dogmatic, and on the other to be exact and scientific linguistically. Thus it is only apparently that Cullmann's structure of time is biblical and non-philosophical.[71]

For Barr it is clear that theologies cannot be built upon lexical structures; such structures are of service, not normative. "A valid biblical theology can be built only upon the *statements* of the Bible, and not on the *words* of the Bible." [72]

There is another critique of Cullmann that is found among the Bultmannians, and this is to the effect that Cullmann's presentation misses the dynamic, the existential impact of the theology of Bultmann. This has provoked one Protestant theologian, dissatisfied with the shortcomings of Cullmann and of Bultmann as well, to remark rather waggishly that Cullmann's content is superb—without an addressee, while Bultmann has the addressee—but no content.

In his remarkable little book *The God Who Acts* Professor George E. Wright maintains that biblical theology is a theology of recital— that is, a theology of proclamation of the mighty acts of God and the inferences that may be made from those actions. "These acts are themselves interpretations of historical events, or projections from known events to past and future, all described within the conceptual frame of one people in a certain historical continuum." Wright feels that his approach not only avoids the conceptual danger of regarding the Bible excessively as "word" but also restores the place of the Old Testament to theology and affirms the essential unity of the Bible as a whole. Thus in beginning his discussion of biblical faith Wright concentrates on history as the arena of God's activity. "Biblical man conceived of himself as existing in a particular, unique history which possessed significance because God through it was revealed as in process of redeeming all history." [73]

From the very beginning biblical man was aware of the chief inference to be drawn from the fact that God's action in history was always mediated; this was the creation of a people through whom He could effect His designs. This is confirmed throughout the Old Testament in the event of covenant. Biblical theology, then, is an interpretation of history itself, the constant confessional proclamation of events as the acts of God. Thus, for example, in the Bible even the concept of God is not abstract, but He is always described *"in relation to* the historical process, to His chosen agents and to his enemies." [74] In proclaiming Christ the New Testament authors use the events of the Old Testament in the historical form of exegesis that we call typology, in order to express the fact that Christ is the event of history that fulfills all that God has done. The earliest forms of kerygma, the Christian proclamation, are therefore confessions of Christ, who claims God's work in history.

Since it is central to Wright's presentation of biblical theology, he is quite explicit as to the facticity of these events, in contrast to the tendency of the Bultmannian and existentialist theologians, who question, or regard as unimportant, the actuality of the events:

> Some biblical theologians are insisting strongly today that the acts of God are visible only to faith. These theologians appear to object to the location of revelation in history because to do so would base the revelation on "objective" evidence rather than on faith alone; it would lead one to trust a "process" rather than God. The current attack on *Heilsgeschichte* (the conception of the Bible as centered in the saving acts of God in a particular history) seems in part to be motivated by this viewpoint. Yet such an exclusive and one-sided emphasis may fail to do justice to the biblical understanding of the "objective" nature of God's acts. These are historical events interpreted and understood by faith, to be sure, but they are none the less real events which cannot be either realized or relegated to the realm of the "spiritual." Biblical realism consists precisely in its refusal to separate a spiritual realm, known only to faith, from the real world known only to the senses. There is only one creation and one God who makes himself known in it, not by the gift of spiritual *gnosis*, but by the evidence of his *activity*.[75]

One of the most important and rewarding features of Wright's thought is his insistence on the community relationship of the individual associated in faith in Christ; this is a liberation of man to true community, where he finds the purpose of his life. His insistence on the Church as community is located within history and provides for the individual a location in history. His illustration is quite illuminating:

> One way of conceiving the biblical doctrine of individual and community is to understand the nature of historical purpose as a series of interlaced or intersecting arches. The purpose of God over-arches all of time. This purpose is being accomplished by means of his election of a people. The time of this people is that needed to fulfill its election, its purpose is a portion of the Divine purpose; its arch is within and organically related to that of God, while at the same time it over-arches the time alloted to each individual of the community. Individuals likewise have their election; but it is one within the temporal arch given the

community. The time, the purpose, the task (i.e., the arch) of each person thus forms a part of the community purpose which over-arches all components within it.[76]

It is also rewarding to note Wright's insistence on the New Testament tension of the "even now—not yet": "The New Testament views of the Kingdom, of the New Jerusalem, and of the redeemed society of the end-time are both futuristic and 'realized.' " [77]

Detailed treatment of the *Heilsgeschichte* marks the bibilical theology of history presented by Professor Eric Rust in his excellent works *The Christian Understanding of History; Salvation History: A Biblical Interpretation,* and *Toward the Theological Understanding of History.*[78] Rust defines history as the totality of events in time wherein the total man is involved. "History is concerned with past human activity in all its diversity, the expression of human freedom as man responds to and struggles with his environment, as man lives in relationship with his fellow man, and as man encounters the ultimate mystery behind the universe." [79] The meaning of history is not to be sought in some metahistorical overview of the entire process but in the purpose of God disclosed in history, particularly the Christ event. "The final meaning of history must be a purpose of redemption which is actualized by God in history itself. Salvation carries this meaning. It occurs within a process of universal estrangement and moral bankruptcy." Morevoer, according to Rust, history is "creaturely time achieving meaning, and that meaning is God's eternal purpose. God created man and gave him time that the divine purpose might be actualized. Thus time always points beyond itself to God and only becomes justified as it becomes the scene of human history." [80]

Rust also faces the problem of human values in the overview of salvation history. But even here he maintains the traditional Protestant difficulty of seeing value in the world itself because of sin. Thus "the world, blind to the true source of its ideals, its cultural meanings, and its creative visions, carries on in its sinful autonomy." And again, "We must not expect to find any triumphant synthesis here and now between Christ's revelation and the world of contemporary culture." [81]

In the company of his contemporaries in biblical studies Rust affirms that the revelation of God in history is a "mediated revelation," which is the actualization of God's purposes in history itself.

Thus God always comes "veiled in flesh," and "the principle of incarnation holds not only of the central redemptive act in Jesus of Nazareth but throughout salvation history. To understand God's revelation we must find him veiled in flesh." [82]

When Rust affirms the facticity of the biblical events over and against Bultmann, he states that Bultmann has not adequately distinguished the primitive world structure from the primitive world view expressed within those structures. He says that these primitive world structures arose out of prescientific thought and may be jettisoned, but the world view, the "revelatory insight," is not outmoded.

In Dodd, Cullmann, Wright, and Rust we have the major theologians of history to be found among contemporary biblical scholars. Their universal dependence on the *Heilsgeschichte* viewpoint is more than obvious, but it is far from universally accepted by biblical scholars. A distinguished New Testament scholar such as C. K. Barrett can effectively enter his own scruples: "Paul sees history gathering at nodal points, and crystallizing upon outstanding figures. . . . These names follow one another in chronological sequence in the history books (in other words, in the Old Testament); but as far as the experience of mankind is concerned they need not be chronologically distinguished. Rather, they make up a dialectical pattern which provides the clue to Paul's understanding of mankind and of its history." [83] In addition, Barrett calls the attention of the *Heilsgeschichte* theorists to the warning of Paul to the Romans: "O the depth of God's wisdom and wealth and knowledge! How unsearchable are his judgments! How his ways baffle our attempts to track them down." [84]

Yet it has been precisely among these scholars that the sense of man's history and the biblical revelation of its meaning have produced major presentations of theologies of history. From a Catholic viewpoint they are more acceptable answers, with reservations, to the problem of history than the existentialist attempts to work out a theology of history that relies totally on the existentialist conception of history. What many find remarkable in these biblical theologians is that in their unanimous affirmation of the eschatological nature of the New Testament revelation the theologies they propound do not involve an "eschatological" flight from the world. By maintaining the bipolar tension of the "even now—not yet" in New Testament

Christianity and the import of Christian mission, witness, and proclamation to the world they provide a relationship of salvation history to secular history.

As a final step in our investigation of the theology of history in contemporary Protestant thought we turn to those works that specifically attempt to present the Christian interpretation of history.

THE THEOLOGIANS OF HISTORY

Professor Roger Shinn reflects the ancient wisdom of Christianity's greatest theologian of history, Saint Augustine. His *Christianity and the Problem of History* indicates a long and complex study of the problem, and he acknowledges a heavy debt to the Augustinian tradition. God has given man, Shinn tells us, a thread to hold while he gropes his way through history, and Augustine gives us three strands, none of which may be ignored without peril: the ultimate eschatological fulfillment giving meaning to history, the significance of the Church within history, and finally, the appreciation of human history itself and its possibilities of achievement.

Shinn's own comments on Augustine's work are based firmly upon one presupposition for any theology of history: "In the last analysis the problem of history for faith is the problem of the sovereignty of God. If God rules the world, then provisional chaos and meaninglessness finally contribute to His purpose, and history is not in vain. If God does not rule, then whatever achievements may be wrought, the final words pronounced upon history are doom and despair." [85]

In commenting on the first of Augustine's strands Shinn says that the eschatological element is the most important of the three. "With it we can say that history derives its meaning from a Kingdom of God. History thus is never bereft of meaning, and it never encompasses its own meaning." Eschatology is the constant guard against all this-worldly schemes for the salvation of man. But eschatology may be exaggerated into an unworldliness that is other-worldliness, and thus the second strand to be emphasized is that which maintains the tension: the creativity and value of human history itself. This is not the restatement of the naïve nineteenth-century view of progress, but the recognition of history as the arena of decision. These strands are intrinsically related for "the dynamic interpretation cannot finally exist at all without the eschatological." [86]

The final strand is that of the Church, the Kingdom here and now, or more properly, an earnest, a first fruit, a sign of the Kingdom of God. This strand, the Church, relies upon the eschatological, and indeed without this concept of the Church "the eschatological loses some of its immediacy and power." [87]

The Christian understanding of history is finally a profession of faith. It is not a philosophy of history; it does not "explain" the detail and minutiae of history, but as a confession of faith it offers a way of life, a way of living within history.

> Thus understood, Christian faith admits a high degree of agnosticism in history. It is, as a matter of fact, more agnostic than any "philosophy of history" and than most of the implied philosophies of historians. But it ends in an assurance—a trust and a commitment. Admitting a great provisional meaninglessness in history, it affirms a final meaning. In the Christian understanding of history we start with mystery verging on chaos: a mystery which we, despite our intelligence, cannot, comprehend; a chaos which we, despite our freedom, cannot govern. By faith we affirm: it is comprehended; it is governed. He is Sovereign Lord, and He shall reign forever and ever.[88]

There is little in Shinn's work with which we may quarrel. It is essentially a modern reaffirmation of some of the elements of Augustine's thinking upon history. This is far from deprecatory, for Shinn demonstrates a wide acquaintance with the problems posed by history vis-à-vis the Christian faith. He will, of course, be criticized for a somewhat unfair conception of Catholic thinking on the subject and a rather insufficient grasp of the dimensions of Catholic theology and of the early Fathers in treating the Church as the prolongation of the Incarnation. Again, the Catholic cannot accept his adaptation of the Calvinist dynamic, or his setting of the "institutionalized" Church over and against the Church as the community of faith. For all of this, however, Shinn's tour through the problem of history, his incisive observations, and his striking reaffirmation of the mystery that lies behind history mark his work as a Christian vision of history.

Professor John McIntyre has attempted to relate the elements isolated by Shinn and other theologians into a coordinated body of doctrine. McIntyre believes firmly that the Christian doctrine of history is not simply the *Heilsgeschichte*, but that since history involves man's activity as well as God's acts, the latter cannot exhaust a description of history. Because this is precisely a Christian doctrine of history, "it will be a doctrine which is in organic union with the whole corpus of the Christian faith." McIntyre maintains that the Christian is not only committed to this doctrine of history but that the doctrine is related "to the central nature of history itself." [89]

In this definition of history as "meaningful occurrence" McIntyre states that such occurrences are constructs of five categories: necessity, providence, Incarnation, freedom, and memory—which are the conditions for the apprehension of reality. History, then, is not the totality of occurrence, nor even of meaningful occurrence, but "it is only when all of the categories are present and operative that historical occurrence takes place." [90] Among these categories a key position is occupied by the Incarnation, which is constitutive of the redemptive and recreative effect in history of Christ. This effect is observed in: forgiveness ("which laid the basis for future possible renewals of personality which may come through the acceptance in faith by believers of the forgiveness that God constantly offers"); reconciliation (since "the Death of Christ sets up a relation between God and the world that did not exist before"); identification ("God effects the identification of Himself with history . . . this history in all its fallenness"); and victory ("God in Christ puts the powers of darkness to final shame and through the victory of the Cross takes the moral ambiguity from history as a whole").[91]

The Incarnation, conceived as an eschatological event, allows McIntyre to make a contribution to the realization of the incarnational-eschatological tension.

> In contemporary usage, then, the idea of the *eschaton* has two elements. First, it means completely accomplished *telos,* the fulfillment of the mighty purposes which God advanced so far in the Incarnation of Our Lord. Secondly, it means *finis,* the end in the ordinary sense that there is just no more to come. It is the presence in the notion of this double element which is the explanation of its apparent versatility. Because it is *telos* it may be projected forward into the events in the theological series previously described which anticipate it. Because it is *finis* it does not hereby lose its position as the end-term in the series. Because it is the consummation of the *series* it is continuous with the proleptic realizations of itself, and, as the Gospels indicate, takes place within this world and the history that we know. Because it is the *consummation* of the series it is discontinuous with the earlier events as embodying something which was absent from them.[92]

McIntyre speaks of Christianity's relation to the structures of history. These structures are: first, that with which the practicing historian deals; second, the comprehensive patterns reflecting the whole system of necessity in which historical man acts, and which are the objects of the philosopher of history; and third, the Christian's knowledge of God's acts culminating in Christ. Each of these possesses a degree of self-sufficiency, and so there are those engaged in each who exclude the higher categories. "It is this relative independence of the structures of each other which makes it possible for different people to accept one in isolation from the rest." McIntyre feels that these structures are related to each other "in terms of dimensions, and that the dimensional description enables us to determine the relations in which the three structures stand to each other." The integration of the lower into the higher structures is seemingly impossible from a purely human point of view, and it is only for God in His omniscience that these structures are perfectly one: "what is fragmentary for us is unitary for him." [93]

In relating these structures to one another McIntyre warns that not all is well, for while we acknowledge that Christianity makes sense out of history, perfectly integrating its structures in a hierarchy, nevertheless it does introduce "profounder depths" of meaninglessness into history. "To my mind man's sinful rejection of God's love does not 'make sense' to a degree which far surpasses all those other events in life that we so often call meaningless. In other words, the affirmation of the higher dimensions introduces an element of meaninglessness into history and into events that occur on the lower dimensions which does not exist for those whose judgments are based simply on empirical observations made at those lower levels." [94]

The distinguished Anglican theologian Alec R. Vidler, in his contributions to a Christian understanding of history, follows the line of thinking developed by F. D. Maurice,[95] and reflects the influence of the French Catholic theologian Yves Congar. Vidler accepts the distinction in Old Testament thought propounded by the biblical theologians between this age and the "age to come," and also the New Testament affirmation that the "age to come" has been inaugurated, not realized, in the Christ event. Thus the problem of history is set within the framework of the tension that follows upon the Christian affirmation of living in two worlds at once, the world of the creation and the new creation. Basic to any theology of history,

Vidler says, is the Will of God; the Christian must hold the tension of co-existing in this age and the "age to come" simultaneously as deriving from the Will of God.

Vidler introduces into the theology of history the very useful distinction between civilization and evangelization. Civilization includes "all that is involved in preserving and developing the order of creation or this age." [96] Evangelization includes the proclamation of the Gospel and the building up of the Church.

> I am not required to argue that Christians are responsible for evangelization; that is obvious. But I am required to argue that Christians are also responsible for civilization. . . . It would be astonishing if it were not so, since the possibility of preaching the gospel and building up the church depends on the maintenance of order and freedom by civil governments. . . . In other words, evangelization presupposes civilization. And I should further be prepared to argue that for this reason church and state ought, insofar as historical conditions permit, to cooperate and actively assist one another in their respective and complimentary tasks.[97]

Why, then, does God maintain this age in existence? Is the purpose of our stage in history solely to proclaim the Gospel, or does our history have a value in itself? Vidler gives no definite answers but offers four "hints" toward the formation of a positive theology of terrestrial values. First: The work of our history is an opportunity given by God to take an active share in the decisive victory of Christ. Second: As God wishes each man to develop his potentialities, so also he wills that the created world utilize as fully as possible the capacities he has implanted. Third: There is a discontinuity between the work of this world and the Kingdom of God, but the doctrine of the resurrection of the body implies also a continuity between human achievement and the Kingdom; "the least we can say is that it is *this* world and not any sort of world that is to be transformed at the final consummation into the world to come." [98] Fourth, and last: No matter how great have been human achievements in history, they are still all man can do, and may end in failure and disaster; the Kingdom of God will not be the fruit of human effort but, ultimately, the gift of God.

Vidler offers a very profound affirmation of the antinomies that establish the Christian understanding of history, and his affirmation of those antinomies is complemented by their mutual tension. He offers no coordinated synthesis that may be called a theology of history, but he does offer, in the tradition of what the Catholic would call "orthodox" theology, a meaningful restatement of the problem and an incisive reprise of its elements.

George A. Buttrick in a recent book, *Christ and History,* relies very heavily on the work and development traced by the biblical theologians. For Buttrick history is a dialogue between God and man in the language of events; the Bible record is to be considered faith history, a term that is not at all pejorative since "secular history, with no room for any belief in God is nevertheless faith history; it assumes that life is merely secular, a poor creature of time and space. . . . Likewise objective history is faith history: it is written in the pretense that there is no subject." [99]

In the dialogue that is history Christ is the middle term of the conversation, "the key to the translation, the light in which the whole pilgrimage can be seen and understood, and the love in which history's brokenness is healed." [100] Human history in itself is a revelation of the mystery of God, it illuminates life and nature, it is newness in that it offers possibilities, and finally, as revelation, it challenges man to decision. In the revelation of creation the "painful knife-edge of our own finitude" exposes the truthfulness of the biblical affirmation of creation; [101] in the revelation of the Christ event history is able to be interpreted; and finally, the Church as event in history is revelation in affirming a continuing revelation of God in our human story. In this is Buttrick's affirmation of hope: "If God in love for men invaded history, and if Christ lived and died in history and then convinced His followers of His presence with them beyond death, what right have we to think of history as hopeless?" [102]

In this dialogue of history, the clue to the meaning of which is the Christ event, which he terms a "Piercing Event," there is to be found resurrection. Here Buttrick interprets the identity of history to "mean" in the Christian theology an identity with the experience of each individual. The individual by meeting suffering sees the dialogue of history in the microcosm of his own life; the individual is called to involvement, by his very existence, in the dialogue. "The only vital way in which history can be known as Dialogue, with Christ as the revelatory Word, is that we try to re-enact in our own finite and individual history the clue and thrust of His Life. . . . We are involved and cannot flee involvement; and the meaning of history becomes clear by involvement, not by philosophizing." [103]

The position outlined by Buttrick is rather difficult to assess. He seems firmly planted within the tradition of regarding history "biblically." Yet he fails to spell out the totality of a full theological view of history. *Christ and History* suffers from moralizing, preachments, and an almost totally homiletic presentation. But despite these faults there is at work an obviously cultured mind, a man of wide reading and evident brilliance. The theologian will be impressed by the frequency of Christian insight into history, but will nevertheless lament the fact that Buttrick has failed to draw a clearer theological perspective.

The late Professor H. Richard Niebuhr of Yale University, brother of theologian Reinhold Niebuhr, has placed the problem of Christianity and human history in the framework of the perennial dispute over the relationship of Christianity to culture. The choice of this framework, or better, this statement of the problem, resulted from Niebuhr's acknowledged dependence upon the work of Ernst Troeltsch. Niebuhr lists five basic answers given by Christians to history and culture, and attempts to state his own reflections, yet he is always conscious, as he puts it, "that Christ as living Lord is answering the question in the totality of history and life in a fashion which transcends the wisdom of all his interpreters yet employs their partial insights and their necessary conflicts." In his interpretation of the problem Niebuhr takes the common man's definition of culture or civilization as "that total process of human activity and that total result of such activity." [104]

The first type of Christian answer emphasizes the opposition between the Christian idea and culture ("Christ Against Culture"). Niebuhr finds the original statements of this tradition in patrology (Tertullian, Didache, Letters of Barnabas and Clement), continued in the monastic tradition, and personified in modern times by Leo Tolstoi. It faces serious theological difficulty in the doctrine of creation, and "at the edges of the radical movement the Manichean heresy is always developing." [105]

The second answer is that which recognizes agreement between Christ and Culture ("The Christ of Culture"). The earliest representatives are the Judaizers in *Acts*, the Gnostics, Abelard in the Middle Ages, and later liberal Protestantism personified in Ritschl.

The position is beset by objections from both the Christian and the secular camps, and the basic Christian difficulties with this position are the established tenets of the Christian faith.

The next school of thought, while it maintains the differences between the principles of Christianity and culture, nevertheless attempts to hold them in some unity ("Christ above Culture"). The protagonists of this school recognize "the primacy of grace and the necessity of works of obedience." However, here Niebuhr distinguishes three groups: synthesists, dualists, and conversionists. The synthesists affirm a "both-and" relationship of Christ and culture, since we are dealing with God in both cases and "in full awareness of the dual nature of our law, our end, and our situation." [106] Representatives of synthesis are Justin Martyr and Clement of Alexandria, pre-eminently Thomas Aquinas, and the Roman Catholic tradition.

The fourth answer is given by those whom Niebuhr calls dualists ("Christ and Culture in Paradox"); here the duality implied by Christ and culture is affirmed, but the opposition between them is also affirmed. This position is marked by existentialist thought, crisis theology, in which the question about Christ and culture "is not one which man puts to himself, but one that God asks him." The dualist differs from the synthesist in his sense of sin and the depth of depravity, in which "the whole edifice of culture is cracked and madly askew." Niebuhr speaks of dualism as a motif, more than a school of thought, and, he maintains, it is to be found in Paul, Marcion, Augustine, Luther, Kierkegaard, and neo-orthodoxy. "Whether or not the dualistic accounts are intelligible from the viewpoint of their inner consistency, they are intelligible and persuasive as corresponding to experience." [107] There is in this, however, a defect: a relativization of laws, occasion for the despairing to throw off the yoke of law in society, rationalizations for refusing to resist temptation.

The final form in which the Christian answer has been framed is that of the conversionists ("Christ the Transformer of Culture"), who seek to convert not only sinful man but also his culture and society. Man is converted "not apart from these, for there is no nature without culture and no turning of men from self and idols to God save in society." [108] The conversionist is deeply concerned about the present as encounter with God in Christ. Again, this is found as a motif in the Johannine writings, in Augustine, Calvin, and the contemporary Anglican theologian F. D. Maurice.

Niebuhr maintains that his study is unconcluded and inconclusive, but that "in theology as in any other science the seeking of an inclusive theory is of great practical importance." A conclusive answer cannot be given, for that would be to usurp the Lordship of Christ, yet through personal decision we "still need to resolve a present issue in specific terms." [109] In this he declares himself in the tradition of Kierkegaard, recognizing the necessity of decision, of moving from history and speculation to action. Yet he rejects the Kierkegaardian emphasis upon the individualistic and the abstract, and the isolation of the individual from society; Niebuhr strikes out for solidarity, not the solitary. Here is Niebuhr's concept of history for the Christian: "The present moment is the time of decision; and the meaning of the present is that it is the time dimension of freedom and decision." It is not synthesis, dualism, or conversionism that he affirms, but rather what might be called "compresence." "What makes the moment of crisis, the critical, decisive present, so pregnant with meaning is not the fact that the self is alone here with the responsibility of decision, but that there is someone compresent with it." [110] The Christian in decision confronts a compresent and contemporaneous Christ.

The key to this relationship must, therefore, be Christian faith. "On the basis of that faith we reason; and much that was unintelligible on the ground of faithlessness or faith in the little gods who are not trustworthy is not illuminated . . . it forms the basis for our reasoning in culture; for our efforts to define a rational justice; for our endeavors after rational political order; for our attempts to interpret the beautiful and the true. . . . To make our decisions in faith . . . is to make them in view of the fact that the world of culture—man's achievement—exists within the world of grace—God's Kingdom." [111]

Professor Niebuhr has left us a marvelous book. The Catholic would, of course, quarrel with certain points and interpretations. Yet any attempt to present, as Niebuhr does, the general answers to the problem of Christ and culture demands that some patterns and categories be structured. The remarkable work that Niebuhr has accomplished is to make the categories seem to grow from the material, which does not give the appearance of being forced into a priori molds. The disagreements one feels should be presented are nowhere in proportion to the many insights and rewarding observations that Niebuhr bestows upon the careful reader. It is regrettable that Niebuhr himself did not develop a more systematic presentation of his own thinking about history; his *The Meaning of Revelation* proclaims his insistence upon our concrete history as the framework for our thought, and indeed for the Christian revelation.[112] Yet a developed response to the problem of history for the Christian, or even within the framework of culture and the value of human achievement in which *Christ and Culture* was written, would be desirable. While the mystery would hardly have been dissipated, we would, no doubt, be richer for his reflection.

Like H. R. Niebuhr, Professor Richard Kroner places the problem of history in the framework of culture. Man's culture is, for Kroner, his attempt to escape contradictions in existence. Although culture is directed to the solution of the existential gaps, it never succeeds, because it is autonomous from religious faith. The unity of civilization now is imperiled by the continuing secularization and divorce of culture from faith. Kroner's answer is the affirmation that religious faith is the "soul" of culture, and it is faith and faith alone that unifies the activities of culture and at the same time consummates them. "Faith can consummate life and culture because it does not belong to culture and therefore offers not a rational, i.e., a cultural, solution but one which is rooted in the fact that man's life and reality as such are of a mystical nature." [113]

This thesis of the consummation of culture by faith does not, however, remove the tension between culture and faith, since culture is not consummated in time nor replaced there by faith. This tension may be expressed thus: "If faith alone succeeds in attaining that goal toward which the activity of culture moves without final success, what validity can this activity or its results claim?" [114] Culture, to maintain its own significance, must resist and reject its consummation in faith. This tension is reflected in Church history in the formulations of the theologians; philosophy, being the adjunct of culture, cannot attempt to formulate religious faith. Unfortunately Kroner's review of Christologies in the Church is almost ridiculous, and his concept of Thomism is also dominated by this a priori assertion that culture must resist and capture the faith.

Basic to Kroner's view, and indeed the essential defect of his attempt, is his experiental definition of religious faith. For him faith is a vague, subjective area of experience without comprehension; it is "mystical." "The moment we try to express what it is, we distort or destroy it." [115] Deprived of mystical experience, religious faith loses its original and true meaning, and "religion" becomes another cultural construct. Kroner's insistence upon the radical discontinuity between God and His creation, his disregard for any valid system of analogy, destroys any real attempt to establish a relationship between Christianity and culture. At times reminiscent of Barth, his error lies basically in a rigidity of distinction between the "mystical" and the "religious" that ultimately on his own terms deprives his own work of meaning.

The variety of strains in modern thinking represented by historicism, existentialism, and the rigors of the Bultmannian system converge in the approach to history of Carl Michalson. In a vigorous and imaginative work, *The Hinge of History,* which has not at all received the attention and discussion it deserves, Professor Michalson strikes out in a bold new reconciliation of the problem of the relationship of Christianity to history.

Michalson expresses his dissatisfaction with the constant dependence of Christian theology upon the categories of philosophy, not that they did not once have their place, but because in our own day Christianity has been radically affected by historical reasoning. The work done by his Protestant contemporaries, he believes, has only severed the true wholeness of the Christian event: "On one side are metaphysical claims which transcend events; on the other side are historical records which trace events." [116] Beginning with the traditional concept of world history (which has happened and is past), he moves to the necessity of history as referring "to events in which subject and object exist in a mode of togetherness," and thence through the tradition of Dilthey and Collingwood to the concept of history represented by Bultmann's disciple Ernst Fuchs, wherein "history is the world in so far as the question about the possibility of meaningful life is opened up." [117] Thus the historian is called to raise the question of the meaning of events.[118]

From the older idea of the historian who evidences the chronology of events Michalson moves to the philosophers of history who try to make the succession of events meaningful. It is "the compelling concern for meaning within world history" that gives rise to the philosophy of history; but it is this concern, this capacity "to negotiate life with meaning" that constitutes what Michalson calls "existential history." [119]

Existential history refers to the paratactic (deficiency in connectedness) structure of history. It is biblical history that supplies explanations for these paratactic gaps; it witnesses to events that are able to fill those gaps. Thus, borrowing Voegelin's term, Michalson calls the biblical events "paradigmatic," for they display the meaning of history. These paradigms that are found in biblical history supply the authentic form for human existence. In view of biblical history the Christian must be impatient with every form of historicism: "Historicism is wrong, however, in refusing to concede as a valid dimension of history events impervious to objective methods. For paradigmatic events are *intrinsically* inaccessible. The events of biblical history are not the events one knows. They are the events *with the help of which one knows*. . . . This is the reason they are called events of revelation. . . . They are not unique in the sense of being isolated events. On the contrary, they are unique in supplying the hinges between events which would otherwise leave our lives in paratactic incompleteness." [120]

Thus when Michalson speaks of biblical events as being historical, their having-happenedness is not what constitutes their being history, but rather the fact that they supply meaning, and so "Christ is the hinge of history, the paradigmatic event which supplies the very form of the Christian man's existence." For Michalson the paratactic gap between Old and New Testaments—although he concedes to some continuity between them—bespeaks something about the Christian structure of history. It is the Old Testament only that witnesses a holy history, a *Heilsgeschichte;* the Christ event is final and complete, and although history (world history) continues, there is no further paradigm. "The appearance of Christ is an event which supersedes all previous events and teleologically suspends all previous acts of obedience by an imperious claim to be the sole authentic form of all existence. Everything hinges on Christ." This last paradigm, by which all others are interpreted and by which all history hangs together, is termed by Michalson "eschatological history": "Biblical history provides a pre-history for the decisive Christian history as world history does not. Nevertheless, Biblical history is superseded by eschatological history. It is so radically superseded, one might almost say that eschatological history reduces Biblical history to the status of world history, or at least to the status of existential history." [121]

In tracing the developing dimensions of history from world history to existential history to biblical history to eschatological history Michalson is not unaware of the contribution of existentialism. When the existentialist is aware of God's turning to man in Jesus Christ he ceases to be an existentialist, although he may maintain the existentialist approach to mysticism by "letting God be." [122]

In Michalson's presentation the Church is a meaningful and responsible community in eschatological history. The Christian lives in two times: that of world history, which continues (*chronos*), and that time of salvation, the time of eschatological history, which redeems world history (*kairos*).

Professor Michalson has managed to convey in his work an ordered and coherent viewpoint of the relationship of Christianity and history. His obvious indebtedness to the historicist and Bultmannian traditions has not prevented him from making his own contribution. The Catholic will have serious reservations about Michalson's emphasis upon the dynamic and subjective character of his basis in existentialist history, and will feel that the attention given to the eschatological nature of the Church remains necessarily incomplete. Indeed, others have criticized Michalson's rigorous distinction between historical and scientific thinking. Walter E. Weist, in reviewing his latest work, accuses Michalson of promoting "a revised version of Descartes' duality of thinking self and 'extended' physical world." [123] But Michalson has made an attempt, and has managed to convey many insights into the theology of history. He has also challenged each Christian and the Church to the New Testament commission: "The Church is fulfilling its redemptive mission in the world when the body as a whole becomes patterned after God's own self-emptying in Christ" (Phil. 2).[124]

Chapter 6

THE CATHOLIC THEOLOGIES OF HISTORY

THE STUDENT of Catholic theology today is faced not only by manuals of theology, traditional since the nineteenth century Leonine revival of Thomism, but by the vast number of new, fresh, and penetrating studies of perennial theological problems. In addition, he is confronted with a host of titles and problems unnamed or disregarded by the theologians of the schools: the theology of history, the theology of the laity, the theology of work.[1] If the student's training has been limited to the manuals, if his vision of theological endeavor has been limited to conciliar decrees culminating in those of the first Vatican council, a real initial problem is presented by the theology of history. Wherein did it arise? For what reason is man's history, as history, now a central theme in theological thought? It is here that some grasp of the revolutionary century through which we have passed is necessary in order to approach the problem and the answers posed by the Catholic theologians of history.

The causes of this new thinking, more precisely of this new application of the Christian revelation to a problem seen in a new light, are indeed manifold. It may be stated that for Catholics as for Protestants the events of our century—two world wars, international organizations, and the constant pattern of change—provide the central historical situation for this development in Christian thinking. In sacrifice to simplicity, and with due allowance for the deceptive nature of the simple, we may divide the influences upon scholarship in the Catholic Church into the extrinsic and the intrinsic.

Extrinsic to the Church are five new and influential movements that have risen to prominence in the last hundred years and that challenge the traditional presentation of the Christian message. These are existentialism, Marxism, historicism, science, and technology. Existentialism in many of its aspects, and especially in most of its current forms, still reflects the historical skepticism of its founder, Sören Kierkegaard. It will not do for the Catholic scholar to hide behind the Thomist revival (and the realist philosophy that it embodies) and say to the existentialist that the problem he places before men's minds is simply his own creation, and that existentialism itself is not possessed of genuine areas of truth. Marxism may well be regarded as essentially discredited in its thoroughgoing materialism, or even castigated as the demonic force in the world today, but this does not challenge the interior dynamic of the Marxist system, nor does such a posture emasculate it of its sense of the inexorable in human history. Historicism has witnessed the triumph of critical methods in historical research and also the rise of new philosophies explaining the "meaning," and in some cases the direction, of history. The Catholic theologian cannot relegate this force in our world of thought to an intellectual cubbyhole under apologetics and forget the intense sense of human history that historicism has awakened. Science and its progressive mastery over the world are not to be deftly assigned a place in the hierarchy of knowledge, and the sense of human genius and value it has unearthed cannot be ignored. In the wake of scientific achievement, its application in the technocracy of our age challenges the Christian theologian to once again affirm and explicate a Christian humanism in the face of the conformity and brutalization of man that technocracy threatens to effect. Thus it is a changing world that is reflected by the Catholic theologians of history, not a changing theology.

Intrinsic to Catholic Christendom are a number of influences that tend to converge with the extrinsic influences. These may be cited as the most significant: the Protestant tradition, the problem of relevance, the magisterium of the Church, the biblical movement, and finally, developments in dogmatic theology reflected especially in ecclesiology. The insistence of the problem created by modern man's sense of history has been coupled with the thrust of the Protestant theologians who took up the initial studies in the development of the Christian theology of history. But these studies have also strongly influenced Catholic scholarship, so that, for example, we find so excellent a Catholic scholar as Père Jean Daniélou first provoked into examination of the problem by the distinguished studies of Dodd, Rust, and Cullmann. The enforced communication of Catholic theologians with the non-Catholic segments of the intellectual community has stimulated, particularly in Europe, new attempts by the theologians to state the Christian proposition in terms of relevance to a world acutely aware of the movement of history.[2] The magisterium of the Church throughout the twentieth century, with its emphasis on the work of the Catholic layman, on Catholic action and the apostolate, has provoked serious theological attempts to establish a basis for such action on ecclesiologies of history. We shall take up the influences of the biblical movement and of the developments in dogmatic theology in our study of the actual courses that the Catholic theologians have followed.

There is a generally accepted division of the Catholic theologies of history along the lines of incarnationalism and eschatology. Though it is a distinction of some merit, commentators unfortunately interpret it in too facile a vein by reference to incarnationalism as optimistic and to eschatology as pessimistic. It cannot be stated too strongly that both general schools of Catholic thought accept the totality of the Christian revelation and the unique function of the Church in the divine plan.[3] Both schools attempt to work out their orientations of a theology of history precisely as theologies, that is, related to and organized about all the data of the Christian revelation without ignoring, suppressing, or rejecting any particular element of data that does not serve to bolster their own peculiar viewpoints.[4]

The observer will of course ask, "Wherein does the difference between the incarnational and eschatological attitudes lie?" This widely admitted distinction has its basic roots in the very paradox of the Christian fact, in the New Testament tension of the "even now—not yet." Incarnationalists concentrate their gaze upon the person of Christ, upon His mission, and upon the Church. They tend to accentuate the importance and the relevance of man's achievements here and now in the divine plan: they emphasize and accentuate not only the Pauline notion of the "building up" of the Church but also the essential goodness and values of the world as the creation of God. When the incarnationalist faces the question of the culmination of this period of the "time between" in the parousia he insists upon the transformation of the world, not its destruction. Eschatologists, on the contrary, are distinguished by a constant focus on the process of salvation history (*Heilsgeschichte*) and, therefore, the essential transitoriness of this stage in which we live. As is implied by their name, a major feature of the eschatologicals' thinking upon history is the parousia, toward which they reflect the New Testament impatience for the final coming of the Lord Jesus.

It should be more than obvious that the incarnational-eschatological distinction is one of orientation; it reflects as basic a theological orientation of the same data of the Christian revelation. It is, for all of this, a real distinction; and when one examines the consequences of the separate views the reality of the distinction is more than apparent. The incarnationalist position produces in its adherents an attitude inclined toward humanism and the values of this world; it is sympathetic toward culture, and it views progress as not only demonstrable but an expected fact. Incarnationalism sees in the spread of Christianity and in scientific progress the expected advance of man toward the final form of the Kingdom of God. Over and against these views we find in the eschatological orientation an attitude reflecting that of Saint Paul, that we are strangers and pilgrims in this world, that we have here no lasting city. The Kingdom of God in its final perfection is not anticipated by a "gradual mastery by Christ of the present world, but by the glorious return of Christ." [5]

When we spoke in general of those extrinsic and intrinsic movements that affect the Church, we merely mentioned the developments in dogmatic theology and the biblical movement as contributory to the current interest of Catholic theologians in the theology of history. It would also seem that in these two parallel and at times interrelated movements we can find a cause for the incarnational-eschatological difference. Catholic thinkers working in the theology of the Church and concerned about the nature and the mission of the Church in the world tend to fall almost totally within the incarnational camp. Catholic biblical and patristic scholars concentrating upon the historical working out of the divine economy of salvation, and deeply affected by the final and decisive event of human history in the parousia, seem to tend totally toward an eschatological orientation. It is to an examination of these developments within Catholic thought and their consequences for the Catholic theologians of history that we now turn.

THE INCARNATIONAL THEOLOGIANS

Theology within the Catholic Church has from the time of the Reformation been hampered by a seemingly defensive stance of apologetics and reaction. The theology of the Church reacted, as might be expected, against the Protestant division by attaching enormous importance to the external and juridical concepts of the Church itself. The years after the Reformation, which brought in their wake Gallicanism, Jansenism, Febronianism, and Josephism served only to strengthen a juridical preoccupation with the nature of the Church, whose roots lay in the late Middle Ages. This understandable though unfortunate theological preoccupation in ecclesiology began to be challenged and reversed in the nineteenth century by the work of the Tübingen theologian Johann Möhler (1796–1838). "The great glory of Möhler shall always be his sublime conception of the Church in its internal and external structure. . . . In a sense, without Möhler it would be hard indeed to imagine the fruits of this revived ecclesiology which we enjoy today." [6] The current theological preoccupation with the identity of the Church and Christ stems not only from the work of the New Testament scholars but also from the recovery by the dogmatic theologians of the internal nature of the Church as the body of Christ, a modern trend that dates its renewal to Möhler. As we shall see, it is in the context of this revived sense of the Church as a totality that incarnational theologians propose their orientation toward human history.

Möhler's thought, which marks the beginning of this modern ecclesiology, seems to have progressed in these stages: (1) insistence upon the juridical concept of the Church; (2) awareness of the Holy Spirit as the interior element in the Church, reflected in his *Die Einheit in der Kirche* (1825); (3) belief that through the operation of the Holy Spirit the Church is the continuation of the Incarnation, that it is the body of Christ—a position he finally adopted in the *Symbolik oder Darstellung* (1835). Möhler's reinsistence upon the too long neglected truth of the Church as the mystical body of Christ did not ignore the traditional or juridical aspect, but rather he attempted a synthesis of both. It is toward an ever more articulate and elaborate synthesis of the internal and external aspects of the Church that modern ecclesiology has veered. "To define the totality of the Church, both of these characteristics must be taken into account. The truth lies in the synthesis of the two. In the words of Yves Congar, to sacrifice the invisible to the visible is a form of Nestorianism; to sacrifice visible to the invisible, a form of Monophysitism." [7]

It was also Congar who summarized the tradition of Möhler's dynamic conception of the Church as it has passed down to our own time: "Möhler begat Passaglia; Passaglia begat Schrader; Passaglia and Schrader begat Scheeben and Franzelin." [8] Into our own time this vibrant sense of the Church as the body of Christ in the tradition of the theologians was borne by Möhler's descendant at Tübingen, Karl Adam.[9] Among the theologians the current tradition of synthesizing the external and internal elements of the Church has also been strengthened by a separate line of inquiry pursued by the biblical theologians, who through the erection of more articulate theologies of the New Testament have reinforced this dynamic conception of the Church.

It is in this tradition, which culminated in the encyclical of Pope Pius XII on the Church as the mystical body of Christ, that incarnationalism has emerged in our time. The incarnationalists lay great stress upon this fundamental doctrine of the Church as the body of Christ in the world, and as the extension of the Incarnation through space and time. Père Paul Henry, professor at the Institut Catholique in Paris, expresses this incarnationalist orientation:

[Incarnationalists]—and I range myself among them—think that the Christian cannot be indifferent to natural values, to human progress; they believe that the Christian has not only the right but also the duty, and, therefore, the possibility, of working with all his forces for the construction of a better world, the natural substructure of a world spiritualized by grace. He has confidence in reason, in thought, in human action, inserted in Christ, and the prolongation of His action in the unfolding of time and in the extension of space. I believe that in the New Testament there are elements which support this conception of a theology of the Incarnation prolonged by the action of the Christian in the bosom of the Church of Christ. Before all else the appeal addressed to Christians is to build the Body of Christ, the Church, a society not only divine but human. By the Incarnation Christ has reconciled us with our "human condition" and invites us to make of this world a real anticipation, a beginning of the world to come.[10]

Henri de Lubac is regarded by many as one of the foremost theologians of our time. He is also one of the serious voices in the incarnationalist camp. Having long wrestled with the problem of establishing a lasting basis for humanism, De Lubac has concluded to the necessity of theism as a first principle for humanism.[11] In itself, he maintains, humanism has not up to this point established itself as essentially Christian, nor can it hope to do so in the future. Therefore true humanism requires God for its basis, and indeed, to be lasting, it requires Christ. "If there be no man without humanity, much less still is there any humanity without men. By calling us back inwards, the Gospel is at the same time calling us back to the truth of human relationships, that truth fatally betrayed by all ideologies and political systems."[12] De Lubac's vision of man and human value, and therefore his vision of the meaning of human history, lies in his conception of the Church. It is, as a matter of fact, the Church that he chooses as the central point of his theology, the vital center around which all other data organically group themselves. Here again De Lubac sounds the theme Möhler was so fond of handling—the Church as the body of Christ:

> If Christ is the Sacrament of God, the Church is for us the sacrament of Christ; she represents him, in the full and ancient meaning of the term, she really makes him present. She not only carries on his work, but she is his very continuation, in a sense far more real than that in which it can be said that any human institution is its founder's continuation.[13] The Church is the sacrament of Christ; which means, to put it another way, that there is between her and Him a certain relation of mystical identity. Here again we encounter the Pauline metaphors and the rest of the biblical images, which the Christian tradition has continually explored. . . . Head and members make one single body, one single Christ; the Bridegroom and the Bride are one flesh. Although He is the Head of His Church, Christ does not rule her from without; there is, certainly, subjection and dependence between her and Him, but at the same time she is His fulfillment and "fulness."[14]

Thus it is that Père de Lubac's incarnational view of human history is not only based upon his presentation of the Church as the extension of the Incarnation but relies solely upon this as the central intuition that gives history any meaning:

> Amid this universal chorus Christianity alone continues to assert the transcendent destiny of man and the common destiny of mankind. The whole history of the world is a preparation for this destiny. From the first

creation to the last end, through material opposition and the more serious opposition of created freedom, a divine plan is in operation, accomplishing its successive stages among which the Incarnation stands out as chief. So in close connection with the social character of dogma there is another character, equally essential, and that is the historic. For if the salvation offered by God is in fact the salvation of the human race, since this human race lives and develops in time, any account of this salvation will naturally take an historical form—it will be the history of the penetration of humanity by Christ.[15]

In this presentation of human history there are a number of practical implications for the Christian. De Lubac sees these as essentially revolving about the concept of the engagement of the individual Christian in the work of the world. It is this engagement that he calls the "law of the Incarnation."

> The Word of God submitted himself to this essential law: He came to deliver us from time, but by means of time. . . . That is the law of the Incarnation and it must undergo no Docetist mitigation. Following Christ's example, "loyally and with no cheating," every Christian must acquiesce in that state of engagement in time which gives him part and lot in all history, so that his connection with eternity is not unrelated to a past that he knows is immense and a future the length of which is hidden from him.[16]

Finally, to understand De Lubac's constant teaching of the Church as the body of Christ we must see that for him it is in the Church that humanism and human values are guaranteed, and that indeed it is the Church that is the fulfillment of creation and of created values. "To see in Catholicism one religion among others, one system among others, even if it be added that it is the only true religion, the only system that works, is to mistake its very nature, or at least to stop at the threshold. Catholicism is religion itself. It is the form that humanity must put on in order finally to be itself." [17]

This premise of the Church as the basis of a theology of history is also to be found in the work of the French Dominican Père M. Montuclard. The unique work of Christ in the Church is paralleled by the work of Christ in history, and the ultimate attainment of the Kingdom of God will be achieved by the Church and by history specifically as the gift of God bestowed upon history. True to his insights, Montuclard did try to establish a *modus vivendi* with what he regarded as the most evident factor in historical development today, Marxism. His *Les événements de la foi* (1952) was put on the Index in 1953; and thereafter he sought and obtained a reduction to the lay state by the Holy See.

Where Père de Lubac and others adopt an incarnational orientation toward history from a consideration of the Church, we find another basis for incarnationalism in the thought of Père Teilhard de Chardin (1881–1955). The basic elements for his view of reality are to be found in his *Phenomenon of Man,* and their implications for the Christian in *The Divine Milieu.*[18] Teilhard de Chardin conceived the evolutionary process not only on a biological level but also as the meaning of all the material and spiritual energy in the world. The appearance of man in the world reflected the convergence of the evolutionary trends of reality, and the nineteenth-century awareness of this evolutionary process was an awareness of the "irreversible coherence" of all that exists. "What makes and classifies a modern man," Teilhard de Chardin comments, "is having become capable of seeing in terms not of space and time alone, but also of duration, or—and it comes to the same thing—biological space time; and above all having become incapable of seeing anything otherwise . . . the consciousness of each of us is evolution looking at itself and reflecting." [19]

In view of this awareness of evolution, human history has a new meaning for modern man:

> Man is not the center of the universe as once we thought in our simplicity, but something much more wonderful—the arrow pointing the way to the final unification of the world in terms of life. Man alone constitutes the last-born, the freshest, the most complicated, the most subtle of all the successive layers of life. This is nothing else than the fundamental vision and I shall leave it at that. But this vision, mind you, only acquires its full value—is indeed only defensible—through the simultaneous illumination within ourselves of the laws and conditions of heredity.[20]

The evolution of man is termed in Teilhardism "cosmogenesis," and the end toward which it proceeds is called the "Omega point." The attainment of point Omega is termed "Christogenesis," and it is this Christogenesis, the perfection of evolution, that is the integration of human personality with Christ. It is incorporation—a total process of wholeness with other men and indeed with life itself. Among the major implications of this total view of life, history, and reality is the affirmation of the particular value of human activity in the plan of God, and the affirmation of the Christian's cooperation in this plan by engagement in the world. "God does not deflect our gaze prematurely from the work He Himself has given us, since He presents Himself to us as attainable through that very work. Nor does He blot out, in His intense light, the detail, of our earthly aims, since the intimacy of our union with Him is in fact a function of the exact fulfillment of the least of our tasks." In carrying through this thinking, Teilhard de Chardin denies the distinction of the Christian's work in the world as "worldly." He says: "By virtue of the Creation and, still more, of the Incarnation, *nothing here below is profane* for those who know how to see. On the contrary, everything is sacred to those capable of distinguishing that portion of chosen being which is subject to the attraction of Christ in the process of consummation." In speaking of the eschatological fulfillment of the parousia as the triumph of cosmogenesis, Teilhard comments: "Then the presence of Christ, which has been silently accruing in things, will suddenly be revealed—like a flash of light from pole to pole." [21]

One of Teilhard de Chardin's most salient critics, Louis Cognet, has pointed out and emphasized the chief difficulty in this presentation: the problem of evil.[22] Teilhard de Chardin's conception of evil in human history, according to Cognet, is unreal; evil as it is presented seems to be merely that of inertia in nature, and the historical reality of sin is inadequately faced. Thus, as Nicolas Corte has remarked:

> That is why he [Teilhard de Chardin] talks readily of the Incarnation but less readily of the Redemption. He often returns to the mystery of the Cross, but he no longer gives it its full meaning. There is a certain aroma of pelagianism in Teilhard's system. Christ for him, as for Pelagius, is first and above all a "sort of universal center of psychic convergence." Christ is a guide, a model, a trainer. It is not made sufficiently clear that He is above all the Savior, the Source of grace, the only Mediator between God and Man.[23]

The French Dominican theologian, Père Th. G. Chifflot, in a remarkable little book published in 1960, surveys the problem of a theology of history through the work of Oscar Cullmann, Louis Bouyer, Saint Thomas, and Teilhard de Chardin. Acknowledging the permanent elements of Christian eschatology to be found in the work of Cullmann and Bouyer, Chifflot uses the traditional construc-

tion of Saint Thomas to point out that it is possible in the eschatological position of the biblical scholars to lose the sense of the real
value and meaning of human history, and by concentrating upon the
linear working out of salvation history to lose the sense of the
"economy" of salvation. He concludes, in his essay on Teilhard de
Chardin, to an affirmation of the intrinsic connection of human history to the whole universe. In fact, it is in Teilhardism that Père
Chifflot finds major elements for a Christian viewpoint on history. In
Teilhard's thought Chifflot finds a fundamental agreement with the
doctrine of creation.[24] More so, evolution as Teilhard presents it
"accords admirably" with biblical thought.[25] With or without the
initial Teilhardism thesis, Chifflot sees in Teilhard de Chardin's
thought implications for life, not only completely Christian but substantial contributions to modern men's thinking on history.

A fellow Dominican of Chifflot's, Marie-Dominique Chenu, one of
the great teachers within the French tradition, has also placed himself in this moderated incarnational position of Chifflot.[26] In fact,
Chenu feels that Chifflot represents almost completely his own position. He states on his own these three basic themes for a theology of
history (themes which he feels are present throughout Chifflot's
work): First: Time and history are to be found in every knowledge of
the Christian mystery. Second: Human time is transfigured by the
"presence" of God as a historical figure. Third: The incarnation of
God's Son, by the operation of the Holy Spirit, extends through history in the Church. Chenu feels that in his own and Chifflot's position a median has been established between the extreme eschatology
of Bouyer and the incarnationalism of Teilhard de Chardin, and
that their position "gives consistency to the Christian-in-the-world
without waiting for the decisive eschatological event." [27]

In the United States the incarnational viewpoint is well represented by Walter J. Ong, who, like Chifflot and Chenu, draws
inspiration from the work of Teilhard de Chardin. Not only, according to Ong, does the Judaic-Christian revelation destroy the
captivity of the cyclical patterns of history, but the modern scientific
sense of evolution destroys them as well. Having made an obeisance
to the biblical insistence on salvation history, Ong does feel that
this biblical sense of linearity "has its disadvantages here, for the
Christian and Hebrew sense of time is by no means so spatialized as
the term 'linear' suggests. It is more interior and psychological, or

'human,' and, besides, it does involve certain considerations which, when they are handled geometrically, are best handled by analogy not with straight lines but with circles." Ong believes that the evolutionary viewpoint of modern science is not only not opposed to, but perfectly suitable for, the Christian. "The world view which is opening out before us in our post-Darwinian world is thus one eminently congenial to a follower of Christ." [28] The Christian vocation in the world, then, is to elucidate God's creation in a Christian framework by developing "the positive habit of thinking of man within the full perspectives of time and space in which he exists in the cosmos." [29]

It should not be thought that for Ong all problems are settled; rather he feels that the Christian is faced by a serious problem—a stunted Christology, and that the need exists for a Christology in which the positive relationship of Christ's work is related "to a world which we now know as pointed into the future in a way earlier man did not suspect." [30] Father Ong has concentrated the application of his thought upon Christian scholars. These he summons not only to Christian but also to secular scholarship:

> Hence the Christian's stake in the advance of secular knowledge is not merely negative. Once the evolutionary growth in the cosmos, in life, in our knowledge, is known, the Christian must recognize as God's work this upward movement in the universe. And if this is God's work, how does the Christian have any choice but to further it? The Church, with her theologians, must keep in touch with the whole universe-in-history, with its sciences and arts especially, in order to preach the gospel to the whole world—to be present with Christ everywhere on the present front of history. It is here in the present that we ourselves live, and it is this present that we must impregnate with Christ.[31]

Incarnational theologies of history have also been ably represented in England, and Abbot Christopher Butler of Downside has made a valuable contribution to them.[32] Butler strikes out vigorously for a Christian humanism, and he feels that the value of human activity lies in its preparation for the Kingdom of God. He interprets the eschatological elements of the New Testament as having their origin in an expected imminent parousia; with the passage of time itself the Christian expectation led to the development of new implications. The presence of Christ in the Church led, therefore, to an understanding of the "time between" as the period in which His Kingdom reached through time and space towards fullness. Christ, then, in this view does not and will not abolish the world or human history, but rather He will transfigure them. The transition between the incarnational and eschatological positions, marked by such distinguished scholars as Léopold Malevez and Yves Congar, stresses the Christian's engagement in the world and at the same time maintains the radical discontinuity that exists between the world and its achievements and the Kingdom of God. Far from adopting such a mediating position, Martin D'Arcy comments upon Butler's full-bodied incarnationalism by thus glowingly evaluating his thought:

> In saying that history is the flowering of the seed whose fruits will be garnered at the end in the kingdom of God, Abbot Butler brings together as closely as possible human life to its supernatural end. No longer have we to accept the discontinuity laid down by Père Congar and Père Malevez. The Christian has not to arrive personally safe but without luggage; he has to take with him all that he acquires on the road. There is no misanthropic unworldliness here! Even the image of the pilgrim with his staff and scrip hastening past Vanity Fairs or valleys of tears must be dropped. We are so accustomed to what Abbot Butler might call the cautionary tales or necessary moods of spiritual writers that we may be at first timid in accepting this challenging and heartening view.[33]

The distinguished dogmatic theologian Gustave Thils, professor at the University of Louvain, has produced one of the most fundamental and articulate presentations of a theology of history ever written by a contemporary Catholic theologian.[34] Thils maintains that the eschatological-incarnational dualism is being forced toward harmony precisely because of constant papal teaching in our time concerning Christian engagement in the world and the importance and significance of the apostolate for every Christian, cleric or lay. Thus Thils feels that a theology of "earthly realities" is incumbent upon the contemporary theologian, and that this theology, from one point of view, may be termed more properly "Christian anthropology." By this he means not only the concept of concrete man but the integral biblical revelation of man as he should be. The deficiency of the older dogmatic theologians, a deficiency he labels "impoverishment," was the too intense conception of man in the abstract, that is, as a rational animal, which ignored the many facets of man-in-history, his cultural, social, economic, and civil progress. While he emphasizes the importance of historical man and man as he is meant to be, Thils also maintains with equal emphasis that the construction of such a theology of earthly values must be integral with the full Christian revelation in the Word of God.

Does human history have value? Thils feels that if one follows the eschatology of Bouyer and Daniélou it is inevitable that one must deny value to the world of our temporal activity. Man's work in the world is to complete Christ, to glorify Him, and man does this by his progressive mastery of the earth. From the viewpoint of the end result, and only from that viewpoint, it does not matter what intention is in the man (whether he works from a Marxist, positivist, or Christian position); when he extends the mastery of man over the world the result is the same, the completion of Christ.

The elements of a theology of history become more evident when Thils posits and answers the question of the direction of history, which he feels is characterized by an elevated motion toward unity. It is the Holy Spirit, he says, who dominates the history of the world and who tends to spiritualize all things. Here there are two facets of unity: first, the transcendent unity of grace, and second, the unity of terrestial life (the harmony and understanding of men's minds and hearts). Thus Thils renews his emphasis upon the fundamental unity of creation (the world) and redemption (Christ) and their eventual identity in the eschatological fulfillment of the Kingdom of God.

Few would quarrel with Thils' fundamental Christian truth of the unity of the orders of creation and grace; he then continues from this initial position to spell out the consequent meaning that he sees in history. The benefits of the Holy Spirit, by which we are "graced" in Christ, are participations in the life of God, but they necessarily call for a "terrestrial translation" in which this profane world is rendered Christian. History, then, is the site of a conflict that is dominated by the Cross, in which the spirit is opposed by the flesh. The Christian's faith in the efficacy of the spirit is total; it extends to natural as well as supernatural efficacy, so that one can see that the good realized in the world by the spirit will eventually dominate. Man, then, moves toward a greater unity and peace under the power of the Holy Spirit.

Human history itself, Thils tells us, can be interpreted in two ways. Either history is seen as a *prefigure* of the Kingdom of Heaven, that is, in the unique involvement of the Holy Spirit in creation, and therefore history is good, but still only an image of what is to come, or history may be interpreted as *prelude* of the Kingdom, that is, the work accomplished in history is definitive and lasting, yet it only partially inaugurates what will later be perfectly achieved under the motion of the Holy Spirit. Thils states that both interpretations are to be found in our history: we find there the real prefigurement of what is to come in the achievements of human technology and the arts, and we also find the preludes of the Kingdom in the historical forms and the arts; likewise we find the preludes of the Kingdom in the historical forms of charity and unity (families, social and political organizations).

Consequent to Thils' thinking about history is the obligation of the Christian to engage in the works of the world that are the prefigures and preludes of the Kingdom, and to have faith in the power of the Holy Spirit to fulfill the natural as well as the supernatural order. Thils' magnificent and singular contribution to a theology of history does not stand alone; true to his vision, he has worked out a total ascetical theology to reflect and complete this theology of history.[35] Although it is possible to disagree with his constructions, no critic of this view can dismiss the enormous erudition, the deep insight, and the evident dedication that Thils has brought to his work. For many Thils' work in the theology of history will stand as a classic elucidation of the incarnational view.

In the United States a former student of Thils and a brilliant, young, and promising theologian, Peter Riga, has presented a survey of the problem of the theology of history.[36] This work, although ostensibly presenting a *status quaestionis* and a bibliography (which is superb), spells out his own position as an incarnationalist much in the tradition of Thils. The eschatologists, with Bouyer in the lead, have frequently vexed the incarnational theologians with their inability to place the Cross of Christ firmly within their positions. Riga replies to this (and follows with a comparable citation from Thils):

Certainly we cannot eliminate the Cross from this perhaps too optimistic view of the elaboration of the temporal order under the inspiration of the Holy Spirit. This historical sequence is not always a forward-moving sequence; it has its backslidings, its failures, its drawbacks; but the Christian should not, and must not, become discouraged. Perhaps these very setbacks will be an occasion, providential perhaps, for purification of intention, renewal of purpose, and dedication for Christ and for men, *instaurare omnia in Christo.*[37]

No eschatologist would find this a very satisfying answer, and indeed it would be considered hardly relevant to the objection. Riga, however, remains with Ong among America's most promising young theologians in the incarnational tradition; he reflects the wisdom of his master, Thils, as Ong reflects Teilhard de Chardin.

The urgency of the problem of history for the contemporary Christian seems to dominate the thinkers at Thils' own University of Louvain. There the vital Christian sense of the philosopher Albert Dondeyne has also attempted to meet the problem along lines that though at times resembling those of Thils are nevertheless more affected by his conversation with modern thought, especially existentialism. Like Thils', Dondeyne's Christian sense brings him to an essentially incarnational position.

For Dondeyne the approach to a solution of the problem of history is made in his dialogue with contemporary existentialism. The progress of modern science coupled with modern man's sense of the future have accentuated the existentialist concept of historicity. The all-important question that the modern world puts to the Christian conscience is whether the belief in God and the afterlife destroys in the Christian any feeling for man and for his history. Thus it is that Dondeyne meets what he feels to be the crucial proposition of Merleau-Ponty: "The metaphysical and moral consciousness dies once it comes in contact with the absolute."

Dondeyne begins with a concept dear to the existentialist and essential to any sense of history—liberty, the possibility of giving things a sense. He continues his argument through to individual historic consciousness as an encounter, "a never-ending dialogue with a world which appears to us as a horizon opening up an indefinite number of perspectives." [38] Thus it is that he relates the three strands that determine historicity for the existentialist: consciousness, the temporal character of man, and the intersubjectivity of man's world. And yet, as he points out, to avoid the inevitability of pure relativism the existentialist, while asserting from his sense of historicity the provisory nature of every human truth, still affirms one positive and absolute truth, namely, the given fact of one's presence in the world. It becomes absolutely necessary for the existentialist to affirm some universal permanent element within history, for historicity is unthinkable without it. This element differs in

Sartre, Merleau-Ponty, and Heidegger; Dondeyne posits God, and moves to reconcile this absolute being with historicity.

Utilizing Thomist philosophy, Dondeyne repeats the dictum of Saint Thomas that although God is the first and absolute in the order of being (*quoad se*), this does not mean that God is the proximate norm of imperfect truths as far as we are concerned (*quoad nos*). This would be to destroy the transcendence of God. The distinction, however, is crucial in the discussion of the basic elements of an argument that he develops later: "But if the foundation and norm of truth for us (*quoad nos*) is not God but our own existence, with the existential orbit that is inseparable from it, it is clear that neither the affirmation of God nor later reflection on His mystery nor a special recourse to God will in any way change this *prius quoad nos*." [39]

In speaking of the problem of history Dondeyne states that there are no specifically Christian views of physics, economics, politics, and so on, for the Christian maintains that there is a sacred as well as a secular history. He disputes Daniélou's conception of sacred history as embracing secular history, and Daniélou's view that it is Christianity that makes history genuine. "This is playing on the word 'history,' and talking as if secular history was somehow not genuine history; the term 'history' has, in fact, different meanings and belongs in the first place to the secular order." [40] The structure of civilizations, Dondeyne states, is one of a hierarchy of value domains: biological, cultural, and moral. The basic values are respect for life and death, the love of truth, love, liberty, and authentically human society.

The basic distinction between the secular and the religious order is a necessary consequence of the existentialist recognition of human existence dominated by two fundamental but divergent intentions. The first is existence as "being-to-the-world"; the other is existence as "being-for-God," a receptivity to the transcendent. The domains of value dependent upon these two intentions are autonomous but related. Here lies the problem of the Christian and man's sense of historicity: "It is very difficult to achieve a synthesis of the religious and the secular nowadays that would not be just a juxtaposition or, worse still, a confusion of the two domains." [41] The distinction between secular and religious in man and the possibility of their union follows upon the understanding of human existence as it is. "The ultimate basis of the possibility to reconcile secular civilization and religious belief must, therefore, be sought in the fact that both spring from *two distinct dimensions of existence,* or more precisely, from two distinct dimensions of freedom." [42]

In this Dondeyne is most anxious to preserve the essential transcendence of God and the essentially religious nature of the Christian revelation. "The religious dimension of our existence is not, properly speaking, a prolongation of its secular dimension. . . . God is not part of this world nor is He the sum of things that go to make it up." Christianity is fundamentally a mystery, adhered to in faith, coming from God and having God as its object. Science and secular culture are not directed to bring us to God and communion with Him, "but to make us at home in the world and bring this world closer to us."[43]

> The progress of science and civilization can neither satisfy nor suppress the need for religion, and conversely there is no danger that religious faith, lived in all its purity, will disturb the work of mankind in search of cultural values. . . . The religious dimension of our existence is not an epiphenomenon or a sublimation of the secular, but springs from another intention, another source, and has a life all its own. . . . As such, Christian faith is meant neither to throw light on nor to perfect the secular life of the Christian.[44]

The evident objection to Dondeyne's thesis—that he implies a duality of existences—is met in his definition of faith as an existential and concrete reply to the supreme question posed by the meaning of existence. The life of faith, since it makes us receptive to the transcendent, affects the self in its deepest levels. "It follows that the life of Faith gathers together within it all the elements of secular and historical existence. It gathers them up, giving them a new sense, a new dimension, without weakening either their specific content or their historical structure." [45] And again, he says elsewhere: "One should not conclude . . . that we are dealing with two worlds existing and evolving in pure *juxtaposition.* Both meet *in man* and impose a task on one and the same human being." [46]

It is Christian morality that provides for Dondeyne the synthesis of the religious and secular within an individual concrete existence.

> It is through the fidelity of Christians to the moral teaching of Christ Christianity is called on to enter into the secular history of the world; it is this, too, which makes Christianity a historical factor of immense

significance for humanism in every age. . . . It is also a humanism, an original, intensely spiritual and personalist way, not only of conceiving human existence, but of accepting it, exercising it, and promoting it for oneself and others.[47]

And so Dondeyne's answer to his world that belief in God, that Christianity, is incompatible with the existentialist recovery of a sense of man's history is a denial in principle, *but* "in practice, it all depends on ourselves." "If our recourse to the Absolute is genuine, if our faith is truly a life of God, a loving openness towards God and, through God, towards man, Christianity cannot fail to express itself in a true and healthy humanism. Not that Christianity is first and foremost a humanism, but it is a humanism none the less." [48]

Incarnationalism has drawn its strength not only from the Church-oriented work of scholars like De Lubac, from the scientific impulse of a Teilhard de Chardin, from the confrontation of contemporary humanism by Dondeyne, and from the elaborate articulation of a Thils, but also from the theological reaction created by contemporary Marxism. The Jesuit Père F. G. Fessard, in a difficult two-volume work, strikes out heavily at the lack of a Catholic theology of history in the face of Marxism.[49] The blame he places squarely upon the shoulders of the Thomists for their constant considerations of being—existence in the two exclusive realms of reason and nature. Against the other extreme, represented by the Catholic left, which seeks to de-atheize or "baptize" Marxism, he argues the impossibility of such an effort because of the atheist posture essentially necessary for the Marxist position. Fessard's work contributes little to the elaboration of a theology of history, but it does serve a purpose in its strident call to the theologians to enter the world of our time, even the political order, with a revived Christian sense of the historical.

Although not *ex professo* a theologian of history, but a popularizer committed to an incarnational viewpoint and its implications, Jean Mouroux has ably stated the case for the incarnational concern with the temporal:

> The Christian loves the temporal first of all because it comes from God. Things, persons and all their innumerable activities spring from the Creative Power of God, and consequently all are good. . . . True, there is sin. But if sin has wounded everything it has corrupted nothing. . . . All is redeemed in Christ in principle; and the divine benediction re-descends on things and men and the efforts of men. . . . Human endeavor

remains always destined to perfect the universe and to save souls. Temporal realities and temporal values may be wounded and dangerous, but they remain innocent, and always worthy of love.[50]

In his theological study of time Mouroux traces the relationship of God and time (time having its roots in eternity and being the measure of creation), Christ and time (time is fulfilled in, and creation takes its meaning from, Christ), and the Church and time (the Church prolongs and manifests the fulfillment and meaning of time in Christ).[51] In a perceptive critique of his work the Catholic theologian Robert Johann states that Mouroux has dealth with time extrinsically, so that he carries none of the insight that "time is rather part and parcel of the creature's structure." [52]

FROM INCARNATIONALISM TO ESCHATOLOGY

There are many theologians very conscious of the historical reality and mission of the Church as the extension of the Incarnation, and also aware of the necessity of a theological basis for humanism and engagement in the world, who cannot subscribe to the extreme statements of the incarnational viewpoint. These theologians feel that in orienting a theology of history about the essential continuity of the orders of creation and redemption one does great harm to the traditional Christian conception of the unique free gift of God in Christ toward sinful man. At the same time they are not willing to adopt an eschatological posture, simply because they feel that the eschatological posture is itself an extreme and one in which no basis at all will be established for personal commitment to work in the world. For these reasons they work to establish a theology of history that will embrace the essential mystery of history in the Christian dispensation: the finality of the Christ event and the realization of the Kingdom of God now in the Church with the necessity of man's engagement in the world. The essential link between eschatology and incarnationalism, then, is the individual Christian; here, in the Christian-in-history, are to be resolved the tensions of ways of looking at history. Foremost among these scholars are Yves Congar and Léopold Malevez.

Père Congar starts from the decisive principle of the total Lordship of Jesus Christ and maintains its application toward God's purpose for the world as His Kingdom. In the divine plan "the

Resurrection, consummated in the Ascension, is the very first achievement in the triumph of the *Pneuma* over nature itself, the reconciliation in Christ of the cosmic order with the order of God's free grace." [53] In this a higher principle emerges, which regulates the lower elements and because of which those elements find the perfection proper to their nature. This principle, Jesus Christ, does not now exert the fullness of power, for He allows nature now to work according to its rules. Christ wills not to exercise His authority over temporalities until the parousia. The final stage of creation will be the complete subjection of creation to the pneuma (the spirit), in which the perfection and integrity of nature will be made manifest.

The peculiar "even now—not yet" tension that dominates in the eschatology of the New Testament is expressed thus by Père Congar:

> Christianity is inconceivable without reference to the final realities, the eschatological consummation, and on the other hand that these eschatological realities are not only things which chronologically will come at the end, they are also present throughout the time of the Church and give this time its insistence that we are living in the last days: but this must not be interpreted apocalyptically as the imminence in time of the end of this world, but in the sense that in a way we are already under that definitive dispensation after which there will be no other, for it is the rule of the Son of God Himself. The final realities are in a sense present and active among us here and now. This is because of Christ and the economy of the messianic work.[54]

Between the Ascension and the parousia there is the time of the Church in which men are called to share in what Christ has done. The question of the meaning of history as Congar poses it is the meaning, then, of this "time between": Is it accidental or is it a positive value for the individual Christian? Man's contribution to the Kingdom of God is quite affirmatively stated in Congar's answer: "The Christian meaning of time as the time of the Church (and also, as we shall see, as the time and history of the world) is to be found in man's co-operation or 'doing' as bearing positively on the final result, the Kingdom of God." [55] In speaking of the eschatological-incarnational viewpoints current in the Church, Congar expresses his appreciation of the principles upon which each has erected its theological orientation, with his own reservations for each position. He seems to feel that the incarnationalists have the better of the argument in that they have seen clearly the *continuity* between the human work of this world and the Kingdom of God, a continuity he thinks the eschatologists have missed. In terms reminiscent of Thils' basic distinction, this sense of continuity is presented by Congar, with its serious consequences:

> In God's unitary design the Church and the world are both ordered to this Kingdom in the end, but by different ways and on different accounts. Church and world have the same end, but only the same *ultimate* end. That they should have the same end is due to God's unitary plan and to the fact that the whole cosmos is united with man in a shared destiny. That they should have only the same *ultimate* end prevents a confusion that would be bad for the Church, as raising a risk of dissolving her own proper mission in that of history, and bad for the world, as raising a risk of misunderstanding and hindering its own proper development. . . . Church and world (or "history," to borrow from Father Montuclard's suggestive vocabulary) have the same ultimate end, but they do not have the same immediate, and, therefore, specifying, end. They serve the same end by different means and on different planes, each keeping its own nature and its own constitution.[56]

Thus it would seem that for Congar the Church and the world, each on its own proper level, prepare for the perfection of the Kingdom of God. The Church as the body of Christ creates through the powers of Christ as priest (sanctifying), prophet (teaching), and king (jurisdictional authority). It is in view of these activities that "the Church indeed deserves the name of seed or germ-cell of the Kingdom." [57] So it is that Congar speaks of the Church as "metahistory" rather than history, for in it are actively present the Christian mysteries that are beyond time.[58] In contrast to the Church, the world (or human history) "strive[s] to attain wholeness and that state of reconciliation in which all the oppositions from which we suffer shall have been overcome; and that is to say that they [it] seek[s] the Kingdom, not so much on its spiritual and religious, as on its cosmic side. The meaning of history (which is the world's movement) and the meaning of culture (which is history's attainments) is the quest for this triumph of good over evil." [59]

This quest of human history is, however, doomed in itself and by its own efforts alone to failure, for the reconciliation of the Kingdom is fundamentally the work of God. The Kingdom, given by God, is, for all this, continuous with human effort and that to which this effort has tended. For Congar this relationship of the Church and history is one in which "a certain conciliation, even a *rapproche-*

ment, of the eschatological and evolutionist-incarnationist theses" is possible.[60]

Congar maintains his reservations about both incarnational and eschatological positions with especial precision concerning the practical demands or attitudes that either position would impose. The incarnational viewpoint seems entirely too optimistic: "They put forward service of God in and through the world's work in such a way that this work seems to be identified with that of the redemption and of the Kingdom of God. . . . But this is to forget that the Church is a different thing from the world, and that the world is not holy by itself but has to be hallowed and saved from without, by Jesus Christ." Eschatologists, on the other hand, seem too negative and dualistic: "Though the work of the world is not the last end, neither is it *solely a means;* subordinate to the absolute end, it partakes of the character of means, but also of *intermediate end,* having its *own* value in its order." [61]

The resolution of the seeming dilemma of incarnational and eschatological theologies of history starts for Congar from the first principle of the divine economy, namely, the divine Will. "We have to start from the Will of God, for it is that that sets the Christian apart from the world to make him a citizen of another city, and at the same time, does not withdraw him from the world but leaves him to work therein." [62] The concept of vocation as the Will of God for man is treated by Congar as the first result of this resolution of the incarnational-eschatological. From vocation he moves on to consider as a consequence the necessity of engagement in the world, and finally he examines the concept of the responsibility of man in the light of his vocation and engagement.

Père Congar finally places the paradox of both man's engagement in the world (incarnationalism) and his concomitant disengagement (eschatology) under the sign of the Cross of Jesus Christ: "The sign of the Cross also marks the Christian's efforts to 'christofinalise' the work of creation and bring about God's reign therein, and this, of course, less in the more technical and 'physical' aspects of temporal activity than in the more human and 'moral' aspects, those most concerned in the achievement of 'civilization.' " [63]

Akin to the initial insights of the Congar position, although not as elaborately detailed, is the work of Père Léopold Malevez. Malevez, like Congar, goes far toward reconciling the incarnational-eschatological differences. He denies the incarnational affirmation of the continuity between this world and the final fulfillment of the Kingdom of God by laying large emphasis upon the Kingdom as being essentially a *gratia*—a gift from God.[64] Having said this, Malevez admits that history becomes a problem for man; man seeks to understand history and the value of his work in the world. Having stated the problem, Malevez maintains that such knowledge of history or clear appreciation of value is impossible for a sinful world. The consciousness of history is in itself meaningful, for it shows that man is struggling for mastery of good over evil, of sight over ignorance. This state for which man is striving is the ultimate gift of God in His Kingdom. Once again, like Congar, Malevez sounds a fundamental note of discontinuity.

In the body of Christ, the Church, the gift of the Kingdom is present in its power—a presence now in time that is sacramental. It is because of the Church, then, that man's striving in history and his work have value. Membership in the Church is a real intrinsic possession, unlike the external relationship represented by the theology of Karl Barth. Malevez is acutely conscious of the difficulty such a view of history as Barth's imposes, and admits the necessity of demonstrating the unity of the orders of creation and redemption. Thus in his work on Bultmann he comments: "To be acceptable to the modern mind, the Christian message must show that it has an affinity with certain human hopes and longings. . . . The theologian and the preacher ought to be able to relate human concerns to Christian doctrine, and to show how its message challenges us, takes us to task, and helps us to understand ourselves." [65]

If Malevez, like Congar, goes far toward a central position by affirming the discontinuity of human achievement and the ultimate reign of the Kingdom of God, like Congar also he rejects an excessive eschatological disdain for the work of the world. The progress represented by man's science, culture, and civilization has a value in the Christian viewpoint, because in the Incarnation Christ reconciled the world to the Father. In a sense, then, for Malevez the mystery of history is the mystery of Christ, because the reality of the Incarnation history not only has value but is a mystery. The illustration that Malevez uses for his position is the image of the teacher who has set a problem for his students, a problem well beyond their capabilities. He does not do this with the expectation of receiving an answer to the problem but because it is good for the student to attempt a solution and because such an attempt at solution will approach the truth.[66] Against the eschatological extremism of withdrawal from the world Malevez invokes as the first and ordering principle for action "Seek first the Kingdom of God"; and against the incarnational extremism of excessively evaluating human activity he invokes and affirms the Cross of Jesus Christ.

THE ESCHATOLOGICAL THEOLOGIANS

In attempting to understand the incarnational theologians of history we have seen that the background from which they emerged was characterized by a revived sense of the Church. To grasp the historical phenomenon of the eschatological school of the Catholic theologies of history it is necessary to see them against a background of revival in biblical studies. No other single movement or event is more vital to the eschatological viewpoint than the past fifty years of biblical research and achievement. Primary among the results of this biblical study has been the isolation and appreciation of the eschatological element in the Scriptures, especially in the New Testament. In the light of what we now know it is inconceivable that one could comment upon the text and meaning of the New Testament without reference to its eschatological elements.

Pre-eminent among the eschatologists, and indeed the most vocal of them, has been the French Oratorian, Père Louis Bouyer. Formerly a Lutheran minister, profoundly affected by the work of Karl Barth, and a devoted student of Oscar Cullmann, Bouyer has taken an unswervingly eschatological position, basing himself firmly on the biblical revelation and a theology of the Word of God.[67] In his commentary on the Gospel of John, Bouyer says that the Johannine view of history is that this is a great mystery. He states:

> St. John's concept of history is only an application of a wider idea, that the material world is not brute chaos impenetrable by spirit, but rather it is the features of the spiritual world wherein close observation may find very deep and recondite truths. . . . Stated more generally, but also more profoundly, the course of human history reveals the action of God's hand accompanying and producing it. Matter, at one with spirit in its fall as in its salvation, discloses to us unsuspected insights into it, and the history of events taking place on the world-stage affords glimpses of the eternal designs.[68]

History, man's work, and the world are all intelligible only in the unity of the mind of God. But history does tell us about God, revealing His creative Word, especially in the person of Jesus. It is in Christ, through His humanity, that a man recovers the original divine image, so that the strictly historical and the meaningful are both essential elements in the Jesus of history. When John speaks of the Word made flesh he allows us to come to the Word sacramentally, through the symbols that are the sacraments. Thus the Johannine vision of the sacraments is one of encounter with the Lord. This sacramentalism of the Fourth Gospel sparks Bouyer's vision of history, giving meaning to our present stage of history: "To say, then, that the sacrament is a visible Word must mean that it is a mysterious event in which the Word touches us directly, not only to enlighten us but to act within us, to change our whole life by bringing to it the life of Christ himself." [69]

> The sacramental world is charateristic of the Faith, and of these "last times" of history in which we are to live, in that the sacramental world effects a paradoxical meeting point between this world of everyday life and the world to come, the world of the resurrection into which Christ has led the way. . . . How are we to conceive the relation between the world to come which is brought into contact with us here and now in the liturgy and in the sacramental order, and the world of everyday affairs? . . . It is to this world that we are to give witness of the divine *agape,* in order to snatch out of its power the children of God who are there enslaved and bring them to liberty. But this task can only be accomplished by means of our cross and theirs, borne patiently and even joyfully as being Christ's own Cross. And thus we shall come to the resurrection, where everything which we had to lose in order to follow Christ will be found once more in the new cosmos, the new order of things and of being, where He is King, having overcome Satan and thrust His power down to hell. [70]

Bouyer is constantly aware of the criticism that this sacramental-eschatological view of human history in the absolute terms of biblical finality apparently serves to weaken the commitment of the Christian in the world. "Every age, especially ours, has reproached Christians with: that the belief in eternal life is liable to weaken their interest in this life." [71] The incarnationalist reply that the Christian is a man who aims at both the salvation of his soul and those of others by bringing about the temporal salvation of humanity, is, according to Bouyer, "too facile to be convincing." These incarnationalist positions satisfy no one and ultimately avoid the problem by equivocation. He maintains:

> Christianity asserts quite unambiguously that neither the individual nor the collective salvation of humanity is possible either on earth or in any possible prolongation of the present state of affairs. Christianity is, as they say, eschatological. That is, it rests on a belief in the end of time. It asserts that human history must end in a catastrophe, that it will be interrupted by the supremely miraculous event, the return of Christ and the universal judgment and resurrection. After that, but only after that, the salvation of humanity will be possible.[72]

This does not mean, according to Bouyer, that the initial objection with which the Christian belief is faced must be admitted. "All objections of this sort fail to take into account the fact that eternal life is only promised to the Christian on condition that he makes a right use of this life." [73]

The eschatological aspect of New Testament Christianity emphasizes, in Bouyer's view, the urgency for the Christian to practice perfect charity. The love of God toward us in the Cross of Jesus Christ determines the life we live here and now. The incarnationalist tendency to by-pass what may be called the "law of the Cross" provokes Bouyer's telling indictment of the incarnationalist position as he sees it.

> Today we meet many people, and often they are in the ranks of the most zealous apostles, who live only for the conversion of the world to the Gospel, but who do not realize that the methods they are using to accomplish this purpose might much better be called an attempt to convert the Gospel to the world. Under the name of "incarnation," such people attempt in all good faith to incorporate all the ideals held by men today into the total ideal of Christianity. But such a Christianity becomes something quite different from the authentic Christianity of the "divinization" of man through the Cross. It becomes instead an unconscious but desperate struggle to avoid the Cross in an effort to "divinize" the world as it is. That is to say, it becomes in fact, under all sorts of Christian phraseology, a purely pagan apotheosis of the created things. . . . One would cease to believe at all in the Christian Mystery if one held that God in Christ is not the only author of man's salvation, but that man, even if he does not wholly accomplish that salvation himself, still contributes something toward it which has saving value of itself, apart from any root dependence on God's own work on the Cross.[74]

Bouyer is not alone among the biblical scholars of the Church presenting definite ideas drawn from sacred Scripture about the meaning of history. Two French scholars in an examination of the Church as the culmination of the Old Testament community have submitted a unique view.[75] For Villain and Baciocchi the Church now bears a distinct relationship to the covenanted community of Israel in the past, and to the coming end of the world. The finality of the Church as the New Testament community demands a universality so that the work of Christ may be accomplished in all nations until the end of time.

This same theme of the Church in history is stressed in the work of the distinguished Canon Lucien Cerfaux of Louvain.[76] The Old Testament people of God are realized in the New Testament Church, and therein it is in the preaching of the apostles that the mystery of the divine plan of salvation is revealed to men. The late Jesuit scripture scholar Joseph Bonsirven also traced the concept of the Kingdom of God in Scripture and its ultimate revelation in Christ.[77] His work stressed the universality, the dynamism, and the periodic "times" of the Kingdom and offered elements for a coherent view of history about the concepts of the Kingdom and the Church.

The work of the French Dominican Benoit Pruche recalls the strong insistence of Bouyer upon the dichotomy that exists between human history and achievement and the gift of eternal Kingdom of God in Christ.[78] The Marxist and existentialist postures of modern man, Pruche maintains, are postures of revolt against the Christian conception of history. Christianity is essentially awaiting the parousia, the open revelation of the Kingdom of Christ; it finds now no other absolute meaning intrinsic in history. History, Pruche says, is for man a mystery hidden in God. While man does, and indeed must, contribute to the development of the world and human history, nevertheless the world and history remain for him the mystery hidden in God.

A French Franciscan, Père Evode Beaucamp, finds in the Old Testament certain enduring elements for a biblical theology of history. History is created by the covenant, wherein God enters into a dialogue with His creatures and directs their destiny toward a specific goal. The revelation of God that we find in the Old Testament is in events, the God of the Bible becomes the Lord of history, so that nature is not seen as the prototype of history. "For life to possess meaning and direction, it is not sufficient for man to be aware of the existence of God, he must be made to feel that he has been taken in hand by God. With the sealing of the covenant mankind has been freed of the great fear of history." [79]

It is the covenant, according to Beaucamp, that determines the Old Testament view of the universe. "The idea of creation came late, however, in the evolution of biblical thought, and it was always treated by the inspired authors in the same context as the idea of the covenant: they present it to use merely as the starting-point of the divine plan of salvation." However, the Bible also presents the universe to us other than in a creation account, but also as in itself bearing witness to God: "For in the very organization of the universe can be found manifested the final triumph of the elect and the broad outline of their destiny." [80]

Thus the sense of history that we find in the Old Testament allows us to see this significance in our universe, a sacrament or a sign of God's concern for His elect. Man is to take possession of the world and to dominate it, and then only will it be truly restored to Him. "The earth, therefore, does not come between man and God; on the contrary, it unites them in a common enterprise of conquest and development." [81] Man's civilizations, his culture, his techniques and sciences, all have their place in God's plan for man's history:

> We may go further and say this: the world will not really belong to God until man has fully taken possession of it in his name; never, for example, was the land of Canaan considered to belong to Yahweh before its conquest by the Hebrews, and it is only with the gesture of God the Son handing over the vanquished cosmos to God the Father that the last page of history will have been written: "And when all things shall be subdued unto him, then the Son also himself shall be subject unto him that put all things under him, that God may be all in all" (Cor. 15:28).[82]

The German Jesuit Werner Bulst moves from salvation history (*Heilsgeschichte*) to a striking contrast with what may be termed secular history.[83] Human history distinguishes between revealed and natural theology, revealed and natural knowledge of God. That which originates in the creation is secular history; it affords essentially a knowledge about God that is impersonal and known by the inquiring mind. Salvation history, on the other hand, arises from God's involvement in time; it confers essentially a knowledge of God that is personal and is known by faith. Although Bulst's distinction of secular and sacred histories may be a useful tool, as all contrasts are useful, the reality of the distinction does not seem to be quite as certain as he insists. The creation is in itself, according to Scripture, part and parcel of the sacred history, and even the Christ event is presented in the New Testament as a new creation.

In his commentary on the Book of the Apocalypse, Père H. M. Feret presents a traditional biblical and eschatological viewpoint on history. In speaking of the general trend of sacred history he considers our present age as the last stage of human history, and although messianism culminates in Christ, the eschatological tradition continues by now being directed toward the consummation of time. The Book of the Apocalypse, Feret tells us, demonstrates by "the concrete realities of history" the present power over history by Jesus Christ.[84]

> We are now, therefore, in possession of the essential factors of the book of history: the irresistible conquests of truth, the great scourges and divine punishment that will overtake humanity, the prayer of the martyrs and saints crying for vengeance against the enemies of God, the cataclysmic catastrophies preceding the final judgment, and then the judgment itself—these are the things the revelation of Patmos invites us to recognize at work in history, while showing us through them that Christ, the overcomer, is completely in command. We also know what all this leads to, and the ultimate success that will justify this long period of waiting, so full of trials and sufferings. The adding up of the final total of the elect is the end to which this whole human cavalcade is moving.[85]

It is in John's Apocalypse that Feret finds a theology of history. "Its author prompted by the first great historical crisis the Church had to face, presents a veritable theology of history, even though he writes in the fashion of his time and in a literary idiom derived from his place of birth." The elements of this theology of history are for Feret basically three. First: Messianism is completed in Jesus the Christ, the only Messiah. Second: Christ and truth are identified in time and history, where the truth of the Gospel prolongs the revelation of Christ. Third: In the victory of Christ is the certainty of victory for the Christian: he cannot possibly fail to triumph in the end. The desire this engenders in the individual for the consummation of the Kingdom is not one that disengages from the world, but rather compels complete engagements. "It is a desire that compels action, that is to say, testimony. Every Christian has the mission to participate in the secular witness by which the whole church, symbolised by the Bride, ardently desires the glorious return of the Lamb and hastens that return by that very desire. 'Yes, I come quickly' answers the Son of Man who reveals these things to John." [86]

In what he calls a "meditation on the philosophy of history" the distinguished German scholar Josef Pieper also works within the eschatological framework of the Apocalypse. Regarding history from its end, or term, described in the revelation of Saint John, Pieper maintains that from this point of view "an inner affinity in principle of an especial kind may, therefore, be said to exist between the philosophy and theology of history." The end of history as presented in revelation is, according to Pieper a "transposition" of the temporal into the untemporal, and it "can be conceived only as effected by a direct intervention of the Creator." The acceptance of this revelation, however, produces a hope "that renders the believer able and willing to act here and now, within history, indeed even to see in the midst of the catastrophe itself a possibility of meaningful action within history." [87] The Christian in the fact of history, according to Pieper, must continually forge a meaningful theology of history in every age:

> Therefore, despite the fact that the Christian's attitude to history includes preparation for a catastrophic end within history, it nevertheless contains as an inalienable element the affirmation of created reality. To create a vital link between these seemingly irreconcilables is a task that challenges the courage of the most valiant hearts, precisely in times when the temptation to despair is strong.[88]

In the writings of the very learned and eloquent confrere of Pieper, Father Romano Guardini, there is also a deep concern for and preoccupation with history. In fact, in his works are to be found what could be termed an apocalyptic vision of human history that not only complements Pieper's thought but stands by itself. Guardini was formerly professor of the philosophy of religion at the University of Munich and has long been a mainstay of Catholic cultural life in Europe. In a brief essay entitled "The Nature of History," [89] Guardini maintains that although history is in effect impenetrable, nevertheless its purport is to make God known. The bafflement that one faces in history is related to the mystery of human freedom, which he calls "the determining factor for the nature of history." In history God "in the immediately perceptible sense, is powerless, for the reason that He willed a free humanity, and respects its freedom." [90] In history there is a relation between freedom and the end:

> On earth, in time, things are obscure in regard to their true nature because of the inadequacy of contingent beings to express their meaning; in regard to one another because each thing can exist separately only by being held distinct from every other thing; in regard to the whole because, by this very separateness, things are fragmentary, obdurate, resistant, and tend to fall apart. Not even in things does God's sovereignty seem to be perfectly fulfilled. But creation is not yet finished, it is in its first, its earthly, temporal stage, one which, for men, is designed for free, decisive choice, for history and its proving. But when man has passed through death, judgment, and purifying suffering and has entered into the second freedom, which is openness to truth, then things, too, having passed through the end of the world and destruction, will enter into their second stage. They will become the "new heaven" and the "new earth." [91]

The meaning of history, then, for Guardini is to be found only in its end—the final act of God, judgment:

> These facts, then, mark the character of history that it is obscure, that men are freed to do wrong, and that evil may at times prevail over good. History cannot, therefore, be its own fulfillment. It points beyond itself. Man's most intimate desire, whether he acknowledges it or not, is that finally light should be thrown on so much obscurity and ambiguity, that the possibility of evil should be canceled out in true freedom, that the good may become the rule of reality, that evil may at last be exposed for the nothingness and void that it is. In short, man must desire the Judgment. [92]

Guardini, in his insistence on the factor of human freedom, is not playing down the traditional place of grace, or of providence, or of Christ in the meaning of history. [93] His time and thought have been spent most fruitfully on a specific reflection, that of our present age of history. Here it is that the apocalyptic nature of his thought is clearly expressed. In speaking of man's present stage of history Guardini presents us with a terrifying analysis of our times in which he discerns the hallmarks that pertain to the essence of the end. The ages of Western man share the continuum of history: they are continual with one another. In the future, however, man will be cut off from his past, and he will stand alone in the universe for the first time. Although the age of Christianity overturned the Greco-Roman world it yet preserved a continuity in its usage of the

Ptolemaic system; in turn, when modern man rejected the Christian revelation he secularized Christian values in his concept of nature (absorbing the world into himself), personality (making himself the lord of his being), and culture (making existence his own creation). In this process the continuum of history is maintained, but now, as Guardini sees it in the title of his frightening little book, comes *The End of the Modern World.*

> My hypothesis has nothing in common, however, with that cheap disposition which revels always in prophesying collapse or destruction. It has nothing in common with that desire which would surrender the valid achievements of modern man. Nor is my hypothesis linked with a longing for a romantically envisioned Middle Ages or with an advance into a glorified utopia of the future. But this hypothesis has its crucial importance; it will enable us both to understand and to master the meanings implicit to the new world that is upon us.[94]

Why is the old order passing, and a new being born? Why do we now stand at what seems to be the end? Nature has been destroyed by man, it has become alien and dangerous, and "this shifting relationship manifests itself even as it leaves itself undefined in the striking complex of knowledge, theory, skill and mode of production summed up in the term 'technics,' that is in technology." The sense of personality is being lost in the emergence of mass man, "fashioned according to the law of standardization, a law dictated by the functional nature of the machine."[95] Culture is giving way to power, and in this power of man over things one single factor stamps the new culture—danger.

Not all, however, in this end of the modern world as we know it is for evil; there are grounds for hope. Although the older order, revolving about the concept of nature, has been destroyed, there is a new religious emotion that "wells up from a sense of the profound loneliness which man knows in the midst of all that is now summed up by the term 'the world'; man's emotion grows out of the realization that he approaches his ultimate decision, that he must face it with responsibility, with resolution and with bravery."[96]

Even technology bears a positive meaning:

> It is found without doubt in the value achieved by man as he shoulders the work of dominating his world. That work will make such tremendous demands of man that he could never achieve it by individual initiative or even by the united effort of men bred to an individualistic way. The

work of dominating the world calls for a union of skills and a unity of achievement that can only grow from quite a different attitude.[97]

These terms are reminiscent of Teilhard de Chardin's vision of man's progress and unity; and what Teilhard de Chardin saw as the emerging progress and unity of the race, Guardini terms "comradeship." "If this comradeship is accepted in accord with the true meaning of 'Person,' it will be the supreme human value to come from the mass, even under the changing conditions brought by the mass, comradeship could help to regain the values of the 'Person': benevolence, understanding and justice." [98]

As for power, that will depend upon how it is used. "Close examination proves that recent years have been marked by a monstrous growth in man's power over being, over things and over man, but the grave responsibility, the clear consciousness, the strong character needed for exercising this power will have not kept pace with its growth at all." [99] Thus it is that the challenge facing modern man is the development of an ethic of power:

> In the coming epoch, the essential problem will no longer be that of increasing power—though power will continue to increase at an ever swifter tempo—but of curbing it. The core of the new epoch's intellectual task will be to integrate power into life in such a way that man can employ without forfeiting his humanity. For he will have only two choices: to match the greatness of his power with the strength of his humanity, or to surrender his humanity to power or perish. The very fact that we can define these alternatives without seeming utopian or moralistic—because by so doing we but voice something of which the public is more or less aware—is a further indication that the new epoch is overtaking the old.[100]

As we witness the end of the modern world and the emergence of a new world we do so precisely in consequence of man's mastery over nature. Guardini offers cause to hope, not in the order of reason or a benevolent principle of nature, but in God. And from God's Will, it is to man, and to man's free decision that history belongs: "If we speak here of the nearness of the End, we do not mean nearness in the sense of time, but nearness as it pertains to the essence of the End, for in essence man's existence is now nearing an absolute decision. Each and every consequence of that decision bears within it the greatest potentiality and the most extreme danger." [101] And in another book he says: "If anything further on the subject

of history can be said, then certainly not that during its course mankind grows better or worse, but that the object of the decision forced
upon it is revealed with increasing clarity; that the option itself
becomes increasingly inescapable, the forces flung into the battle
ever weightier, the Yes! or No! increasingly fundamental." [102]

The apocalyptic nature of Guardini's vision of history and of our
time does not find a ready acceptance among many; [103] his thesis
remains a thesis and a point of view. But what Guardini does offer
the theologian who examines the problem of history is a renewed
and vital sense of faith over and against history. As Frederick D.
Wilhelmsen has commented of Guardini in an introduction to *The
End of the Modern World:* "He offers us faith, neither in man nor
in history, but in God alone and in His Providence." [104]

The Apocalypse has not, however, been the only viewpoint from
which eschatologists have framed the theology of history. In one
of the most remarkable products of contemporary biblical theology,
Père F. X. Durwell's study of the resurrection of Christ, the theological problem of history is presented in terms of the paschal mystery. At our present moment of history, Durwell writes, "the Church
moves ever deeper into the splendour of Easter, looking forward
to the perfection of that splendor in the parousia; it is as though
Easter is for her only the morning, and the day is yet to come." He
affirms that the Cross and resurrection of Jesus form the eschatological moment, cosmic in its dimensions: "They stand for the end of
this world and the beginning of the resurrection of the
dead." [105]

But the resurrection is not to be separated from the parousia,
nor, despite their chronological separation, are they to be envisioned
as intrinsically separate or historically unrelated.

> Thus, from the moment of his glorification, Christ's parousia has been
> in the world. It overtakes different men at different times, some soon,
> some in the distant future; in the course of history it becomes multi-
> plied, but in itself and in the mind of Christ, it is a single reality and
> already present. . . . Christ's resurrection and the manifestations of
> His glory, together with his final coming, form a single mystery of the
> parousia, revealed gradually in the course of history. Time, which for us
> flows continuously between Christ's resurrection and the parousia, is as
> it were contracted in Christ's exaltation; for us on earth it shows one by
> one the effects of the parousia of Christ which will eventually be re-
> vealed as a whole.[106]

Durwell stoutly maintains that in the light of the New Testament event of Jesus Christ, history and the mystery it bespeaks must be stated in eschatological terms:

> Despite often considerable differences in their points of view, the sacred writers agree in seeing Easter as the eschatological event that brings history to a close. They know, however, that time still flows on; they realize that they are caught up in history and they look forward to its end. A theologian who wants to reconcile these contrary ideas would say that God's action in the parousia is the same as that action of raising which has been wholly accomplished in the man Christ Jesus, and which will one day be brought to bear upon the entire world.[107]

The point of the Book of the Apocalypse is, according to Durwell, that the Resurrection is wholly turned toward the parousia, that the final resurrection is realized in Christ's, and that history is the gradual realization of Christ's resurrection until its manifestation in the parousia. "The Church is the *pleroma* of Christ in the receptive sense of the word, for she contains his fullness; similarly, history is the *pleroma* of Christ's victory, a victory whole and complete in Christ himself, but which must be accomplished step by step in the world." [108]

For Durwell, to state the theology of history in the terms of the Church and our present era is to say that the Church is "detained" in the kingdom of this world: the Church exists in time and eternity, leading her heavenly existence in mystery and her visible earthly existence in history. In both senses is she related to the Resurrection: "Whereas in his individual body, Christ is beyond the reach of sense, in his mystical body he remains in space and time. The fact of being engaged in history is an imperfection for God's people; it indicates an incomplete evolution of their resurrection in Christ." [109]

Finally, it would be a mistake to present Durwell's Resurrection-centered theology as one in which the identity of the Easter event and parousia in the one mystery blurs our vision of the work of the Church in the present time:

> However, although for Christ personally the parousia and the Resurrection are one thing, there is a difference for the Church; for her Easter is a vast potentiality and the parousia a full realization. Time can add nothing to Christ, but it enriches the Church with all the treasures of her Saviour. When Christ is considered in his identification with the Church, then even for him the parousia is a different thing from the

Resurrection. In Christ's individual humanity the mystery of the parousia is complete. . . . But to Christ, as identified with the Church, all things are not yet subject (1 Cor. 15:24; Heb. 2:8), the material world is not reconciled (Rom. 8:19–20), the resurrection of the dead is only beginning. Thus Christ's resurrection has not yet achieved its full significance throughout the world, for it is in bodily man that the powers are or are not vanquished, and the material world is or is not crucified and saved. . . . In short, the parousia, both actual and final, adds nothing to God's action in raising Christ; but it bestows on the Church the blessings of that raising action, and in the Church, it manifests the risen Christ to the world—for it is through the Church that the risen Christ is in the world. History enriches Christ, not in himself, but by bringing about the realization of him in the Church.[110]

The work of the German theologian Hans Urs von Balthasar toward articulating a theology of history is not unrelated to that of Père Durwell. Balthasar states that the Incarnation of the Word of God has made all history "sacral," and that the Church as the extension of the Christ makes by its very presence a single total history of man—not two histories (the one sacred, the other secular). The distinction between eschatological and incarnational is a false setting for the theology of history, for if Christ is the norm of history, both positions must be chosen; the eschatological determines the keeping of "distance" from the world, and the incarnational determines the choice of a position in the world under Christ, the norm of history. "In Jesus Christ, the Logos is no longer the realm of ideas, values and laws which governs and gives meaning to history, but is Himself history. . . . The historical life of the Logos—to which His death, Resurrection and Ascension belong—is, as such, that very world of ideas which, directly or reductively, gives the norm for all history; yet not as coming forth from some non-historical height above, but from the living center of history itself."[111]

For Balthasar the meaning of the Incarnation is to do the will of the Father, so that the basis for the time of the Son is His receptivity to God's will. The Christian virtues of faith, hope, and charity are, then, the powers by which He brings the eternal into time. "Only thus can we perceive the inward meaning of the following of Christ, as an imparting of that spiritual life, the life to which all of our Lord's discourses, from the Beatitudes onwards, invite us."[112]

Human history in the deepest sense is an opening within the freedom of God, and "within this space man is free to make history happen. But since this space belongs to Christ, it is in no sense an empty space but one that is shaped and structured and completely conditioned by certain categories. The framework of its meaning is constructed of the situations (the interior situations) of Christ's earthly existence." Grace, then, is that which places us in the Christological situation; it "is inwardly historical and shapes history: not because it is a sort of Something above history which man can draw into his history or not, as seems good to him, but because it bears within itself the measure and meaning of history as foreseen in every moment." [113]

In the work of the Holy Spirit, Balthasar points out, the individual existence of Christ is universalized, so that He is constituted as the norm for every individual in history. Precisely here Balthasar chooses the New Testament account of Christ's risen life, the forty days after Easter, as illustrative of Christ as the norm of history:

> Since it is not possible that the mode of time belonging to the risen Christ should have altered with his Ascension (this being rather in the nature of a signing-off gesture, purely for our benefit), it is necessary to grasp that the mode of time revealed during the forty days remains the foundation for every other mode of his presence in time, in the Church, and in the world. . . . Yet the time of these forty days is not a self-contained time (such as the time of Paradise or the time after the Judgment), for it exists to serve as a bond between his earthly life and the time of the Church. . . . By interpreting history in both senses, from fulfillment to promise and from promise to fulfillment, he performs, here within history, an act which involves both the end of history and its totality: for us the end of history, the *eschaton,* he is present at its center, revealing in this one particular *kairos,* this historical moment, in which he is present both to prove that he himself is alive and to be the self-utterance of the Kingdom.[114]

In the development of his theology of history Balthasar reechoes the central Christian proposition of Congar and Malevez, that God's work in Christ is absolutely gratuitous. In commenting upon the parable of the Kingdom in Matthew 21, he states: "The action of the feast, the miracle in the midst of it, depends simply and solely on the appearance and royal character of the King." There are not two histories, secular and sacred, but one, and the

Incarnation is not only the goal of the history of Israel, but Israel itself in its historical experience stands as the "guarantee of the ultimate indivisibility of sacred and secular history." [115] The realization of the inauguration of the eschaton in Christ is the realization that "no upward advance can ever even draw near to that, let alone catch up to it and pass it." [116]

Among the foremost theologians now writing in the theology of history is the French patristic scholar Jean Daniélou. Biblical and eschatological in his presentation, Daniélou relies heavily upon the thinking and the expression of the Fathers. Central to the method of his approach is his appreciation of typology, an exegesis of biblical texts in which events are seen as foreshadowing events. "That the realities of the Old Testament are figures of the New is one of the principles of Biblical theology. This science of the similitudes between the two testaments is called Typology." [117] And typology, he maintains, has a historical dimension: "Typology, being historical in character, is a new thing, depending on the occurrence, at given moments of time, of particular divine events in the historical process of redemption." Finally, typology, and the exegesis it represents, is essentially eschatological: ". . . not a sense of Scripture but a sense of history. It begins in the Old Testament, where episodes in the past of Israel are presented as a figure of what shall come to pass in the end of time. It is thus originally and essentially eschatological." [118]

For Daniélou, Christ is the decisive moment of human history. Beyond Christ there can be no further development for the world. Once again, in Daniélou, we find the absolutist affirmation of the echatological position:

> Granted that the Person of Christ is the point of intersection of the two Old Testament themes, there is a further stake to make good, namely to grasp that this is not simply a point among others, a term of reference for a continuous line, but an absolute termination, in the sense that there can be nothing beyond: the possibilities of development are exhausted. Here we face a characteristic paradox of Christianity. Although the time process continues, and the last day, or chronological end of the world, is in the future, yet the ultimate reality is already present, in the Person of the Incarnate Word; there is not, because there cannot be, anything beyond this.[119]

The incarnational position as it is represented by the Teilhardists, the disciples of Teilhard de Chardin, is therefore as reprehensible to Danièlou as to Père Bouyer. And even the possibilities for development held out in the theology of Thils are summarily dismissed in view of the eschatological nature of the Christ event.

> Christ's resurrection being the decisive event in all history, nothing that will ever happen will equal it in importance. This disposes at once of all the errors of evolutionism. No progress now can ever bring about for us what we have already got in Christ; that which is beyond all progress is here and now in Him; the last state exists already in the Christian mysteries. Consequently no identification is permissible between the Christian hope and a belief in progress: they are radically different things.[120]

It should not be imagined that Danièlou's vision of history is not realistic, or that time after Christ is meaningless, "but that time which follows Him is in some sense interior to Him and is constituted by the extension of His dimensions, until the Church, which is his body, has attained its fullness." This last period of history in which we live is one in which we "observe the full deployment of the historical process in the Church, the Sacraments being the decisive events of this period." [121]

Karl Rahner, S.J.: Implications for a Theology of History

Any attempt to work out a theology of history, or even to take some faltering steps toward a statement of such a theology, requires the affirmation of the essential elements in both the incarnational and the eschatological positions. Such a theology will attempt to maintain the bipolar tension of both schools in commenting upon what is essentially a mystery. It would seem that there is an area in which the theology of history can be stated, and to which we will turn in the last part—explicating the mystery of history and its meaning in Christ in a theology of the Word of God. It is within the expression of such a theology that the tension required by the simultaneous affirmation of the incarnational and eschatological insights can be maintained.

In such an attempt an enormous amount of preparatory work has already been done in the metaphysical system of the eminent German theologian Karl Rahner.[122] Rahner's work seems to provide necessary theological background for a theology of the Word, and within his work are to be found many elements that provide profound implications for any attempt to formulate a theology of history.

Few theologians witness in their own lifetimes the importance and influence of their thought upon their contemporaries as has Karl Rahner. A student of Heidegger at Freiburg, Rahner frequently reflects the stance and vocabulary of the existentialist within the Thomistic tradition of the school of Marechal. His first works in philosophy (*Geist in Welt* and *Hörer des Wortes*) have been succeeded by his frequent and influential theological writings. He formerly held the chair of dogmatic theology at the University of Innsbruck and is now at Munich; he edits the *Lexicon für Theologie und Kirche,* and is a *peritus,* over the objections of more traditional scholars, at the Vatican council.

It is characteristic of Rahner's thinking that he begins with the consciousness of man in seeking the meaning of being, of his being a spirit in the world who in his intellectual apprehension grasps the Infinite Absolute "as the real term of its a-priori drive to self-perfection through intentional assimilation of realities other than itself." The interpersonal relations of man and God follow upon this: "Man's will is free because, as an appetite specified by his intellect, it is in its turn a drive toward the infinite Absolute; and so none of the finite participants of God's reality which are the objective terms of its desire can satiate it. God then appears once more as the 'horizon,' the transcendental condition of possibility, of the free acts in which the human spirit, precisely as free person, tends to self-fulfillment." [123]

In this view of man and the nature of human personality there is a demand for communication, so that "the necessity of society, language, and culture has as its ground, therefore, the essential structure which determines the nature of an incarnate person's self-perfection through conscious activity." The extrinsic dependence upon matter demanded by the personality's knowledge and acts of will makes these acts of knowledge and will share the successive character of events, and at the same time "the intrinsic independence of matter enjoyed by the self-determining spirit gives to his [man's] choices their character of personal uniqueness and unpredictability. Man is not only a temporal and social being; he is essentially historical." [124] The relevance of Rahner's concept of personality to theology, and particularly to a theology of God's Word, is indicated by Father McCool:

> If, then God should determine to communicate His personal revelation to man, He would be compelled to do so by means of some sensible symbol, a "word," a spatiotemporal perceptible event, which will carry God's message to man. If there is to be a revelation, it must be a unique, historical event. Thus philosophy brings man to the threshold of theology. For if man, by his essential structure, is potentially a "hearer of the word" of God, it is his duty to study his history attentively to see whether in fact God has spoken such a word.[125]

Against this philosophical background Rahner elaborates two problems in theology that are basic to his thought—the concept of theology itself and the relationship of the natural order to the supernatural. Rahner believes that Catholic theology has always implicitly accepted the inadequate distinction between theology as the study of God (theological theology) and as the study of man in relation to God (theological anthropology). The inadequacy of the distinction arises from the fact of the Incarnation, and consequently all theology is in a sense anthropology, and theology finds its content in the revelation of the Incarnate Word.

The Incarnation, Rahner maintains, destroys once and for all those endless conflicts provoked by later scholasticism's abstractions and reflections upon pure nature.[126] Basic to theology is, however, the question of the relationship of natural and supernatural. Rahner's rejection of the manualistic approach and his own approach to the problem of the natural and supernatural is basic to his theological thought. In his rejection Rahner states that "if man, just so far as he experiences himself existentially by himself, is really nothing but pure nature, he is always in danger of understanding himself merely as a nature and of behaving accordingly. And then he will find God's call to him out of this human plane merely a disturbance, which is trying to force something upon him . . . for which he is not made." [127] Thus Rahner's point is that man, the world, and history are dependent for precisely what they are upon God. "If God gives creation and man above all a supernatural end and this end is first 'in intentions,' then man (and the world) *is* by that very fact always and everywhere inwardly other in structure than he would be if he did not have this end, and hence other as well before he has reached this end partially (the grace which justifies) or wholly (the beatific vision)." [128]

This, then, is the starting point in any attempt to speak of the concrete quiddity of man. Man, in traditional scholasticism, has an "obediential potency" toward God as the place of connection between nature and supernature; for Rahner this "obediential potency" connotes more than a simple openness to the supernatural. Man possesses, in Rahner's terms, an *übernaturliches Existentiel* (supernatural existential), which is a bent or direction toward the supernatural and exists in man's concrete nature. This supernatural existential is as unmerited and unexacted as grace itself and corresponds to God's gracious Will. "This central, abiding existential, consisting in the ordination to the threefold God of grace and eternal life, is itself to be characterized as unexacted, as 'supernatural.' " [129] Thus in the thorniest of contemporary theological problems, bordering upon a theology of history, Rahner preserves not only the existential insight of modern thought but the gratuity of the supernatural order. As Father McCool comments:

> In the dynamism of historical human nature, even though it be deprived of grace, there is always a longing for God which has its metaphysical ground in the supernatural existential. Experience presents the philosopher with a drive which is supernatural; only a theological anthropology, with its more accurate awareness of the limits of human nature, can recognize that drive as supernatural. [130]

In the first volume of his *Schriften zur Theologie* Rahner offers a masterful projected scheme for an entire treatise of dogmatic theology based upon his metaphysics. [131] There, under the Church, he presents an outline for the "historical theology of the Church," in which he provides for a formal and material theology of history. Under the formal elements are the possibility of a theological periodization of Church history, the historical forces within the Church, the eschatological element, and the growth and development of the Church. Under the material elements he lists the Church of the Old Covenant, the Church of the Gentiles, the Church of the Roman Empire, the world Church, the Church of the last days, and the "Church" of eternity. It is unfortunate that Rahner's thinking on this question has not developed further than the sketch he provides. Within his system, however, he does provide us with his sense of history as the arena in which his theology of the Word is developed. "God's revealing word is directed through the medium of the historical process at the total history of humanity." [132]

Rahner, with co-author Herbert Vorgrimler, sketches his view of a theology of history under the title "Geschichtstheologie" in the *Kleines Theologisches Wörterbuch.* There he lists the beginning and end of history as data from revelation, nevertheless maintaining their character as events. The whole of history is subject to God's free disposition, and its unity or "economy" is revealed in the progress of history. God enters the world in Jesus Christ, and the concept of a salvation history as distinct from profane history can only be made in faith by one who has heard God's Word in Christ. Man is called to be a free partner in this plan, so that revelation and covenant become essential factors in a theology of history. From what God does and from man's answer to it arise in a real historical fashion ever new ages of salvation history, and the theology of these periods of God's plan of salvation is the proper task of any systematic theology of history that will serve as the basis of a truly theological Church history and a genuine pastoral theology.[133]

Nor does Rahner slight the eschatological nature of God's Word incarnate in Christ:

> To start with, Revelation is not the communication of a definite number of propositions, a numerical sum, to which additions may conceivably be made at will or which can suddenly and arbitrarily be limited, but an historical dialogue between God and man in which something *happens,* and in which the communication is related to the continuous "happening" and enterprise of God. This dialogue moves to a quite definite term, in which first the *"happening"* and *consequently* the communication comes to its never-to-be-surpassed climax and so to its conclusion. Revelation is a saving happening, and only then and in relation to this a communication of "truths." This continuous happening of saving history has now reached its never to be surpassed climax in Jesus Christ: God himself has definitely given himself to the world. . . . *Now* there is nothing more to come: no new age, no other aion, no fresh plan of salvation, but only the unveiling of what is already "here" as God's presence at the end of a human time stretched out to breaking-point: the last and eternally the latest, newest day. It is because the definitive Reality which resolves history proper is already here that Revelation is "closed." Closed, because open to the concealed presence of divine plenitude in Christ.[134]

There is, for Rahner, in God's plan one central, definitive and saving act, which is "precisely for that reason different from all the others," and this is the "single utter unity of Incarnation, Cross and Resurrection." [135] The divine plan, and this central decisive moment of the divine plan, are necessary to view or understand the inner connection of God's historical activity in the world; furthermore, any given act in this saving history can only become meaningful or understandable from the viewpoint that allows one to see it as an element of the whole.

From this viewpoint history cannot be regarded as the unraveling of the divine plan in that sense of predestination that destroys real human freedom. Rather God's "Word and Act are free in the further sense that they are freely directed to men already in existence, and so are essentially Event and History, not Thing, metaphysical Idea or Norm." Thus human history is *not* the result of some unchanging predetermined norm, "but the free, incalculable ever new Event of God's activity." Over and against this we must see that "God's freedom has determined from the very beginning a goal for the world and for men which is in fact infallibly pursued and attained in the history of the world." [136] Here Rahner returns, as all Christians must, for a reconciliation, not an explanation, in the mystery of God: "God's plan of salvation has rather been an absolute secret of His, concealed from all other earlier ages and generations, and which only now, in the last times, becomes objectively real and thereby makes itself known." What is still to come, in its concrete form in history, remains under God's Lordship, and remains for us a mystery "only fully to be unveiled at the end of all the ages." [137]

It is in history that God confers upon man the power to make a genuine free response to His Word, "and so makes his own further Word dependent upon the way in which man does in fact freely answer." [138] Thus it is that throughout his theological synthesis Rahner strongly insists upon the freedom that characterizes human history and the deadly seriousness that it reflects:

History is not just a play in which God puts himself on the stage and creatures are merely what is performed; the creature is a real co-performer in this humano-divino drama of history. And so history has a real and absolute seriousness, an absolute decision, which is not to be relativized as far as the creature is concerned with the remark—at once true and false—that everything rises from God's will and nothing can resist it. The Scriptural basis for what has just been said lies in the simple and yet incomprehensible fact that in the Bible the Almighty, Absolute, the pantokrator (Apoc. 1:8), through His own personally expressed Word, calls upon his creature, the work of his hands, to do his will; and that accordingly this Word which calls upon someone else cannot be meaningless, although it proceeds from him who has the power to do all things.[139]

PART FOUR

TOWARD A THEOLOGY OF HISTORY

Introduction

IN CONSIDERING the problem that history poses for modern man, the theologian brings to any approach to solution the data of revelation. It is the theologian's job to reflect upon and to penetrate God's Word in the Church; theology itself is a way to understand God's revelation. The theologian does not merely gather data for a specific problem; he must organize it, make it the object of reflection, see it related to the other truths of the faith, and so come to a deeper grasp of what is believed. In specific problems, as, for example, the one of history, the data of revelation may not be addressed to the problem as such. Here the theologian's job becomes difficult, for his function will now embrace the framing of the proper questions to be put to the data and the organization of the data. Lacking a final solution, he must (at least) locate the problem in the divine economy and explicate the precise nature of mystery reflected by the problem.

The essential problem in the development of a theology of history is to apply theological principles and the biblical revelation precisely to the line of human history, and to examine the purely historical accomplishments of man against the revelation of God's Word. In a true sense any explanation of history lies under the judgment of God's Word.

It does not do simply to proclaim Christ as the Lord of history and to let it go at that. One cannot affirm an eschatological interpretation unless one is willing not only to explore the ranges of meaningfulness this implies but also to take cognizance of the real difficulties and objections such a viewpoint encounters. Nor, on the other hand, is the affirmation of an incarnational viewpoint, the stressing of the progressive or evolutionary trends of human history, always a meaningful treatment of the problem. The assertion that the Christ event divinizes human activity, or that the Kingdom of God is appreciably added to by human effort, must be aligned with and understood in the eschatological dimension of the New Testament.

But perhaps there remains another way. Perhaps there is a viewpoint, a way of looking at human history, that can properly stress the validity of man's efforts in the arena of time and, by the same token, affirm the essentially eschatological character of Christianity. It is our opinion that perhaps for too long a time the problem has been stated too strongly from one or another viewpoint alone, that a dichotomy has been forced upon the Christian, and that there exists another position from which to view human history, a position in which the valid insights of both eschatology and incarnationalism can be preserved.

Certain principles must, however, guide such a theology of history. Although Sacred Scripture does not treat the problem, nor even define it in the way that modern man poses it, yet God's Word provides for the Christian the necessary insights from which such a theology must be taken. The method to be followed here is aptly stated by Père Daniélou: "The use of scriptural principles for the resolution of questions to which these principles were not, in Scripture, explicitly applied." [1]

Oscar Cullmann treats the problem of history by a masterful dissection of time as presented in the New Testament. But must the theologian necessarily limit the discussion of this problem to the area in which Cullmann has placed it? Cullmann's work allows us to see the mind of the New Testament authors more clearly, but it does not prohibit the discussion from proceeding from *other* biblical principles that are also operative in this area. It would therefore seem to be a legitimate endeavor for the theologian to construct a viewpoint by abstracting his principles from Scripture, and then to arrange all the principles pertinent to the problem in another synthesis. Thus he is better able to deal with a problem not explicitly handled by the biblical writers. The end result may well be subject to the objection of being "unbiblical" in an organizational way, that is to say, in the pattern it adopts; but if biblical principles are totally utilized and explicitly adhered to, the total solution will in no way merit the pejorative adjective "unbiblical."

Chapter 7

THE WORD OF GOD AND HUMAN HISTORY

THROUGHOUT the Old and the New Testaments there is a developing theology of God's Word in which the place and the meaning of human history may be found. This theology becomes full blown in the Johannine prologue, wherein the eternal Word's pre-existence is directly related to the redemptive work of Christ, the center or "hinge" of human history. John, it may be presumed, was not ignorant of both the Greek and Hebraic notions of the Logos (Word), and in order to grasp the Johannine presentation it is necessary to see what John saw in this concept of Logos.

The Logos concept was very familiar in the ancient world. Among the Greeks, from Heraclitus through Plato, the Logos concept was always a process of rational abstraction, but was never hypostasized (identified as a personality). The Greek philosophical tradition did, however, influence the pre-Christian Hellenized Jews; this is evident in Philo's intermediate being. Rudolf Bultmann tentatively speaks of the Gnostic *Logos* as an intermediary being who is creator, revealer, and redeemer. "But Bultmann assumes too quickly that the pre-Christian Gnostic teaching was a fixed and completely apprehensible entity when he considered its *Logos* doctrine as the one and only source of the Johannine *Logos*." [2] At the time of the writing of the Gospel of John the *Logos* concept was extremely widespread in a large and divergent number of distinct traditions; and with John this concept was completely transfigured.

For the people of the Old Testament that which they understood by the term "Word of God" underwent considerable development.[3] The older cultures of the Near East, Israel's neighbors, conceived of the word of the gods as a being in itself, powerful, irresistible, and partaking of the qualities of the gods themselves. The Israelites, however, in speaking of God's Word attribute speech to Him only in an analagous manner. The term itself, "word," connotes a certain *power* and *permanence* in the events it effects: it externalizes an interior reality, and "if the will is strong enough, the reality which is posited by the word will infallibly come into being." [4] For the Israelite the Word was a dynamic reality because of the dynamism of the person who performs it. This dynamism is evident in the Hebrew for "word," *dabar,* which can mean not only "word" but "thing" or "deed." Thus it is evidently opposed to the Greek conception of "word" as opposed to "deed."

For the Prophets it is the Word of Yahweh that marks the prophetic experience: it is dynamic, real, received by the Prophet from Yahweh. "It is the conscious possession of the word which distinguishes the true prophet from the false." [5] For Isaiah (6:1 ff), Ezekiel (1:1 ff., 8), Amos (7:7-9; 8:1-3), and the other Prophets this Word of Yahweh renders the prophetic vision intelligible. In short, then, for the knowledge we have of the Word from the Prophets, "it is not enough to represent the biblical conception of the prophetic experience of the word as a simple hearing. It is the experience of a distinct and compelling reality." [6]

In addition to this prophetic conception of the Word as a dynamic reality, the Prophets make the *power* of this word abundantly clear. In a sense the Word is sacramental; it inevitably effects what it signifies. The Prophets do not exemplify so much that which we have frequently conceived of as verbal prediction and real fulfillment, but rather they are the spokesmen of God pronouncing the Word of Yahweh which itself accomplished its purposes by the power inherent in it. "So shall my Word be that goes forth from my mouth; it shall not return to me void, but shall do my will, achieving the end for which I sent it." [7]

The creative nature of this Word of God marks the development of Hebrew thought at the time of the Deutero-Isaiah. [8] At the time of the Deuteronomic reform (c. 621 B.C.) another addition is made to this developing notion of the Word of Yahweh: the notion of its identity with the Law. "Deuteronomy extends this conception of word to the entire law given in the book." [9]

The wisdom literature, influenced by Hellenism, provides for us specific examples of personification. [10] This pre-existent wisdom is identified with the Law (Torah) in late wisdom literature. [11] Still later not only the Torah but all of the sacred books were identified with God's Word. The dynamism of the developing Israelite conception of the Word passed to the collection of writings handed down to us as the Old Testament.

To summarize the developing Old Testament concept of God's Word: "word" as such is a reality possessing the power of its speaker; the Word of Yahweh bears the irresistible power of God Himself and therefore it is creative, eternal as He is eternal, and revelatory of the God who utters it. This Word of God to the world is, however, never considered as a definite historical earthly human being.

In the line of this Greek and Hebrew tradition, the New Testament Johannine conception cannot be regarded simply as Hellenization: the dependency John manifests is primarily on the Hebraic tradition, a tradition that does share, in later Judaism, a Greek influence. The Word of the Old Testament, the dynamic, real, eternal, creative and revealing Word is hypostatized by John: he identifies it as the personality of Jesus Christ. The developing Old Testament theology of the Word reaches the Johannine crescendo: "And the Word was made flesh." "Nothing more clearly shows the Hebraic and biblical character of Johannine thought than its insistence upon the incarnation of the Logos." [12] A radically new conception of God's Word enters with John's Gospel: its identification of the Word with a concrete event—Christ! It is in Jesus Christ that the Word of the Old Testament is fulfilled: a distinct being, creative, inevitably effectual, the revelation of God, and consequently the meeting place of God and man.

The reality of the eternal Word of God, as being in nature God Himself, is affirmed at the very opening of the Gospel of John. He, the Word, is distinct from God ("The Word was *with* God"); and He is a distinct person ("The only-begotten of the Father"), relatively opposed to the Father, God; and He is God ("And the Word was God"). The divine nature of the Word of God is incontestable because of the attribute of creation that is given to the Word ("All things were made by Him"), and finally, because the Word is constantly presented as the light, the source of life, the dispenser of truth.

It is not only in the Gospel of John that we find evidence of the pre-existence of Jesus and of His special relationship to the Father as Son; we find in St. Paul: "one Lord, Jesus Christ, through whom are all things . . .[13] " "He is the image of the invisible God, the first-

born of every creature. For in Him were created all things. . . . " [14]
Also, in the Epistle to the Hebrews: "God . . . last of all in these
days has spoken to us by His Son, whom He appointed heir of all
things, by whom also He made the world." [15]

The New Testament identification of Jesus as the Word of God
has still deeper implications. Jesus, the Word of God, is the revelation of God. The New Testament no longer means by the Word
of God just the individual instruction of the Old Testament *dabar
Yahweh,* but rather it is the proclamation of God's salvation, the
final and definitive revelation. To "hear" this Word in the New
Testament is to believe—to have faith.[16] Jesus *is* the Word of God.
"In the Gospel of John a direct line leads from the theologically
charged concept of the proclaimed word to the Logos who became
flesh in Jesus. This is indeed the meaning of the Gospel: it intends
to show that the total human life of Jesus is the centre of the revelation of divine truth." [17]

The Word of God, now identified as the person of Jesus Christ,
maintained those elements that marked the development of the
Word. The Word of God remains creative; its efficacy is now
obvious, for the Word is a divine person, God Himself. Creative,
the Word effects what it says; thus election, revelation, and regeneration are not verbal invitations extrinsic to a man, but constitute
what the New Testament calls "the new creation." When God's
Word is spoken to us in Christ we are re-created as His sons. Thus
in Christ we find the fulfillment of the *dabar Yahweh.* He is the
God-Who-Acts precisely as the Word of God.

Christ is the Wisdom (sophia), the Law (torah), and Word (logos)
of God; and the Johannine prologue makes quite evident that in the
incarnation of Jesus Christ the Word of God, "tabernacles," dwells
with us. This recalls the Old Testament Shekinah, the presence of
God in the ark and later in the temple. Christ identifies His body as
the place of the presence when He identifies it with the temple.[18]
Thus in encountering Christ the Word of God is spoken to man. The
encounter has not been reserved to the actual period of Christ's
physical presence but has been maintained in a new people for a
new and everlasting covenant—the Church. Christ, the Word of
God, is now physically present with the Father, but he maintains
in mystery and sacrament His presence to be encountered in the
people of the new creation. Consequently in the Church (an exist-

ing reality, a perduring state, a new creation, a permanent alliance) Christ is encountered and consequently God's Word is heard.

It is not strange that many Catholics should find this presentation of old concepts new, strange, different, for they are long used through education to the abstract, and sometimes philosophical presentation of the Christian message. The content of a theology of the Word of God is no different from the content of the great medieval synthesis that has been handed down to Catholics in catechisms and textbooks; but it is different in this, that it relies more on the biblical presentation, with its inherent dynamism, than upon the sometimes static presentation of the syllogism. The value of a theology of the Word of God is that it more closely approximates the actual historical events in which God reveals Himself.

From the events of the Old Testament, from the historical event par excellence, Jesus Christ, we have known the actions of God in time. Thus it is in history, not in abstraction, that God has been revealed to us. Our knowledge of God, His revelation of Himself, is not an abstract set of principles given to us but is first and foremost the actions of God in history. From what He does we have come to know the God-Who-Acts. From what He does we acquire knowledge of what He is like.

Using these events as a basis, the theologian can formulate the interplay of relations between God and man; he can affirm the Trinity of persons and the Unity of nature in God. For the theologian to speak of God is to speak of the Trinity and thus to speak of two terms: the unity of nature and the Trinity of persons. Neither the Unity nor Trinity precedes the other in any way, for it is no less correct to speak of the three persons in one God than to speak of one God in three persons. The Western intellectual tradition, which formulates the mystery by starting with the unity of God and proceeds in time to the Trinity, is not erroneous, but it is in a sense unfaithful to the New Testament; "hence it is a poor preparation for understanding fully the true Trinitarian dimensions of the view of the world proposed in the New Testament." [19]

Beginning with the biblical proclamations of God's mighty acts we can reason from the plurality of persons in the opposite direction and affirm the unity in divine nature. The advantage in this procedure is that it allows us to distinguish in the very beginning the God of the Bible—Father, Son, and Holy Spirit—from a too strictly abstract "rationalist" God. Closer to the "sources" of Christian faith, this way of thinking about God follows a more biblical attitude, more concerned about the relations of God with our world and our history. "In brief, the attitude is that of the historian rather than the philosopher." [20]

The dialectic of the divine economy, the mystery of God's saving Will, is essentially Trinitarian. Because the central link of the divine economy is the work of the Word-made-flesh, this fundamentally Trinitarian viewpoint from another point of emphasis can be called Christological. Saint Paul puts it thus: "Yet for us there is only one God, the Father from whom are all things, and we unto Him; and one Lord, Jesus Christ, through whom are all things, and we through Him." [21] The whole divine economy, then, as such, issues *from* the Father, and the Father is its term, or end. The one through whom God's plan is effected is the Son, the eternal Word. Wherein is the work of the Holy Spirit? He is intrinsically related to the whole divine economy; vis-à-vis the Word of God the Holy Spirit is the power that acts *in* and *through* the Word of God. God's design, effected through the Word, is accomplished *in* the Holy Spirit.

The awesome mystery of God's Trinity, known in God's action in time, is explicated by traditional Christian theology along these lines: the relationship of Father and Son is simultaneous, and it is eternal; it can never be properly perceived in any time sequence. The Word is God's eternal utterance of Himself, always Son to the Father in an eternal generation. Proceeding from Father and Son in a simultaneous eternal spiration is the love between them, the third person, the Holy Spirit. The Word of God, generated in the eternal act of cognition of the Father, has long been the object of theological reflection; while theologians have long debated the object of the divine act of cognition, all affirm the Word of God as His own Son, distinct from the Father, eternal and possessing the divine nature.

It cannot be too strongly emphasized or too often repeated that this knowledge we have of God in Himself was not confided to us as the abstract propositions that we have presented here, but that it is arrived at through the action of God in history. And history begins with His act—creation. History is determined in origin, meaning, and completion in the utterance of God's Word. A theology of the Word immediately relates the beginning of history (creation—mediated by the Word), redemption (effected by the Word incarnate), and the end of history (when the Word incarnate comes again).

It is in the light of a theology of God's Word, as we have sketched it here, that human history may be seen, so that both the insights of eschatology and incarnationalism are to be preserved and the problems of their relationship approached. Here we may develop the theme of universal history about what we have chosen to call the three utterances of the Word of God—three moments of progressive articulation of God's Word *ad extra*. These momentous utterances of God's Word may be called (1) the creative utterance (creation), (2) the eschatological utterance (the redemptive mystery of Christ), and finally, (3) the apocalyptic utterance (parousia).

The first and the third utterances of the Word of God, the creation and the parousia, serve as the border line of history—the beginning and the end. As we shall see, God's eternal Word is to be identified in each as the beginning and the end, the Alpha and Omega of the Book of the Apocalypse. The mid-period marked by the Word made flesh embraces (1) the preparation for Christ, (2) Jesus Christ—the center of history, and (3) the present period of the Church. These three stages of human history and development are called "salvation history" (*Heilsgeschichte*) and are characterized in all their stages by relationship to the eschatological utterance of the Word—Christ.

To each of these three utterances of the Word (creation-eschaton-parousia) we will now turn, and having developed lines of thinking along the paths indicated by a theology of God's Word, we shall return to the specific question of our own stage in human history and of the principles that will therefore govern our involvement both in the city of man and the City of God.

THE CREATIVE UTTERANCE OF GOD'S WORD

When we speak of the Word of God in creation it is necessary first of all to speak of the account of creation given in the Book of Genesis. This involves of necessity some critical background, although the limits of our subject do not allow a complete treatment.[22] The Book of Genesis is a work composed of three narrative sources, which are usually given letters to distinguish them. The first and oldest source, called the Yahwist (from the name given God throughout the source, Yahweh), is dated at about the tenth century B.C., and is sometimes designated as the J source (for the old form, Jahweh). The second, called the Elohist (also from the name given God in this source, Elohim), is dated at about the eighth century B.C., and is designated as the E source. The third is designated D and derives from the Deuteronomic reform at the time of Josiah, about the seventh century B.C. These three documents, J, E, and D, were all collated, edited, and added to after the exile by a priestly group (whose work is itself in certain parts pre-exilic), and are therefore designated as P. Sacred tradition, oral forms, the memory training of the ancient Near East all undergird these written elements of Genesis, so that the whole work as we possess it considerably reflects the most ancient traditions of Israel, back to Moses himself, as well as the theology and traditions of the Deuteronomic and postexilic eras. Even though the Catholic critic acknowledges this briefly sketched theory of the sources of the Book of Genesis (and the first six books of the Old Testament), he maintains the substantial Mosaic authorship of the first five books, the Pentateuch.

The Genesis account of creation (Gen. 1:1–2:4) is basically from the priestly source; while its traditions are old and it reflects a long history of oral and written sources, the date of the completed literary composition as we have it here would be postexilic. This should not be exaggerated, for the importance of the P source is that it reflects not only very old traditions but also a significant theological tradition.

> Here everything is written after reflection; nothing is without theological relevance, for in this work we have the essence of the theological labor of many generations of priests. . . . Even though it may really have received its final form only in the postexile period, still, along with later material and material that has been considerably revised theologically, it also preserves very ancient matter in almost unchanged archaic garb.[23]

Since the priestly document is basically concerned with the heart of Old Testament theology, namely, God's election of His people, the creation account must not be considered as the point of the document but rather as the priestly authors' linking of the events of salvation history back to the very beginning. Yahweh, who makes a covenant with Abraham and Moses in history, is the Creator of the world and the Lord of history.

> The biblical doctrine of creation is a derivative of history, the sacred history of the chosen people. The creation account in Genesis I is not only prologue to the history which follows it and thus to be read in relation to it, but it is also a development of the election-historical life, of the redemptive history which has the Exodus as its center. It is a product of the mature reflection of Israel upon the meaning of her history within the purpose and grace of God.[24]

Since we have seen that the account of creation is a priestly one, and therefore has been carefully drawn and deliberately reflects a long theological tradition, we can now find in this account a number of specific truths. While the account cannot be considered as giving an explicit statement that God's creative activity brought into existence that which had previously not existed, this concept (elaborated in later Jewish theology) is certainly implied in the account. The chronicle of the days of creation that it narrates reflects the cosmology and the scientific knowledge of the authors' time, but it also allows "the orderly presentation of individual fundamental elements of the Old Testament belief in creation." [25]

Significantly the creation of the world is presented as having occurred by the Word of God. This affirmation of the activity of God's Word rules out the possibility of the world being considered an emanation of God; it marks the radical distinction between the Creator and His creation. Finally, this creation of God's is therefore essentially good; evil, experienced by man, must have its origin elsewhere. The concluding verse of the creation account, "God saw that all he had made was very good," reaffirms this essential goodness of God's creation.[26] As a preview of what is to come, Von Rad has commented on the significance of creation by God's Word: "One must remember that this method of creation gives the world a susceptibility to God's word, which will have eschatological consequences." [27]

A number of truths may be drawn from this concept of God's creation. First: Creation is not necessary—the sovereign Lord is in no way constrained to create. God does not have to create from either an internal or external necessity. Thus creation, as God's free act, is marked by pure gratuity. So, for example, the sacred author refers to God as "resting" on the seventh day, thus implying His freedom.

Second: All of creation is essentially one in the viewpoint of God, for it—in all its admitted complexity—is *created,* and as created it stands over and against God the Creator. God, then, is the only absolute. God and every level of creation are on different levels of being. Thus God is transcendent to His creation, so that there is an eternal real, qualitative distinction between God and every level of creation.

Third: The action of creation extends as well to time, the measure of created being. Eternity is not that which exists before and will exist after time, rather it is the measure of God, and time coexists with it. Time, then, does not unfold: "In biblical metaphysics God creates gratuitiously. Time is the creation in process; eternity is the Creator's point of view." [28]

Fourth: History, in lieu of creation, has meaning because it has beginning and end. (Later revelation, especially in the New Testament, as Cullmann has shown, demonstrates that between the beginning and the end time has it own stages, or "times," called *kairoi* (see Matt. 26:18, John 3:1). Over and against the Genesis account, we find in the last book of the Bible that history makes its way to a final stage.[29] Creation, then, implies God's providence, His ruling and directive power over His creation, which proceeds according to His plan.[30]

Fifth: The doctrine of creation leads man to a new appreciation of the problem of evil. Evil is not caused by the innate limitations of created matter (for these are good, as the products of God's hand: "God saw that all he had made was very good" [31]). Evil can be understood only in terms of man's freedom (a freedom that God has graciously bestowed, even allowing man to sin against Him). In our own time this creation concept has served to refute the popular myth that it is through the progress of unfettered reason alone that evil can be overcome. History becomes the arena of cooperative action: that of the creative activity of God's Word and of free man. It is not an arena foreordained, but one in which freedom has its part under the provident rule of God.[32]

Sixth and last: In creation God enters into community with man. Again, freely and gratuitously God chooses to enter into this community, and this remains the radical cause of man's supremacy over creation recorded in Genesis. Of man's creation we are told that God said: "Let us make man in our image, after our likeness." [33] Man's likeness to God, His "image" of God, consists in this, that God has established with him a peculiar and personal relationship through His free election. The control over creation, of which man is capable through his intelligence, does not cause God's election but is consequent upon it. "God gives to man, with whom He has established this personal intercourse, a share of His own dominion over the world." [34]

The biblical account of Genesis is not the only one that gives prominence to the activity of the Word of God in creation. Throughout the Old Testament there is a constant tradition of the Lordship of God over His creation attested to in the affirmations of the creative activity of the Word. The songs of prayer and praise, the Psalms, repeat this tradition: "Let the whole earth hold the Lord in dread, let all the inhabitants of the world stand in awe of Him; He spoke and they were made . . ."; "let all these praise the Lord; it was His command that created them." [35] The wisdom literature and later traditions of the Old Testament have "personalized" wisdom and pictured it as present in creation. [36]

The New Testament throws more explicit light upon this conception of the creative Word of God. In the prologue of Saint John's Gospel the role of the eternal Word in creation is stated: "Everything was by Him; and without Him nothing was." God and His Word exist before anything comes to be: "Thou hast loved Me before the creation of the World." [37] The coming to be of that which exists outside of God is effected through the Word of God. The negation of the Johannine prologue—"and without Him nothing was"—indicates both a strong separation of the Word from all things that come to be and their coming into being in the Word. [38]

Saint Paul also, but in another metaphor, speaks of the creative activity of the Word in the beginning of that which comes to be. "He is the image of the invisible God, the firstborn of every creature. For in Him were created all things in the heavens and on the earth, things visible and things invisible, whether thrones, or Dominations or Principalities, or powers. All things have been created through and unto Him, and He is before all creatures, and in Him all things hold together." [39] Both in his Epistle to the Colossians and his First Epistle to the Corinthians Paul speaks of the Word of God in creation as the wisdom present at the moment of the creation. In the opening of the Epistle to the Hebrews we read of the Son, God's Word, "being the brightness of His glory and the image of His substance, and upholding all things by the word of His power." [40]

Theologians have long regarded the operation of creation as one in which all the persons of the Trinity are involved. Since it is an operation terminating outside the divine (*operatio ad extra*), it is produced by the divine nature, which is one, so that all the persons are involved. However, it does seem clear from Scripture that the Word, the second person of the Blessed Trinity, is involved in some special way in the operation of creation.

The precise relationship of the Word to creation as presented in the New Testament, particularly in St. John, is given by Père Boismard:

> It is, therefore, probable that for St. John also the Word of God plays a part in creation because it is the pronouncement of an idea, of a name, and not because it is endowed, as such, with effectiveness. All things have been created in and by the Word, in this sense that God proclaimed their "name," their essence, to enable them to come into existence. But by the very testimony of St. John, the Word existed in God long before the creation; its existence could not depend on the work of creation. We must then conclude, even though St. John does not say so, that the Word, since it is the expressing of a "name," is essentially the expression of that eternal Name, the divine essence: it is the Word which God conceives when He reflects upon Himself. [41]

Thus the Word contains within Himself an expression of God's plan for the world, and He breathes forth the Spirit of God, who causes the order of those things which come into being, so that it can be said that all things were created in and by the Word. The New Testament revelation leads us to see that the Word of God in creation, in the choosing of a people, is His own Son.

> The eternal Word that God speaks to the world is in reality His Son; and all the words that God has spoken since the world began are gathered up in the mystery of this single Word. In Him alone is the meaning and secret of creation revealed to us. The mystery of creation is a mystery springing from the depths of love. The creative will of God is a will motivated by love. It creates an object to love, and wishes to be loved in return. [42]

One of the most striking features about the activity of God's Word is that of revelation. The acts of God are always revelatory of Himself: His word always communicates to man knowledge about the Godhead. The utterance of God's Word in creation is also the speech of God to us, if we but have ears to hear it. In the initial act of creation God has revealed something of Himself, and because of His place in the creative process the Word is present in that creation.

Theologians have long referred to the knowledge of God that is arrived at through an observation and study of created things. This "natural" theology is spoken of by Paul: "For since the creation of the world his invisible attributes are clearly seen—His everlasting power also and divinity—being understood through the things that are made." God communicates to man in creation not only knowledge of Himself but also natural law: "When the Gentiles who have no law do by nature what the Law prescribes, these having no law are a law unto themselves. They show the work of the law written in their hearts." [43] Thus the Word of God fulfills in the beginning that which always marks His presence: communication with man, revealing to him God and laying upon him the response of action or ethic that is called law.

One of the more significant conclusions that consideration of the Word's presence in creation leads to is the a priori certainty that there can be no conflict between the truths of faith and science. Creation is known and explored by our human science, and although it may adequately explore and explain created events in lower orders of causality (for example, evolution), this does not affect the ultimate question of their being. Humanity and its accomplishments, including the sciences, have not only their ultimate origin but also their constant foundation in existence in the Word of God, in whom we live, and move, and have our being.

Finally, it should be remembered that the historian also is profoundly affected by the doctrine of creation. This doctrine is the necessary basis for a Christian view of history, and in the Judaic-Christian heritage it constitutes the linear view of human history. Creation guards the Christian historian from the cyclical notions of history, since it indicates the beginning of time and creation from the hand of God. And while it has been serviceable for the historian in the past, it still provides an advantage for the historian today, teaching him that the time process is not self-explanatory. Traditionally the creation doctrine has been of advantage to all historians, for because of it the possibility of universal history is clearly recognized. Universal history and its concomitant sense of human solidarity seemed to be impossible because of the subjective elements involved and because of the depth of historical ignorance. "In Christian theology, history is conceived in universal terms because the universal God is its originator and stands at its end." [44]

The linear conception of history deriving from the Christian view of creation has ultimately served as the basis for modern (Western) progress in the sciences. Acknowledgment of God's act in creation allows man to see nature for what it is: neither divine, (if divine, not to be tampered with); nor as intrinsically corrupt, (if corrupt, exploration would be fruitless). It is upon this ground of Western religious heritage, based on the distinction between God and His creation, and historically only upon this ground, that modern science has developed. "It may well be that, even as modern historical consciousness required the soil of a prophetic-Christian attitude towards history, so also modern science required an attitude toward nature which could be furnished only by the Christian idea of creation." [45]

But the science that has grown in the soil prepared by the Christian concept of creation has itself broken from its traditional mooring in the creation event and taken on, if not the nature of an opponent of Christian truth, at least the place of one that regards the Christian position as irrelevant. The progress of modern science in tracing the lines of causality in the orders of life, nature, and the cosmos frequently blinds the observer to the question of ultimate causality. The most advanced of the sciences does not answer the ultimate question of being as opposed to nonbeing, nor does it face the mystery of the whole complex represented by reality. The sciences, in the words of Niebuhr, "renounce the final mystery behind every problem of meaning by raising no ultimate questions." Thus to the modern who finds history and its processes self-explanatory, through scientific investigation is opposed the biblical insistence upon creation and the ultimate cause of being in the Creator. Niebuhr, taking a cue from Bergson, refers to the modern inclination, based on the scientific world view, to substitute time for God. Time is made the clue to the mystery of existence, and thus there arises a modern fascination with progress as a substitute for the classical Christian conception of a purposive end to human history. "The conception of time as God undergirds the conception of history as redeemer in modern thought." [46]

As we move on to consider the two further utterances of God's Word in Incarnation and parousia, the fundamental identity of the Word in creation, Incarnation, and parousia must be constantly stressed. In the words of Von Rad which we have cited, creation must be regarded as "susceptible" to God's Word. The work of creation is a stable and lasting entity, and although sin and evil will enter into that creation through man's freedom, it is still fundamentally good, brought into and sustained in being by the Word, and consequently susceptible to that same eternal Word of God.

THE ESCHATOLOGICAL UTTERANCE OF GOD'S WORD

The history of salvation (God's plan within history) is traced completely in the biblical record. We cannot perforce but highlight here God's Word as the active agent in this process. Reviewing salvation history, we can see the Word as creative, choosing, effective, and revealing God as the sovereign Lord of history.

1. The Old Testament Preparation. The world, good from the hand of God, did not long remain so. Man in his freedom sinned against God; and in the wake of sin followed suffering, pain, evil, and death.[47] "Therefore . . . through one man sin entered into the world and through sin death, and thus death has passed unto all men because all have sinned." [48] Human history was delivered over to the demonic powers; in fact, not only was human history marked by sin from the beginning but the Fall was itself a cosmic event. The whole world was brought under the reign of Satan and suffered for its wages both death and corruption.

The Genesis account of the Fall should not be seen as an abstract presentation of the source of evil but rather as a literary account stating the fact of the fall of the first parents of the human race.[49] The consequences of this fall, of this rejection of man's initial election in the creation, are spelled out in the chapters that follow: the loss of primal innocence, the experience of estrangement from God, the disruption of right order in man's relationship to the world, the punishment of God. The story of Cain exemplifies the terrible consequences for man of this original sin.[50] But even within this terrifying context of the Fall, God speaks His Word of promise that one day a Saviour will be born in history, descendant of Eve: "And I will put enmity between thee and the woman, between thy offspring and hers; he will crush thy head, while thou dost lie in wait for his heel." [51]

The history of man is continuous from Adam, and within that history what gives it meaning is God's plan (salvation history), which begins with God's Word coming to Abraham. Freely, gratuitously, Abraham was selected within history to initiate God's saving purpose. "The Word of God came to Abraham," and at His command Abraham obediently journeyed from Ur to the land of Canaan. Abraham's faith is his "hearing" of God's Word, his obedience and commitment to God's command. For this God says "I will make of you a great nation . . . in you *all the families of the earth will be blessed.*" Because he heard God's Word, in all the depth that the biblical "hearing" conveys, we read that this faith of Abraham's justified him: "He believed the Lord; and he accounted it to him as righteousness,"—a global designation of the entire process by which Abraham was brought into right relationship with God.[52]

The people of the promise received its transmission through Abraham's son Isaac and through his son Jacob and through his twelve sons. The migration of this people to safety in Egypt under Joseph evolved through the centuries of their sojourn into slavery. And now God "heard their groaning, and God remembered his covenant with Abraham." Again God spoke His Word, now to Moses calling him to save His people.[53] The Word spoken by God effected this salvation; it spoke of it in the Exodus. God led his people from slavery; through Moses He covenanted with them in the desert; and finally he brought them to the promised land. Once again God's Word *elected* (Moses and the people of Abraham), *revealed* (His name), *created* (the nation in the covenant), and *communicated* (the Law).

The Exodus-covenant is the central event of the Old Testament, and it is, as we shall see, the core of the continuing proclamation (kerygma) throughout the history of Israel. When Moses announces the Word of God to the people, they "hear"—the Jews accepted and committed themselves to this Word: "All that the Lord has spoken we will do." [54] Their covenant sacrifice of ratification was in obedience to the demand of the Word. Thus the covenant was founded not upon Israel's choice or her merit, but rather she was welded together as a nation—elected by God's free and choosing Word. Israel was brought into existence as a nation by God's Word in the continual course of human history in order to be the instrument and the sign of His salvation to come. "And the word 'sign' in this connection means an event that already contains within itself something of the reality to which it is pointing." [55]

The possession of the land recorded in the Book of Joshua was marked by the presence of the Word, by the constant commands of God. God's Word (*dabar*) is act; the Jews were successful because God's Word accomplished in them that of which it spoke. During the period of the Judges, the disorganization of the people was reflected by the biblical comment: "The Word of the Lord was precious in those days." This age was closed when the Word of the Lord came to Samuel.[56] Samuel initiated at God's bidding the Kingship marked so pre-eminently by David.[57] It was not Israel but God who selected David: "And now the Lord said: up, anoint him, this is *My* choice." And, again, the event of the Davidic kingship is to be an instrument and a sign of what the Word of God will do.[58]

Israel experienced the crucial period of her history from the eighth through the sixth centuries—the age of the Prophets. The era is considered crucial from many viewpoints: military and political history, biblical formation, doctrinal development, messianism, and Israel's understanding of her own history. The Prophets were intimately related to the emergence of God's Word in history: they were His spokesmen, the mouthpiece of God, the bearers of the Word. They were called and elected by God's Word (the first and fundamental meaning of "prophet"); although we often consider them (with some justification) to be "fore-tellers", they were primarily "forth-tellers." They spoke His Word, which was necessary for Israel's continuance in existence. Thus, for the Prophets no greater punishment could be envisioned than the lack of God's Word: "Yes, days are coming, says the Lord God, when I shall send famine upon the land: Not a famine of bread, or thirst for water, but for hearing the word of the Lord." The Prophets were, in short, the articulation of God's Word, and not by merit or by personal choice but by election: "The lion has roared; who will not fear? The Lord God has spoken; who can but prophesy?" [59]

Elias announced God's Word of judgment against the northern kingdom, and it came to pass.[60] Isaiah bore the same Word of judgment to the southern kingdom, and again it was effectual.[61] Jeremiah presented God's Word of restoration, and under Cyrus (538 B.C.) Jerusalem was restored. In the disasters that marked the end of the two kingdoms the Prophets are not concerned with "prediction" but with preaching the sinfulness of His people, and the consequent instrumentality of the conquering nations in God's plan.

When the Prophets spelled out the meaningfulness of history they did so not simply by telescoping the orders of causality and asserting God as an immediate cause of every event, rather they proclaimed that history had a goal, and that God had elected Israel to play a role in the historical events that constitute the divine plan. For the Prophets the disasters of the sixth century were not to be explained in the order of causality so much as in the order of God's purpose: the redemption of the world.

The spokesmen for God's Word have in common this doctrine of God's Lordship over history; they communicate to Israel the meaning of her historical experience. God's Word in prophetism, then, *reveals* God's plan as the meaningfulness of history. Through the Word the Prophets were able to penetrate "the political surface of contemporary events and found within them the righteous acts of God, the outcropping in history of his purposeful government of the world." [62]

During the age of the Prophets Israel did, as a matter of fact, turn again to "hear" God's Word. The reform of Josiah in 621 was marked by the discovery of the Deuteronomic Code and its promulgation.[63] The people were convoked by God's Word rediscovered by the high priest; God's Word in Deuteronomy was heard, accepted, ratified by sacrifice.

In the final periods of Israel's history before Christ, in the postexilic period, the age of the Prophets slowly gave way to an age of the Law. From 538–332 the Jews were ruled by the Persians. Nehemiah rebuilt the walls of Jerusalem while Ezra published the Law and undertook to reconstitute the temple worship. The people at the time of this renewal, in hearing the Word, recalled the acts of

God in the past, and slowly became aware of their eschatological significance as they realized them to be the tokens of greater deeds to come.[64] There was an emphasis upon the priest, the congregation, the Levitical Law of holiness, and the temple (where now the Psalter receives its finalized form). There was a redaction of the Pentateuch by the priestly editors, and gradually—through the influence of the priests—ritual law was raised to the status of moral law.

The development of Israel immediately after the exile was, therefore, marked by reliance on the Scriptures, the priests, and the later Prophets, especially the Deutero-Isaiah. Through the Deutero-Isaiah came God's Word concerning the new Israel and the idea of her universal destiny; in the Servant Songs Israel becomes conscious of her role in God's plan. Over and against the personal piety that marks this period of "hearing God's Word" a dry legalism gradually began to emerge. In 332 Alexander the Great inaugurated the period of Greek influence marked by the emergence of the Scribes and the importance of the Book of God's Word. The Hellenized Jews, supported by the Greeks, fought with the orthodox, thus inviting the intervention of Antiochus Epiphanes and the consequent violation of the temple and persecution of the Jews. Judas Maccabaeus' successful revolt on behalf of the Hasmoneans (a priestly tribe) secured a period of independence. Pompey's conquest (63–61) ended this period of independence.

It should be noted that progressive foreign rule and oppression intensified the sense of Jewish patriotism, legalism, the tradition of separatism, and the religious thought of the Jews concerning the problem of suffering and the meaning of Israel in history. From the postexilic period dates the wisdom literature, books of the Bible that reflect a practical philosophy of life and, by comparison to the rest of the Old Testament, a sometimes areligious outlook. Nevertheless, the wisdom literature does make noticeable achievements in the question of the mystery of the afterlife. Of greater significance, however, is the teaching in the wisdom literature about wisdom itself *(sophia)*, about the Law *(torah)*, and ultimately about the identification of wisdom, law, and the Word.

In postexilic Judaism the Torah reflected the whole of religion as revealed by God, although the translation in Greek by the Septuagint of *torah* is *nomos,* a term which reflects only that aspect of revelation known as law. That unfortunate choice of the Greek *nomos* for the Hebrew *torah* seems to have been determined by the later legalism that dominated the period of translation. Rabbinic Judaism identified the Torah as the life of the age to come, the water that gives life, the bread of life, the light of the world; furthermore, the Torah was regarded as pre-existent to creation and indeed the agent of creation.

The concept of wisdom in Job[65] is specifically hypostasized in Proverbs, wherein wisdom appears as a person pre-existing creation: "The Lord begot me, the first born of his ways, the forerunner of his prodigies of long ago; from of old I was poured forth, at the first, before the earth . . . while as yet the earth and the fields were not made, nor the first clods of the world." [66] So also do we find the concept in Sirach, and again in the Book of Wisdom, wherein it is, like the Torah, the active agent of creation, light and life.[67] Thus we find that late in Judaism *torah* and *wisdom* are identified.

These concepts are also identified with the Word of God. In Sirach we are told, "From the mouth of the Most High I came forth . . ." [68] Thus it is that against the rabbinic traditions of speaking of the Word of God in the Torah-wisdom motif must be read the prologue of St. John's Gospel, wherein the Incarnate Word is spoken of with all the attributes of Torah-wisdom-Word. Thus, for John, in the incarnation of the Word the dwelling motif of Torah and wisdom is fulfilled. It is against this tradition that we are to read the whole of John's Gospel and his identifications of Christ as life and light, his eucharistic theology revolving about bread and wine, and the theological use of wisdom by Paul in speaking of Christ.

The last two centuries of Jewish history were marked by the appearance of apocalyptic (revelation) writings dealing with the new age and with formal attempts to penetrate the meaning of history and the divine purpose. The apocalyptic writings identified the great divine action coming in the new age as one embracing the universal Kingdom, the resurrection of the righteous, and a final judgment. The Book of Daniel pictures this age as one of victory for God's elect in order to comfort a persecuted Israel by the vision of God's victory.[69] God's Kingdom is to be established and to mark the end of history. "Israel's faithful completely give up an expectation that the Kingdom of David will be established in the future by men's efforts. They expect it to come by a mighty act of God who will break into the course of history and thus bring it to an end. From this time on David is no more than a figure pointing toward this Kingdom to come, a Kingdom that will be the Messianic Kingdom." [70]

2. *The Old Testament and History.* In the Old Testament view God is the Creator of the world, the Lord of History, who reveals Himself—speaks His Word—in acts. The Word of God is His deed. There is a certainty that God rules the course of human history and that history is the arena of God's activity. Life is meaningful because of its place in God's plan, and central to that plan is God's gracious election of His people.

The biblical view is tied not to abstractions but to history. The Israelite feasts were feasts based upon the historical actions of God toward His people; their confessions of faith were proclamations of what He had done. G. E. Wright has pointed out that biblical theology is essentially a theology of recital, and that the Old Testament itself is a reflection on the meaning of God's acts. The implication this bears is that "biblical man conceived of himself as existing in a particular unique history which possessed significance because God through it was revealed as in process of redeeming all history." [71] At the center of this history for the Old Testament was the Exodus event, God's choosing of His people.[72]

The meaning of Israel, the point of the phenomenon in which Old Testament man shared, was that God had chosen her. Her "greatness" (certainly a poorly chosen term on the scales of the values of world history) lay for the Jew in the election of God, in His "choosing" Word. The history of Israel embraced her failures and her sins, so that the Jew could see no intrinsic merit as the cause of election, but only God's gratuitous love.

A new element necessarily entered Old Testament theology, and this was Israel's expectation of the future, of the goal of the process of election. This we call eschatology. Election pointed to the future, so that the message of the Prophets, interpreting history, became inevitably eschatological. This was not a new element in the sense of invention, but rather "had its roots in the presuppositions of the older histories and in the attempt to interpret the work of God in the current crises of history." [73] God's election, in short, conferred upon the experience of Israel a meaning in His divine plan: it pointed forward to the fulfillment of history. And let it be repeated, this election in Exodus and covenant was a real and actual historical event, throughout Israel's history enshrined in kerygmatic proclamation. The kerygma, then, was not a set of ideas propounded, but a confessional recital of events, God's acts; the kerygma was not a historically developed or developing doctrine, but an interpretation of history.

The eschatological hope expressed in the Old Testament experience looks forward to another event in history, an event that will involve a new covenant,[74] a new Israel,[75] and their proclamation (kerygma) throughout time and history. The New Testament kerygma, which is the first proclamation of God's eschatological and decisive act in Christ, relies on the Old Testament proclamation, and now proclaims that Testament's fulfillment and history's fulfillment in Christ. In fact, New Testament typology sees the acts of the Old Testament (Israel, covenant, Passover) fulfilled in the *mirabilia dei,* the wonderful works of God it (New Testament) proclaims.

This biblical grasp of history and its meaningfulness in God's effective utterance of His Word does not ignore the problem of man's freedom, and, therefore, of man's responsibility. Reconciling in a purely rational way both God's effective Word and man's freedom and responsibility is impossible. It is not accomplished in the Bible, for the Bible witnesses to the mystery that surrounds God, the ultimate ground of the God-man relationship. In the Old Testament man is good, precisely as the product of God's creative activity. From the Word's activity in creation man is "susceptible" to the influence of the Word; he is capable of God's revealing Word in the deeds of history, and it is precisely here that the Bible places man's importance—his encounter with the Word of God. "The focus of attention is not on man's inherent or natural dignity and value because his works exhibit the very reverse of dignity and a betrayal of value."[76] Encounter with God's Word as the field of man's value derives from the biblical view of history as itself the utterance of God.

The anthropology, as it were, that the Bible presents to us is dynamic, it is the God-man relationship, not the later abstractions of the philosophers and the theologians, legitimate as such endeavors may be. Sin is *not to hear* God's Word; sin is directed against God, not against a legal statement; sin is a violation of man's relationship (election) with God, of which he is susceptible from the very beginning in the creative activity of God's Word. Sin is essentially disobedience to God; it is not to trust, not to believe, not to wait upon God acting in history; it is, in short, the lack of total commitment to God. To hear God's Word is experience, not abstraction; it is existential, implying an involvement or engagement. The Gospel of John in its concept of faith (life) vis-à-vis sin (death), reflects the absolute nature of the commitment involved in the hearing of God's Word. Faith, which is the hearing of God's Word in a wholehearted manner, is the response demanded of biblical man.

And this response of hearing God's Word is required as well of the covenant community. To keep the covenant is to hear Yahweh's Word; to break its provisions is sin. The heart of this adherence to God's Word is, of course, the encounter with God: it is the God-man relationship in His election. The later juridical traditions of the Jews, which ignored the encounter in history, brought upon the Jews the judgment of God's Word in the Prophets and the promise of the new and everlasting covenant.[77] The challenge to this traditional biblical view presented by individual sin and suffering—what the West has come to call in its philosophy the problem of evil— was handled late in Israel's history. The wisdom literature, particularly the Book of Job, affirms the element of mystery in God's dealing with men, so that faith in God's Word and in His plan for human history is not shaken.

McKenzie states in regard to the biblical belief in the Word of God:

[It shows] the Israelite conception of history as a process governed by Yahweh and moved to a term intended by Him. History also is "the word of Yahweh," a reality which fulfills the utterance of Yahweh. The word of history is dynamic and dianoetic: dynamic in that it accomplishes what it signifies, dianoetic in that it makes the historical process intelligible. History is then revelation of the purpose of Yahweh, but it is more; as the word is a release of the psychic energy of the personality, so history is a revelation of the character and personality of Him whose Word it is. The word affirms not only the thing signified but also the person who utters it.[78]

We will now turn to a consideration of God's Word as it culminates this progressive revelation of history and in history in Jesus Christ, the Word of God in human flesh.

3. Jesus Christ: The Word Made Flesh. "And the Word was made flesh and dwelt among us. And we saw His glory—glory as of the only-begotten of the Father—full of grace and truth." Jesus Christ is the crucial moment of God's plan, the turning point of time, the center of history. The divine Word, existing from all eternity, active from the first moment of creation, the light and the life of men, became man in Jesus Christ. The progressive articulation of the Word in salvation history is perfected. "It was, if I may call it so, the paroxysm, the climax, of divine effort that brought the Word in the flesh." [79] God's promise to "presence" among His people is fulfilled when John states simply of the Word made flesh that "He dwelt among us." [80] God's plan, hidden from all eternity yet always operative in history, is, according to Saint Paul, manifested in Jesus Christ.[81] The developing articulation of the Word culminates, according to the Epistle to the Hebrews: "God, who at sundry times and in divers manners spoke in times past to the fathers by the prophets, last of all in these days has spoken to us by His Son." [82] And God's Word, the *dabar Yahweh,* is also God's deed, His act: God's Word is not an abstraction, nor a rationale, but a person who reconciles the world to God.

One cannot rip the person of Jesus Christ, Word made flesh, the supreme deed of the God-Who-Acts, from the context in which He came, for the mystery of Christ cannot be separated from the revelation history of the Old Testament. It is the Old Testament that revealed the acts of God, it is the Old Testament that reflected the emergence of the Word, and it is the Old Testament that protects the New Testament focus upon God's act of salvation in history. The New Testament itself makes clear the meaningfulness of the Christ in the Old Testament line of history: "The *time* is fulfilled and the Kingdom of God is at hand." [83] So "for the Christian, Christ is the key to the central concepts of the Old Testament, but at the same time it is the Old Testament which provides the clue to Christ." [84]

The history of the Old Testament can be viewed, as we have noted, from the point of departure provided by the progressive emergence of God's Word. God's Word is His act—the creation of His people—first in the Exodus event; and His constant Word recreates and holds in existence that community. The Israelites themselves were conscious always of being the people of the Word, God's chosen ones in history; and they were always aware through that Word of the meaningfulness of history; and, finally, they looked forward to the realization of God's plan in an age to come. In the new covenant the Christian Church, established by Jesus, constantly saw itself as having heard and received the supreme utterance of God's Word, Jesus Christ, and it recognized itself as the heir to Israel, as God's people.[85] The Christian Church was and still is held in existence by God's Word made flesh, to whom it bears witness. As the Old Testament reflected the progress of the people of the Word through the vicissitudes of history, the New Testament directs itself primarily to the action and the person of the Word, Jesus Christ.

The meaning of Christ, the nature of God's eschatological utterance of the Word, can be found in the books of the New Testament that bear witness of Him. Throughout all these books there is a fundamental unity in their proclamation (kerygma) or Gospel ("good news"). This is essentially: (1) The eschaton, the new age toward which the Old Testament looked, had begun in Christ. (2) The Messiah is Jesus, who worked "mighty Deeds," was put to death, and rose again. (3) This Jesus has been exalted, and will come again as the revelation of the eschaton. (4) Let each man repent and be baptized for the remission of sins.

The fundamental notion in this proclamation is its eschatological nature. The Christ event opens the new age: Jesus' ministry is the fulfillment of time and the presence of the Kingdom of God,[86] and thus the New Testament consciously relates itself to the Old Testament as the fulfillment of all that it pointed to and longed for. Christ comes not to destroy but to fulfill. The Old Testament, which spoke of the coming of God's rule, is climaxed by the New Testament affirmation of the Kingdom begun in Christ. "The New Testament has introduced what we might call a tremendously significant change of tense." [87]

The Day of the Lord, the eschaton to which the Old Testament looked forward, would be the final deed of God: no further Word of God would be spoken beyond that final day. As the eschatological event it bore certain characteristics: the revelation of God's purpose in history, the victory of God over the powers of evil, new life, and a new beginning.[88] The New Testament proclamation of the eschaton in Christ recounts its fulfillment: the establishment of the Kingdom of God and the meaningful pattern of human history laid bare in God's Word made flesh, Christ's power over the evil spirits, and in His Cross and resurrection conquest over the devil.[89]

In speaking of the eschatological nature of God's Word made

flesh we see Christ as the fulfillment of the Old Testament themes that give meaning not only to Israel's history but to all of human history. In Christ the themes of Old Testament history that progressively articulate the Word are supremely fulfilled in the perfect historical articulation of God's Word. The life, work, passion, death, resurrection, and ascension of Jesus Christ represent the realization of the eschaton.

In meeting Christ the Jews of His time were heir to the Old Testament and especially to the eschatological expectations marking the postexilic period immediately preceding His appearance. In the New Testament we find the Old Testament themes applied to Christ in the titles with which He is honored: Prophet, Suffering Servant, Priest, Messiah, Son of Man, Lord, and Saviour.[90] These great Christological titles provide a biblical evaluation of the life, work, and person of Jesus.

In the Old Testament tradition the Prophet was such because he was called, seized by the Word of God, which he delivered to the people as the meaning of their historical situation. The demise of prophecy after the exile brought Judaism to expect its resumption,[91] a resumption that would mark the "age to come."[92] Christ is presented in the New Testament if not explicitly as *the* Prophet whose appearance marks the last days, certainly at least as a prophet.[93] John identifies the Word of God (characteristic of prophecy) as a person: Jesus. Christ when He preaches does so on His own authority ("*I* say unto you . . ."). He announces the immanent Kingdom of God. His message is final, and response to it is decisive. Christ is a true prophet of God, and His appearance signifies the last days; and this title of "Prophet," while it does not exhaust the full meaning of the Christ event, does at least indicate the eschatological nature of the words and work of Christ.

In the figure of the Suffering Servant of God prophesied in the Old Testament two significant works are attributed to him: vicarious suffering and the re-establishment of the covenant.[94] Late Jewish apocalyptic writings tend to identify the Messiah and the Suffering Servant by affirming some actions to both. Jesus begins His public ministry with the baptism of John, and the voice from heaven that testifies to Jesus used an almost exact quote from Isaiah.[95] On another occasion Jesus specifically cited Isaiah of Himself;[96] and again, He alluded to both the fifty-second and fifty-third chapters of Isaiah.[97] At the Last Supper the works of the Suffering Servant (vicarious suffering and re-establishment of the covenant) are explicitly linked with His own redemptive work on the following day: "This is my blood of the *new covenant,* which is *being shed for many.*" [98] The identification of Jesus as the Suffering Servant of Yahweh predicted in Isaiah is, according to Oscar Cullmann, "the only way we can understand the witness of the Baptist when he says 'Behold the Lamb of God, who takes away the sins of the world.'" [99] The New Testament writers understood and reflected the appropriation of the theme of the Suffering Servant by Jesus Himself; and so in the Gospel of Matthew there is a direct reference to this theme in Isaiah,[100] and in the *Book of Acts* Philip exegetes the Suffering Servant: ". . . beginning from this Scripture he preached Jesus to him." [101] Thus from the very beginning the Church saw in Christ the fulfillment of the eschatological theme of the Suffering Servant of Yahweh; and the importance that is to be attached to this identification is the significance of the death of Christ. The death Jesus freely undergoes is, therefore, the central act of God's saving plan, it is in the blood of Jesus that the new covenant is drawn, and this death is on behalf of all men for their salvation.

The conjunction of priest-king themes in later Jewish eschatology was reflected in the books of Genesis and the Psalms, as well as by a considerable corpus of the extrabiblical literature.[102] In all of these there was a tendency to identify the Messiah as Priest. The New Testament Epistle to the Hebrews attributes to Jesus this concept of the great high priest, sees His atoning death, which culminated in His ascension, as a priestly work, and also insists upon the decisive character of that priestly work as the perfection and fulfillment of the Old Testament priesthood.[103]

When we speak of Jesus as the Christ we speak of His being the Messiah. The Hebrew *mashiach,* meaning an anointed one (the king), is translated into Greek as *Christos;* one may therefore appropriately read for Jesus Christ "Jesus-Messiah." The term arose naturally in Hebrew history from the period of the monarchy; and in the destruction of the monarchy Jewish thought turned to the future and the hope of an eschatological king in the line of David. Accentuated by the travails that followed the Exile, the late Jewish tradition of the expected Messiah devolved into various concep-

tions, all tinged with political hope. Throughout His public ministry Jesus sought to purify this notion of the Messiah (for example,
the account of the Temptation, which reflects Jesus' concept of His
messianism, the confession of Peter, and Jesus' own answers to the
high priest and Pilate before His death).[104] In attempting this purification Jesus sought to disengage the notion of Messiah from any
idea of political, economic, or social redemption. Consequently the
public life of Jesus is marked both by His avoidance of the title and
his constant attempts to disengage it from Judaic political expectations by calling the attention of his listeners to His coming passion
and death. Thus Jesus wished to bring His followers to see in His
messianic destiny his fulfillment of Israel's *role* in history. The
nationalist overtones connoted by "Messiah" had their origins in
this concept of the Messiah as a fulfillment of the history of Israel.
The constant New Testament designation of Jesus as Christ, the
Messiah, is the result of the experience of the Resurrection and His
expected second coming. From its very beginning the proclamation
of Jesus by the Church is Jesus Christ, the fulfillment of Israel's task
and the central link between the old and new covenants, between
Israel and the new people of God.

In the process of disengaging the title "Messiah" from its political
and nationalistic nuances, Jesus deliberately substituted the title
"Son of Man," and thus purposefully evoked the Old Testament
concept of the son of man. This theme occurs first in Daniel as a
collective representative of God's holy ones,[105] and by the time of
late Jewish apocalyptic writings the Son of Man was believed to be
a single eschatological figure—the heavenly man who appears at the
end of time on the clouds of heaven to judge the world. Jesus' constant use of the term was a claim to the decisive and central role in
the eschatological event. Furthermore, involved in Jesus' designation
of Himself as the Son of Man was the claim to be Judge.[106] Through
the principle of collective representation Saint Paul conceives of
Christ, the Son of Man, both as the Suffering Servant and as the
second Adam.[107]

From the very beginning of her existence the Church spoke of
and prayed to Christ as Lord (*Kyrios*). From the Hellenic background of late Judaism and from the Septuagint translation of the
Old Testament the full divine significance of the title "Lord" is
constantly evident.[108] But beyond even this understanding of the

person of Jesus as divine, which the title Lord signifies, the title speaks volumes for the constant Christian conception of the work of Jesus. It is only after His resurrection and ascension, and because of this glorification, that the term comes into the common and even usual designation of Jesus "whom God hath made both Lord and Christ." [109] The usual prayer and eucharistic proclamation of the early Church, "Maranatha—Come, Lord," evidences the eschatological nature of the Christ event, that in Him the decisive moment had come and that His resurrection had already inaugurated the eschaton, which remained to be perfected in His revelation to all men as Lord (in the parousia). The nature of Christ's work in the interim, the time between the Resurrection and parousia, was to be essentially one of Lordship.[110] The ascription to Jesus of the title "King" and the statement of His "sitting at the right hand of God" are concepts directly related to His Lordship. One further conclusion follows from the risen, eternal Lord idea: because Christ is the risen Lord, He is not bound by space and time, and consequently is at every age, as Lord of the Church, a contemporary to every Christian who confesses His Lordship.

The title "Saviour" occurs in the Old Testament primarily in reference to God who delivers His people. The early Church speaks of Jesus as Saviour because of His work of salvation from sin and death accomplished in His Cross and resurrection.[111] This accomplishment of salvation in His suffering is not directly related to the Suffering Servant theme, for "in the concept *Soter* (Saviour) the suffering for forgiveness of sins is understood entirely from the divine ratification of that suffering in Jesus' exaltion to Kyrios." [112]

The great Christological titles of Christ adequately affirm the New Testament conception of the life, work, and person of Jesus, and although they do not exhaust the dimensions of the meaning of Christ, they especially indicate the eschatological nature of the Christ event. These titles reflect the fulfillment of the Exodus-covenant theme, which is the basic kerygma of the Old Testament, in the theme of the new covenant established by God in the eschatological utterance, Christ. The New Testament proclamation, like its Old Testament predecessor, also bears a law. In Christ there is a new commandment,[113] a new law.[114] This is the law of love, for it is the love of God toward man that characterizes the Christ event: "God so loved the world that He gave His only-begotten Son that those who believe in him may not perish, but may have life everlasting." [115]

There are in the New Testament many specific instructions for the behavior of the Christian (the Sermon on the Mount, the Pauline Epistles), but all forms of ethical behavior are presented in the context of God's love for us. Morality is viewed in the light of what God has first done for us: "Let us love therefore, because God first loved us." [116] This may be illustrated in Paul's exposition of marriage: "Husbands, love your wives as Christ loved the Church and gave Himself up for it." [117] So the specific ethic of married life that Paul preaches is based primarily upon the deed of God in Christ for us. The essential note of the proclamation of Christ is therefore also the core of the Law; and in the New Testament there exists no antagonism or opposition between the concepts of Gospel and Law.

4. Saint Paul and the Mystery of Christ. Saint Paul speaks of Jesus Christ as the realization of God's plan in history under the aspect of *mysterion*—mystery. The Christ event as the deed of God is a mystery because it has been hidden from eternity in God; it is the divine economy, God's plan for *all* creation uttered in His Word. This mystery is identified with God's eternal Word, for it is one with Christ, the Word incarnate, who is in Paul's words the *pleroma* —the fullness: "And this His good pleasure He purposed in Him to be dispensed in the fullness of the times: to re-establish all things in Christ, both those in the heavens and those on the earth." [118] "For it has pleased God the Father that in Him all His fullness should dwell, and that through Him He should reconcile to Himself all things, whether on the earth or in the heavens, making peace through the blood of the Cross." [119] "For in Him dwells all the fullness of the Godhead bodily, and in Him who is the head of every Principality and power you have received of that fullness." [120]

Thus for Paul, Christ the risen Word incarnate reveals the fullness of God's intention: the Incarnation, like Creation, is revelatory of God; the distinction lies in the completeness of revelation in Christ. Christ is, then, the perfection of God's plan and the fullness of God Himself. In the light of Pauline teaching the first act of creation and consequent human history are not purely external to God but that in which He has freely chosen to be bound up. In history Christ stands revealed as the final achievement and perfection; and just as in Christ, God and man are one reality, so we know in Christ man's destiny as God's real (although adopted) children. God's eschatological utterance of His Word is the perfection of His creative utterance: "But we all, with faces unveiled, reflecting as in a mirror the glory of the Lord, are being transformed into his very image from glory to glory, as through the Spirit of the Lord." [121] Thus, although man has sinned, he is called by God's Word in the eschatological utterance of Christ not only to reconciliation but indeed to authentic existence.

How is God revealed in this mystery of which Paul speaks? For Paul, God is revealed in this: that we have known His love.

> It is the Cross which is the revelation of the divine love for us because it is in the Cross that we know that God's love for us does not demand us to merit it. Rather it is a generous love in that it does not need some good in us to love, but makes us good by loving us as only God can love. "For," as St. Paul says, "scarcely in behalf of a just man does one die; yet perhaps one might bring himself to die for a good man. But God commends His charity towards us, because when as yet we are sinners, Christ died for us." [122]

Thus it is that God has perfectly revealed Himself in His Word as a person; Christ is the decisive moment of human history; Christ is not only the intervention of God in history, he is as well the revelation of God's love for us, a love in which there is a new creation; therefore it must be stated that there is an intrinsic relationship between the creative and eschatological utterances of His Word.

Paul's exposition of Christ as the mystery of God develops not only in a specific historical circumstance, but, as W. D. Davies has shown, in considerable dependence upon it.[123] In the tradition of rabbinic Judaism Christ was identified by Paul with the Torah—not simply *torah* as law, but *torah* as the totality of revelation from God: the attributes of *torah* are made the attributes of Christ.[124] The tradition of wisdom as a person is maintained in Paul, who also identifies Christ and wisdom: "From him you are in Christ Jesus, who has become for us God-given wisdom." [125] Therefore, for Paul the work of wisdom is attributed to Christ.[126] The significance of the personified wisdom tradition as we find it in Paul is that it throws further light upon what we have stated as the intrinsic relationship between God's creative and eschatological utterances of His Word. Although man has fallen in sin, the redemptive activity of God's Word made flesh and our consequent share in the Christ life indicate that what is most opposed to God's Will in creation is man's sin (not the sonship to God by man); and it is precisely the rectification of this situation to which the eschatological utterance is ordered. "In teaching that Christ was the agent of creation Paul too, we cannot doubt, was seeking to express a similar truth; that to love after Christ is the natural life, that the creator is the redeemer, that nature and grace are related not antithetical." [127] We shall shortly see the necessity of so strongly stating the fundamental continuity of the creative and eschatological utterances of God's Word.

Before we move on to the third element in the eschatological utterance of God's Word, the present age as one of proclaiming Christ, the thought of Saint Paul allows us a natural transition. His figures of the Church as the "extension" of Christ, as His mystical body, have the obvious inference of a theological understanding of history. George T. Montague has summarized this thought of Paul:

> Paul's complex thought is this: Christ, pouring His life into the Church, is in turn achieving a cosmic completion by reason of the solidarity which His members have with the universe—a solidarity which transcends and transfigures the universe because of their union with Christ. . . . Thus the dynamic of the Church and of cosmic history is charity. To no other "world soul" is the engine of progress to be reduced than to *agape*, the divine love that descends from Head to members, uniting them and spurring them each to contribute his characteristic gift to the corporate growth of all, leading them upward toward the Head, and sweeping into their ascent such as will let the divine love draw them. This is how Christ progressively achieves His conquest of the universe, for it was the aim of His ascension to the Father—"that he might fill the universe." Thus the Christian bears in his heart the destiny of the universe and contributes to its realization in the measure in which he lends himself to the dynamic and progressing rhythm of the divine love flowing from the Head and circulating in the members, uniting them and making them grow together unto the spiritual stature of the one perfect Man, Christ. It is Christ's love, shared and circulated by His members, that does all (I Cor. 12:4–7).[128]

5. *The Church and the Age of Proclamation.* In the Ascension of Jesus,[129] the Church sees the completion of His Resurrection, celebrates His exaltation, proclaims His Lordship. The Ascension is "the Father's response to the voluntary humiliation of His only Son, the proclamation of his victory over all the enemy powers, the enthronement of Christ as Victor and Ruler." [130] The ascended Christ,

God and man, brings with Him into the very Godhead His human-ity and ours, "in order that we might be partakers of His Di-vinity." [131] In His glorification Christ is the first of many.[132] This exaltation of Christ is frequently referred to in the New Testament as Christ's being seated "at the right hand of God," the fulfillment of the promise in the first verse of Psalm 109. And in the first sermon in the Church on Pentecost Peter proclaims: "God has made both Lord and Christ, this Jesus whom you crucified." [133] It is this Lord-ship of Jesus *now* that defines the Church even for us.

The Lordship of Jesus is universal, total, complete, and cosmic. "All power on heaven and on earth has been given to Me." [134] Therefore God also has exalted him and has bestowed upon him the name that is above every name, so that at the name of Jesus every knee should bend of those in heaven, on earth and under the earth." [135] The victory of Christ in His Cross and resurrection is total over every power.[136] Thus it is that in Jesus begins the new age, a new creation, and the presence of the Kingdom of God.[137] The basis of the Lordship of Jesus lies in His Cross, in His obedi-ence to the Will of the Father.[138] And in His exaltation as Lord, Jesus is also our intermediary with God.[139]

The first action of His Lordship toward us is the fulfillment of His promise of the Spirit,[140] and on Pentecost the Spirit creates the Church. It is on Pentecost that Saint Peter declared the eschatologi-cal nature of the Church, that its existence is the opening of the new age. "But this is what was spoken through the prophet Joel 'and it shall come to pass in the last days, says the Lord, that I will pour forth of my spirit upon all flesh.' " [141] As Christ is the eschatological event, so the Church of Christ recognized in herself the eschatologi-cal community, the new creation.

The Church is, then, the new Israel of God,[142] and as such is called into existence and maintained in existence to proclaim the God-Who-Acts, just as the Old Testament Israel did. Like the old Israel, the Church bears God's Word to all men: "You, however, are a chosen race, a royal priesthood, a holy nation, a purchased people; that you may *proclaim* the perfections of him who has called you out of darkness into his marvellous light." [143] The Church fulfills Isaiah's words about the remnant,[144] and is the new covenant pre-dicted by Jeremias.[145] The Church is the revivified Israel predicted by Ezechiel, for "even when we were dead by reason of our sins, he brought us to life together with Christ." [146] This revivified Israel possesses the Spirit of Jesus: "then he who raised Jesus Christ from the dead will also bring to life your mortal bodies because of his Spirit who dwells in you." [147]

The Church, born of the Spirit of Jesus, is not only the new Israel but the new temple of God; and as the Old Testament temple bore the Shekinah, the divine presence in Jesus is continued through Jesus' presence in His Church. The Church is built upon Jesus as the chief cornerstone, and "in Him the whole structure is closely fitted together and grows into a temple holy in the Lord, in him you too are being built together into a dwelling place for God in the Spirit." [148] The Church fulfills the temple-presence motif because it is in some mysterious way the body of Jesus: "and him he gave as head over all the Church, which indeed is his body." [149] "For as the body is one and has many members, and all the members of the body, many as they are, form one body, so also is it with Christ. For in one Spirit we were all baptized into one body. . . ." [150] "So we, the many, are one body in Christ." [151]

We come, then, to the essential work of the Church: the proclamation of God's Word, of His mighty deed in Christ that all men might be saved. The Church, the new Israel, the temple of God, the eschatological community, the body of Christ, bears the incarnate Word through space and time. The bearer of the Word, the Church's ministry, is the reconciling ministry of Christ: the Church is the place of encounter of God's final Word (Christ) and man. Thus from the first day of its existence the Church has steadfastly performed its divine commission. When Peter first proclaimed the Word, his bearers, confronted by the Word, asked what to do. "Repent and be baptized every one of you in the name of Jesus Christ for the forgiveness of your sins, and you will receive the gift of the Holy Spirit. For to you is the promise and to your children and to all who are far off, even to all whom the Lord our God calls to Himself." [152] This essential role of the Church, proclaiming the Word, marks its progress through history.

How does the Church proclaim the Word? Basically, the Church fulfills her mission in three ascending forms of proclamation: Word, sacrament, and Eucharist. Her ministry of the Word is the Scripture, the preaching, and her teaching, in which God's Word in Christ confronts man with what God has done and demands from him the response of faith. The sacraments are "visible words," the actions of Christ through His ministry in the Church. They, as actions of Christ, partake of His nature as God's Word by effecting that which they indicate or signify. Finally, the Eucharist is the supreme act of the Church, the covenant meal, the making present of Christ's sacrifice, and the anticipation of the parousia: "As often as ye shall eat this bread and drink the cup, you proclaim the death of the Lord until he comes." [153] This supreme proclamation of the Word made flesh in the Eucharist is commanded by Jesus: "Unless you eat the flesh of the Son of Man, and drink his blood, you shall not have life in you." [154] In the next chapter we shall return to a more detailed examination of the Church's function in our stage of history as proclaiming the Word.

The proclamation and presence of the Word in the Church marks the last stage of salvation history; Jesus assures us that the proclamation of the Word is the last stage of history: "And this gospel of the kingdom shall be preached in the whole world, for a witness to all nations; and then will come the end." [155] The proclamation of the Word in history evokes and demands the response called faith. Jesus opened His ministry with this demand,[156] and Israel's refusal to hear God's Word in her rejection of Christ brings down upon her the judgment of God. Hearing God's Word, faith, is not merely the assent of the mind, but rather the reception of God's Word by the whole man, by the totality of person; and so, hearing God's Word is more accurately identified as commitment.

Proclaiming the Word is the offer of salvation; the proclamation itself is necessary, but "faith then depends on hearing, and hearing on the word of Christ." [157] Faith is the personal response in the here-and-now to this proclamation; it is obedience to God's call. Jesus constantly linked the hearing of the Word to the doing of it.[158] Thus the full biblical meaning in hearing God's Word incumbent upon man is assent, obedience, decision, and trust: it is the full commitment of a person to the Word. In this proclamation God's Word remains a choosing Word; it is selective, for the hearer undergoes election by God. "For by grace you have been saved through faith; and that not from yourselves, for it is the gift of God." [159]

Since a man remains constantly free, he is free also to reject God's Word at any time. Man may choose not to hear. Faith, then, cannot be one act of man's life, but is rather a constant and abiding

gift (assented to freely), which partakes of the nature of a relationship with God. Not to hear God's Word when proclamation has
been made and recognized as such is sinful. "To many in the
modern world, the statement that unbelief is sin seems a hard saying, but it is the consistent biblical point of view. Men who are
concerned wholly with this world, its values and pleasures, resist
the Christian Gospel because it makes a demand upon them; atheism
is often the rationalization of the refusal to face the challenge of
obedience. 'It is so hard to believe,' said Kierkegaard, 'because it is
so hard to obey.' "[160]

In the wake of faith, in the hearing of God's Word in Christ proclaimed by the Church in Word and sacrament, a man undergoes
the new birth, he becomes a new creation. The old creation died
with Christ, the new occurred in His resurrection. The individual
is joined to Christ by the sacrament (by "hearing" the Word) of
baptism, and he dies and rises again, walking in a newness of life.[161]
Thus through proclamation of the Word and obedience to God the
Christian is rightly called a new creation.[162] When one comes,
therefore, to accept the redemption won for us in Christ, there is
an ascending order: (a) the Word of God in Christ, (b) the proclamation, and (c) "hearing"—instruction, commitment, and baptism.

Finally, the Church as the proclaiming presence of the Word in
history bears a relationship to the world and human society. All
power is given to Christ the Lord, [163] and, therefore, as all authority
derives from God, man in society owes obedience to lawfully constituted authority.[164] Prior loyalty to Christ alone fixes the limit
to created authority.[165] The theology of Church-State relationships
is clearly set forth by Christ: "Render, therefore, to Caesar the
things that are Caesar's, and to God the things that are God's." [166]
Vis-à-vis the state there is a priority in proclaiming the Gospel,[167]
thus Peter and John answered the authorities: "Whether it is right
in the sight of God to listen to you rather than to God, decide for
yourselves. For we cannot but speak of what we have seen and
heard." And on the occasion of another arrest: "We must obey God
rather than men." [168]

And so the Church, bearing the Word, held in being by the Word,
whose duty it is to proclaim the Word, continues through history
conscious of its presence in the world and its mission there, but also
mindful of its non-worldly origin. "If the world hates you, know

that it has hated me before you. If you were of the world, the world would love what is its own. But because you are not of the world, but I have chosen you out of the world, therefore, the world hates you." [169]

THE APOCALYPTIC UTTERANCE OF GOD'S WORD

Jesus specifically instructed His apostles that at some future date He would come again to judge the world, that He would "come in His majesty, and all the angels with Him, then He will sit on the throne of his glory." [170] At the time of the Ascension the apostles were told, "This Jesus who has been taken up from you into heaven shall come in the same way as you have seen Him going up to heaven." [171] And in the opening of the Book of the Apocalypse Saint John speaks of Jesus as "who is and who was and who is coming." [172] Throughout the New Testament, then, there is a firm and unwavering belief in the coming again of Christ in glory, to which is connected the note of the final and perfect manifestation of the glory of God in Christ. This we speak of as the apocalyptic utterance of the Word.

The Greek verb from which the English "apocalyptic" is derived has the meaning "to uncover" or "unveil." The parousia, or second coming of Christ, has this specific note in the New Testament, that it will be apocalyptic-revelatory. Faith is to give way to sight—all will on that day "hear" God's Word—the open manifestation of Christ will be unmistakable.[173] But to share in that glory it will be necessary to have first heard the Word in its eschatological utterance. Man is free to accept or reject Christ now and to bear the consequences of that decision; when He comes again everyone shall know Him, only not as Saviour but as Judge. Thus the eschatological Word, the Christ event, is decisive and final, and the apocalyptic utterance of that Word is the open and clear manifestation of the Word to all men. Those who have rightly heard the Word in the decisive eschatological utterance, and only those, will be brought to perfection: "For I reckon that the sufferings of the present time are not worthy to be compared with the glory to come that will be revealed to us. For the eager longing of creation awaits the revelation of the Sons of God." [174]

The identity of the apocalyptic Word with the Word in creation, incarnate in Christ, is made in John's Apocalypse. Operative in the beginning, in creation, He is identified as operative in the end of history: "I am the Alpha and the Omega, the beginning and the end." [175] In the prologue to his Gospel John stressed the activity of the Word in creation and in the new creation, and he completes this thought in the Apocalypse, wherein the eternal Word is not only the beginning of the historical process but also its *telos*—end; He is the final amen to all history.[176]

The expectation of the second coming of Christ, which was rightly perceived by the early Church as intimately related to the eschatological event in Christ, was understood as a rather early return precisely because of the decisive nature of the Christ event. As time went on, the awareness grew of a period of waiting, and of the time of the Church and the hidden time of the parousia sometime in the future. Scoffers asked, "Where is the promise of his coming? For since the Fathers fell asleep, all things continue as they were from the beginning of creation." [177] Saint Peter, instructing the early Church and answering these questions, pointed out the importance of this growing "time between," the period of proclaiming God's Word in Christ: "But, beloved, do not be ignorant of this one thing, that one day with the Lord is as a thousand years, and a thousand years as one day. The Lord does not delay in his promises, but *for your sake* is long-suffering, not wishing that any should perish but that all turn to repentence." [178]

Saint Paul also speaks of the apocalyptic utterance of the Word, and sees in it the completion of the work of Christ: "Then comes the end, when he delivers the kingdom to God the Father, when he does away with all sovereignty, authority and power . . . and when all things are made subject to him, then the Son himself will also be made subject to him who subjected all things to him, that God may be all in all." [179] The "subjections" of which Paul speaks when he refers to Christ being subject to the Father are a subjection of sonship: Son to Father, not a metaphysical subjection. Significantly, then, theologians have long spoken of the eternal life of the faithful, who are subject to Christ, and Christ to the Father, as sharing intimately in the life of the Trinity. For Paul, Christ the "wisdom" of God present in the creation, is the climax and decisive moment of history, is also the culmination of history under the imagery of being the last Adam.[180]

It is interesting to note, and also significant for any understanding of the Book of the Apocalypse, that all the New Testament writers use the metaphors of battle and conquest to speak of the reconciling work of Christ. While the New Testament affirms (through the activity of the Word in creation) the essential goodness of the created, it does allow that through the sin of Adam, Satan gained power over the world,[181] and that in the Cross and Resurrection, Christ has accomplished a victory over the satanic power. The eschatological event of Christ continues in the present stage of salvation history through its proclamation, and this period of proclamation, or time of the Church, is pictured as one of warfare: "These will fight with the Lamb, and the Lamb will overcome them"; ". . . and he went away to wage war with the rest of her offspring, who keep the commandments of God, and hold fast the testimony of Jesus." [182] The Antichrist, whether one understands it to be a singular or a collective figure, shares in this battle against Christ. The hostility and the warfare reign even until now, although the decisive battle has been fought in the Christ event; the tension of the "even now" and the "not yet" marks this period of proclaiming the Word. The revelation of Christ, the last apocalyptic utterance of the Word marks the final destruction and imprisonment of the satanic force.[183]

The end of the world (the *telos*) of which the New Testament speaks must not be merely envisioned as an end point. It is not an Oriental submergence of the distinct into a simple unity, but it is rather the manifestation of the new creation in Christ; it is the revelation of a new world that is completely transcendent to the old. The New Testament resort to image and metaphor to describe the apocalyptic utterance is understandable, for "Eye has not seen nor ear heard, nor has it entered into the heart of man, what things God has prepared for those who love him." It is only because we have heard God's Word in Christ that we are able to speak of that last day; no one can know about that day, except, as Paul says, "But we have the mind of Christ." [184]

It is for that last day, for that end, that the whole of creation yearns.[185] This transcendent state of the world is the Sabbath rest of God Himself, for again, in the Epistle to the Hebrews, we meet the connection of creation-redemption-apocalypse: "There remains, therefore, a Sabbath Rest for the people of God. For He Who has entered into his Rest, has himself also rested from his own works, even as God did from his. Let us, therefore, hasten to enter into that Rest." The apocalyptic utterance of the Word must of necessity imply at that time a judgment: "For the Word of God is living and efficient and keener than any two-edged sword, and extending even to the division of soul and spirit, of joints also and of marrow, and a discerner of the thoughts and intentions of the heart." [186] The Sabbath rest, then, toward which history presses as to its end, is of God. "This is not the rest of death nor the abolition of all distinctions, but the rest of perfection. The stream of time, which presses forward, will flow into the deep sea of eternity." [187] The picture of the end presented by John fulfills the "tabernacling" theme of the incarnation of the Word ("And I heard a loud voice from the throne saying: 'Behold the dwelling of God with men, and he will dwell with them' ") and of its meaning in the end ("And I saw no temple therein. For the Lord God Almighty and the Lamb are the temple thereof").[188]

One point remains to be stressed about that last day—the relation of the eschatological and apocalyptic utterances of the Word. The apocalyptic utterance of the Word should not be envisioned as the new creation, for that has already taken place in Christ. This utterance is to be the revelation of that new creation in Christ: "For as in Adam all die, so in Christ all will be made to live. *But each in His own turn,* Christ as first fruits, then they who are Christ's, who have believed, at His coming." [189] Thus the new creation has occurred in the Cross and Resurrection, in the eschatological utterance, and now awaits its revelation. It is the Christian's sharing of the Resurrection that makes him partake of the new creation in Christ,[190] and it is for the manifestation of this that the Christian looks: "For you have died and your life is hidden with Christ in God. When Christ, your life, shall appear, then you too will appear with him in glory." [191] Thus when the Apocalypse speaks of the new creation; it speaks of the eschatological utterance, and then it goes on to speak of the manifestation of that new creation in the last day.[192] It is because of the new creation that Paul can say, "for this world as we see it is passing away." [193] Our incorporation into the risen Jesus is real but not now manifest; it is decisive but not now revealed. Our hearing of God's Word in the eschatological utterance is comparable to a sowing; the harvest will occur, when that Word is spoken in the Apocalypse, and "what is sown in corruption rises in power; what is sown a natural body rises a spiritual body. . . . But when this mortal body puts on immortality, then shall come to pass the word that is written, 'Death is swallowed up in victory.' 'O death, where is thy victory? O death, where is thy sting?' . . . But thanks be to God who has given us the victory through our Lord Jesus Christ." [194]

And so it is that the moment of revelation in the eschatological utterance of the Word of God is directly related to the paschal victory of Jesus. That final victory, of which the theologians speak as the resurrection of the body, is the manifestation of that which is spoken by God to man in the resurrection of Jesus. Eric Rust states it thus: "Through the resurrection of the Lord, re-creative and redemptive forces were released in history and in our world. History and nature are thus moving towards a climax in which what is now working in a hidden way will finally be disclosed. The resurrected Body of Christ carries within itself the meaning of all created existence, and, just as this is the work of God, so also will be the resurrection of the believer, the fulfillment of history, and the re-creation or resurrection of the cosmos." [195]

The Relationship of the Divine Utterances of the Word

The Word of God is operative in the creation of the world, and thus we speak of the creative utterance of the Word. While consideration of this utterance of the Word guards the Christian against any manichean tendency to disdain the fruit of God's creative action, it also poses the problem of God's eschatological Word in Christ and their relationship. Modern theologians, pre-eminently Barth, Niebuhr, and Löwith, have long shared a common stress upon the absolute discontinuity of God's Word in Christ with human history. Thus neo-orthodoxy has been marked by its seemingly cavalier dismissal of natural theology in favor of accenting God's transcendence and man's sin. Catholic eschatologists have tended also to favor absolutist ways of speaking about God and man. Although such theologies and eschatological presentations are attractive—as extremes are always attractive—their attention to the essential goodness inherent in God's creative purpose has been less than satisfying. Their problem, however, remains also our problem:

How are we to envision the distinction of the creative and eschatological utterances of the Word? To affirm the identity of these utterances precisely as utterances of the one Word of God, and to affirm
their distinction precisely as utterances, is to avoid the problem by
terminological restatement.

The solution, oddly, seems to lie in the neo-orthodox and eschatological insistences upon man's sin. God's creative purpose has been
truly thwarted in his free creatures by their use of that very freedom
to sin. Human history in its origin has been deformed through sin,
God's purpose has been thwarted; to be homely: the well water is
bad because the spring has been poisoned. And while sin and evil
persist in the world—and they will persist until the last day—the
Christian nevertheless affirms that in Christ a new creation has
occurred, the evil of sin has been repaired, and the decisive battle
over the powers of evil has been won.

Human history, having both its origin and its maintenance in
being in God's creative utterance of His Word, always remains susceptible to the Word of God. The transcendence of the all-holy God
is reflected in the doctrine of God's immanence in His creation. It
is not the created precisely as created that is evil; rather, as created,
it is good and susceptible to the Word. Not man's freedom to sin
but his choice to do so irreparably destroys his relationship to God
ex parte hominis (insofar as man himself might be able to repair it).
It enslaves him and the world, by free choice, to the powers of evil
and the fruit of death. Man, by sin now freely constituted as a
sinner (because in him God's creative purpose of sharing a special
relationship has been thwarted) has been seriously affected. And yet,
although man has fallen short of the glory of God by sin, and although he is now powerless to repair that wound of sin, yet as God's
creation, *and precisely as His creation,* there still remains the
possibility of the Creator's altering man's interior constitution as
a sinner; man still remains susceptible to the creative and life-giving
Word. The *possibility* of redemption is metaphysical, i.e., the sinner
as a being (and, therefore, the result of God's creative utterance).
Man's in-existence, therefore, is the connecting link of the creative
and eschatological utterances of the Word.[196]

The eschatological utterance of God's Word, the Christ event,
is the restoration of God's purpose in His creation thwarted by sin.
Like the creative utterance, it is God's free act directed toward us,

motivated only by His love. Saint Paul, applying the traditional Judaic conception of the solidarity of corporate personality, sees a new Adam in Christ, so that we who hear the Word, we who are in Christ, have conquest over sin and death in His conquest, the Cross and Resurrection.

> But not like the offense is the gift. For if by the offense of the one the many died, much more has the grace of God and the gift in the grace of the one man Jesus Christ, abounded unto the many. . . . For if by reason of the one man's offense death reigned through the one man, much more will they who receive the abundance of the grace and of the gift of justice reign in life through the one Jesus Christ. Therefore as from the offense of the one man the result was unto condemnation to all men, so from the justice of the one the result is unto justification of life to all men. For just as by the disobedience of the one man the many were constituted sinners, so also by the obedience of the one the many will be constituted just.[197]

So we find in Paul the constant New Testament theme of man and the world being enslaved by the demonic powers *through* Adam's sin. When Paul tells us that it is *"through* one man sin came into world," and not *"because* of one man," the distinction to be preserved is crucial; for Adam is not the origin of sin, but through his sin man and the whole world fall captive to the power of Satan. Creation is thus under bondage, and in Christ, the new Adam, the definitive victory over the power of Satan is achieved. Karl Heim illustrates the Pauline conception masterfully:

> As a result of the Satanic Fall, which led Adam astray so that he lost fellowship with God and wished to glorify himself a Satanic power has broken into the world, which has spread like an avalanche through the world of human history, and has assumed more and more sinister dimensions. . . . Paul is convinced that in this physical resurrection of Jesus Christ a cosmic event took place. Christ is, as Paul says, the "first-fruits" of a new, world-embracing event, which like the cosmic event of original sin must go on like an avalanche until it reaches its goal.[198]

Nor is Paul's use of the wisdom tradition and his identification of wisdom and Christ to be lost sight of here. Wisdom personified was viewed as active in the creation, so that it is in man's free sin and the entrance it affords the satanic power, not in the essentially dependent nature of creation, that the problem of corruption and death is to be placed. The Pauline wisdom-Christ theme is a powerful antidote for the theologian fascinated by neo-orthodox and

eschatological absolutes. The disrespect of natural theology en-
gendered in the neo-orthodoxy of the Barthians falters in the face
of the Pauline use of wisdom; and "we may go further than this
and say that it ignores the doctrine of Christ as the Wisdom of God
which we found in Paul." [199]

The first stage of salvation history, of the eschatological utterance
of the Word, was essentially one of preparation. The old covenant,
precisely as preparation, could not of itself repair the wound of
death—sin. "For the Law, having but a shadow of the good things
to come, and not the exact image of the objects, is never able by
the sacrifices which they offer continually, year after year the same,
to perfect those who draw near; for in that case would they not
have ceased to be offered, because the worshippers, once cleansed,
would no longer have any consciousness of sin." The sacrifices of
this preparatory phase, in which the Word progressively emerges
in human history, are essentially temporary, "imposed until a time
of reformation." [200] Israel possessed only the hope of a redemption
and perfect reconciliation with God in the *eschaton*.[201]

The Christ event, chronologically central to salvation history, is
the eschatological utterance, and Christ the Word perfectly effects
"at the set time" the reconciliation made necessary by sin.[202] So
Paul tells us of the work of the Word: "But now in Christ Jesus
you, who were once afar off, have been brought near through the
blood of Christ," [203] and that in Christ the Father reconciles all
things, "making peace through the blood of the Cross." [204] In this
reconciling work of the Word we have peace with God.[205] And the
dimensions of this work are phenomenal, for God has not only
reconciled us in Christ but also the whole of creation: "For God was
truly in Christ, reconciling the world to himself." [206] In this reconciling work of His Cross, Christ has become the one mediator of a
new covenant, and a new Covenant People.[207] Just as the Word of
God was operative in the creation of the world, the eschatological
utterance of the Word is His operation in the new creation.[208] "If
then any man is in Christ, he is a new creature: the former things
have passed away; behold, they are made new! but all things are
from God, who has reconciled us to Himself through Christ.[209]

The final stage of salvation history is the proclamation of the
Word, in which each man is faced with the eschatological Word
and called to decision. "How then are they to call upon him in
whom they have not believed? But how are they to believe him

whom they have not heard? And how are they to hear if no one preaches? And how are men to preach unless they be sent?" [210] The Church, sent ("apostoled") into history by Christ, bears to man the Word that reconciles all creation to God: "On behalf of Christ, therefore, we are acting as ambassadors, God, as it were, appealing through us. We exhort you, for Christ's sake, be reconciled to God." [211]

God's Word, then, has been spoken in our midst in all its fullness, so that He perfects His creation through incarnation. Human history now is to hear this reconciling Word and undergo the new creation that restores man's authentic existence destroyed in sin. Therefore, this is the meaning of the Church's proclamation of the Word in Word, sacrament, and Eucharist; she is sent by Christ, as He was sent by the Father, so that the Word of God will reach out to all men, for the Church, "always possesses the Word itself in its entirety, both spoken and speaking in her midst." [212] Father Bouyer beautifully expresses this meaning of the Church in our stage of history: "In order that the eternal gift of God in the procession of His Word, the eternal gift of His love, that is of His deepest being, should replenish and fulfill all time by becoming the fulness of all being, newly created in Christ." [213]

New Testament imagery describes this decisive eschatological utterance in picturing Christ as the Lamb of God, the completion of the paschal type, who has redeemed us in His blood.[214] Even under this eschatological imagery the pre-existence of the Lamb is affirmed, "foreknown, indeed, before the foundation of the world," and His apocalyptic function as well.[215] Those who have heard the saving Word in the eschatological utterance of the Christ event are pictured as those who "have washed their robes and made them white in the blood of the Lamb." [216]

> The Mystery of the Lamb is the mystery of selfgiving love, the mystery of God Himself. This is the love that governs every moment of world history. It is the love that inspires God's creative act of calling the world into being. It is the love that inspires all of his subsequent gracious acts throughout the course of history until the final act that will destroy the last manifestations of death and inaugurate the reign of victorious love.[217]

We have to come to see, then, that the New Testament constantly affirms the identity of the Word in creation and redemption—that the creative and eschatological events are both utterances of the one

Word; it also now affirms the identity of this same word with the apocalyptic utterance.

How is the apocalyptic utterance of the Word distinct from the eschatological? How can there be another utterance of the Word really distinct from the decisive Christ event, which is intrinsically eschatological? Here again we must keep in mind first, the fundamental identity and unchanging nature of God's Word in all three utterances, and second, the distinction in each, a distinction in history based upon the progressive articulation of the Word in the actions of God toward us. Thus the essential distinction possessed by the apocalyptic utterance is precisely "apocalypse"—revelation. As the Christ event revealed the divine plan in Christ, the person of the Word, nevertheless such a revelation remains from man's point of view one based on faith. The apocalyptic revelation is to be one of sight—all will see and know the divine Word. "Behold, he comes with the clouds, and every eye shall see him," for "we see now through a mirror in an obscure manner, but then face to face." [218] So the salvation of the individual is related to the eschatological utterance: by hearing God's Word in Christ a man receives the saving Word and is joined to it. The apocalyptic utterance is essentially the final word of salvation, for Saint Peter tells us that having heard the eschatological utterance, he now looks forward to sharing the essentially revelatory note of the apocalyptic utterance, for he is "the partaker also of the glory that is to be revealed in time to come." [219]

The decisive moment for human history is the eschatological utterance of the Word, so that the stages of salvation history revolve about the Christ event as a central pivot, and it pleased God that "through him he should reconcile to himself all things." [220] This is the eschatological utterance, for it is God's last utterance to man, the very person of the Word,[221] an utterance fulfilling creation by calling sinful man to authentic existence. Faith, or hearing that utterance in this world, is also, therefore, eschatological, and awaits now the final revelation and perfect manifestation of that same person of the Word in the apocalyptic utterance.

Chapter 8

OUR TIME:
THE AGE OF PROCLAMATION

IT IS IMPOSSIBLE to avoid the comfortable intellectual feeling that comes with the possession or imagined possession of the meaning of history. The Christian, no less than the idealist philosopher or Marxian economist, also possesses the comfort that his vision of history affords him. And while the Christian readily admits that the comfort is no test for the validity of his vision, he is also aware that the source of this meaning of history is transcendent to reason and is achieved in faith. He is aware, in addition, of the incompleteness of his view, which is due to his expectation of God's final utterance of His Word in the revelation of the end. Thus it is that the New Testament itself reflects not only the certainty that gives comfort but also the tension that avoids complacency. The "even now" and the "not yet" of our eschatological age reflect this "time between" in which we live: a time of certainty and a time of tension, a time of possession and a time of expectancy.

If we have found valid principles for our over-all understanding of history along the lines of a theology of the Word, yet it still remains for us to examine more closely this time, or era, in which we live. While the general process of our history is grasped as meaningful from our theology, there still remains the problem of exploring the implications of such a theology *hic et nunc*—at our present moment. We have seen that this time we now share is held in being by the creative utterance of the Word, and that it has been determined in a decisive manner in outcome by the eschatological utterance of the Word, and also that it awaits His revelation in the end. Nevertheless this present stage of salvation history, this last time, must have its own specific principles of understanding drawn from our general theological grasp of history.

There is a difficulty here. The difficulty is rooted in the manifold approaches to the one reality revealed in the New Testament which provides adequate evidence for considering human history in its present stage as the new creation or eschatological age, or again, as the age of the Church, or as the age of the Resurrection and the resurrection body of Jesus. From other points of view we might call this age that of the Spirit, the age of faith, or—as Cullmann would prefer—the age of the Lordship of Jesus. All these depend upon the organizational principle adopted from the data of revelation. Our problem, then, is one of organizing the data of revelation about a theme or synthesis that will adequately reflect each insight and relate it meaningfully to a view of the whole. The theme chosen must be itself adequate to the historical line as such. Thus, as we have taken a general viewpoint from a theology of the Word, we now take the position that this synthesis may be adequately represented by seeing this age of ours as the age of proclamation.

What is meant when we say that this present stage of history in which we are is the age of proclamation? It is that this last stage of salvation history is marked by proclamation of the Word of God throughout time and space. The age of proclamation is the *proclamation of the Word,* which is God's deed in Christ, *to* all men *for* their salvation *in* His community, the Church, *through* Word and sacrament, pre-eminently the Eucharist, *by* the power of the Holy Spirit. The age of proclamation is, in short, the articulation of the Word in history; it is the effecting of Christ's reconciling ministry until time is filled and the Word itself stands revealed.

Thus the proclamation of the Word is the present and last stage of the history of redemption. It is now intrinsically bound up with the decisive deed of God in Christ, which is His victory through the Cross and Resurrection. The proclamation is now necessary that men be brought to salvation. Between the victory of Christ and His parousia the "good news" of this decisive deed, this eschatological Word, is to be proclaimed "and then will come the end." [1] "And the Gospel must first be preached to all the nations." [2] The universal Lordship of Christ, indicated by His resurrection and ascension, demonstrates the universal nature of this mission: the proclamation is not to be bound by geography or time.

The proclamation is the present stage of the eschatological utterance of the Word; it is for us intrinsically connected to the redemptive act of Christ. "How then are they to call upon him in whom they have not believed? But how are they to believe in him whom they have not heard?"[3] As the present stage of the eschatological utterance of the Word, proclaiming that Word is now itself an eschatological act: the "time between" is bordered by the resurrection of Christ and the resurrection of the dead, and the Spirit of God is poured out upon the Church precisely that it may proclaim Christ to the very ends of the earth.[4] The finality that proclamation bears to salvation history is itself indicated by Christ, and more so than indicated, even commanded, for the mission of His witnesses guarantees His presence: "And behold, I am with you all days, even to the consummation of the world"; and again, "They went forth and preached everywhere, while the Lord worked with them and confirmed the preaching by the signs that followed."[5] Where the Word is proclaimed, then is Christ Himself present. Christ's power is there and the proclamation is itself the work of Christ.[6]

In our present time it is the proclamation of the Word that unites our concepts of the creative, eschatological, and apocalyptic utterances of the Word. These are meaningfully present in the proclamation. There is an awareness of the Word in whom we live and move and have our being, of the eschatological nature of that Word, for we share the victory of Christ and are a new creation in Him, and thus we really anticipate the glory of Christ that is to be revealed.

THE MEANING OF PROCLAMATION

There are very definite meanings that pertain to those concepts about which we organize the theological understanding of the history of our present age. It is this stage in which we are that we have chosen to designate as the age of proclamation. How and in what way is this proclamation constituted? Again, we must turn for our answers to the New Testament.

The core of New Testament Christianity, the very heart of the message that is proclaimed in every book of the New Testament, is called, as we have seen, the kerygma, or proclamation. Frequently English translations of "kerygma" use the expression "preaching". While at first it would seem easy to understand the kerygma in the sense of its being simply the core of the message, the heart of the Christian religion, the facts that constitute the essence of Christianity, nevertheless it seems that in the New Testament the term means something more. Saint Paul in writing to the Corinthians says that "it pleased God by the foolishness of our preaching [kerygma] to save those who believe." [7] This seems to indicate that in Paul the sermon is part and parcel of the saving act of God. Kerygma is more than just the verbal articulation, the preaching action in itself, it is—in Paul's mind—not only the preaching but the message preached; kerygma, rightly understand, includes the message preached, which is the Christ event. Because the Word of God, Jesus Christ, is present in the message proclaimed, that message becomes able to save the hearer. The Word of God makes Himself accessible to men by clothing Himself in humanity in the Incarnation, and continues that incarnation by taking on the words of the creature in the proclamation. Where Jesus is proclaimed, therefore, in words (verbal or visible) Jesus makes Himself present for the salvation of the hearer.

The New Testament, in a more famed instance, chooses the word "evangelion," or "good news," or "Gospel." There is according to the New Testament only *one* Gospel, only one announcement of good news, only one proclamation—that of Jesus Christ. Significantly, the Evangelists introduce their books as "The *Gospel* according to . . . " This Gospel, or "good news," is the content itself—the Christ event.

Any authorized proclamation, any "apostled" (sent) proclamation of the Christ event, is the making present of that one same saving event. It is kerygma. The Christ event is proclaimed wherever the eschatological Word is proclaimed, that is, where the Cross and resurrection of Jesus are communicated. And again, this communication may be through human words (literally, preaching) or in sacraments (which are signs, or "visible words") by those sent to do so by the Word. As to purpose, the event of God in Christ reconciling man to himself is to be proclaimed in words and sacraments precisely in order that men may come to salvation. The knowledge of what God has done in Christ, that is, of the historical order of the events alone, the knowledge of the historicity of 33 A.D., is not enough. The *meaning* of those events as saving events must be grasped by the whole man so that he is truly constituted as a "hearer" of the eschatological utterance of God's Word in order that he be brought to salvation. The most detailed history books of the first century A.D. do not of themselves lead to salvation for the hearer or reader, for this is accomplished only by the foolishness—in Paul's words—of the kerygma or proclamation. The most detailed historical information is as nothing against the authorized forms of proclamation in words (Scripture, the teaching Church, the Christian preaching) or sacraments (visible "words"), which, making present to the hearer the saving event of Christ, lead to salvation.

Moreover, we may state that the proclamation of the Word also possesses a significance of discourse as the very term "word," or "Logos," itself indicates. It is in consequence, and only in consequence of this Word, or deed of God, that we can speak at all of revelation. In other words, from our viewpoint the divine Word is first a person, not a doctrine; to speak of God's Word is not to speak of a thing, but of a person. Therefore, priority is given not to what is said in the utterance of God's Word, but to God's act. This is not to say that the revelatory function of the Word is not present when the Word is proclaimed—quite the contrary; rather, it is to say that the priority of man's reception of the Word is the reception of the living person of the Word, and in consequence, in the person of the Word, the revelation of God.

Furthermore, the discourse significance of the Word also implies immediately a dialogue relationship where the Word is uttered. God's Word never exists in a vacuum; men are not, as it were, unnecessary to the consideration of the utterance of the Word *ad extra*. In surveying sacred history we find not only the creative nature of God's Word but also its selective nature; the Word chooses—and this is more than evident in one of the basic themes of scripture: covenant-election. The fundamental unity of all salvation history is God *and* His people; the Word of God creates and holds in existence a people. Thus in concept and in history the Word without a hearer is inconceivable; the dialogue relationship is established by the Word where it is uttered, for God's Word is always God's Word to man.

Those constant features of the Word that mark its appearence are perforce always present in the dialogue relationship. Thus the Word, where uttered, is creative and life-giving: it calls into existence, or into a *new* existence. The Word is free, it is uttered unconditionally and always independently of man's merits. The Word is effective, that is, the Word alone effects forgiveness, regeneration, reconciliation—not man's response or reception.

The second party to the dialogue relationship is man. The dialogue is not terminated by the Word of God, but is completed by the active response of man. Man receives God's act, he "hears" God's Word in a personal decisive act in which he is totally involved and to which he is drawn by the power of the Word itself.

The appreciation of the dialogue relationship of God-man involved in all utterances of the Word demands a final consideration of the encounter itself, the field of contact of the Word and man. This point of connection, or encounter, is the sounding, or heralding, of the proclamation. The solemn and authorized communication of the Word in human words or signs is the vital and necessary moment when the Word and man meet, it is the point of encounter. Thus it follows from a consideration of the very nature of the Word and from a consideration of the dialogistic relationship established from the moment of encounter in proclamation, that proclamation itself is necessary for man to recover his authentic existence, his true constitution in creation.

The Word of God in Christ, the eschatological utterance, is at this stage of salvation history a proclaimed Word. Our age of proclamation is the last stage of the eschatological utterance of the Word. It is maintained further that the crucified and risen Christ is present in the proclamation, for, as we shall see, the theology of mission guarantees the presence of Christ in the proclaiming community and in the proclamation itself. Thus it is that for the Christian the theological construction of the proclamation in our time must grant the priority of the presence of the Word as proclaimed Word, and therefore also the priority of the proclaiming community or Church. But the Church herself, the sacrament of Christ, proclaims Christ in two modes: word and sacrament.

In the first mode we find the human words in which Christ is proclaimed. The authorized community proclamation and its inspired verbal crystallization (Scripture) are necessarily infallible. There are in the Church not two sources of her proclamation, but one, namely the Word itself proclaimed in living tradition, of which Scripture is, as we have said, a verbal crystallization under the power of the Spirit. In addition to this infallible proclamation in human words there are also verbal but fallible forms of proclamation in the ordinary teaching office of the Church and in the day-to-day preaching of authorized preachers. Thus in the Sunday sermon and in any authorized preaching and teaching, the Word is truly proclaimed, for in preaching Christ, the Word of God is set forth. The second mode of proclamation is the "sign," that is, the sacraments of the Word. Thus Paul says: "As often as ye break the bread and drink this cup, ye proclaim the death of the Lord until He comes." [8] The sacraments are the actions of the Word in His community effected by His Holy Spirit.

Finally, we may state that in both modes of proclamation the dialogue relationship is present. In both modes God in Christ, in the Cross and resurrection of Jesus, effects the salvation of him who truly hears. The supreme moment of proclamation in our age is, as we shall see, in that action of the community when Christ is proclaimed both in word and in sign—the Eucharist.

THE CONTENT OF PROCLAMATION: THE RESURRECTION AGE

What is to be proclaimed? Simply, the Word of God. The Gospel, or "good news," the kerygma, or heralding of God's deed in Christ, is the Word of God. To see how Christ is present in this proclaimed content it is necessary to examine the ministry of the Church. To this we shall turn shortly, but first let us see the Word itself that is to be proclaimed.

The Lord sends men to speak, He pours out upon them His Holy Spirit to effect this mission, and He guarantees His presence in their proclamation. The New Testament speaks of the deed of God in Christ, wherein He reconciles the world to Himself as "kerygma" and "gospel," terms that imply a messenger, herald, or apostle. The Word is God's Word, and the Word is flesh in Christ, and Christ is present in the proclamation of that Word. Thus it is that the New Testament presents the public proclamation of Christ first in its one basic kerygma (for this denotes not only the message but the content as well), and then, basic to the kerygma, the Gospel, that is, the Christ event, which is the Cross and resurrection of Jesus.

Critical examination of the New Testament books has isolated for us a number of confessions, confessions of faith in the early Church and apostolic era that all possess the element of unity that is Christ Himself. Christ is the center of their affirmations, and all anchor themselves in the specific historical event of Jesus Christ. This critical dissection also expresses clearly the unifying element in all the

New Testament books, their common core in the proclamation of the kerygma. Since it is the kerygma that essentially marks the fundamental preaching of the Church (which is not to say that it exhausts the total message confided to it by the Lord), it is the kerygma that is to be examined closely; for it is the kerygma, the heralding and the content, by which it pleases God to save those who believe.[9]

The letters of Saint Paul are the earliest of the documents of the New Testament, and these present a problem in isolating the kerygma, for they are written to already believing Christians and therefore presuppose the kerygma; "They expound and defend the implications of the Gospel rather than proclaim it." [10] In his letters to the Corinthians Paul himself clearly makes this distinction, and again in his metaphor of the foundation and the superstructure. He begs his readers to "recall to your minds, brethren, the gospel that I preached to you." [11] It is certain that a constant note in the Pauline preaching was the fact that Christ died and rose again "according to the Scriptures," that is, that Paul preached the Christ event in a meaningful setting of the history of salvation—God's plan for saving men. So Professor Dodd comments: "The Pauline *kerygma* was a proclamation of the facts of the death and resurrection of Christ in an eschatological setting which gives significance to the facts." [12] Finally, we may state that throughout his writings Paul stoutly affirms the identity of this gospel he preached with that proclaimed by the apostles.

We may set out the elements of the Pauline kerygma, found throughout his epistles, in this manner: (1) Christ fulfills the prophecies of the Old Testament and inaugurates the new age. (2) He was put to death and was buried. (3) He rose again. (4) He is exalted at the right hand of God and is now Lord of all. (5) He will come again.[13]

In the Book of the Acts we do have records of what seems to be the earliest forms of the kerygma in the Church: Peter on Pentecost Sunday, and later addresses of Peter to the people, to the Sanhedrin, and to the family of Cornelius.[14] Even those biblical critics who have cast doubts upon this record of speeches as preserving the actual words of Peter nevertheless admit that Acts does present in these instances the kerygma of the Church at its earliest period in Jerusalem. This representation of the kerygma may be summarized thus: (1) There is a new age in Jesus Christ. (2) The ministry, death, and resurrection of Jesus inaugurate this new age. (3) Jesus has been exalted in His resurrection and constituted Lord of all. (4) He pours forth His Holy Spirit upon all who obey Him. (5) He will return. (6) An appeal by the preacher for repentance, faith, and baptism.[15]

Again, as in the case of Paul, we have essentially the proclamation of the death and resurrection of Christ within an eschatological setting. Where other New Testament authors use the terms "gospel" or "kerygma," it is significant to note here that Saint Luke speaks of this as the "Word of God" or the "Word of the Lord" for the content of the proclamation. In presenting the apostles as witnesses to Jesus in Jerusalem he speaks of them as proclaiming the Word of the Lord. The great reliability that is to be attached to these particular sections of the Book of Acts is based upon the apostolic transmission of the Christian kerygma and the evident apostolic control over the material testified to in Acts itself.[16]

The Gospel documents represent for us the later expansion of the historical sections of the kerygma; they all concentrate their concluding chapters upon the death and resurrection of Jesus. Mark represents the closest approximation of the other forms of the kerygma,[17] while Matthew and Luke represent a departure from the kerygma in the way that they organize the content of the apostolic preaching. John, in turn, also presents the historical elements of the kerygma, but he places far more emphasis upon the eschatological significance of Jesus' life as well as of His death and resurrection. While Paul and John emerge from our study of the New Testament as the theologians par excellence and as representative of significant development of kerygma, nevertheless the kerygma constitutes the basis and core of their theologies.

Thus for all their diversity the books of the New Testament present a fundamental unity in their common proclamation of the Word, Jesus Christ. They proclaim the Word, and as kerygma, they herald the one Gospel; their confessions of faith are essentially confessions of Jesus Christ. The essential elements of the kerygma may be summarized, then, as the Christ event, that is, the life, death, and resurrection of Jesus Christ. A New Testament scholar such as Oscar Cullmann can sum up this proclamation of the Word now in the confession of the Lordship of Jesus. This is also why there are theologians who speak of our present stage of history as the Resurrection age, because of the central place of the Resurrection in the proclamation of Christ. That the Resurrection is absolutely intrinsic to the Gospel and its heralding, and indeed essential to any proclamation of the Word, is more than evident. As Saint Paul says: "And if Christ has not risen, vain then is our preaching [*kerygma*], vain too is your faith." [18]

The Place of Proclamation: The Age of the Church

To speak of our present time as one of Proclamation, it is necessary, in view of a specific element of the New Testament revelation, to speak also of this period as the time of the Church. It is the Church, the witnessing community, that proclaims the Word. In hearing the Word a man is constituted a member of that eschatological community of the Word—the new Israel. The Church is constituted by the Will of Christ about the apostolic ministry; as Christ received His mission from the Father (He is sent, "apostled" by the Father), so also He sends others (apostles); Christ transmits His mission to the Church. Sent as He was sent, the Church possesses the power of Christ; the Church, as the sign or sacrament of Christ, is therefore the presence of the Word in history's successive stages until the end. The Church proclaims the Word both in human speech and in the sacraments.

Jesus Christ, the Word Incarnate, is sent into the world to effect its salvation.[19] God's utterance of His eternal Word in time is the sending of the Word; Christ is, to use the Greek, therefore "apostled" by the Father; He is *the* apostle. Christ Himself makes this idea of mission abundantly clear: "And the Father himself, who has sent me . . ."; [20] "With me is he who sent me, the Father . . ."; [21] "I must do the works of him who sent me . . ."; [22] "My teaching is not my own, but his who sent me." [23] To hear the Word in its eschatological utterance is therefore to hear the Father: "He who believes in me, believes not in me but in him who sent me. And he who sees me, sees him who sent me." [24] "Now this is everlasting life, that they may know Thee, the only true God, and him whom Thou hast sent, Jesus Christ." [25] The parables of the Good Shepherd and of the vine dressers, also indicate the mission of Jesus.[26] There is, then, an identification of Jesus, the Word, with Him who sent or uttered Him.

But in the New Testament we find not only that Jesus is the apostle of the Father but also that he apostles his followers as the Church. "Even as thou hast sent me into the world, so also I have sent them into the world." The Church is the resurrection body of Jesus, it is the temple of his presence in the world; it is after the Resurrection that Jesus mandates the apostles as those whom he sends: "As the Father has sent me, I also send you." [27] Moreover the Old Testament pastoral image of Israel and God as sheep and shepherd (Ps. 22) was deliberately evoked in the New Testament to illustrate the apostolic nature of the Church, and was used in this manner by both Peter and Paul.[28]

Just as there is an identification of Jesus and the Godhead, there is also, in the mandate of the apostles as those sent by Christ, an identification of the Church (the new Israel) and Jesus. The Church is the community of the Word and so proclaims the Word; the actions or "signs" of the Church that constitute this proclamation are in this same process of identity the actions of the Word. Thus in a definitive sense where the Church proclaims in speech or in sign, in word or in sacrament, there the Word is present.

Thus it is that we speak of the Church as the *locus* or proper place of proclamation. The eschatological utterance of the Word of God, the Christ event, can be proclaimed in no other place than within this community of the believers and the apostled. The Church as the mandated or apostled community is the visible sign itself—*the* sacrament—of Christ. The Church is identified with Christ: "Who hears you, hears Me . . . "; [29] "Behold, I am with you all days . . ."; [30] "Where two or three are gathered together, behold, there am I in the midst of them . . ."; [31] "It is Me whom thou persecutest." [32]

However, the proclamation of the Word in word and sacrament in this community has, so to speak, both horizontal and vertical direction—it is both intensive and extensive proclamation. It is vertical or intensive when we speak of this proclamation *within* the community; to use a metaphor from physics, the proclamation is centripetal, that is, the saving event of the Cross and the resurrection of Jesus is continually addressed to the believer. The Christian proceeds "from faith to faith," and his initial commitment to the deed of God in Christ is ever deepened and strengthened both in the verbal proclamation of Scripture and the teaching Church and in the sacramental proclamation. For this reason we will be able to speak of the Eucharist as the pre-eminent proclamation of the Word, so that in this sense the Eucharistic celebration can be seen as the very core of the Church, as the ultimate intensive form of the presence of the Word to the believers as community and as individuals.

The horizontal direction of the proclamation of the Church, the centrifugal force of proclamation, is extensive to space and time. This is to say that the Word is proclaimed to all peoples without exception; it is represented by the universal nature of the mission given the proclaiming community. Finally, in both the intensive and extensive directions of the proclamation, since it is the Word that is proclaimed, the dialogistic relationship of the Word to man is always present.

The Church is presented to us in the New Testament under another very important image. It is described as the kingdom of God established in Christ Jesus. Because of the teaching of Jesus, the Easter experience, and the gift of the Holy Spirit on Pentecost, the New Testament presents the Church as the Kingdom in the community of the believers in Jesus who have received the Spirit. But this idea of the Church as the Kingdom is evidently one that shows a development in various places in the New Testament. It is arrived at through the guidance of the Holy Spirit in the Church's penetration into the meaning of the universal mission she has received from her Lord. The transformation by which the Church came to understand herself as the Kingdom of God was accomplished over a number of occasions recorded in the Book of the Acts.[33]

The *first* of these was Pentecost. That the apostles were living in messianic times was evident to them in the gift of the Holy Spirit; they were the new Israel, and the last age into which they had now entered must be envisioned in two stages: preparation (their period of mission) and parousia (the second coming). The *second* occasion was the martyrdom of Saint Stephen. The Hellenist Christians, especially Stephen, reminded the early Church that "it was in this world that they must struggle, even to death, to establish the kingdom." [34] The conversion of Cornelius marks the *third* stage of development. Peter's vision and the baptism of Cornelius led to the realization of the universality of the Kingdom, and the Antiochean Christians exemplified this by putting Stephen's principle to work.[35] The *fourth* stage is represented by Saint Paul. The older belief that the parousia is to come when the Jews as a people enter the Kingdom still remains, but now this is postponed by Israel's rejection of the Gospel until the full number of the Gentiles has come in.[36] *Fifth* and last we have the Council at Jerusalem. This is the last function of Jerusalem Christianity, and it grants the charter of Christian liberty at that Council. Thus it is that Saint Luke's theology, as we find it in the Book of the Acts envisions the Christ event as inaugurating the Kingdom, and that as the Church proclaims Christ, "to reject the church is to refuse God's kingdom; the coming of that kingdom upon earth was effected by the apostolic organization of the church among the Gentiles." [37]

One point remains for our study, however, and that is the gift of the Holy Spirit by whose power the Church is brought into existence upon Pentecost. It is through the operation of the Holy Spirit that Christ as risen Lord is present in the community; thus the signs of His presence now in the community are like those of the time of His public ministry.[38] The effective agent of the Church, the Kingdom of God, the mystical body of Christ, the new Israel, is the Holy Spirit whose presence indicates the last days.

The place of the Holy Spirit in the New Testament presentation of Jesus Christ is essential. Throughout the period of Christ's public ministry the striking feature of the absence of the spirit from the apostles was constant: "He said this, however, of the Spirit, whom they who believed in him were to receive; for the Spirit *had not yet been given,* since Jesus had not been glorified." [39] The Spirit was absent, therefore, because His presence was to be eschatological; that is the mark of the last days established in the Cross and resurrection of Jesus. Thus Saint Peter in Acts 2 on Pentecost explains the presence of the Spirit as an eschatological sign, and like John, specifically links it to the glorification of Jesus.[40]

It is worthwhile to note that Jesus' promise of the Spirit specifically linked the gift of the Spirit to the preaching of the Gospel: "And when they lead you away to deliver you up, do not be anxious beforehand what you are to speak; but speak whatever is given you in that hour. For it is not you who are speaking but the Holy

Spirit." [41] The gift of the Spirit is also connected to the task of Christian witness.[42] Saint Luke reflects a specific theological approach to history by presenting a detailed account of the gift of the Spirit on Pentecost in Acts 2 in which the gift of the Holy Spirit is primarily related to the apostles going about preaching "the wonderful works of God," accompanied by the gift of tongues; and on the occasion of the next major proclamation of Christ, that is, to the Gentiles, the Spirit is again present, so that the universal nature of the proclamation is evident.[43]

In the fulfillment of the prophecy of Joel (2:28) the Holy Spirit is present to all men in the Church. This Spirit of God is the Spirit of Jesus testifying to Christ and teaching all truth.[44] Thus the Spirit is the effective power in any proclamation of the Word: He guards and guarantees the Word proclaimed. Scripture is inspired by the Spirit, and the Word in Scripture is thus understood rightly only in the Church or community wherein the Spirit has been given. Doctrine develops as the Holy Spirit constantly and continually witnesses to the living Word in the Church. In short, the Holy Spirit witnesses to Christ, not to Himself; the Spirit manifests Christ to the believer, and He is the effective agent in the presence of the Word. The Church in her teaching and doctrine, in all her formulations of the Word, does so only in view of the possession of the Holy Spirit and of His inner testimony.

So it is that so distinguished a New Testament scholar as Oscar Cullmann can remark: "It is the presence of the Holy Spirit which makes the action of the church, as such, eschatological." The church, possessing the Holy Spirit, is for that reason eschatological. Cullmann continues: "The church itself is an eschatological phenomenon. It is the center of the present lordship of Christ. It was constituted by the Holy Spirit at Penetcost. That is why the task of the church consists in the proclamation of the Gospel to the whole world. This is the very essence of the Holy Spirit's work, and the meaning of the miracle of Pentecost. . . . Precisely in the period to which we belong—between the Resurrection and the return of Christ—it is the duty of the church to go out 'into all the world, and preach the Gospel to every creature,' looking toward the end." [45]

THE OBJECT AND PURPOSE OF PROCLAMATION: THE AGE OF FAITH

Among the more ancient formulas giving a sermon of Peter, a form of the kerygma in the early Church, are these words: ". . . and he charged us to preach to the people." [46] Until He comes again Christ is to be preached, and if this Word of God, Jesus Christ, is to be proclaimed authoritatively within the community, which He established and endowed with the Holy Spirit, through whose operation He is present, that same Word must also be heard. The Word now is truly word when preached, heralded, or more properly, proclaimed. The Word of God is the one gospel to all, "that you may believe that Jesus is the Christ, the Son of God, and that believing you may have life in his Name." [47] Thus it is that Saint Paul speaks of the Word of God in Christ as "the message of reconciliation," confided to be proclaimed by those whom he has sent, "God, as it were, appealing through us." [48] Just as God's purpose in proclamation is the same as that of the Christ event proclaimed, namely, reconciliation through the Cross and resurrection of Jesus, so also it must be clearly stated that the proclamation has man for its object.

Jesus Christ is God's eternal Word uttered definitively in history: He is the manifestation in the flesh of God's love. In the New Testament to "hear" this Word is to believe in Christ and to accept God's gracious and loving offer of Himself in Christ. It is in the writings of Saint John that we find an intrinsic relationship established between this initial and continuing faith and the basic demand of love.[49] The implications of faith are most clearly stated in and made evident by Saint John; there the dialogistic relationship of God's Word to man is clearly drawn.

God's Word is the object of faith; therefore Jesus Christ as the object of faith leads to eternal life.[50] To reject Christ is not only to reject God's revelation of Himself but it is also to reject the possibility of sharing God's life by refusing the offer of God in Christ to participation in divine life: "No one who disowns the Son has the Father," and "this is the testimony, that God has given us eternal life; and this life is in his Son. He who has the Son has life. He who has not the Son has not the life. These things I am writing to you that you may know that you have eternal life—you who *believe* in the name of the Son of God." [51]

The initiative in the dialogistic relationship of the Word of God to man in proclamation still remains that of God, and this also is presented to us in St. John. Man does not make himself a son to God in faith, but rather he accepts God in Christ, the same God who makes man his Son: "But to as many as received Him *He* gave the power of becoming the Sons of God; to those who believe in His Name." [52] This Johannine doctrine is not always so explicitly stated in the New Testament, but it is everywhere implicit. "Unlike Paul, John does not repeatedly emphasize this point by insisting e.g. that faith removes all grounds for boasting. He does not need to stress the gratuity of justification, since he is not like Paul writing against those who vaunt the value and merit of man's works. An evident truth needs emphasizing only when someone denies it." [53]

Man's reception of God's Word in Christ bears an intrinsic relationship to God's creative utterance. Man was made to the image and likeness of God; in creation he was elevated to the state of special friendship with God. Through the exercise of freedom man defaced God's creative Word; it is man who initially brings about estrangement from God. It is this that God rectifies in His eschatological utterance of the Word in Christ that each man is to hear. Thus, in the truest sense, man when he hears the proclamation of the Word receives what Bultmann has chosen to name a call to "authentic existence." This, the new creation in Christ, the restoration of man's friendship with God, the reconciliation effected by the Cross and resurrection of Jesus, is what man is called to; it is this that constitutes for man an authentic existence.

The righteousness effected by the Word of God to man restores the image and the likeness of God in creation; defaced by man's free choice, it now constitutes man as God willed him to be. To hear the eschatological utterance of God's Word is for man to recover his authentic existence; that is, his state of special relationship of man to God established in the creative utterance is restored when man hears the eschatological utterance. In the language of the dogmatic theologian, this is to ask the question, "Is this special relationship to God 'natural' to man?" Can it be stated that since the eschatological utterance is a call to authentic existence that man has a natural end in the possession of God?

Any answer to this problem must regard the terms in which it is set and the frame of reference in which the problem is stated. As we have stated it, the answer must be "no," for what the theologian, working in the Thomist tradition, understands by the term "natural" end of man, is essentially a philosophical rendition of the problem. Taking the term "natural" in its context, then, the possession of God can by the definition of those theologians never be natural to man but always supernatural.

But again, there is a widespread school of existentialist philosophy; there are such thinkers as Bultmann and Heidegger, and what they address themselves to in the term "authentic existence" is the elevated state that did exist from the beginning, by the will of God, and now exists as a possibility in Christ.

It would be better to say that philosophy seems to remain irrelevant to the basic data of revelation, namely, that God did create man in a state of elevation and that God, in redeeming man, restored that elevated state to him. Thus from man's viewpoint, God's creative and eschatological utterances of the Word remain identical, and man, the object of those utterances, is by them and only by their God-initiated utterance constituted in God's image and likeness.

PROCLAIMING CHRIST: WORD AND SACRAMENT

The proclamation of the Word is the proclamation of the risen Christ who now lives and pours forth His Spirit, gathering men into His Kingdom, where they are reconciled to the Father. The primary forms of this proclamation by the Church are word and sacrament. The Church proclaims and makes present the saving Christ in word infallibly through her Scriptures and teaching, and fallibly through every authorized preaching of Christ.

How is the Bible understood by the Church as "the Word of God?" Basically the Church recognizes in the Scripture a derived presence of the living Word through the medium of mission. The Word is articulated in the proclamation by those whom the Word has sent, and their proclamation has been crystallized, under the inspiration of the Spirit whom he has given, in the books of Sacred Scripture. It is simply that the Bible is the authentic proclamation of the Word, inspired by the Spirit: there, then—in those words—

is the Christ, the Word of God, present to us in a mysterious manner. We might speak of the proclaimed word as "incarnated" in the human words inspired by the Holy Spirit.

And there, in the Sacred Scripture, once again the dialogue relationship is present, as it is always present where the Word is proclaimed. In reading or hearing the Scriptures God truly speaks to men and demands response, for wherever the Word is authentically proclaimed the relationship of dialogue is established. The verbal "finalization" of the official proclamation is represented by the inspired Scriptures, themselves the Words of God in dialogue with man. Thus the words of Scripture from this point of view "possess an inherent light and force which surpass the light and force of human words, and give them a singular and unique authority and power." [54]

The Word proclaimed in the Bible is the living, creative, and eternal Word enshrined in man's words: to hear the Scriptures is to hear the living Word of God. The presence of the Word in Scriptures is as real as is His sacramental presence in the Eucharist but the manner of presence is different. But, like all the sacraments, this presence is not prior to His mysterious presence in the Church, but is immediately derived from it. It is because the Church, the place of proclamation, is the body of Christ vivified by the presence of the Word through the operation of the Holy Spirit that the inspired form of His proclamation also bears His presence.

In taking up the Bible itself a word remains to be spoken about the relationship of the Old Testament and the New Testament, that is, about the relationship of the Old Testament proclamation of the Word to the definitive proclamation of God's Word in Christ. Here attention must be given to the essentially preparatory phase represented by the Old Testament; when the New Testament is studied we can clearly see those elements of the New Testament proclamation drawn by the New Testament authors themselves from a consciousness of the intrinsic harmony between both Testaments. So, in proclaiming the eschatological utterance of God's Word in Christ, Paul states of the Old Testament, "now these things came to pass as examples to us," and again, "for whatever things have been written, have been written for our instruction." [55]

Therefore one should not look to find in the New Testament a simple verbal fulfillment of the Old. Rather can we see clearly in the New Testament proclamation of the Christ event, God's Word made flesh, the complete historical articulation of the Word. The Old Testament is *historically* fulfilled in the New; the slow emergence of the Word in the Old Testament phase of history climaxes in the Incarnation. The acts of God recorded and proclaimed in the Old Testament culminate in the New Testament act of God in Christ. The New Testament, then, is the historical fulfillment of the Old; and the gift of the Holy Spirit opens to the New Testament authors the realization of the identity in pattern of both old and new covenants, so that from the very beginning of the Church it is Old Testament history and concepts that are used to express the meaning of the Christ event. So it is that the essential harmony of Old and New Testaments, the intrinsic relatedness of the Christ event to the events and stages of the Old Testament, is not a "spiritual" or "new" way of interpreting the Scriptures but rather the Spirit-inspired interpretation of the New Testament itself.

Christ, the eschatological Word, is proclaimed infallibly by the Church in the Scriptures and also in her authentic teaching. Let us see now why the Word proclaimed in Scripture is the same infallibly proclaimed Word by the Church herself. The Word is present in the apostolic proclamation because it is the proclamation of those sent as Christ Himself was sent. It is apostolicity, or mission, that guarantees the presence of the Word now in His body, the Church. As faith comes through hearing, the Word is present in the proclaiming Church, and it is of the essence of this Church to proclaim infallibly the Word, since it is for that that she is apostled. So the Church settles all arguments and her decision is final. The Bible crystallizes the apostolic proclamation, and yet it is the Church that establishes the canon of books that make up the Bible and it is the Church that determines the biblical form as adequate and true proclamation. It is the Church that guarantees their inspiration by the Holy Spirit, and the last appeal in every theological dispute is to the apostled community. It is as the Church-guaranteed verbalization of God's Word that the Scriptures are themselves rightly called the Word of God. Priority, as is evident, therefore belongs to the living Church in existence as the *locus* or place of the Word, and it is in the Church and only in the Church that the Word is truly proclaimed. It is the Church that determines and interprets, it is the Church that proclaims God's Word in Scripture.

Again, one may look at the problem from the awareness of the Scripture as God's Word: although the presence of the Word in the Church infallibly guarantees the recognition by the Church of the Word in Scripture, yet the Church also declares that these books have the Holy Spirit as their principal author, and so it is that these books express the object of her faith adequately. Once again priority rests with the official, the authorized, the missioned and apostled community, the Church.

In view of these facts it goes without saying that the major body of revealed truth must then be present in the Church's guaranteed Scripture. This presence may be either explicit or implicit. The theology of tradition (called by the bibilical scholars *paradosis*) therefore determines not only the priority of the Church but also allows us to affirm that some revealed truths are only implicitly in Scripture while evidently in the tradition of the Church. "To recognize tradition . . . as not only governing the interpretation of Scripture but as occasionally supplementing it does not forbid us to regard Scripture and tradition less as two separate sources of dogma than as a single twofold source." [56]

These considerations offer us not only immediate and considerable insight and understanding into the Church as the extension of the incarnate Word but also a fruitful avenue of investigation in which a new and fresh approach may be made to long-standing theological problems. The identity of the content of the Word proclaimed in every age leads to a consideration of the problem of development of doctrine within the Church. For this perplexed problem solutions are to be sought along the lines of the presence of the Word in the Church—which by definition is the resurrection body of the Word—as well as in the presence of the Holy Spirit in the Church bringing that resurrection body to life. With this new line of investigation one must not of course neglect the influence of history itself, that is, the historical development of the Church, in which specific areas of the message confided to the Church are highlighted and examined.

Within the Church there is not only her infallible proclamation of the Word in Scripture and tradition but her fallible proclamation in every authorized preaching of the Word. This most closely affects us, those of us called and commissioned to preach the saving Word of God in Christ and those of us who hear Christ preached at the Eucharistic celebration of His community.

The preaching of Christ in the Church is constituted as a true, but fallible, preaching of the Word when that preaching is authorized. The preacher must be called, must be "ordained" for this end. If he is to make present the Word in his words, then he must be truly sent ("As the Father has sent Me, I send you"), for that presence is freely given not by man but by God. The commission of the Church is necessary to validly proclaim and make present the Word of God confided to the Church. Catholic theologians have seemingly labored for too long a time under the shadow of what they have regarded as Protestant excess in this matter. Thus an occasional moral theologian takes up the problem of the obligation to preach in one "ordained" for the Word, and this normally within the context of pastoral responsibility. Too little positive theological attention has been given to the actual importance of preaching, to the unique "event" in the life of the Church constituted by the sermon.

The sermon, delivered by the authorized preacher, particularly at the Eucharist, is here and now the continuation of Jesus, the Word of God. It is "the act of the Risen Lord through the Holy Spirit in the 'communion of the saints.'" [57] The authentic presence of the Word through the apostled preacher is here and now God's action in the present stage of salvation history. It is in the here and now that the sermon occupies its place through the gracious Will of God as the offering of the saving act to man. Ordained to the service of the Word, the priest therefore holds a serious obligation to preach; the instrument of salvation, the priest cannot be misled by a juridical conception propagated by some moralists that he must preach "at times." It would seem that moral theologians must investigate the severity of the obligation to preach the Word, for in the New Testament it is hard to avoid the conclusion that this is a most certain mark of the Church—"to preach the Gospel."

Preaching, however, must not be regarded as an infallible form of proclaiming the Word. The possibility of defect is not from the part of God (who acts through the medium of mission) but from the part of man (who is the one sent and is, of his nature, an imperfect instrument). For all that, however, preaching as we find it in the New Testament and in the constant experience and tradition of the Church is an event, an event of major consequence because it is the Word.

God's word to us, Jesus Christ, is not only proclaimed in the words of human speech (Scripture, tradition, and preaching), He is also proclaimed in sign. The seven signs or sacraments of this proclamation can only be clearly seen when the identity of the Church as the body of Christ the Word, vivified by His Holy Spirit, is kept resolutely in view. Pauline scholars have long highlighted this essential identity of the Church and Christ.[58] For Saint Paul, as Cerfaux has pointed out, the mystery of God's saving plan is not only effected in Christ, it is to be identified with Christ. Christ is the content of this eternal mystery, so that to preach the Gospel or to herald the Word is essentially "to preach Christ." God's power now at work in the world, reconciling it to Himself, is centered upon the risen body of Christ, wherein the members of the Church are members of that body of Christ and share the fullness of Christ. To speak of the Church as the mystical body of Christ is not to speak simply the language of metaphor but of reality; it is to affirm the realism of Paul's language.

> The teaching of Paul on the body of Christ is eminently simple. For him all union is the surrender of the body of the Christian in the semitic sense of self to the body-self of the risen Saviour, thus forming with Him only one body. The conclusion is inescapable. This union is an existential contact and a dynamic identification between the faithful and the body charged with power; especially is this true in baptism (Rom. 6:3–11; Gal. 4:27–28) and in the eucharist (I Cor. 10:16–17; 11:24–30). The life that is in the body becomes the life of those who are its members. Whether in the first moment of union or in the moment of Parousia consummation, both the Christian and Christ are inseparably united.[59]

Modern theologians, especially Karl Rahner, Otto Semmelroth, and Edward Schillebeeckx, like their confreres in biblical study, place the prior attention of sacramental theology upon the identity of Christ and the Church. Thus all identify the Church as the *Ursackrament,* that is the first, primal, or prior sacrament (sign); they identify the Church as the sacramental Christ; the Church is itself the sign of the definitive entrance of God's saving grace in the world. Thus for Rahner the Church is the *Realsymbol* of God's grace, and the sacraments are the actions of the Church, her essential works by which she authenticates herself.[60] The Church, the body of Christ in the world, must perform these actions, and these actions, or sacraments, were instituted by Christ simultaneously with His institution of the Church. Father Semmelroth also sees the sacraments as rooted in the structure we call the Church, the divine and human reality that extends the Incarnation.[61] Because of Christ's essential work as mediator, Semmelroth relates the preaching of Christ and the sacraments in the twofold notion of mediator; so that the preaching of Christ is symbolic of God's coming to man in Christ, and the sacraments are symbolic of man's movement to God.

Father Edward Schillebeeckx has refined and developed these notions with particular attention to the sacraments themselves.[62] The progressive revelation of the Word in history from creation through the Old Testament to Jesus culminates in Jesus, and it is there that God definitively invites us to personal communion with Him. Christ, the Word made flesh, makes perfectly visible God's action to us. Thus it is the man Jesus Christ who is the *Ursackrament,* the first sacrament of man's communion with God. The identification of Christ with his Church allows us still to find the dimension of encounter with God in visible signs, for the Church is the visible sacrament of Christ the Lord, the definitive sacrament. What we call the seven sacraments are, then, the visible signs of encounter with the saving work of God in Christ. Thus, Schillebeeckx says of the Church: "The church is the visible historical representation of the accomplished redemption. As the earthly channel of God's revelation, she is essentially both sacrament and word. . . . Christ sent the Holy Spirit, but He also sends His apostles. Both missions are organically connected: Pentecost, the day on which the church is fully revealed in her sacramental and kerygmatic action, is the mystical manifestation of both missions precisely in their cooperative union—a union whose vitality springs from the common source of the Christ-life." [63]

It should not be thought that these dynamic conceptions and approaches to understanding the sacraments as the actions of the risen Lord by the operation of the Holy Spirit lose their eschatological significance. They remain as preludes of the parousia, since they are encounters with the Word who is to come in His glory.

Like the threefold proclamation of the Word as word (Scripture, magisterium, and preaching), the sevenfold proclamation of the Word as sign authenticates man's existence in Christ and anticipates the revelation of the glory with which God has graced us in Christ. The actions of the Church in word and sign are the actions by which the Church most completely realizes herself as the risen body of Christ in the world.

From the viewpoint of symbolism these seven signs possess a natural symbolism (bread, wine, oil, water), but their fundamental symbolism as signs of the end—as actions of encounter with the eschatological Word of God in Christ—should be kept in view. It is upon this eschatological symbolism that the theology of the sacraments in the New Testament itself rests. In the New Testament we find the constant perception of the stages of world history as salvation history, that is, of the progressive utterance of the Word. Here the sacraments are considered as by their nature signs of the end, as eschatological events in which the Christ event is experienced and effectively shared by all generations of believers.[64] Thus in the Johannine teaching on the Eucharist, as we find it in the sixth chapter of John's Gospel, there is an intrinsic relationship between the Eucharist (in which Christ pours forth the Holy Spirit upon the faithful) and the eschatological event of His resurrection and the Pentecost. This relationship of the sacraments to the events of salvation history we will find most salutary. "The efficacious symbolism of the Eucharist, for example, as the 'divine bread from heaven' 'giving life to the world' comes not only from the words of institution but also from the feeding of God's people with manna." [65] Such a symbolism, as Father Stanley points out, serves to express the efficacy of the sacraments and at the same time to guard against any idea of the sacraments as magic. But it also serves to throw light upon the sacraments as the acts of God in Christ toward man now at this stage of history. Just as we have seen that the proclamation of the Word in human words introduces the dialogistic relationship (thus constituted as an all-important present event in the life of the individual believer and the community), so also the proclamation of the Word in these seven signs is both for the believer and the community an event in which the encounter or dialogistic relationship of the Word is present.

Therefore the Word of God in the Church, the body of the Word, is proclaimed both in word and sacrament; so it is fitting that we should conclude with a consideration of the proclamation of the Word par excellence: the Eucharist. There in the meal of the Christian community, celebrated by the assembly of the believers with their apostled representative, the priest, is God's Word —the Christ—proclaimed both in word and sacrament. This, therefore, is the central action of the Christian Church; and its permanence in the experience and tradition of the Church, its central place in any presentation of Christian theology, its constancy in Christian history, is easily understood. The Eucharist is the preeminent form of proclamation and consequently is the basic action of the Church by which it is most essentially the Church and by which eschatology is realized in its truest and deepest sense.

The Christian community has awaited the parousia from its earliest days. This waiting for the apocalyptic utterance of the Word marks the pages of the New Testament and every era of Christian history. The waiting was fixed upon the day of Christ's universal Lordship, his resurrection, therefore Sunday. The token of His coming was always celebrated upon that occasion in the supremely eschatological act of the Church by which the Apocalypse was anticipated, the Eucharist. In the period of the Old Testament, the Passover and the feasts of the Sinai, or Exodus event, were the supreme events in the life of the community; they were the events of the community by which the present was linked with the past event of the Exodus and by which the future action of God in human history was anticipated. So now, in the New Testament, each Eucharist is the event in the present stage of the Church by which the events of salvation history are realized in the present. When the Church celebrates the Eucharist she celebrates and proclaims in word and in sign the eternal saving act of God in Christ, that is, the eschatological utterance of the Word of God, the passion, death, and resurrection of the Lord Jesus Christ. Not only does this action of her Lord transcend time as He transcends time, and thus may be made present in the Eucharist, but the open revelation of this action as the definitive act of God, the apocalyptic utterance of the Word, is anticipated. And this Eucharistic action is essentially the one proclamation under both word and sign. The eschatological Word is proclaimed in Scripture and the preaching of the Gospel, creating His community and entering into the relationship of dialogue; but He is also proclaimed in the signs of the bread and wine, for in the words of Saint Paul, "as often as you eat this bread and drink of the cup, you proclaim the death of the Lord, until He come." [66]

This eschatological dimension of the Christian Eucharist is not only one of theoretical acknowledgment of the Christ as the eschatological utterance, but is deeply rooted in the constant experience, practice, and tradition of the Church from the time of Pentecost until now. The Eucharist in the early Church was looked upon as the anticipation in the present of the eternal Kingdom of God. The Kingdom of God to be revealed, the eternal banquet mentioned in the Gospel of Mark (14:25), is inseparably linked with the here and now celebration of the Eucharist. Thus the earliest of the Eucharistic prayers, and one which closes the text of the New Testament revelation, is that of "Maranatha" ("Come, Lord"), linking the Eucharist with the parousia.[67]

There are, then, two actions in the Eucharist, word and sign, that are basically one: the proclamation of the Word. The first action of the Eucharist celebration by the Church is the speaking and the hearing of God's Word in Christ through the instrumentality of the apostolic ministry. This proclamation of Christ in word, this ceremony of the Synaxis, is not to be thought of as purely limited to the Gospel message. "That word, of course, is always and forever that which is given to us *through the whole history of redeemed mankind. . . .* Therefore, in as much as we are what we are as the result of the one and complete history of mankind of which we are the heirs, so we must hear the Word throughout all the phases of its proclamation to mankind in order that we may be able to understand the final and full Word of God in the Gospel." [68] The Word of God is in the practice of the Church proclaimed in the foremass and heard in an ever-deepening dimension that culminates in the eschatological utterance of Christ. It is precisely here that preaching properly so-called takes place so that the Word might be proclaimed as relevant to our own time and translated in the language and situations in which man here and now finds himself. The prayers and hymns of praise that surround this heralding of the Word in the community are evoked by the Word Himself, and at the same time are the responses of men to the heralding of God's Word.

The second part of the Eucharistic celebration, the sacrificial and sacramental, is continuous with the first. It is the proclamation in sign of that same Word of God in Christ. As Father Bouyer has pointed out, Christ Himself fulfilled and gave a new meaning to the Jewish Eucharist and its return of thanks to God.[69] Thus when we ask why Christ is present in the Eucharist, why the Church's action in the Eucharist is the same as that of Christ, that is, why the Eucharist and the Cross are identical, the answer is ever the same: "These three questions have the same answer: in Christ, the Word of God himself now makes His own the thanksgiving which man makes over the world in which and by which he is to live; the world itself, therefore, is now filled by the Word incarnate; the Word conforms to itself all the men who receive it. Finally, as a result of all this, the church in all that she does and in all that she is, is nothing less than 'the fulness of Him Who is completely filling up all things' (Eph. 1:23)."[70]

Thus in a very real sense a Christian theology of history leads up to a consideration of the Eucharist as the event par excellence, and conceivably a theology of history can be written about the theme of the Eucharist. As one theologian has expressed it:

> At the Sacrificial Banquet, we are called and we gather together both to encounter Christ and to await His final Coming in Glory. As we partake of the Eucharistic Meal we participate in the Death and Resurrection of the Lord, and we "proclaim the Death and Resurrection of the Lord until he comes." Nourished by the Body and Blood of the Word made flesh, assimilated to Him and He to us, we already share in the life of the Risen Lord. But also we prepare ourselves and in ourselves the material world, for the universal resurrection. We live now between the resurrection of Christ and our own, when He shall come again. Our worship reveals to us the eschatological dimension of our lives. Our contact with Christ in the liturgy, though not perfect, is the highest function of our work—assisting Christ in bringing the historical dimension of *all things to fulfillment.*[71]

Proclaiming Christ to the World: Salvation History and Secular History

When one attempts to understand human history in the light of a theology of God's Word, and to maintain that the present age of history is to be understood as the age of proclaiming that Word,

the difficulties proposed by any theology of history are evidently
not settled. There are any number of problems in human history
whose answers may be proposed within the framework of the proclamation of the Word. Basically these problems, long perplexing
to the theologians, deal with the relationships of saving and human
history, the relationship of Christianity to other religions and to
non-Christian cultures, the place of Israel, and what is most perplexing, the meaningfulness of human achievement. Among these
problems let us now see what our understanding of history as the
proclamation of the Word tells us of the relationship of secular to
saving history.

There is, as we have remarked, a very real distinction between
the creative and eschatological utterances of the Word, between the
creation as God willed it to be and man's despoiling sin that required God's redemptive act in Christ. There is, then, from this
viewpoint, every reason to speak of secular and salvation history;
and it has been the constant temptation of many theologians of history to place the problem of history in the relationship of these
"two" histories. But although we can maintain a distinction in
utterance of God's Word, the corollary distinction of two histories,
secular and sacred, does not seem to be required. The implication
that there are two lines of history leads to the assertion that, for
the Christian, faith is revelatory of another or "inner" history
(saving history) that gives meaning to the entire historical process.

However, if this world and human history take their origin from
the creative utterance of God's Word, it must be asked, then,
whether the eschatological utterance of that same Word in Christ
is truly distinct as Word; in other words, is salvation history absolutely discontinuous with secular history? From the viewpoint of a
theology of God's Word it would seem that we must deny as unreal the distinction between sacred and secular history; these are, it
seems, not two histories, but one. The question is not to find the
relationship of one history to the other, but rather to see that one
is a dimension of the other, one is the perfection of the other. It
is God's Word that effects man's existence and his relationship to
God; and while man's sin destroys the initial relationship, God's
Word in Christ restores it.

Thus the Christian, like the non-Christian, as he faces history,
does not find two histories, but one. The difference between them

is that the Christian, having heard God's Word in Christ, hears the same Word active in creation. The Christian is aware through faith of the true dimension of human history; the Christian possesses, therefore, the key to human history, not to another history.

It follows, then, that Christianity must be considered by the believer as a priori compatible with every form of human culture, and again, incompatible with every form of history. Christianity is, to use the language of neo-orthodoxy, at once continuous and discontinuous with human history. God's Word in Christ may thus be uttered in any culture and in the human trappings and clothing of that culture. What God has done for man in Christ can be translated into all languages, all thought forms, all traditions. But at the same time that we affirm this fact it must also be stated that once God's Word in Christ is spoken and heard, then that same reconciling word stands in judgment upon that culture.

This radical discontinuity of the Word, or its judgment, is spoken in a human culture that, to the degree that the culture is itself an achievement of man, is an achievement of sinful man; no human activity or human achievement, nor the sum total of human activity, can accomplish the God-man relationship (election) intended in the creation and restored in the redemptive activity of Christ. When we speak of Christianity in history, of the actual moment of a real incarnation in a specific time, place, and cultural form, we must speak of that time, place, and culture as under the satanic power released into the world by man's initial sin. While Christ may be proclaimed in any cultural form or milieu, and while He may be for that culture "incarnated" by the Church that proclaims Him, yet He is always proclaimed, and thus always present, as opponent and victor of the satanic power. In short, all culture and all the activity of man maintain their susceptibility to the Word that brought them into, and still holds them in being. But at the same time, human achievements are unable to effect reconciliation, which is the work of God's Word in Christ.

Therefore, within the framework of this relationship of salvation history to secular history, we must now apply the theological understanding of the meaningfulness of human achievement within the divine plan.

PROCLAIMING CHRIST IN THE WORLD: THE MEANINGFULNESS OF HUMAN ACHIEVEMENT

Modern man witnesses more dramatically than at any time in the past a confrontation of Christianity and non-Western culture. In the Arab world, in the Asian subcontinent, and in Africa the Christian religion is frequently regarded as the baggage of the colonials, and the attempt to Christianize these areas has forced the Church to state the Christian fact as disengaged from the achievements of Western civilization. Thus the missionary thrust and the challenge of evangelization have forced the Church to sharpen ever more clearly the relationships of the Gospel and cultures. In answer to this problem the distinguished Père Jean Daniélou has proposed that "the civilization itself must first be Christened before its leaders can be converted." [72] However, it does not seem to us that the essential proclamation of God's Word to these cultures is a distinctively separate task as proclamation, although certain difficulties present themselves.

It should be remembered that in principle the question of intercultural proclamation is also related to intracultural proclamation. As the final act of God, and as His proclaimed Word, Christ is not and cannot be intrinsically joined to any one culture or civilization. Interculturally the conversion of the Greco-Roman world represented a translation of God's need in Christ, but intraculturally Western civilization maintains a degree of Christianity directly proportionate to the translation of the proclamation in terms of its progressive cultural stages. Thus the demand for speaking God's Word in the present language of men is not merely the task of the foreign missionary but indeed of the whole Church in every time and place. To proclaim God's Word in man's words is just as necessary in the urban industrial areas of Paris and New York as in Brasília and New Delhi. This translation into the language of the men to whom it is proclaimed is just as necessary at every stage of cultural development as to every culture.

This is not to deny that there are specific differences, and indeed difficulties. The religious beliefs of non-Western cultures, the delicate nuances of meaning betrayed by linguistic translations, and the differing psychologies of peoples all serve to complicate the task of Christian proclamation. The service to be rendered to the Church by its intellectuals, although a seemingly secular one, takes from this point of view an importance and even a necessary position vis-à-vis the proclamation of the Word. Not only do the Orientalists, the specialists in Hindu and Islamic cultures, dedicated students of African development offer the Church an indispensible service preparatory to and necessary for proclamation; they also—within a given culture such as our own—offer services preparatory to proclamation in such areas as anthropology, economics, sociology, and psychology. The Word is one, and the service preparatory to proclaiming the eschatological Word is essentially one of seeing all creation as susceptible to the Word.

There is, then, for the Christian's understanding of the mission of proclaiming the Word, no such idea as a theology of the mission exclusively concerned with the foreign missions. Foreign lands and the intercultural proclamation may indeed present specific problems of their own, problems as interminably multiplied as the mission areas, but fundamentally the basic theology of mission is as applicable to the parish priest as to the missionary. The principles involved in proclaiming God's Word are identical, although circumstances may differ. If the minister of God's Word is to contribute his own poor talents to the effective proclamation of the Word, then at least from his human viewpoint he must study in his audience the created susceptibilities to that Word.

That fashionable concern of Western Christians for the intercultural proclamation of the Word, for the translation of God's Word in Christ into the forms and languages of non-Western cultures, is actually a missionary concern for the Church. But frequently as we see and hear this concern elucidated in journals of Christian opinion, we see also a forgetfulness of the same necessity and the same concern for intracultural proclamation. The forms and languages of our Western cultures are presumed too easily to be Christian, whereas in fact the science, economics, technology, politics, arts, and entertainment forms of the West have served to blind modern man to the ultimate question of human destiny and have produced ever larger and more chronic areas of deafness to God's Word. In the so-called Christian West many popular cultural forms have conspired not only to sound out God's Word but even to condemn it to irrelevance.

It would seem, therefore, that ecumenicism is among the primary intercultural and intracultural problems of proclamation that face the Church. Both to the people of our own culture and to the non-Christian peoples of the world the division within Christendom is a scandal. Indeed, from the viewpoint of proclamation it is the most serious of problems, in that it divides and confuses the Christian witness in proclamation. And even if Protestant and orthodox Christians are from the Catholic viewpoint "separated brethren," nevertheless as Christians they do feel the necessity of the Christian commandment of proclamation and the Christian duty of witness. The challenge, then, of intercultural proclamation takes on a note in our world much like that of intracultural proclamation, that is, it demands a unified Christian proclamation of the one Word of God. As Barbara Ward has commented: "The modern scientific and materialist world view challenges the Christian communions to much more than an inner realization of how much they have in common. It poses to the human race urgent problems and agonizing difficulties which might perhaps be more impressively and effectively answered if the Christian voice were less muffled by interior disputes." [73]

PROCLAIMING CHRIST TO THE WORLD: THE DIVIDED CHURCH

When we speak of the age in which we live as the age of proclamation we affirm the importance of the community of the Word that proclaims Him. The evident division of Christendom, then, constitutes a problem when history here and now is affirmed as meaningful because it is the era of proclamation. In speaking, as we do here, of the Catholic position, it should not be thought that the critique of Protestantism is one that sees either ignorance or disregard of God's Word in the Protestant experience; nor should it be thought that any such criticism of the Protestant experience is implicit. The proclamation of God's Word in Christ, the articulation of the Word in history, has to a great degree been maintained in the historical forms and structures of the Protestant experience.

This Protestant tradition of devotion to the Word is more than evident in the serious reliance that is placed upon the Sacred Scripture in their traditions, and in the extensive place that the preaching of the Word holds in their manifold forms of worship.

The Catholic critique, honestly carried on in an atmosphere of interconfessional respect and love, admits the Protestant concern for the Word of God but is leveled at the content of the proclamation as we find it in Protestantism. The first and most serious question that the Catholic must address to his Protestant brother is how closely the proclamation of the Word in modern Protestantism agrees with the proclamation witnessed by the New Testament. In addition, there are other subsidiary questions the Catholic addresses to the Protestant tradition of proclamation.

These, then, are the four areas to which the Catholic addresses himself in his dialogue with the Protestant: first, the content of the proclamation; second, theology (that is, the science of formulating and proposing the content of the proclamation); third, apostolicity (that is, the mission of the Church, apostleship as the basis for the claim to proclaim the Word authoritatively); and fourth, practice (the effectual Christianization of the world in the proclamation).

As to the content of the proclamation, it may certainly be stated that where Protestantism is preached in its fullest and most traditional sense the basic element of the proclamation is present—God's saving act in Christ. The Catholic does maintain, however, that the total revelation of God in Christ, the fullness of the Word, must be proclaimed. Thus, the Catholic view of the Christian community, the Church, is that it is brought into existence by the Word and that it is kept in existence by the Word for the purpose of proclaiming the Word, and furthermore, that in this Church there are certain basic elements put there by the Word of God. The Catholic affirms not only the organization of the Church about the historic Christian episcopate, which preserves her apostolic nature and guarantees the mission of the Church, but he also affirms that the episcopate is organized about the historic Papacy, representing the fullness of jurisdiction and guaranteeing the authenticity of doctrine. The nature of the Church is not extrinsic to the proclamation, and the theological formulations concerning its nature and organization are not regarded as of their nature speculative or dependent upon historical circumstances. This Church in the fullness of its organic unity is essential to the total proclamation of the Word, it is part and parcel of our age in the history of salvation. And although we must admit that in non-Catholic Christianity basic elements of the proclamation are found in varying degrees of completeness, the Church does affirm that in its organization around the bishops and the Pope the organic fullness of the proclaiming community as Christ intended it to be is evident.

In the realm of theology the Church faces the inherently difficult problem of proposing the content of revelation with the tools of human reason and language. Thus, the Church has always affirmed the essentially subordinate role of philosophy, and although historically it has elevated the realism of Saint Thomas Aquinas to the state of a quasi-official philosophy, it always maintains the essential priority of the eschatological Word in the Church and the essential philosophical freedom of the Church. The Protestant principle of subordinating man's achievements, and therefore his philosophies, to the judgment of the Word in Sacred Scripture has not historically preserved the Protestant confessions from a subordination of the proclamation to philosophy. Cut off from their moorings in the whole Church and from the teaching authority of the Church, the Protestant confessions have historically been easy victims (and are still today) of every modern intellectual current and of new and untried philosophies. The sad spectacle of the nineteenth-century liberal Protestants, the witness even of Karl Barth to his previous existentialist position, and especially today the systems of Bultmann in Scripture and Tillich in religious philosophy, all these demonstrate the theological ambivalence of Protestantism. It is interesting, and indeed encouraging, to note that where the Protestant principle is rigidly adhered to and followed in an intelligent and constant appeal to the Scriptures there is an evident tendency toward a Catholic orthodoxy. For the Catholic, the Protestant principle can only be rightly understood and fulfilled within the Church, and her organic fullness in the possession of the Word guarantees the ultimate judgment of the Word upon man's achievements.[74]

Authoritative proclamation of the Word is involved in the Catholic discussion with Protestantism. The maintenance of the Word of God in the Bible by Protestantism does present it with authorized preaching, for the words there preserved are those of authoritative and authentic preachers with their mission from God Himself. It is precisely insofar as he hears the Word proclaimed in Scripture that the Protestant hears the Word officially proclaimed. Indeed, with the Word in Scripture, the teaching of the Fathers, and the influence of the Church's teaching, a further development is preserved in Protestant traditions. Theologians now allow a wide field to Christian witness and instruction requiring no special mandate; that is, in view of baptism every Christian possesses a certain mission.[75] Thus it is maintained that the Protestant ministry itself may, in the opinion of these theologians, possess an *authentic mission* as a charisma related to the Church over and above that proper to each baptized, and more, that the ministry as an institution representative of good faith may to a degree possess a special grace of state.[76]

Finally, it must be noted that since God wills all men to be saved, it does not seem that efficacy (that is, the success in practice of the dissident proclamation) can be denied a priori to the Protestant ministry. As orthodox or schismatic administration of the sacraments are efficacious, so also "while Protestantism is undoubtedly displeasing to God in so far as it diverges from Catholic truth and unity, it by no means follows that God does not wish there to be salutary ministries within Protestantism."[77] The perdurance of Protestant dissidence throughout four hundred years attests by its in-existence to a "vestigium ecclesiae." The successes that attend Protestant evangelism, foreign missions, and even parochial life have from the Catholic viewpoint their effective cause in those elements of the proclamation that have been maintained even in dissidence.

The task of ecumenism, which faces the Catholic with the terrible urgency of a unified proclamation of the Word and a common witness to our world, is one of great difficulty. It must be carried on in charity, but it is always incumbent upon the Church to witness her own organic fullness as the authorized community of proclamation. The Catholic is called upon to state that the perils of the Protestant experience (that is, its sectarianism created by those certain centripetal tendencies of fundamental Protestantism) evidence a certain incompleteness of proclamation. Those large bodies of Protestant confessions that deny the extremely realistic sacramental system found in the New Testament have, in the Catholic view, cut off a significant area of proclaiming the Word. And, as we have seen, certainly where the Eucharist is not celebrated as the authoritative and full and definitive expression of proclamation, there is a truly severe dessication of proclamation.

Conclusion: The Meaningfulness of Human Achievement

Once one has admitted the eschatological nature of God's deed in Christ, and has explored the nature of the tension affirmed in the New Testament of the "even now—not yet," then most clearly the real problem of the meaningfulness of human achievement is highlighted. The problem, stated in the terms of Oscar Cullmann, is one of coexistence, the coexistence of two ages; again, it is one of creating beings living now in the new creation. In the terms of a theology of God's Word the problem may be framed by asking the relationship of God's creative and eschatological and apocalyptic utterances of His Word. Although we have previously treated the interrelationship of these utterances, there still remains the necessity of investigating the value of human achievement.

One primary truth should be clearly stated: that this "time between," this time of tension, this age of the old and the new creations, is willed, as such, by God. The remainder of human history left to us is part of the divine plan. Our attempt to understand this age in the terms of human work, of terrestrial values, depends first upon this fundamental fact of the divine Will. To proclaim the eschatological Word of God now requires the acceptance of the world as it is; and the attempt to penetrate more deeply into the relationship of the creative and eschatological utterances of the Word must always be done in reference to this fact.

And so it is His Will that our age is good, even though it has been complicated by man's sin and God's saving action. Because it is the handiwork of God this world is good. Sin, and the mastery over the world that it affords the satanic power, do not totally corrupt that which God has created, and in the eschatological utterance of the Word in Christ that same sin and that same satanic power are defeated. If God's action in Christ is truly eschatological, it by no means follows that what is left (human culture, achievement, progress) is purely illusory. They do have meaning and value in themselves insofar as they manifest the will of God, the Sovereign of time and the Lord of history.

Even if we were to leave one one side this argument for human values from God's Will, human achievement still maintains a positive value by the relationship that it bears to the proclamation of the Word. As Professor Alec Vidler has remarked, "evangelization presupposes civilization." [78] This is to say that the eschatological utterance of the Word presupposes the creative utterance, and it is precisely the susceptibility of the created to the Word that is prior to the eschatological utterance. The Church, which is the body of the Word and His proclaiming community, demands for the accomplishment of its universal mission the existence of human forms, that is, some structures of civilization and culture. Without order, government, and law, without the insights and the knowledge that seemingly secular studies bring, the proclamation of the Word would be severely hampered. In the practical arena of mission, therefore, there is truly evident the presupposition of intrinsic values in creation, values necessary for proclamation. In speaking of the relationship of non-Christian cultures and civilizations to the proclamation of the Word we have seen the real similarity of both intracultural and intercultural proclamation. What this indicates is, in short, the necessity of some culture or civilization for proclamation. The proclamation of God's saving act in Christ takes place always within some culture or civilization. The Word when now proclaimed is still to some degree "incarnated" in the words, the language, the thought forms and the achievements of a culture. The development of Christian theology in the West, for example, utilized the traditions and rationale of Hellenic-Roman civilization, and was thus the "incarnation" of the proclaimed Word in and through the human achievements of the West. The biblical witness to God's act in Christ, inspired by the Holy Spirit and verbally crystallized in the Pentecost community, was for the most part an "incarnation" of the proclaimed Word in and through Hebraic thought forms, literary genres, and cultural achievements. The proclamation of the Word, then, does not exist in a vacuum; it is not an infinite echo resounding in some ethereal void, but it is always the Word of God to someone—to man in all the cultures, civilizations, and manifold achievements of his hands.

There is also the relationship of the eschatological Word in proclamation to the open revelation of the Word in the end. The apocalyptic utterance of God's Word is precisely that, an apocalyptic— open, manifest, and therefore completely and perfectly effective. The age of proclamation remains the age of faith and of freedom. It is willed by God that none should be coerced or forced against his will to accept what it is He has freely done from love. And this aspect of His love is made manifest in this age by His constant faithfulness to the gift of freedom that He initially bestowed in creation. History would make much more sense, its processes would be more evident, without the complicating factor of our freedom, the precious gift by which man can even sin and refuse to hear the Word or acknowledge His deed. The apocalyptic utterance of His Word, the parousia, will mark the end of this age, the end of faith, the perfection of proclamation in the perfect articulation of His Word.

In addition to the divine Will, and to the service creation renders the proclamation of Christ, there is still another viewpoint from which to see the meaningfulness of human achievement. As we have seen, unless God had first uttered the creative Word there could be no eschatological utterance in Christ. Man exists, and consequently his civilizations and cultures exist, because of God's creative utterance that brought man into and sustains him in existence. The reconcilement of God's purpose in this creative utterance (which was required because of man's defiling sin) was effected in Christ, and thus it is that the eschatological Kingdom inaugurated in Christ is both continuous and discontinuous to creation. It is discontinuous for it is essentially God's Kingdom established by Him in the reconciling work of His Son Jesus Christ—and this absolutely without man's contribution. But while affirming the absolute "givenness" of the eschatological deed of God in Christ, there is an area of continuity based primarily upon the creative deed. It is man, historical man, who is reconciled to God; it is the world, this historical world, that is being transformed in Christ; it is man and his world that await the consummation and manifestation of God's power and purpose in the Apocalypse, when God "shall be all in all."

It would seem, then, that it is here that the progressive nature of man's historical development can be rightly understood. Perhaps provision may even be made for so revolutionary a vision as that of Teilhard de Chardin—human history articulates God's creative utterance as proclamation articulates His eschatological utterance. The revelation and the manifestation we await in the Apocalypse is, then, the manifestation of the Word (experienced by man's historical existence in three utterances) as essentially the one eternal utterance of God Himself—the Word from all eternity.

Thus man's daily work, his secular pursuits, his terrestrial values, are really values as man's share in the articulation of the creative Word of God. When human history has progressed to its ultimate point of development, when every potentiality placed by God in creation is utilized, when man so cooperates as to give perfect resonance to God's creative utterance, then will man see that his most advanced and perfect state remains ultimately in dependence upon God's Word, and the necessity of His reconciling Word in Christ will be manifest, so that man's historical peak will be the necessity of the Apocalyptic cry to the Lord of History: "Come, Lord Jesus."

NOTES

1. A very instructive account of the cyclical theories of history common to ancient and Oriental civilizations may be found in Grace E. Cairns, *Philosophies of history* (New York: Citadel Press, 1962), and also in R. C. Dentan, ed. *The Idea of History in the Ancient Near East* (New Haven: Yale Univ. Press, 1955). A sometimes useful survey of philosophies of history may be found in Alban G. Widgery, *Interpretations of History: Confucius to Toynbee* (New York: Humanities Press, 1961).

2. Mircea Eliade, *Cosmos and History* (New York: Harper Torchbook, 1959). See also his "History and the Cyclical View of Time," *Perspectives*, V, No. 3 (May–June 1960), 11–14.

3. That the Greeks actually held cyclical conceptions of time is debated by G. Delling in *Das Zeitverständnis des neuen Testaments* (Gütersloh, 1940), and in his article, "Kairos," in Gerhard Kittel's *Theologisches Wörterbuch zum Neuen Testament*, II, 456–465. It is also debated by James Barr, *Biblical Words for Time*, Studies in Biblical Theology (Naperville, Ill.: Allenson, 1962), pp. 137 ff.

4. Arnaldo Momigliano, "Pagan and Christian Historiography in the Fourth Century," *The Conflict Between Paganism and Christianity in the Fourth Century* (Oxford Univ. Press: Clarendon, 1963), p. 85. A short but good introduction (with selections) to the elements of a theology of history in the Fathers may be found in Pietro Chiocchetta, *Teologia della storia* (Rome: Editrice Studium, 1953). See also R. L. P. Milburn, *Early Christian Interpretations of History* (New York: Harper, 1954).

5. Momigliano, p. 83.

6. This relationship of the Old Testament to the New Testament was a constant historical problem in the early Church. Thus the thrust of Marcion, who opened the door to allegorical interpretations. That this problem persists to our own day is evident in the varieties of solutions to be found in the collection edited by Bernhard W. Anderson, *The Old Testament and Christian Faith* (New York: Harper & Row, 1963).

7. D'Arcy's view is disputed by Père Dominique Chenu, O.P., who claims for Saint Thomas at least a reflection of a theology of history. See his *Introduction à l'étude de S. Thomas d'Aquin* (Paris: Vrin, 1950). See also the work of Johannes Metz, *Christliche Anthropozentrik* (Munich: Kosel, 1962).

8. Giovanni Vico, *The Autobiography* (Ithaca: Cornell Univ. Press, 1944), and *The New Science* (Ithaca: Cornell Univ. Press, 1948). See also Martin D'Arcy, S.J., *The Meaning and Matter of History* (New York: Farrar, Straus & Cudahy, 1959), pp. 122 ff.

9. See the treatment of Kant in W. H. Walsh, *Philosophy of History* (New York: Harper Torchbook, 1960), pp. 119 ff.

10. Georg W. F. Hegel, *The Philosophy of History* (New York: Dover, 1956).

11. William F. Albright, *From the Stone Age to Christianity* (Garden City: Doubleday Anchor, 1957), pp. 88–89.

12. See R. G. Collingwood, *The Idea of History* (New York: Oxford Galaxy, 1956), pp. 126 ff.

Chapter 2: FROM HISTORY TO PHILOSOPHY

1. An introduction and selections from Dilthey may be found in H. P. Rickman's *Pattern and Meaning in History* (New York: Harper Torchbook, 1962). Also see H. A. Hodges, *The Philosophy of Wilhelm Dilthey* (London: Routledge & Kegan Paul, 1952).

2. Rickman, p. 33.

3. Benedetto Croce, *History, Its Theory and Practice* (New York: Russell & Russell, 1960), and *History as The Story of Liberty* (London: Allen & Unwin, 1941).

4. R. G. Collingwood, *The Idea of History* (New York: Oxford Galaxy, 1956).

5. T. M. Knox in the introduction to ibid., p. xv.

6. Paul Weiss, *History, Written and Lived* (Carbondale: Southern Illinois Univ. Press, 1962).

7. For a summary of Heidegger's thinking see Thomas Langan, *The Meaning of Heidegger* (New York: Columbia Univ. Press, 1959); also see I. M. Bocheński, *Contemporary European Philosophy* (Berkeley: Univ. of California Press, 1961), pp. 161–172. A far more accurate commentary, however, is given in James M. Robinson and John B. Cobb, *The Later Heidegger and Theology* (New York: Harper & Row, 1963). Heidegger's own classic work is published in English as *Being and Time* (New York: Harper, 1962).

8. David E. Roberts, *Existentialism and Religious Belief*, ed. Roger Hazelton, (New York: Oxford Galaxy, 1959), p. 160.

9. Rudolf Bultmann, *History and Eschatology* (New York: Harper Torchbook, 1957), p. 155.

10. Morris R. Cohen, *American Thought* (New York: Collier, 1962), p. 81. See also his *Meaning in Human History* (La Salle, Ill.: Open Court, 1948).

11. A. H. Johnson, *Whitehead's Philosophy of Civilization* (New York: Dover, 1962), p. 85. See also the sympathetic discussion of Whitehead's philosophy of history in Marie C. Swabey, *The Judgment of History* (New York: Philosophical Library, 1954), pp. 205 ff.

12. See Charles A. Beard, "Written history as an Act of Faith," in *The Philosophy of History in Our Time*, ed. Hans Meyerhoff (Garden City: Doubleday Anchor, 1959), pp. 140–152.

13. Peter Geyl, *Debates with Historians* (New York: Meridian, 1958), and *Encounters in History* (New York: Meridian, 1961).

14. Raymond Aron, *The Opium of the Intellectuals* (New York: Norton, 1962), p. 136. See also his *Introduction to the Philosophy of History* (Boston: Beacon, 1962).

15. Alan Bullock, "The Historian's Purpose," in *The Philosophy of History in Our Time*, p. 293.

16. Karl Popper, "Has History any Meaning?," ibid., p. 310. See also his *The Poverty of Historicism*, (New York: Harper Torchbook, 1964).

17. Edward H. Carr, *What Is History?* (New York: Knopf, 1962), p. 35.

18. Ibid., pp. 60–61.

19. William F. Albright, *From the Stone Age to Christianity* (Garden City: Doubleday Anchor, 1957), p. 102.

20. Oswald Spengler, *The Decline of the West* (New York: Knopf, 1926, 1928).

21. See H. Stuart Hughes, *Oswald Spengler* (New York: Scribners, 1962).

22. In addition to the commentators cited here, see also Douglas Jerrold, *The Lie About the West* (New York: Sheed & Ward, 1954). See also Peter Geyl, Arnold Toynbee, and Pitrim Sorokin, *The Pattern of the Past* (Boston: Beacon, 1949).

23. Eric Voegelin, "Toynbee's History as a Search for Truth," *The Intent of Toynbee's History,* ed. Edward T. Gargan (Chicago: Loyola Univ. Press, 1961), p. 190.

24. See also Toynbee's *A Historian's Approach to Religion* (New York: Oxford Univ. Press, 1956).

25. Hughes, *Oswald Spengler,* p. 185.

26. C. S. Lewis, "Historicism," *The Month,* (1950), pp. 230–242.

27. See Maurice Nédoncelle, *Is There a Christian Philosophy?* (New York: Hawthorn, 1961).

28. Not only the possibility but also the necessity of a Christian philosophy of history is maintained by Msgr. Francesco Olgiati in the abstract "Theology and History," *Theology Digest,* II, No. 2 (Spring 1954), 111–117.

29. A. Robert Caponigri, "Philosophy and History," *Modern Catholic Thinkers* (London: Burns, Oates, 1960), p. 475.

30. Jacques Maritain, *On the Philosophy of History* (New York: Scribners, 1957).

31. Ibid., p. 11.

32. William F. Albright, *History, Archeology, and Christian Humanism* (New York: McGraw Hill, 1964), pp. 140–141.

33. Albright, *From the Stone Age to Christianity,* p. 116. See also *History, Archeology and Christian Humanism,* pp. 26 ff.

34. *From the Stone Age to Christianity,* pp. 118, 123, 126.

35. William F. Albright, "Eric Voegelin," *Theological Studies,* XXII, No. 2 (June 1961), 272

36. Butterfield's perception of sin in human history may also be found in the work of Gerald Heard, *Is God in History?* (New York: Harper, 1950), and in Enrico Castelli, *Les présupposés d'une théologie de l'histoire* (Paris: Vrin, 1954).

37. Bernard J. Lonergan, S.J., *Insight* (New York and London: Longmans, Green, 1957; students' ed.).

38. Ibid., pp. 209, 125–126, 126.

39. Ibid., pp. 210, 210–211, 211.

40. Ibid., p. 743.

41. Christopher Dawson, "The Christian View of History," *Modern Catholic Thinkers,* p. 481.

42. Ibid., p. 481. An equally extreme antiphilosophical position by a Protestant scholar may be found in Graham Neville's *The Advent Hope* (London: Darton, Longmann Todd, 1962).

43. H.-I. Marrou, "From the Logic of History to an Ethic for the Historian," *Crosscurrents,* XI, No. 1 (Winter 1961), 68.

44. Ibid., p. 69.

45. Ibid.

46. Mircea Eliade, *The Sacred and the Profane* (New York: Harper Torchbook,

1961), p. 112. See also his *Cosmos and History* (New York: Harper Torchbook, 1959), pp. 147 ff.

47. Mircea Eliade, *The Sacred and the Profane*, p. 112. For an analysis of Eliade's thought see Thomas J. Alitzer, *Mircea Eliade and the Dialectic of the Sacred* (Philadelphia: Westminster, 1964).

48. Josef Pieper, *The End of Time* (London: Faber & Faber, 1954).

PART TWO: THE JESUS OF HISTORY AND THE CHRIST OF FAITH

1. C. K. Barrett, *Yesterday, Today, and Forever: The New Testament Problem* (Durham: Durham Univ. Press, 1959), reprinted in his *Biblical Problems and Biblical Preaching* (Philadelphia: Fortress Press Facet Books, 1964), pp. 1–27, from which quotations here are taken.

2. Ibid., pp. 7–8.

3. Ibid., p. 25.

Chapter 3: THE JESUS OF HISTORY

4. Avery Dulles, S.J., refers to this late nineteenth- and early twentieth-century Catholic apologetic as a "historicist" apologetic. See his excellent survey and critique of the problem, *Apologetics and the Biblical Christ* (Westminster, Md.: Newman, 1963).

5. Heinz Zahrnt, *The Historical Jesus* (London: Collins, 1963), p. 19.

6. An adequate review of this period may be found in Giuseppe Ricciotti, *The Life of Christ* (Milwaukee: Bruce, 1947), pp. 179–216.

7. James M. Robinson, *The New Quest for the Historical Jesus, Studies in Biblical Theology* (Naperville, Ill.: Allenson, 1959), pp. 38–39.

8. Ibid., pp. 28–29. See also pp. 66 ff.

9. John MacQuarrie, *Twentieth-Century Religious Thought* (New York: Harper & Row, 1963), p. 143.

10. C. H. Dodd, *The Apostolic Preaching and Its Developments* (London: Hodder & Stoughton, 1944; 2d ed.).

11. Robinson, p. 49.

12. Ulrich Wilekens, *Der Missionsreden der Apostolgeschichte* (Neukirchener Verlag, 1961).

13. Rudolf Otto, *The Kingdom of God and the Son of Man* (London: Hodder & Stoughton, 1938).

14. Zahrnt, p. 80.

15. Ethelbert Stauffer, *Jesus and His Story* (New York: Knopf, 1960), and *New Testament Theology* (London: Student Christian Movement Press, 1963).

16. See Robinson, pp. 59 ff.

17. Zahrnt, p. 78.

18. Ibid., p. 81.

19. Robinson, p. 81.

20. Ibid., pp. 89–90.

21. Bultmann and his critics have carried on a written debate over the years 1948–55, which has been published in five volumes in German, *Kerygma und Mythos*, ed. H. W. Bartsch. Reginald H. Fuller has translated a representative selection from Vols. I and II, published as *Kerygma and Myth I* (New York: Harper Torchbook, 1958), and a selection from Vols. III–V, *Kerygma and Myth II* (Harper Torchbook, 1962). See also Fuller's *The New Testament in Current Study* (New York: Scribners, 1962), passim.

22. Fuller, *The New Testament in Current Study*, p. 14.

23. Paul Althaus, *Fact and Faith in the Kerygma of Today* (Philadelphia: Muhlenberg, 1960), p. 18.

24. Ibid., p. 39.

25. Ibid., p. 40. See also Eric Rust, *Salvation History* (Richmond, Va.: John Knox, 1962), pp. 49–90.

26. For evaluations of Bultmann's pupils by Catholic scholars see Raymond E. Brown, "After Bultmann, What?" *Catholic Biblical Quarterly*, XXVI, No. 1 (Jan. 1964), 1–30, and P. Joseph Cahill, S.J., "Rudolf Bultmann and Post-Bultmannian Tendencies," *Catholic Biblical Quarterly*, XXVI, No. 2 (April 1964), 153–178. See also the collection by various scholars edited by Carl E. Braaten, *The Historical Jesus and the Kerygmatic Christ* (Nashville: Abingdon, 1964), Hugh Anderson, *Jesus and Christian Origins* (New York: Oxford Univ. Press, 1964).

27. Zahrnt, p. 112.

28. John MacQuarrie, *The Scope of Demythologizing*: Bultmann and His Critics (New York: Harper & Bros., 1960), p. 247.

29. Zahrnt, pp. 112, 115.

30. Ibid., p. 137

31. Günther Bornkamm, *Jesus of Nazareth* (New York: Harper & Bros., 1960), p. 14.

32. Ibid., p. 183.

33. William F. Martin, in the *Dunwoodie Review*, III, No. 2 (May 1963), 251.

34. Neill Hamilton, in *Theology Today*, XX, No. 1 (April 1963), 126.

35. Rust, p. 74.

36. Paul J. Achtemeier, "Is the New Quest Docetic?" *Theology Today*, XIX, No. 3 (Oct. 1962), 362–363.

37. Althaus, p. 60.

38. Ibid.

39. Vincent T. O'Keefe, S.J., in *Theological Studies*, XXI, No. 4 (Dec. 1960), 645.

40. Alan Richardson, *Christian Apologetics* (London, S.C.M., 1947), *An Introduction to the Theology of the New Testament* (London: S.C.M., 1958), *The Bible in the Age of Science* (London: S.C.M., 1961), and *History Sacred and Profane* (Philadelphia: Westminster, 1964).

41. Richardson, *History Sacred and Profane*, pp. 127, 152.

42. Ibid., p. 153.

43. Richardson, *Christian Apologetics*, pp. 94, 98.

44. Richardson, *History Sacred and Profane*, pp. 186, 189.

45. Ibid., p. 195.

46. Ibid., p. 210. This view of Richardson's is, of course, dependent upon his concept of historical thinking.

47. Ibid., p. 224.

48. Dodd, p. 65.

49. Ibid., p. 42.

Chapter 4: THE CHRIST OF FAITH

1. George Ernest Wright, *The God Who Acts,* Studies in Biblical Theology (London: S.C.M., 1952).

2. Alan Richardson, *The Bible in the Age of Science* (London: S.C.M., 1961), p. 141.

3. Louis Bouyer, *The Meaning of Sacred Scripture* (Notre Dame: Univ. of Notre Dame Press, 1958), p. 36.

4. Richardson, p. 174.

5. Jer. 31:31–33; see also 32:38–40.

6. Heb. 1:1–2.

7. See the studies of Jean Daniélou, S.J., *The Bible and the Liturgy* (Notre Dame: Univ. of Notre Dame Press, 1956), and *From Shadows to Reality* (Westminster, Md.: Newman, 1960). Also see George A. F. Knight, *A Christian Theology of the Old Testament* (Richmond, Va.: John Knox, 1959).

8. Richardson, p. 178.

9. Ethelbert Stauffer, *New Testament Theology* (London: S.C.M., 1963), p. 51.

10. I Peter 1:20.

11. Eph. 1:3–5.

12. Oscar Cullmann, *Christ and Time* (Philadelphia: Westminster, 1950), p. 51.

13. Matt. 26:18.

14. I Peter 4:17.

15. Rom. 8:19–21.

16. Rom. 1:20–21.

17. John 7:18, 21:19.

18. John 1:14.

19. Apoc. 21:3.

20. Heb. 4:9.

21. Stauffer, p. 231.

PART THREE: HISTORY AND THE THEOLOGIANS

1. Roger Shinn, *Christianity and the Problem of History* (New York: Scribners, 1953), p. 96; John Cogley, "On Christian Culture," *Christianity and Culture* (Baltimore: Helicon, 1960), pp. 10–11.

2. An interesting and illuminating presentation of the problem and possible answers in Christian thought may be found in John Courtney Murray, S.J., *We Hold These Truths* (New York: Sheed & Ward, 1960), pp. 175–196.

Chapter 5: THE PROTESTANT THEOLOGIES OF HISTORY

3. See the treatment of Nels F. S. Ferré, *Searchlights on Contemporary Theology* (New York: Harper, 1961), pp. 79–144.

4. Ibid., p. 87.

5. Shinn, p. 191.

6. Jerome Hamer, O.P., *Karl Barth* (Westminster, Md.: Newman, 1962), p. 32.

7. Ibid., p. 118.

8. Martin D'Arcy, S.J., *The Meaning and Matter of History* (New York: Farrar, Straus & Cudahy, 1959), p. 170.

9. Georges Casalis, *Portrait of Karl Barth* (Garden City: Doubleday, 1963), p. 123.

10. Karl Löwith, *Meaning in History* (Chicago: Univ. of Chicago Press, 1949), p. 184.

11. Ibid., p. 191.

12. Ibid., p. 195.

13. Charles C. West, *Communism and the Theologians* (New York: Macmillan paperback, 1958), p. 151.

14. Gustave Weigel, S.J., "Authority in Theology," *Reinhold Niebuhr*, ed. Kegley and Bretall (New York: Macmillan, 1956), p. 372.

15. Robert E. Fitch, "Reinhold Niebuhr's Philosophy of History," ibid., p. 310. See Fitch's own little work, which reflects much of Niebuhr's thought, *Kingdom Without End* (New York: Scribners, 1950).

16. It should be noted that in Sweden no major figure in the tradition of Barth or Bultmann (that is, dialectical theology) has emerged. See Leiv Aalen, "Principal Systematic Problems of Present Day Scandinavian Thought," *Lutheran World*, III (1956), 45. See also Nels F. S. Ferre, *Swedish Contributions to Modern Theology* (New York, 1939), and W. M. Horton, *Contemporary Continental Theology* (New York, 1938).

17. Gustaf Aulen, *Christus Victor* (London: S.P.C.K., 1931).

18. Anders Nygren, *Agape and Eros* (London: S.P.C.K., 1953), p. 42.

19. D'Arcy, p. 79.

20. Bernhard Erling, *Nature and History* (Lund: C.W.K. Gleerup, 1960), p. 239.

21. Ibid., p. 252.

22. Gustaf Wingren, *Theology in Conflict* (Philadelphia: Muhlenberg, 1958).

23. Gustaf Wingren, *The Living Word* (Philadelphia: Muhlenberg, 1960), p. 53.

24. Rudolf Bultmann, *History and Eschatology* (New York: Harper Torchbook, 1957), pp. 140, 146.

25. Ibid., pp. 151, 152.

26. Ibid., p. 153.

27. Ibid., p. 155.

28. Leopold Malevez, S.J., *The Christian Message and Myth* (Westminster, Md.: Newman, 1959), pp. 43–44.

29. Among the significant attempts being made to align the work of Rudolf Bultmann and Karl Barth is that of a former student of both, Heinrich Ott, successor to Barth at the University of Basel. An introduction to Ott, his work, and intentions may be found in Robert C. Johnston, "Who Is Heinrich Ott?" *New Theology* No. 1; eds. Martin E. Marty and Dean G. Peerman (New York: Macmillan, 1965), pp. 34–43.

30. Günther Bornkamm, "Enderwartung und Kirche im Mattausevangelium," *The Background of the New Testament and Its Eschatology*, ed. W. D. Davies and D. Daube (Cambridge: University Press, 1956), pp. 222–260.

31. James M. Robinson, *The Problem of History in Mark*, Studies in Biblical Theology (Naperville, Ill.: Allenson, 1957). This work represents Robinson's earlier phase when he was strongly influenced by Oscar Cullmann.

32. Hans Conzelmann, *The Theology of Saint Luke* (New York: Harper, 1960), p. 14.

33. Ibid., p. 208.

34. John MacQuarrie, *Twentieth Century Religious Thought* (New York: Harper & Row, 1963), p. 366. See also MacQuarrie's treatment of Bultmann vis-à-vis Buri in his incisive *The Scope of Demythologizing* (New York: Harper, 1960), pp. 129–153.

35. MacQuarrie, *The Scope of Demythologizing*, pp. 232, 236.

36. Ibid., p. 243. MacQuarrie's affirmation of paradox is contested by another Bultmannian critic of the left. Schubert Ogden maintains that MacQuarrie is guilty of inconsistency, not paradox. The New Testament, he maintains, is to be demythologized to a theocentric approach, because the only basis for salvation is the love of God for men. See his *Christ Without Myth* (New York: Harper, 1961).

37. Paul Tillich, *The Interpretation of History* (New York: Scribners, 1936), and *Systematic Theology* (Chicago: Chicago Univ. Press, 1951, 1957, 1963).

38. William F. Albright, *History, Archeology and Christian Humanism* (New York: McGraw-Hill, 1964), pp. 14–15.

39. See the fine commentary on Tillich by the Catholic scholar George H. Tavard, *Paul Tillich and the Christian Message* (New York: Scribners, 1961), and the collection of essays by Kegley and Bretall, *The Theology of Paul Tillich* (New York: Macmillan, 1952).

40. Martin E. Marty, from his introduction to the collection of essays, *The Place of Bonhoeffer* (New York: Association Press, 1962), p. 10. A fine introduction to Bonhoeffer may be found in John Godsey, *The Theology of Dietrich Bonhoeffer* (Philadelphia: Westminster, 1960).

41. Dietrich Bonhoeffer, *Ethics* (New York: Macmillan, 1955), p. 63.

42. Ibid., p. 72.

43. Dietrich Bonhoeffer, *Prisoner for God* (New York: Macmillan, 1957), p. 126 —letter of May 5, 1944.

44. James Richmond, "Beyond All Reason," *Four Anchors from the Stern* (London: S.C.M., 1963), p. 45.

45. For example, see the recent little treatise on the meaningfulness of time by Olivier Clement, *Transfigurer le temps* (Neuchâtel: Delchaux and Niestle, 1959).

46. See particularly Nikolai Berdyaev, *The Meaning of History* (New York: Scribners, 1936), *The Destiny of Man* (New York: Scribners, 1935), and *The Beginning and the End* (New York: Harper, 1952).

47. Donald A. Lowrie, *Rebellious Prophet* (New York: Harper, 1960), p. 253.

48. E. Lampert, *The Apocalypse of History* (London: Faber & Faber, 1948), p. 41.

49. Ibid., p. 53.

50. Ibid., p. 57.

51. It is not our intention to exclude many of the neo-orthodox and existentialist theologians from the category of "biblical"; the classification is used here to refer principally to more traditional biblical theologians.

52. C. H. Dodd, *The Apostolic Preaching and Its Developments* (London: Hodder & Stoughton, 1944; 2d ed.). See also his *History and the Gospel* (London: Nisbet, 1938).

53. C. H. Dodd, *The Parables of the Kingdom* (London: Nisbet, 1935).

54. R. H. Fuller, *The Mission and Achievement of Jesus,* Studies in Biblical Theology (Chicago: Allenson, 1957); W. G. Kümmel, *Promise and Fulfillment,* Studies in Biblical Theology (Naperville, Ill.: Allenson, 1957); James M. Robinson, *The Problem of History in Mark,* Studies in Biblical Theology (Naperville, Ill.: Allenson, 1957).

55. A distinction has been introduced into Dodd's theory between the anticipatory events ("the eschatological man") and the eschaton itself (the eschatological event) by D. J. Selby, "Changing Ideas in New Testament Eschatology," *Harvard Theological Review,* L, No. 1 (Jan. 1957), 21–36. See also Claude H. Thompson, *Theology of the Kerygma* (Englewood, N. J.: Prentice Hall, 1962).

56. C. H. Dodd, *The Fourth Gospel* (Cambridge: University Press, 1960), p. 447, n. 1; Joachim Jeremias, *The Parables of Jesus* (New York: Scribners, 1963), p. 230, n. 2.

57. C. H. Dodd, *The Bible Today* (Cambridge: University Press, 1960), p. 132.

58. Ibid., pp. 134, 138.

59. Ibid., pp. 140–141, 142–143.

60. Oscar Cullmann, *Christ and Time* (Philadelphia: Westminster, 1950), and *The Christology of the New Testament* (Philadelphia: Westminster, 1959).

61. Cullmann, *Christ and Time*, p. 23.

62. Ibid., pp. 67, 75.

63. Ibid., pp. 145–146.

64. Ibid., p. 155.

65. Ibid., p. 156.

66. Thus, for example, we have the favorable comparison of Luigi Bini, S.J., *L'intervento di Oscar Cullmann nella discussione Bultmanniana*, Analecta Gregoriana 114 (Rome: Libreria Gregoriana, 1961). See also Jean Frisque, *Oscar Cullmann: Une théologie de l'histoire du salut* (Paris: Vrin, 1961). Frisque claims that Cullmann's weakness is that he really does not see the place of Scripture in the Church, so that the Church being transformed at the death of the last apostle can no longer explore the meaning of Scripture in tradition. One Catholic critic has said this position of Cullmann reflects a "theological ice age."

67. MacQuarrie, *Twentieth Century Religious Thought*, pp. 327–328.

68. MacQuarrie, *The Scope of Demythologizing*, pp. 62–63.

69. James Barr, *Biblical Words for Time*, Studies in Biblical Theology (Naperville, Ill.: Allenson, 1962), pp. 49 ff.

70. Ibid., p. 50.

71. Ibid., pp. 133–134.

72. Ibid., p. 147. Barr's critique of biblical theologians who rely excessively upon lexical structure is also leveled at the work of John Marsh, *The Fulness of Time* (New York: Harper, 1952), and his article, "Time," in *A Theological Wordbook of the Bible,* ed. Alan Richardson (New York: Macmillan paperback, 1962), pp. 258–267. Barr has made it quite clear that he accepts the basic notions of *Heilsgeschichte*, although he objects to the imposition of modern concepts such as "history" upon the biblical material; see his "Revelation Through History in the Old Testament and in Modern Theology," in *New Theology* No. 1, pp. 60–74.

73. George Ernest Wright, *God Who Acts*, Studies in Biblical Theology (Naperville, Ill.: Allenson, 1952), pp. 11, 42.

74. Ibid., p. 58.

75. George Ernest Wright, *The Biblical Doctrine of Man in Society*, Ecumenical Biblical Studies (London: S.C.M., 1954), pp. 67–68, n.

76. Ibid., p. 100.

77. Ibid., p. 120.

78. Eric Rust, *The Christian Understanding of History* (London: Butterworth, 1948), *Salvation History: A Biblical Interpretation* (Richmond, Va.: John Knox, 1962), and *Toward the Theological Understanding of History* (New York: Oxford Univ. Press, 1963).

79. Rust, *Salvation History*, p. 12.

80. *Towards a Theological Understanding of History*, pp. 114, 217.

81. Ibid., pp. 247, 248.

82. Rust, *Salvation History*, p. 23.

83. C. K. Barrett, *From First Adam to Last* (New York: Scribners, 1962), p. 5.

84. Rom. 11:33.

85. Shinn, p. 247.

86. Ibid., pp. 263, 266.

87. Ibid., p. 268.

88. Ibid., p. 272.

89. John McIntyre, *The Christian Doctrine of History* (Edinburgh and London: Oliver and Boyd, 1957), pp. 9, 11.

90. Ibid., p. 14.

91. Ibid., pp. 77, 78, 78–79, 80.
92. Ibid., pp. 89–90.
93. Ibid., pp. 109, 110, 112.
94. Ibid., p. 115.
95. Alec R. Vidler, *The Theology of F. D. Maurice* (London: Hodder & Stoughton, 1948).
96. Alec R. Vidler, *Christian Belief and This World* (Greenwich, Conn.: Seabury Press, 1957), p. 44.
97. Ibid., p. 45.
98. Ibid., p. 51.
99. George A. Buttrick, *Christ and History* (New York: Abingdon, 1963), p. 20.
100. Ibid., p. 44.
101. Ibid., p. 105.
102. Ibid., p. 117.
103. Ibid., p. 137.
104. H. Richard Niebuhr, *Christ and Culture* (New York: Harper Torchbook, 1956), pp. 2, 32.
105. Ibid., p. 81.
106. Ibid., pp. 119, 122.
107. Ibid., pp. 150, 155, 185.
108. Ibid., p. 45.
109. Ibid., pp. 232, 233.
110. Ibid., pp. 246, 247.
111. Ibid., pp. 255–256.
112. H. Richard Niebuhr, *The Meaning of Revelation* (New York: Macmillan paperback, 1962).
113. Richard Kroner, *Culture and Faith* (Chicago: Univ. of Chicago Press, 1951), p. 217.
114. Ibid., p. 239.
115. Ibid., p. 187.
116. Carl Michalson, *The Hinge of History* (New York: Scribners, 1959), p. 22.
117. Ibid., p. 31.
118. In his latest work Michalson strictly distinguishes science (concerned with objects) from history (which makes "others" present to us). Faith, he says, accords only with historical thinking. See *The Rationality of Faith*, (New York: Scribners, 1963), passim.
119. Michalson, *The Hinge of History*, p. 35.
120. Ibid., p. 41.
121. Ibid., pp. 42, 45, 47.
122. Ibid., pp. 103 ff.
123. Walter E. Wiest, *Theology Today*, XX, No. 4 (Jan. 1964), 578.
124. Michalson, *Hinge of History*, p. 245.

Chapter 6: THE CATHOLIC THEOLOGIES OF HISTORY

1. The significance of the historical dimension in contemporary Catholic theology may be seen in the dogmatic theology text of Michael Schmaus, "Von den letzten Dingen," Vol. IV, Pt. 2 of *Katholische Dogmatik* (Munich: Hueber, 1953). Schmaus introduces his treatment of the last things with an "eschatological" theology of history. In moral theology see Bernard Haring, C.SS.R., *The Law of Christ* (Westminster, Md.: Newman, 1961), I, 87 ff. Although he pays little attention to the development of historical thought since Dilthey, there is a

good treatment of the sense of history in theological methodology in Jean-Marie Levasseur, *Le lieu théologique "Histoire. . . ."* (Trois-Rivières: Éditions du Bien Public, 1960).

2. See Charles Davis, "The Danger of Irrelevance," *Downside Review*, LXXIX, No. 255 (Spring 1961), 93–104.

3. The necessity of affirming both the incarnational and the eschatological viewpoints at the same time and in tension with each other is presented by Jean Lacroix, *Histoire et mystère* (Paris: Casterman, 1962).

4. Surveys of Catholic positions may be found in Gustave Thils, "Bibliographie sur la théologie de l'histoire," *Ephemerides Theologicae Lovanensis*, XXVI (1950), 87–95; Roger Aubert, "Discussions récentes autour de la théologie de l'histoire," *Collectanea Mechliniensia* (1948), pp. 129–149; and Léopold Malevez, S.J., "Deux théologies catholiques de l'histoire," *Bijdragen* (1949), pp. 225–240.

5. Kenneth S. Latourette, *The Twentieth Century in Europe* (New York: Harper, 1961), p. 113.

6. Peter Riga, "The Ecclesiology of Johann Adam Möhler," *Theological Studies*, XXII, No. 4 (Dec. 1961), 564. This compact and thorough essay provides an excellent introduction to the thought of Möhler and a more than adequate bibliography.

7. Ibid., p. 566

8. Ibid., p. 564.

9. See Karl Adam, *Spirit of Catholicism,* (Garden City: Doubleday Image, 1954).

10. Paul Henry S.J., "Christian Philosophy of History," *Theological Studies*, XIII, No. 3 (Sept. 1952), 431.

11. Henri de Lubac, S.J., *The Drama of Atheist Humanism* (New York: Sheed & Ward, 1950), and *The Un-Marxian Socialist* (New York: Sheed & Ward, 1948).

12. Henri de Lubac, *Further Paradoxes* (Westminster, Md.: Newman, 1958), p. 38.

13. Henri de Lubac, *Catholicism* (New York: Sheed & Ward, 1946), p. 29.

14. Henri de Lubac, *Splendor of the Church* (New York: Sheed & Ward, 1956), p. 151.

15. De Lubac, *Catholicism,* p. 69.

16. Ibid., p. 71.

17. Ibid., p. 153.

18. Pierre Teilhard de Chardin, S.J., *The Phenomenon of Man* (New York: Harper, 1959), and *The Divine Milieu* (New York: Harper, 1960). Père de Lubac points out that these works are on two levels; the first, however, leads to and is complemented by the second. De Lubac's study of Teilhard de Chardin is one of the most significant contemporary contributions toward grasping the theological implications of Teilhardism. See Henri de Lubac, *La pensée religieuse du Père Teilhard de Chardin* (Paris: Aubier, 1962).

19. Teilhard de Chardin, *The Phenomenon of Man*, pp. 217, 220.

20. Ibid., p. 223.

21. Teilhard de Chardin, *The Divine Milieu*, pp. 33, 35, 133.

22. Louis Cognet, *Le Père Teilhard de Chardin et la pensée contemporaine* (Paris: Flammarion, 1952).

23. Nicholas Corte, *Pierre Teilhard de Chardin* (London: Barrie and Rockliff, 1960), pp. 93–94. A Protestant theologian in a highly sympathetic work advances a criticism basic to Corte in that Teilhard de Chardin did not use all the relevant biblical data available but rather deliberately and arbitrarily chose from the Bible. See Georges Crespy, *La pensée théologique de Teilhard de Char-*

din (Paris: Éditions Universitaires, 1961). See also William F. Albright's cutting criticism, "This Travesty of New Testament Eschatology" in his *History, Archeology and Christian Humanism* (New York: McGraw-Hill, 1964), p. 80.

24. Th.-G. Chifflot, O.P., *Approches d'une théologie de l'histoire* (Paris: Cerf, 1960), pp. 73–104, 115.

25. In this, Chifflot relies heavily upon the work of Claude Tresmontant, *A Study of Hebrew Thought* (New York: Desclée, 1960). Tresmontant's work has been well received, but with some important demurrers. Tresmontant is a rather notable Teilhardist. See his *Pierre Teilhard de Chardin* (Baltimore: Helicon, 1959), and Corte's critique in his own work, pp. 95, 98–102.

26. M.-D. Chenu, O.P., "Histoire sainte et vie spirituelle," *La vie spirituelle,* CIV, (1961), 506–513, translated and abridged as "Time in Theology," *Theology Digest,* X, No. 4 (Autumn 1962), 203–206.

27. Ibid., p. 206.

28. Walter J. Ong, S.J., "Evolution and Cyclicalism in Our Time," *Darwin's Vision and Christian Perspectives* (New York: Macmillan, 1960), pp. 136, 146.

29. Ibid., p. 146.

30. Walter J. Ong, "Christian Values at Mid-Twentieth Century," *Theology Digest,* IV, No. 3 (Autumn 1956), 156. See also his *Frontiers in American Catholicism* (New York: Macmillan, 1957), pp. 86–103.

31. Walter J. Ong, "Secular Knowledge and Revealed Religion and History,' *Theology Digest,* VI, No. 2 (Spring 1958), 89. Fordham University's W. Norris Clarke, S.J., editor of the International Philosophical Quarterly also reflects the influence of Teilhard de Chardin. See his "Technology and Man," *Catholic World,* LXI, No. 1172 (April 1962), 4–20.

32. Christopher Butler, O.S.B., "The Value of History," *The Downside Review,* LXVIII, No. 2 (Summer 1950), 290–304.

33. Martin D'Arcy, S.J., *The Meaning and the Matter of History* (New York: Farrar, Straus & Cudahy, 1959), pp. 183–184.

34. Gustave Thils, *Théologie des réalités terrestres* (Paris: Desclée de Brouwer, 1948–1949). See also his later comments in *Orientations de la Théologie* (Louvain: Ceuterick, 1958), pp. 114 ff., 120 ff., 134 ff., 154 ff.

35. Gustave Thils, *Christian Holiness* (Tielt, Belgium: Lanoo, 1961).

36. Peter Riga, *Catholic Thought in Crisis* (Milwaukee: Bruce, 1963).

37. Ibid., pp. 42–43.

38. Albert Dondeyne, *Contemporary European Thought and Catholic Faith* (Pittsburgh: Duquesne Univ. Press, 1958), p. 45.

39. Ibid., p. 164.

40. Ibid., p. 181.

41. Ibid., p. 190.

42. Albert Dondeyne, *Faith and the World* (Pittsburgh: Duquesne Univ. Press, 1963), p. 90.

43. Dondeyne, *Contemporary European Thought and Christian Faith,* pp. 192, 193.

44. Ibid., p. 193.

45. Ibid., p. 194

46. Dondeyne, *Faith and the World,* p. 92.

47. Dondeyne, *Contemporary European Thought and Christian Faith,* p. 197.

48. Ibid., p. 198.

49. F. G. Fessard, S.J., *De l'actualité historique* (Paris: Desclée de Brouwer, 1959–1960).

50. Jean Mouroux, *The Meaning of Man* (Garden City: Doubleday Image, 1961), pp. 20–21.

51. Jean Mouroux, *Le mystère du temps: Approche théologique* (Paris: Aubier, 1962).

52. Robert O. Johann, S.J., in his review in *Theological Studies*, XXIV, No. 2 (June 1963), 325.

53. Yves Congar, O.P., *Lay People in the Church* (Westminster, Md.: Newman, 1957), p. 60.

54. Ibid., p. 62.

55. Ibid., p. 65. See also Congar's treatment in *The Mystery of the Temple* (London: Burns, Oates, 1962), pp. 107 ff.

56. Congar, *Lay People in the Church*, p. 88.

57. Ibid., p. 91.

58. See also the collection of Yves Congar's studies on the nature of the Church, *The Mystery of the Church* (Baltimore: Helicon, 1960).

59. Congar, *Lay People in the Church*, p. 92.

60. Ibid., p. 96. See also his "Heaven, Salvation, and World History" in the collection of his essays, *The Wide World, My Parish* (Baltimore: Helicon, 1961), pp. 44–61.

61. Congar, *Lay People in the Church*, op. cit., pp. 399–400.

62. Ibid., p. 401.

63. Ibid., p. 427.

64. Léopold Malevez, S.J., *Nouvelle révue théologique*, LXXI (March 1949), 244–264.

65. Léopold Malevez, *The Christian Message and Myth* (Westminster, Md.: Newman, 1959), p. 121.

66. *Études* (Feb. 1948), p. 214.

67. Louis Bouyer, "Christianisme et eschatologie," *La vie intellectuelle*, XVI (1948), 6–32, and "Où en est la théologie du Corps mystique," *Revue des sciences religieuses*, XXII (1948), 313–333.

68. Louis Bouyer, *The Fourth Gospel* (Westminster, Md.: Newman, 1964), p. 13.

69. Louis Bouyer, *The Word, Church, and Sacraments* (New York: Desclée, 1961), p. 71.

70. Louis Bouyer, *Liturgical Piety* (Notre Dame: Univ. of Notre Dame Press, 1955), pp. 257–258.

71. Louis Bouyer, *Christian Initiation* (New York: Macmillan, 1958), p. 112.

72. Ibid., p. 113.

73. Ibid., p. 114.

74. Bouyer, *Liturgical Piety*, pp 265–266.

75. Maurice Villain and Joseph Baciocchi, *La vocation de l'église* (Paris: Plon, 1954).

76. Lucien Cerfaux, *Christ in the Theology of Saint Paul* (New York: Herder & Herder, 1959), *The Church in the Theology of Saint Paul* (New York: Herder & Herder, 1959), and *Le chrétien dans la théologie paulienne* (Paris: Cerf, 1962).

77. Joseph Bonsirven, S.J., *Le règne de Dieu* (Paris: Aubier, 1957).

78. Benoit Pruche, O.P., *Histoire de l'homme: Mystère de Dieu* (Bruges: Desclée de Brouwer, 1961).

79. Evode Beaucamp, O.F.M., *The Bible and the Universe* (Westminster, Md.: Newman, 1962), p. 11.

80. Ibid., pp. 36, 88.

81. Ibid., p. 141.

82. Ibid., p. 118.

83. Werner Bulst, S.J., *Offenbarung: Biblischer und Theologischer Begriff* (Düsseldorf: Patmos Verlag, 1960).

84. H. M. Feret, O.P., *The Apocalypse of Saint John* (Westminster, Md.: Newman, 1958), pp. 89, 91.

85. Ibid., p. 107.

86. Ibid., pp. 217, 225.

87. Joseph Pieper, *The End of Time* (London: Faber & Faber, 1954), pp. 25, 68, 76.

88. Ibid., p. 137.

89. Romano Guardini, *The Last Things* (New York: Pantheon, 1954), pp. 79–89.

90. Ibid., pp. 81, 83.

91. Romano Guardini, *The Faith and Modern Man* (London: Burns, Oates, 1952), p. 28.

92. Guardini, *The Last Things*, p. 83.

93. See Guardini, *The Faith and Modern Man*, pp. 33–46, 67–81, 82–101; also his *Freedom, Grace and Destiny* (New York: Pantheon, 1961), passim.

94. Romano Guardini, *The End of the Modern World* (New York: Sheed & Ward, 1956), p. 69.

95. Ibid., pp. 73, 77.

96. Ibid., p. 75.

97. Ibid., p. 84.

98. Ibid., p. 85.

99. Ibid., p. 101.

100. Romano Guardini, Introd., *Power and Responsibility* (Chicago: Regnery, 1961), p. xiii.

101. Guardini, *The End of the Modern World*, p. 133.

102. Romano Guardini, *The Lord* (Chicago: Regnery, 1954), p. 513.

103. See the articles from *America* published in June 1958 as a pamphlet by America Press: *End of the Modern World?* by W. Norris Clarke, S.J., and Frederick D. Wilhelmsen.

104. Guardini, *The End of the Modern World*, Introd. p. xiii.

105. F.-X. Durwell, C.SS.R., *The Resurrection* (New York: Sheed & Ward, 1960), pp. 250, 254.

106. Ibid., pp. 254–256.

107. Ibid., p. 263.

108. Ibid., p. 268.

109. Ibid., p. 270.

110. Ibid., pp 286–287.

111. Hans Urs von Balthasar, *A Theology of History* (New York: Sheed & Ward, 1963), pp. 18–19.

112. Ibid., p. 42.

113. Ibid., pp 66, 68.

114. Ibid., pp. 84, 85, 86.

115. Ibid., pp. 114, 133.

116. Ibid., p. 135. Von Balthasar expresses this same thought in his slashing attack on the ascetical attitudes reflected by Teilhard de Chardin in *The Divine Milieu*. See *Wort und Warheit*, XVIII (1963), 339–350.

117. Jean Daniélou, S.J., *The Bible and the Liturgy* (Notre Dame: Univ. of Notre Dame Press, 1956), p. 4.

118. Jean Daniélou, *The Lord of History* (Chicago: Regnery, 1958), pp. 140, 141. See also his *From Shadows to Reality* (Westminster, Md.: Newman, 1960).

119. Daniélou, *Lord of History,* op. cit., p. 190.

120. Ibid., p. 7.

121. Jean Daniélou, *The Scandal of Truth* (Baltimore: Helicon. 1962), p. 71, and *The Lord of History,* p. 203.

122. Gerald A. McCool, S.J., "The Philosophy of the Human Person in Karl Rahner's Theology," *Theological Studies,* XXII, No. 4 (Dec. 1961), 540. This presentation of Rahner is indebted to Father McCool's study.

123. Ibid., p. 541.

124. Ibid., p. 543.

125. Ibid., pp. 543–544.

126. Karl Rahner, S.J., *Schriften zur Theologie* (Benziger Verlag: Einsiedeln-Kohn, 1955), II, 89.

127. Karl Rahner, S.J., *Theological Investigations* (Baltimore: Helicon, 1961), I, 300. See also his *Nature and Grace* (London: Sheed & Ward, 1963), and his essay "The Order of Redemption Within the Order of Creation" in *The Christian Commitment* (New York: Sheed & Ward, 1963), pp. 38–74.

128. Rahner, *Theological Investigations,* pp. 302–303.

129. Ibid., pp. 312–313.

130. McCool, pp. 547–548.

131. Rahner, *Theological Investigations,* pp. 20–37.

132. Ibid., p. 47.

133. See Rahner's "The Present Situation of Christians," in *The Christian Commitment,* pp. 3–37.

134. Ibid., pp. 48–49; see also pp. 117–118.

135. Ibid., p. 88.

136. Ibid., p. 87.

137. Ibid., p. 108.

138. Ibid., p. 109.

139. Ibid., p. 111.

PART FOUR: TOWARD A THEOLOGY OF HISTORY

1. Jean Daniélou, S.J., *The Lord of History* (Chicago: Regnery, 1958), p. 3.

Chapter 7: THE WORD OF GOD AND HUMAN HISTORY

2. Oscar Cullmann, *The Christology of the New Testament* (Philadelphia: Westminster, 1959), p. 253.

3. See the synthesis, to which we are indebted here, of John L. McKenzie, S.J., "The Word of God in the Old Testament," *Theological Studies,* XXI, No. 2 (June 1960), 183–206.

4. Ibid., p. 188.

5. Ibid., p. 192.

6. Ibid., p. 195.

7. Isa. 55:11.

8. Isa. 40:26; Gen. 1; Ps. 33, 147.

9. McKenzie, p. 203.

10. Prov. 8:22-26; Eccli. 1:1 ff., 24:1 ff.

11. Sirach 24:22; Bar. 4:1.

12. Alan Richardson, *An Introduction to the Theology of the New Testament* (London: S.C.M. 1958), p. 162.

13. I Cor. 8:6.

14. Col. 1:15–16.

15. Heb. 1:1–2.

16. John 5:24.

17. Cullmann, p. 260.

18. John 2:21.

19. Cyprian Vagaggini, *The Theological Dimensions of the Liturgy* (Collegeville: Liturgical Press, 1959), p. 108.

20. Ibid., p. 109.

21. I Cor. 8:6.

22. The reader is referred to the works of Bruce Vawter, *A Path Through Genesis* (New York: Sheed & Ward, 1956), and Peter Ellis, C.SS.R., *Men and Message of the Old Testament* (Collegeville: Liturgical Press, 1963).

23. Gerhard von Rad, *Genesis* (Philadelphia: Westminster, 1961), pp. 26–27.

24. James Muilenburg, "The Biblical View of Time," *Harvard Theological Review*, LIV, No. 4 (Oct. 1961), 242.

25. Von Rad, p. 49.

26. Gen. 1:31.

27. Von Rad, p. 50.

28. Claude Tresmontant, *A Study of Hebrew Thought* (New York: Desclée, 1960), p. 35.

29. Apoc. 1:3.

30. Eph. 1:10.

31. Gen. 1:31.

32. Acts 1:7.

33. Gen. 1:26.

34. Karl Heim, *The World: Its Creation and Consummation* (Philadelphia: Muhlenberg, 1962), p. 79.

35. Ps. 32:8–9, 148:5.

36. Wisd. 7:15 and Wisd. 9; Prov. 8:22–31.

37. John 17:24.

38. See M. E. Boismard, O.P., *St. John's Prologue* (London: Blackfriars, 1957), pp. 10–11, 102 ff.

39. Col. 1:15–17.

40. Heb. 1:3.

41. Boismard, pp. 104–105.

42. Suzanne de Dietrich, *God's Unfolding Purpose* (Philadelphia: Westminster, 1960), p. 33.

43. Rom. 1:20, 2:14–15.

44. Roger Shinn, *Christianity and the Problem of History* (New York: Scribners, 1953), p. 203.

45. Reinhold Niebuhr, *Faith and History* (New York: Scribners, 1949), p. 53.

46. Ibid., pp. 43, 45.

47. Gen. 3.

48. Rom. 5:2.

49. On the concept of the literary genre among Catholic scholars see Pius XII, *Divino afflante,* and the work of Jean Levie, S.J., *The Bible: God's Word in Man's Words* (New York: Kennedy, 1962), pp. 133 ff., 214 ff.

50. Gen. 4.

51. Gen. 3:15.

52. Gen. 12:1, 2–3, 15:6.
53. Ex. 2:24, 3:4.
54. Ex. 24:3.
55. De Dietrich, p. 71.
56. I Kings 3.
57. I Kings 16:12.
58. I Kings 12:20.
59. Amos 8:11, 3:8.
60. IV Kings 19:1–9; 21:17–24.
61. IV Kings 19:20–24.
62. E. W. Heaton, *The Old Testament Prophets* (Baltimore: Penguin, 1958), p. 126.
63. III Kings 23.
64. II Esd. 8:17, 13:1.
65. Job 28:12–27.
66. Prov. 8:22–23, 26.
67. Sirach 24:1–24; Wisd. 7:15–8:1, 8:9.
68. Sirach 24:3; also Wisd. 7:25 and Prov. 2:6.
69. Dan. 7:27.
70. De Dietrich, p. 147.
71. George E. Wright, *The God Who Acts,* Studies in Biblical Theology (Naperville, Ill.: Allenson, 1952), p. 42.
72. See Walter Eichrodt, *Theology of the Old Testament* (Philadelphia: Westminster, 1961), passim.
73. Wright, p. 51.
74. Luke 22:20.
75. I Peter 2:9–10.
76. Wright, p. 87.
77. Jer. 31:31–34, 32:40; Isa. 54:10, 55:3.
78. McKenzie, pp. 199–200.
79. Alexander Jones, *God's Living Word* (New York: Sheed & Ward, 1961), p. 24.
80. Joel 4:17–21; Zach. 2:9; John 1:14.
81. Eph. 3:9.
82. Heb. 1:1.
83. Mark 1:15.
84. Wright, p. 29.
85. Gal. 6:16; I Peter 2:9.
86. Mark 1:14–15.
87. John Bright, *The Kingdom of God* (Nashville: Abingdon, 1953), p. 197. See especially the study of the theme of the Kingdom in Rudolf Schnackenburg, *God's Rule and Kingdom* (New York: Herder & Herder), 1963.
88. See C. H. Dodd, *The Apostolic Preaching and Its Developments* (London: Hodder & Stoughton, 1956), pp. 79 ff.
89. Matt. 12:28.
90. We are indebted to Oscar Cullmann for the enumeration and masterful treatment of the Christological titles in his *The Christology of the New Testament* (Philadelphia: Westminster, 1959).
91. Joel 2:28 ff.
92. I Mac. 4:44; 14:41; Ps. 74:9.
93. Luke 7:16; Matt. 21:11; Mark 6:16, 8:28; John 6:14; Acts 3:2 ff.
94. Isa. 42:1–4, 49:1–7, 50:4–11, 52:13, 53:12.

95. Isa. 42:1; Mark 1:11.
96. Isa. 53:12; Luke 22:37.
97. Mark. 10:45.
98. Mark 14:24.
99. Oscar Cullmann, p. 67.
100. Isa. 53:4; Matt. 8:16.
101. Isa. 53:7, 9; Acts 8:35.
102. For example, Gen. 14:17 ff.; Ps. 109:4.
103. Heb. 9.
104. See the splendid little work of T. W. Manson, *Servant Messiah* (Cambridge: University Press, 1961).
105. Dan. 7:13.
106. Matt. 25:31 ff.
107. I Cor. 15:45-47.
108. So, for example, the Old Testament passages about God (Isa. 45:23) are predicated of Christ (Phil. 2:10).
109. Acts 2:36.
110. Cullmann, pp. 207 ff.
111. Acts 5:31.
112. Cullmann, p. 243.
113. John 13:34; I John 2:7-11.
114. Eph. 2:15.
115. John 3:16.
116. I John 4:19.
117. Eph. 5:25-33.
118. Eph. 1:10.
119. Col. 1:19-20.
120. Col. 2:9-10.
121. II Cor. 3:18.
122. Louis Bouyer, *Liturgical Piety* (Notre Dame: Univ. of Notre Dame Press, 1956), p. 104.
123. W. D. Davies, *Paul and Rabbinic Judaism* (London: S.P.C.K., 1958).
124. Ibid. See especially the essay, "The Old and New Torah," pp. 147-176.
125. I Cor. 1:30.
126. See Wisd. 11:4 and I Cor. 10:1-4.
127. Davies, p. 174.
128. George T. Montague, S.M., "The Idea of Progress in the Early Church," *The Bible Today* (Feb. 1964), pp. 640-641.
129. Luke 24:50-53; Acts 1:9-11.
130. De Dietrich, p. 209.
131. Preface of the Mass for the Feast of the Ascension.
132. I Cor. 15:20.
133. Acts 2:36.
134. Matt. 28:18.
135. Philipp. 2:9-10.
136. Col. 2:14-15.
137. Col. 1:13.
138. Philipp. 2:8-11; Heb. 2:5-18.
139. Rom. 8:34; Heb. 8-10.
140. John 14:16.
141. Acts 2:16-17.
142. Gal. 4:16.

143. I Peter 2:9.
144. Isa. 10:22–23; Rom. 9:27-28.
145. Jer. 31:31–34 and Heb. 8:8 ff.; II Cor. 3:4 ff.
146. Eph. 2:5.
147. Rom. 8:11.
148. Eph. 2:21–22; see also I Peter 2:5 and Heb. 3:6.
149. Eph. 1:22.
150. I Cor. 12:12–13.
151. Rom. 12:5.
152. Acts 2:38–39.
153. I Cor. 11:26.
154. John 6:54.
155. Matt. 24:14.
156. Mark 1:15.
157. Rom. 10:17.
158. Luke 6:47, 11:28; Matt. 7:24.
159. Eph. 2:8.
160. Richardson, p. 31.
161. Rom. 6.
162. II Cor. 5:17; Gal. 6:15.
163. Eph. 1:20 ff.
164. Rom. 13:1.
165. Matt. 10:37. See Oscar Cullmann's treatment in *The State in the New Testament* (London: S.C.M., 1957).
166. Mark 12:17.
167. Mark 13:9–10.
168. Acts 4:19, 5:29.
169. John 15:19.
170. Matt. 25:31.
171. Acts 1:11.
172. Apoc. 1:8.
173. Apoc. 1:7.
174. Rom. 8:18–20.
175. Apoc. 21:6, 22:14.
176. Apoc. 3:14.
177. II Peter 3:4.
178. II Peter 3:8–9.
179. I Cor. 15:24, 28.
180. I Cor. 15:45–49.
181. Rom. 5:17; I John 5:19.
182. Apoc. 17:14, 12:17.
183. Apoc. 19:19–20, 10.
184. I Cor. 2:9, 16.
185. Rom. 8:19.
186. Heb. 4:4, 12.
187. Heim, p. 117.
188. Apoc. 21:3, 22.
189. I Cor. 15:22–23.
190. See Rom. 6.
191. Col. 3:4.
192. Apoc. 21:1–3, 4–5.
193. I Cor. 7:31.

194. I Cor. 15:42–44, 54–55, 57.
195. Eric C. Rust, *Towards a Theological Understanding of History* (New York: Oxford Univ. Press, 1954), p. 262. See also the suggestive essay of Karl Rahner, S.J., "The Resurrection of the Body," in *Theological Investigations* (Baltimore: Helicon, 1963), II, 203–216.
196. In the context of a different problem Karl Rahner states substantially the same point, the order of presentation being reversed: "The supernatural order is that order established by the gracious will of God in which God's creation exists as a necessary factor and presupposition, so that the supernatural order is related to the natural as whole to part" *The Christian Commitment* (New York: Sheed & Ward, 1963), p. 41.
197. Rom. 5:15–19.
198. Heim, p. 133.
199. Davies, p. 175.
200. Heb. 10:1–2, 9:10.
201. See Luke 24:21.
202. Rom. 5:6.
203. Eph. 2:13.
204. Col. 1:20.
205. Rom. 5:1.
206. II Cor. 5:19.
207. I Tim. 3:5; I Peter 2:10.
208. See Eph. 2:15; Col. 3:10; Gal. 6:15.
209. II Cor. 5:18.
210. Rom. 10:14.
211. II Cor. 5:20.
212. Bouyer, p. 28.
213. Ibid., p. 107.
214. John 1:29; I Cor. 5:7; I Peter 1:18–19.
215. I Peter 1:20; Apoc. 21, 22.
216. Apoc. 7:14.
217. De Dietrich, p. 270.
218. Apoc. 1:7, 13:12.
219. I Peter 5:1.
220. Eph. 1:20.
221. John 1:1 ff.; Heb. 1:1.

Chapter 8: OUR TIME: THE AGE OF PROCLAMATION

1. Matt. 24:14.
2. Mark 13:10.
3. Rom. 10:14.
4. Acts 1:8.
5. Matt. 28:20; Mark 16:20.
6. Rom. 15:18–19.
7. I Cor. 1:21.
8. I Cor. 11:26.
9. I Cor. 1:21.
10. C. H. Dodd, *The Apostolic Preaching and Its Developments* (London: Hodder & Stoughton, 1942), p. 9.
11. I Cor. 1:23, 2:2–6, 3:10, 15:1.
12. Dodd, p. 13.

13. See Dodd, pp. 17 ff.
14. Acts 2:14–39, 4:8–12, 5:29–32, 10:34–43.
15. See Dodd, pp. 25 ff. for a comparison of the kerygma in Paul and Acts.
16. Acts 1:1, 6:4. See also Burgar Gerardson, *Memory and Manuscript* (Copenhagen: Munksgaard, 1961).
17. Dodd, pp. 47–52.
18. I Cor. 15:14.
19. John 3:17; I John 4:14.
20. John 5:36.
21. John 8:16; see also John 8:29.
22. John 9:4.
23. John 7:16; see also John 14:24.
24. John 12:44–45.
25. John 17:3.
26. Luke 15:3 ff.; Mark 12:1 ff.
27. John 17:18, 20:21.
28. John 21:15–17; I Peter 5; Acts 20:17.
29. Luke 10:16; see also John 13:20.
30. Matt. 28:20.
31. Matt. 18:20.
32. Acts 9:5.
33. See Hans Conzelmann, *The Theology of Saint Luke* (New York: Harper & Bros., 1960). Also see David M. Stanley, S.J., in his excellent "Kingdom to Church," *Theological Studies*, XIV, No. 1 (March 1955), 1–29.
34. Ibid., pp. 13–14.
35. Acts 11:20.
36. Rom. 11:25–26.
37. Stanley, p. 21.
38. Acts 9:18, 3:8, 9:31, 20:9–12.
39. John 7:39.
40. Acts 2:37 ff.; John 2:33.
41. Mark 13:11.
42. John 15:26–27.
43. Acts 2:4–11, 10:45 ff.
44. Gal. 4:6; Acts 16:7; John 16:14 and John 16:13.
45. Oscar Cullmann, "Eschatology and Missions in the New Testament," *The Theology of the Christian Mission* (New York: McGraw-Hill, 1961), p. 46.
46. Acts 10:42.
47. John 20:31.
48. II Cor. 5:19–20.
49. See the study of Thomas Barosse, C.S.C., "The Relationship of Love to Faith in Saint John," *Theological Studies*, XVIII, No. 4 (Dec. 1957), 538–559.
50. John 6:29, 40.
51. I John 2:23, 5:11–12.
52. John 1:12.
53. Barosse, p. 541.
54. Cardinal Bea, as quoted by Avery Dulles, S.J., in "The Protestant Preacher and the Prophetic Mission," *Theological Studies*, XXI, No. 4 (Dec. 1960), 555.
55. I Cor. 10:6; Rom. 15:4.
56. Anthony A. Stephenson, S.J., "The Development and Immutability of Christian Doctrine," *Theological Studies*, XIX, No. 4 (Dec. 1958), 495. See also George Tavard, *Holy Writ or Holy Church* (New York: Harper, 1959).

57. Dietrich Ritschel, *A Theology of Proclamation* (Richmond, Va.: John Knox, 1960), p. 45.

58. See especially the works of Msgr. Lucien Cerfaux, *Christ in the Theology of Saint Paul* (New York: Herder & Herder, 1959), *The Church in the Theology of Saint Paul* (New York: Herder & Herder, 1959), and *Le chrétien dans la théologie paulienne* (Paris: Cerf, 1962).

59. Barnabas Ahern, C.P., "The Christian Union with the Body of Christ," *Catholic Biblical Quarterly*, XXIII, No. 2 (April 1961), 208–209.

60. Karl Rahner, S.J., *The Church and the Sacraments* (New York: Herder & Herder, 1963).

61. See Otto Semmelroth, S.J., "Towards a Unified Concept of the Church," *Yearbook of Liturgical Studies*, II (Notre Dame: Fides, 1961), 85–102; see also his *Mary Archetype of the Church* (New York: Sheed & Ward, 1963).

62. See especially E. H. Schillebeeckx, O.P., *Christ the Sacrament of the Encounter With God* (New York: Sheed & Ward, 1963).

63. E. H. Schillebeeckx, O.P., "The Sacraments, An Encounter with God." *Theology Digest*, VIII, (Spring 1960), 119; condensed from *Fragen der Theologie Heute* (Zurich: Benziger Verlag, 1957), pp. 379–401.

64. See David M. Stanley, S.J., "The New Testament Doctrine of Baptism," *Theological Studies*, XVIII, No. 2 (June 1957), 169–215.

65. Ibid., p. 173.

66. I Cor. 11:26.

67. See Oscar Cullmann, *The Christology of the New Testament* (Philadelphia: Westminster, 1959), pp. 211 ff.

68. Louis Bouyer, *Liturgical Piety* (Notre Dame: Univ. of Notre Dame Press, 1954), p. 108.

69. Ibid., pp. 115–128.

70. Ibid., p. 127.

71. Joseph L. Cypriano, "Christian Worship and the Historical Dimension," *The Commonweal*, LXXVI, No. 19 (Aug. 1962), 468. See also P. E. Roy, "Eucharistie et histoire," *Revue de l'Université d'Ottowa* (April 1957), pp. 233–267. The excellent little work by Dom Edmund Flood, O.S.B., *In Memory of Me* (New York: Sheed & Ward, 1963), reflects a formal presentation of this relationship of Eucharist to history.

72. Jean Daniélou, S.J., *The Lord of History* (Chicago: Regnery, 1958), p. 36.

73. Barbara Ward, "The Quest for Christian Unity," *Atlantic Monthly*, CCX, No. 2 (Aug. 1962), 125.

74. Louis Bouyer has produced a splendid treatment of the fulfillment of the Protestant principle in Catholicism in his *The Spirit and Forms of Protestantism* (Westminster: Newman, 1956).

75. Avery Dulles, pp. 556 ff.

76. Ibid., pp. 562, 566–578.

77. Ibid., p. 575.

78. Alec R. Vidler, *Christian Belief and This World* (Greenwich, Conn.: Seabury Press, 1957), p. 45.

INDEX OF NAMES

Burckhardt, 80
Burke, Edmund, 80
Buri, Fritz, 68, 125
Bury, J. B., 24
Butler, Christopher, 166–167
Butterfield, Herbert, 40, 45–46, 49
Buttrick, George, 147–148

Cahil, P. J., 205n.26
Cairns, Grace, 291n.1
Calvin, J., 107, 108, 150
Caponigri, A. R., 41–42
Carr, E. H., 33–34
Casalis, George, 113n.9
Castelli, Enrico, 293n.36
Cerfaux, Lucien, 182, 272, 312n.58
Chenu, Marie-Dominique, 165, 291n.7
Chifflot, Th. G. 164–165
Chiocchetta, Pietro, 291n.4
Clarke, W. N., 302n.31, 304n.103
Clement, Oliver, 298n.45
Clement of Alexandria, 6, 148, 149
Cogley, John, 106
Cognet, Louis, 164
Cohen, Morris R., 32n.10
Collingwood, R. G., 27, 28–29, 32, 33, 80, 120, 152, 292n.12, 292n.4
Comte, Auguste, 15, 17, 34
Congar, Yves, 145, 160, 167, 174–177, 178, 192
Conzelmann, Hans, 122, 123–124, 311n.33
Corté, Nicolas, 164
Crespy, Georges, 301n.23
Croce, B., 27–29, 32, 33, 80, 292n.3
Cullmann, Oscar, 85, 95, 99n.12, 123, 133, 134–138, 141, 156, 164, 179, 204, 205n.2, 208n.17, 214, 231, 233n.110 and 112, 259, 264, 286, 307n.90, 309n.165, 312n.67
Cuneo, Ernest, 35
Cypriano, Joseph, 277n.71

Dahl, N. A., 65, 122, 123
Daniélou, Jean, 156, 168, 171, 193–194, 204, 280, 296n.7
D'Arcy, Martin, 8, 40, 44, 45, 46, 49, 112n.8, 117, 167, 291n.7 and 8
Davies, W. D., 235, 236n.127, 248n.199
Davis, Charles, 301n.2
Dawson, Christopher, 40, 47–48, 50
de Dietrich, Suzanne, 216n.42, 221n.55, 224–225n.70, 236n.130, 249n.217
Delling, G., 291n.3
Dentan, R. C., 291n.1
Descartes, Rene, 9, 108, 154
Dibelius, Martin, 64
Dilthey, Wilhelm, 26–27, 30, 32, 33, 80, 152, 300n.1
Dinkler, Erich, 122
Dodd, C. H., 62, 63, 84, 132–134, 141, 156, 229n.88 258n.10 and 12, 259n.15 and 17
Dondeyne, Albert, 170–173
Dostoevski, Fedor, 130
Dulles, Avery, 285n.75, n.76, n.77; 294n.4, 311n.54
Durkheim, Emile, 34, 43
Durwell, F. X., 189–191

Ebeling, Gerhard, 122
Eichrodt, Walter, 225n.72
Eliade, Mircea, 3, 49, 291n.2
Ellis, Peter, 306n.22
Erling, Bernhard, 117–118
Eusebius, 6

Feret, H. M., 184–185
Ferre, Nels, 108n.3 and 4, 109, 297n.16
Fessard, F. G., 173
Fichte, Johann, 13
Filson, Floyd, 63
Fitch, Robert, 116n.15

INDEX OF BIBLICAL PASSAGES

NEW TESTAMENT

MATTHEW

MARK

LUKE

ROMANS